Contemporary Issues in Marketing

Martin Evans
and
Luiz Moutinho

First published 1999 by
PALGRAVE MACMILLAN
Houndmills, Basingstoke, Hampshire RG21 6XS and
175 Fifth Avenue, New York, N.Y. 10010
Companies and representatives throughout the world

PALGRAVE MACMILLAN is the global academic imprint of the Palgrave Macmillan division of St. Martin's Press, LLC and of Palgrave Macmillan Ltd. Macmillan® is a registered trademark in the United States, United Kingdom and other countries. Palgrave is a registered trademark in the European Union and other countries.

ISBN 0–333–67774–9

This book is printed on paper suitable for recycling and made from fully managed and sustained forest sources.

A catalogue record for this book is available from the British Library.

10   9   8   7   6   5   4   3
11 10 09 08 07 06 05 04

Printed in Great Britain by
J W Arrowsmith Ltd, Bristol

Contents

Contents

Part 3   Issues in Strategic Marketing Planning

Foreword

As a young reporter on *Marketing Week*, I was once contacted by Anita Roddick, chief executive of the Body Shop. She was about to deliver a speech to the *Marketing Society*, but confessed to a small problem. No one she had asked was able to provide a succinct definition of the term 'marketing'. Could I help?

A facetious question, of course, from someone who was indisputably one of Britain's leading marketing practitioners. But it amply illustrates a point. Marketing is not just a set of pat definitions and abstract principles distilled into a business science. To succeed, the marketer needs much more: above all – like Roddick herself – abundant energy, vision and purpose.

It is this realisation which has led to the publication of a new and very different kind of guide for would-be marketers: *Contemporary Issues in Marketing* by Martin Evans and Luiz Moutinho.

Quite properly, the book approaches marketing through a scholarly, logical schema. But it draws additional inspiration from the more haphazard reality of daily business life, as seen through the prism of our weekly news magazine.

That should give it, like any good new product development launch, a few advantages over the competition. First, it will be a more lively, approachable read, not least because it blends the everyday language of journalism with that of academe. Second, the juxtaposition of core text with news and features articles enhances the book's practical relevance for the many students who themselves aspire to be marketers.

Finally, I hope that this book will, in a modest way, convince new entrants to the world of marketing that our magazine is indispensable reading.

STUART SMITH
Editor, Marketing Week

Preface

Many courses in marketing are based on one of the major textbooks. No surprise there – that's why those books have been written! What we have produced in this volume is a collection of themed readings from the marketing press, which supplement and complement the core text.

Our own experiences of teaching marketing plus our – and Macmillan's – research among other marketing teachers have revealed the need for a vehicle to put some of the textbook content into a highly recognisable and practical contemporary context. That is the idea behind this book, and we have been lucky to join forces with *Marketing Week*, one of the supplementary readers most recommended by marketing teachers. This book contains over 70 key articles ('clippings') from *Marketing Week*, covering some of the more significant developments and issues affecting contemporary marketing. Some of these issues are not always explored fully in the 'core textbook' format, so our intention is to fill this gap.

The book is divided into three parts covering three marketing themes: issues in market analysis and customer behaviour, issues in marketing programmes

and issues in strategic marketing planning. Within each is a collection of highly topical issues upon which to base seminar discussions, assignments and course work. In addition, the readings act as the context in which to apply concepts, theories other course materials.

For each issue we have provided some additional notes that delve further into the topic and in some cases reflect more recent research in that area. Most of the issues are covered by more than one clipping from *Marketing Week* to demonstrate either the multifaceted nature of the issue, or how its impact and implications 'moved on' in the period between the publication dates of the articles in question.

We hope you enjoy this book and that it helps to enrich your marketing course. We are also keen to receive your suggestions for improvement and hear what you like about the book. You can contact us via the publisher. Enjoy the clippings!

MARTIN EVANS
*University of the
West of England*

LUIZ MOUTINHO
University of Glasgow

Part 1
Issues in Market Analysis and Customer Behaviour

Introduction

In this first part we have selected some clippings that reflect developments and trends in several areas. First, in Chapter 1 we examine the marketing concept itself, via two clippings that not only discuss the concept but also challenge the *status quo*.

Another aspect of marketing explored in this part is what might be described as 'the marketing environment' (Chapter 2). Contemporary issues here include changes in market behaviour in terms of ethical consumerism and the increasingly important – but often ignored – environmental constraint, posed by the law.

The next group of clippings in Chapter 2 are based on the market. This is at the heart of marketing – indeed marketing takes its direction from the market, so we don't need to spell out the importance of understanding those market events which do or might affect our particular marketing operation.

Essentially, marketing is concerned with understanding the needs and requirements of consumers and providing them with what they want – and in a way that is both profitable to the marketer and satisfying to the purchaser. To put it more formally, the Chartered Institute of Marketing in the U.K. defines marketing as follows: 'Marketing is the management process that identifies, anticipates and supplies customer requirements efficiently and profitably'. In this way marketing matches what the market wants with what the organisation offers.

The marketing concept requires market or consumer orientation as opposed to product or production orientation. One obvious way of summarising this is to think in terms of a customer orientation that leads us to 'make what we can sell, rather than sell what we can make'. But we can go a little further and try to discover what it is that people do buy. A Revlon cosmetics executive is reported as saying: 'In the factory we make soap; in the market we sell hope.'

On this basis Chapter 3 includes a number of clippings on the theme of consumer behaviour and addresses some contemporary developments, including changes in consumer profiling – demographics and psychographics in particular. The use by marketers of psychological peripheral cues to influence consumer perceptions and behaviour, sometimes without them being aware of being influenced, is also explored. Other groups of clippings delve into age segmentation, especially the increasing importance of the over fifties and, at the other end of the age scale, the growing targeting of 'pester power'. More topical segmentation and targeting dimensions are examined through a group of clippings on gender stereotypes.

The role of marketing research and information is also clear with regard to the implications of the marketing concept. Chapter 4 therefore includes clippings that explore some contemporary issues in market research and information. These include the increasing use of technology, the nature of 'panel' research and debates on survey research, and also the move towards increasingly personalised consumer data – even 'biographic' data.

1 The Marketing Concept

- The marketing concept
- Market and product orientation
- The role of marketing research
- The marketing mix
- The changing nature of marketing

Preparing a winning formula

Where Clive Sinclair led, others follow. McDonald's has just broken the golden rule of marketing by trying to guess what the customer wants – and got itself into a pickle

IAIN MURRAY

With a candour that is at once engaging and shocking, the president of McDonald's UK declares he has just discovered marketing. "Asking customers what they want is a simple and effective idea," says Paul Preston. "It saves a hell of a lot of wasted time in the boardroom by executives trying to second-guess what people may or may not like."

This dollop of self-evident common sense was revealed to McDonald's with the force of a blinding, unexpected thunderbolt when its McPloughman's cheese, salad and pickle sandwich was rejected by a public whose expectation was a hamburger.

"If we had taken the time to put the concept of McPloughman's through the discovery stage and done some market research we would have found out this was not a highly desirable product," says Preston, whose penitence is as touching as his candour.

That McDonald's got where it is today (the world's biggest restaurant chain with 14,000 outlets in 72 countries and a Big Mac in a million bellies at each turn of the globe) without pausing to ask the customers what they want is truly remarkable. It is an achievement that places the hamburger alongside the wheel in the annals of human invention.

For not every new product is first put to the test of the many-headed monster of the pit. The unsung caveman or cavewoman who rough-hewed the first granite wheel was engaged in one of those rare leaps of human achievement that are inspirational and need no further justification.

Marconi, Edison and Faraday all pressed ahead without reference to the likely end-user. But all were geniuses. Now, it seems, we must place Ronald McDonald alongside those giants – resplendent on a plinth of his own in the pantheon. In the catalogue of creativity wireless telegraphy is at one with the Chicken McNugget.

Ralph Waldo Emerson has a lot to answer for, including, posthumously, the McPloughman's. The notion that if a man makes a better mousetrap than his neighbour the world will beat a path to his door lends an unfortunate credibility to production-led thinking. True, old Ralph was talking about improvements to existing products but the vision of a market rushing, tumbling and tripping over itself to buy is so enticing that the wilder presumptions of the innovator germinate like yeast. Sir Clive Sinclair had that problem with the C5 electronic tri cycle.

But the world's unwillingness to beat a path to a cheese and pickle sandwich in a bar made for hamburgers or to a form of personal transport that places the driver's nostrils on the same plane as a diesel exhaust is no deterrent. In the feverish quest for commercial triumph the lessons of the past go unlearned. That is no bad thing as long as one recognises there is but a single speck of gold for every thousand gallons of dross.

Japanese scientists are confidently – and no doubt eagerly – awaiting the sound of full-bosomed womanhood pounding on their door. In the belief that there is originality in synthesis, they have taken the metal wire used in earthquake-resistant skyscrapers and embodied it in a brassiere. At first this seems to give an insight into a muddled oriental view of the percussive potential in the female form, but there is more to it.

Woven into the fabric, the alloy of nickel and titanium gives the bra the ability to become firmer and more supportive as greater stress is placed on it. According to Dr Clifford Friend of Cranfield University, they don't go out of shape. "And they can take much more weight than a bosom," he adds, leaving the significance of that comment tantalisingly unspoken.

The woman who walked out of the Royal Mint's Essex depot with £20 notes stuffed into her underwear would have appreciated a bra fashioned from titanium and capable of extending her daily haul by £2,000 in coinage (equally divided).

Whether the Smart-bra, as it is known, proves a commercial success or just another cold cheese and pickle sandwich will be decided by the market. I suspect that the Japanese scientists were too excited in their work and too reticent in their manners to test the female appetite for a bra capable of bringing ashore North Sea oil.

Oleg Cassini was on safer ground when he devised his product. In a leaflet distributed by Fayed's Knightsbridge emporium, and which ought properly to be passed on to the Advertising Standards Authority, Cassini trumpets his range of cosmetics for men. "The art of seduction . . . A powerful, erotic masterpiece, a fragrance for the Nineties man, laced with an element of real aphrodisiac, Oleg Cassini has designed a stimulating and seductive scent, irresistible to women, essential for men!"

Who would have thought that more than a century on from the shameless huckstering of our Victorian forbears advertising copy such as that could be written? Ever since man had to forswear the club-on-the-back-of-the-head technique of winning a mate he has sought in vain some magic that – crossed eyes, warts and jug ears notwithstanding – would make him irresistible to women.

But century after endless century the foolproof aphrodisiac proved as elusive as Scotch mist, and as phoney as alchemy. Has Cassini finally cracked it? Will he, too, be up there with the Wright brothers and Ronald McDonald? I wouldn't bet on it. As an inducement to invest in his "sensuous new fragrance" he offers a jet-set travel bag in navy blue "faux" lizard, with signature crest logo. For "faux" read "fake".

Better luck to SP Tyres UK and Dunlop who are introducing a rose-scented tyre. No claims are made that it is irresistible to women run over by it. Fitted to a spare wheel, say the makers, it will freshen your car boot. What, in the way of market research, do you imagine went into that?

A time for marketers to boldly go

The general feeling which emerged from last week's Marketing Forum was that the industry is facing a 'mid-life crisis'. Yet the present climate of change offers marketers prepared to take risks for the sake of innovation an unparalleled opportunity.

ALAN MITCHELL

In search of excellence? Pah! If your life is anything like mine, you never quite reach a position where you really get that search going. You're always just on the point of getting on top of things when the dishwasher breaks down (that's £40, for starters), the cat triumphantly does its business on Johnny's pillow (for the 132nd time – we really must have it put down), and Auntie Meg falls ill and must be visited (there goes that time you had set aside to clear out the loft). And so forth.

As at home, so in work. People you're relying on don't deliver, important considerations get overlooked, competitors do something unexpected, decisions have to be revisited. There's always too much to do in too little time: it's all about firefighting, compromising, ducking, diving, making do. Surviving. Sod excellence, surviving is hard enough.

But is it enough? That was the question posed sharply at last week's Marketing Forum. In his opening address, George Bull, chief executive of Grand Met, declared "the evidence of failure [to apply marketing skills] is all around us". Former Lever Brothers chief Andrew Seth gave an impassioned call for better innovation warning, however, that to do so means going against the grain of our culture: "It's not something that will respond to tinkering. It's fundamental."

Simon Broadbent of the Leo Burnett Brand Consultancy told delegates that unless marketers tackle the issue of measuring effectiveness and becoming more accountable "we're dead", while HHCL & Partners' Adam Lury, declared that the traditional concept of the brand is now "pretty defunct". One large consultancy admitted privately that many clients were sheepishly admitting they no longer know how their markets tick.

Then there was McKinsey strutting its stuff. It coined the term "Marketing's Mid Life Crisis" and, returning to the theme, principal Anthony Freeling warned that "marketing's role as a specific function is under threat . . . Everyone's agreed it must change. But there's no consensus as to how." At which point, the Henley Centre's Nigel Willmott chimed in: "The environment has changed, but the marketing model hasn't."

Indeed, a major thread running through the floating conference's estimated 3,500 talks and seminars was

the notion that nowadays marketing is in some sort of a struggle for survival. Once upon a time, every individual piece of the marketing jigsaw seemed to fit snugly, helping all the other bits to lock into a coherent whole like some Chinese puzzle. But now all these bits seem incongruent.

Just think of the business turmoil of the past ten years: the rise of retailer power and of global competition; a roller-coaster of boom and bust; the powerful impact of benchmarking and process re-engineering; computerisation and ever-accelerating technological change, including an ongoing media revolution (only 500 TV channels in the UK by the year 2005?). Markets and firms are being transformed and, like that Chinese puzzle, none of the pieces seem to fit snugly any more.

In such a context it's perfectly understandable that marketers should feel that things are getting out of control. If all the pieces have been tossed into the air, no one is quite sure what pattern they'll make when they come down – indeed, if they make a pattern at all. Yet the role of marketing's various sub-disciplines and the people who have invested their professional lives in them depend on the outcome. Hence all that survival talk and, perhaps, Forum speakers' ever-recurring plea that short-term tactical considerations should not be allowed to crowd out longer-term strategic thinking.

But how many of us will ever get to the happy state when everything is under control and can we really concentrate on strategy, on "excellence"? Running to a standstill seems to be more the nature of things. Even the mighty lion – king of the jungle – has to sleep 20 hours a day to conserve

energy. And if for some reason it doesn't make a kill, within a day or two it's getting too weak to hunt.

One of the feelings left by the Forum is that marketing is in danger of falling into that trap. It is debilitated by a lack of recent triumphs. However, if the world is changing so fast – and what was fixed is becoming fluid – then now, as never before, marketers have the opportunity to make their mark. Unlike those who went before them, this generation of marketers has room to be more than mere practitioners. Instead of applying rules that are so well known they're encapsulated in text books, their chance is to create the new models: to be the raw material for the next generation of text-book authors.

Can they, for instance, create a new view of branding that moves marketing on from the classic fmcg model of standalone product to the umbrella and corporate brand. Can ideas such as staff as a key communication channel, the creation of a "total brand experience" and the brand as a "unique organising proposition" really work?

It's the need for bold moves such as this that prompted exhortations from Forum speakers like Seth and Freeling. When it comes to innovation, "you can do it!" cried Seth. "Break out of the doldrums. Dare to be great!" declared Freeling.

Just one caveat. In the search for the big new ideas of marketing, don't forget the day job. For, as often as not, it's the little, apparently insignificant, initiatives that are made in the day-to-day struggle for survival that grow up to be big ideas, and not the other way around.

ISSUES

1 What is market orientation and is it at the heart of the marketing concept?

2 What is the role of market information within the marketing concept?

3 What is the role of the marketing mix within the marketing concept and is marketing on the brink of some quantum leap?

EXPLORATION OF ISSUES

1 Murray's article operates at two levels. First, the traditional view of the marketing concept is brought out. Second, it is shown that although the concept is extremely simple to comprehend, it can also operate at too simplistic a level operationally.

The concept is basically one of understanding the market and providing marketing offerings that satisfy customers, and this is the means to the end of achieving the goals of the organisation.

Some of the examples in the article demonstrate a clear lack of market orientation. The Sinclair C5 is often wheeled out as an illustration of product orientation. Had the market been more thoroughly researched, the limitations of the vehicle 'in traffic' would have been more obvious. At the same time niches might have been identified, such as a small but potentially lucrative market for a golf buggy, or similar off-road uses.

The simplicity of the marketing concept is demonstrated by another example. A manufacturer of men's leather wallets had success in the UK with its brown leather wallet, which had a red lining. The company decided to expand into the French market but failed. They couldn't understand why so conducted some market research – group discussions with Frenchmen. The problem turned out to be the red lining, which was considered to 'flashy' and ostentatious by most of the Frenchmen (who were rural dwellers and perhaps less flamboyant than their urban counterparts).

The solution was obvious – the lining was changed to brown and the company became successful in France.

This story is a simple but powerful illustration of the importance of being customer orientated. It does, however, raise the question of how and when to start understanding customers. All too often, even today, companies appear to be product orientated – or just arrogant – and assume that because they have what they think is a good product, the market will beat a path to their door.

Market information is the key and it needs to be gathered and acted upon constantly.

2 The McDonald's story is interesting in terms of market information. In the early 1970s the company decided to research the UK market with a view to entering it. A substantial amount of market research was conducted. In competitive terms, McDonald's identified fish and chip shops and the old style Wimpy Bars as being the main threats, but it was thought that these would actually provide little competition. The 'chippy' was seen as having a rather old fashioned, greasy image and the Wimpy Bars did not seem to be run in an efficient manner. Some customers were taking a whole afternoon to have a coffee and a Wimpy – it had become a social gathering venue at which there was more talk than revenue.

McDonald's also conducted consumer surveys to discover what the British liked and disliked about eating out. There was a big 'thumbs down' to bright lights, counter service and no cutlery – all ingredients of the McDonald's experience in the United States. Instead the British wanted to put their own salt and pepper on their chips, be waited on in a less brightly lit restaurant and so on.

But what were we given? McDonald's came over to the UK with test branches in and around London, and apparently none of the market research had been taken on board. They were very cautious in those days and it was many years before branches were set up away from London – it took ten years to reach Newcastle and Cardiff, for example.

The issues here are clear: why conduct market research at all, and does the above case demonstrate that McDonald's forte is not market orientation?

One of the problems, of course, with such research in the early 1970s was that consumers could not relate to the McDonald's concept – travel to the United States was not as common as it is today and the British public had no experience of anything like the McDonald's approach. How, therefore, could we respond to questions that had no point of reference?

One of the knacks in reading the market is to go beyond the 'words' of a survey and adopt the techniques of environmental scanning, which can help us to look further ahead in time and take a good guess at how lifestyles and social attitudes might evolve. In this way, although a survey might produce a negative result, a projection of trends and events in the marketing environment might indicate opportunities later on.

3 The traditional view of marketing is that the marketing mix – the 4Ps – 'go out' from the organisation to influence the market and satisfy it. That is, we develop the right product at the right price at the right time and promote it in the most relevant way for the market segment we are targeting.

In this way satisfied customers will repeat buy and/or spread goodwill about the marketing offering, and as long as the organisation bears in mind its cost structures and overall objectives with regard to profit or whatever is their *raison d'être*, then the system works to the benefit of supplier and buyer.

A more recent conceptual development is that marketing should be concerned with more than this – it should be about developing relationships and the 'mix' concept has had its day. Indeed, simplifying marketing to the 4Ps has perhaps attracted a degree of derision from those outside the profession on the basis of simplification *per se*. The 4Ps approach has also been labelled as more concerned with transactions than with longer-term relationships. But the jury is probably still out on this issue – the relationship marketing paradigm promises much but research is still at too early a stage to determine what it really means in practice.

2 The Marketing Environment

Ethical Consumerism

KEY CONCEPTS

- The new ethical consumer
- The 'consciousness' paradigm
- Consumerism; conspicuous consumption
- Organised buying boycotts; consumer organisations
- Safety regulations

The power of ethical branding

Ethics have gone up the business agenda in recent years and are a potentially powerful influence on consumer decisions. **ALAN MITCHELL** says brands need to look carefully at these changes and to prepare for a deep shift in public expectations of what they do, and what they stand for

What effect does a changing political climate have on brands? As an issue, ethics has been going up the business and branding agenda for many years. Now, judging by the new Government's first few weeks in office, its impact on the political agenda will also be palpable.

Already, there's little doubt that ethical considerations are a potentially powerful influence on consumer purchasing decisions. As Shell has found out with its environmental policies and its treatment of indigenous peoples,

and Nike with its cheap labour sourcing policies, if a brand gets its ethical stance wrong, it can dog the business wherever it goes and whatever it does. And as brands like the Body Shop, and more recently, the Co-op Bank have shown, wearing your ethical heart on your sleeves can do wonders for sales. But how strong will the pressure on brands to display ethical credentials really become?

Arguably, what happened in the polls recently merely reflects the yearning for less "meism" and more

"usism" that market researchers began finding among the British public ten years ago. According to Richard Adams, managing director of the fair trading retail organisation Out of this World, best estimates from all research so far suggest there are 15 million ethical consumers in the UK – consumers who would prefer to choose positively "ethical" products and companies as against those which are not.

And, as Roisin Rowbotham-Jones, project director at BBH Futures, told a recent BBH seminar on subject, the shift in the balance of power between consumer and producers, the devastating impact of the media exposé, and relative prosperity – which give us the luxury of worrying about these things a little more – all mean that consumers can and do vote with their purse.

Whether it's specific issues such as environmental impact or exploitation of child labour, or a more general pressure on corporations to "give something back" to society through charitable donations, contributions to local communities or support for the arts and sports, every brand is needing to take a conscious decision as to what sort of ethical stance to take.

Yet it's very easy to misjudge the ethical playing field. As the Green bandwagoners of the late Eighties discovered, a key issue is judging an acceptable price to pay for principles. Being efficient doesn't usually allow sentimental considerations to get in the way, and when offered the choice between the sentimental and the lowest cost operator, markets tend to choose the latter. As Adams told the BBH Futures seminar, most of his 15 million consumers have so far proved to be armchair ethicals who are "radicals in the surveys but reactionaries at the checkout".

Besides, it may just be that now that the Government has taken ethics on board, some of the middle class guilt that's driven so much of ethical consumerism thus far will be assuaged, and that the pressure to "do good" will be redirected from business and back to government.

Either way, marketers need to take the ethics challenge seriously, if only because it is so easy to misunderstand what it represents. The big mistake is to see it as an isolated issue, to be treated separately from the rest of the brand's strategy. It's a mistake because the chances are that it's merely a symptom of a much deeper sea-change. Every successful brand has to adapt to stay in tune with its times. But ethics is not just another social trend to be adapted to and ridden, such as the changing role of women in society. It's an advance warning of a deeper shift in public expectations of what brands do and what they stand for.

Put simply, consumers want brands to stop being two dimensional. The whole history of branding has taught marketers the power of packaging, so that the core skills of brand management often amount to little more than the art of facade management: how to paint a pretty enough picture of your particular bundle of emotional and functional attributes to close that sale.

Now, for all the familiar reasons – increasing marketing literacy, the rise of the pressure group, the development of the consumer press – consumers are realising that these bundles do not exist in isolation from society but are deeply embedded within it. If the BSE crisis did nothing else, it rammed down our throats that what we buy is the product of a long and complex series of behind-the-scenes decisions and actions which can affect us profoundly.

No matter what a marketer does to bolster his brand facade, consumers are increasingly looking behind it, and treating it as a facade: increasingly, brands are rightly seen not as representatives of products or even companies, but of supply chains. And they are expected to manage their supply chains both efficiently and responsibly.

One misconception is to assume that the future lies with corporate brands as opposed to standalone brands. This is not necessarily true. It may help, but it's the marketing approach that really matters. A worse misinterpretation is that the assumption that companies need therefore to adopt politically correct motherhood-and-apple-pie "values". Not so. All the evidence is that consumers trust people and companies who clearly believe in what they do, not those who just want to appear nice.

This is where the real force of so-called ethical consumerism lies. It is the most visible expression of a slow, faltering, confused and groping search by consumers for a new relationship between themselves and brands: evidence of a shift in their focus of trust, from the integrity of the product to the integrity of the people behind it.

When the question is no longer "Can I trust this brand to deliver attributes X or Y?", but "are the people who bring me this brand the sort of people who I can trust to do X or Y?" (not destroy the environment, not rip me off) the nature of brands – and brand management – begins to change irrevocably.

ISSUES

1 Comment on the increasingly important role of the consumerist movement.

2 Discuss some key ethical issues in marketing and give examples related to the marketing mix.

3 Misconceptions about the nature of behaviour modification or applied behaviour analysis rest on two major questions concerning the nature of the behavioural approach in general and its application in marketing in particular:

(a) Are behavioural approaches manipulative and unethical?

(b) Do behavioural approaches deny that people can think?

EXPLORATION OF ISSUES

1 The number and power of special interest groups have increased over the past three decades. Political action committees (PACs) lobby government officials and pressure business executives to pay more attention to consumer rights, women's rights, senior citizens' rights, minority rights, gay rights and so on. Many companies have established public affairs departments to deal with these groups and issues.

An important force affecting business is the consumerist movement – an organised movement of citizens and government to strengthen the rights and powers of buyers in relation to sellers. Consumerists have advocated and won the right to know the true cost per standard unit of competing brands (unit pricing), the basic ingredients in a product, the nutritional quality of food, the freshness of a product and the true benefits of a product. In response to consumerism, several companies have established consumer affairs departments to help formulate policies and respond to consumers' complaints (for example the installation of freephone numbers for consumers to use if they are dissatisfied with products or services, and expansion of the coverage of product warranties and wording them in clear terms).

Clearly, new laws and growing numbers of pressure groups have put more restraints on marketers. Marketers have to clear their plans with the company's legal, public, relations, public affairs and consumer affairs departments. Insurance companies directly or indirectly influence the design of smoke detectors; scientific groups influence the design of spray products by condemning aerosols. In essence, many private marketing transactions have moved into the public domain.

2 An individual will make an ethical decision only when he or she recognises that a particular issue or situation has an ethical or moral component thus developing awareness of ethical issues is important in understanding marketing ethics. An ethical issue is an identifiable problem, situation or opportunity requiring an individual or organisation to choose from among several actions that must be evaluated as right or wrong, ethical or unethical. Whenever an activity causes consumers to feel deceived, manipulated or cheated, a marketing ethical issue exists, regardless of the legality of that activity.

Ethical issues typically arise because of conflicts between individuals' personal moral philosophies and the marketing strategies, policies and organisational environment in which they work. Ethical issues may stem from conflict between a marketer's attempts to achieve organisational objectives and the customers' desire for safe, fair and reliable products. Similarly, organisational objectives that call for increased profits or market share may pressure marketers to steal competitors' secrets, knowingly put an unsafe product on the market or engage in some other questionable activity.

Regardless of the reasons behind specific ethical issues,

once the issues are identified, marketers and organisations must decide how to deal with them. In marketing many different ethical issues arise, and although it is not possible to review them all here, the following examination of some key issues provides some direction and should lead to an understanding of the ethical problems that marketers must confront.

Product-related ethical issues generally arise when marketers fail to disclose risks associated with the product or information about its function, value or use. Competitive pressures can also lead to product-related concerns. As competition intensifies and profit margins diminish there may be pressure to substitute inferior materials or product components so as to reduce costs. An ethical issue arises when marketers fail to inform customers about changes in product quality; this failure is a form of dishonesty about the nature of the product.

Many companies, of course, take care to emphasise product safety concerns in their advertising. Such messages send a signal to all employees in the organisation, as well as to customers, about the company's ethical standards.

Promotional issues. The communication process involves a variety of situations that can create ethical issues; Such as false and misleading advertising and manipulative or deceptive sales promotions, tactics or publicity efforts.

Unethical actions in advertising can destroy the trust customers have in an organisation. Sometimes advertisements are questioned because they are unfair to a competitor.

Misleading advertising can range from exaggerated claims and concealed facts to outright lies. Exaggerated claims cannot be substantiated. Concealed facts are material facts deliberately omitted from a message. When consumers learn that a promotion messages is untrue, they may feel cheated and refuse to buy the product again; they may also complain to the government or other regulatory bodies. Consequently marketers should take care to disclose all the important facts and avoid making claims that cannot be supported. For a while, Sainsbury's refused to stock brand leader Perrier because it considered that the wording on the label misled consumers. Also, vague messages remain an ethical issue in advertising.

Personal selling. A common problem with personal selling is ascertaining what types of sales activity are acceptable. Consumers may perceive sales people as unethical because of the common belief that sales personnel often put pressure on customers to purchase products they neither need nor want. Many companies' sales forces know that they must act ethically or risk losing valuable customers and sales. Although most sales people are ethical, some do engage in questionable actions. For example some use very aggressive and manipulative tactics to sell almost worthless gemstones, holidays or other products over the phone. Even though these sales people may be fined for their activities, their unethical and often illegal actions contribute to consumers' mistrust of telephone selling and personal selling in general. At one time or another, most sales people face an ethical conflict in their jobs. For example a sales person may have to decide whether to tell a customer the truth and risk losing the customer's business, or somehow mislead the customer in order to appease him or her and ensure a sale.

Frequently the problem of ethics has a snowball effect. Once a sales person has deceived a customer, it subsequently becomes increasingly difficult to tell the truth. The way in which a sales person deals with an ethical issue can therefore have far reaching consequences for both the individual and the firm.

When payments, gifts or special favours are granted to obtain a sale or for some other reason, there is always some hint of bribery. A bribe is anything given to influence improperly the outcome of a decision. Even when a bribe is offered to benefit the organisation, it is usually considered unethical, and it damages the organisation in the long run by jeopardising trust and sense of fairness. Bribery is pernicious, for it stifles fair competition among businesses and limits consumer choice.

Pricing issues. Price fixing, predatory pricing and failure to disclose the full price associated with a purchase are typical ethical issues. The emotional and subjective nature of price creates many situations in which misunderstandings between the seller and buyer cause ethical problems. Ethical issues may crop up when a company seeks to earn high profits at the expense of its customers.

Distribution issues. Ethical issues in distribution involve relationships between producers and marketing middlemen. For example producers can expect retailers to honour payment agreements and keep them informed of inventory needs. Failure to make payments in a timely manner may be considered an ethical issue. Manipulating a product's availability for purposes of exploitation and using coercion to force intermediaries to behave in a specific manner are particularly serious ethical issues in the distribution sphere.

③ There is no question that behavioural approaches

involve changing behaviour. They have been criticised as manipulative and unethical because they attempt to change behaviour in a systematic way. In fact most human interactions are concerned with attempting to change the behaviour of other people. Behavioural approaches should not be singled out as manipulative and unethical solely because they involve systematic methods for doing what most of us are attempting to do anyway.

The ethical question involved in attempts by marketing managers to coerce consumers into changing their behaviour goes beyond questioning the use of behavioural technology. In fact consumer choice is seen as essential in a competitive, capitalistic system. Companies that survive and prosper in this system are those that are most effective at modifying consumer behaviour and encouraging purchase and repurchase of their products and brands.

Even the cognitive approach to marketing and consumer behaviour can raise questions of manipulation. The reason why we study cognitive variables in marketing and consumer behaviour is because they are believed to influence overt behaviour. In some cases marketers try to influence cognitive variables in order to develop more efficient marketing strategies aimed at changing behaviour without changing the cognitive variable. That is, the needs and benefits sought by consumers are often an issue when segmenting markets, where the knowledge gained is used to develop products and marketing strategies to reach a particular market segment that requires certain benefits or need satisfactions. In neither case is the cognitive approach of much value unless the company develops a marketing strategy that effectively changes consumers' behaviour so that they actually purchase a product.

In summary, a major concern of human activity in general and of marketing in particular is to change or maintain overt behaviour. Our personal interactions cause this to occur, and in many cases society, encourages it. Strategy development in marketing is clearly concerned with influencing overt consumer behaviour, irrespective of whether behavioural or cognitive approaches are used. The claim that behavioural approaches are unethical and manipulative, but that societal, marketing and cognitive approaches to marketing are not, does not seem to be logical.

The conventional wisdom is that behaviouralists see people as at the mercy of their surroundings. In fact, while many behaviouralists believe that behaviour is controlled by the environment, few would argue that there is nothing going on in people's brains. At the same time we acknowledge that a major mistake of marketing and consumer research has been to ignore overt behaviour.

The Legal Environment

- Privacy issues
- The legal environment
- Database marketing

Utilities data taxes Labour

Faced with a £3bn 'windfall tax' bill, the utilities have opened secret talks with Labour to win changes in data protection laws in exchange for their silence. **SEAN BRIERLEY** investigates post-election promises.

Strange days indeed when the party that added Clause Four to the dictionary runs election broadcasts promoting itself as the "natural" party of business.

But the revelation that the Labour Party is secretly offering an olive branch to the utility companies over restrictions on the use of data (*MW* April 10) indicates that the party's new found *realpolitik* may be more than just rhetoric.

The party's election commitment on not raising taxes has provided it with the very real problem of finding supplementary finance. The one-off windfall tax on the privatised utilities, when it was first proposed by shadow chancellor Gordon Brown in October 1994, was seen as a convenient way to address some finance-raising difficulties.

But last week share prices soared among the major utilities following the news that the Labour Party will seek a much lower sum, estimated at £3bn, rather than the previously quoted £5bn to £10bn. At the same time, the utility companies appear to be shifting their stance from almost total opposition to the tax, amid threats of legal action, to one of benign acceptance.

The reasons for this change of heart are varied – the utility companies do not want to be in conflict with a new administration from day one. But more significantly they believe that their intense lobbying of New Labour, since the windfall tax was proposed, could reap rewards.

Shadow energy spokesman John Battle, along with Brown and other shadow treasury figures, has been the main target of the lobbying on the windfall tax which has come down to the utilities trying to wring concessions out of any new Labour administration. And Labour could be vulnerable to persuasion because it needs the money – it would after all be disastrous for Labour to spend the next two years tied up in legal challenges when it needs the windfall money to pay for its policies.

The utility companies do not want to pay a one-off £3bn, but know that a relaxation of data protection laws to allow the full exploitation of databases is far more valuable because it will allow them to compete across the whole energy sector. While the ability to carry piggy-back mailings is important, the ability to market other energy services is the real Holy Grail.

Any reform would require amendments to the gas, electricity and water Acts, but would not require primary legislation and could, in theory, if the Data Protection Registrar agreed, be in place by the autumn. Each act governing electricity, water and gas privatisation includes sections that preclude use of the utility licence holders database for any use other than supply.

On the surface, it appears that the utility companies' biggest complaint is with the Registrar, Elizabeth France, who has ruled that they cannot cross-market other goods and services to its customers.

The outgoing Conservative Government relaxed the rules on utility companies to allow takeovers and mergers by US utility companies and the growth of super utilities which straddle water, electricity and gas markets. However, it did not relax regulations governing the use of data.

British Gas intends to become a major player in the national electricity supply business. "The result is that we will be allowed to sell electricity, which we are very keen to do, but the inability to use our own database means competition is a farce," says a British Gas source. "We pointed out to the Labour Party that if we are to be penalised with the windfall tax, and have to suffer the additional burden of full competition with Ofgas' additional restraints on prices, then we are also facing further unfair restraint on trade imposed upon us because we are not allowed to use our own database.

"The pro-consumer lobby is much less effective in the Labour Party than it used to be, and there is a convincing argument that some data protection legislation acts as an effective restraint on trade," says the same source.

The sentiment is echoed by United Utilities, owner of North West Water and Norweb, which has also had secret talks with Labour. "We have a number of plans in the pipeline to become total energy providers, but current legislation appears to prevent us from doing that," says a UU source.

Existing DPR rules governing utilities are also holding back the wider plans of non-utility companies, such as retailers like Tesco, Asda and Marks & Spencer, to market energy supplies. For instance, if Tesco were to gain a gas supply licence, it could not send Tesco Clubcard vouchers and information of Tesco Clubcard Plus to potential consumers. If it then entered the electricity market, it could not combine gas and electricity billings. As a result, Tesco is understood to have abandoned plans to enter the own-label gas and electricity supply markets (*MW* September 6 1996) and Sainsbury's pulled out last week.

Other supermarkets and non-utility groups are also understood to have abandoned such plans. A source from one of the big four high street banks says: "We looked into the possibility of entering the gas and electricity markets, but the rules governing use of data were an absolute minefield."

Of the 61 licensed industrial and commercial gas suppliers, there are no retailers. Only petrol companies such as Elf, BP and Texaco have joined the deregulated fray in the South-east and South-west.

The DPR first issued a formal warning to the regional electricity companies in March 1996 – specifically against SWEB for selling gas in the South-west during a deregulation trial. The DPR asserted that using the SWEB database for anything other than supply contravened the Electricity Act.

But many of the Regional Electricity Companies (RECs) have flouted or ignored the DPR recommendations. Seeboard and Eastern Electricity publicise their own subsidiaries and carry inserts for others; Northern Electric publicises other services to customers; Midlands and East Midlands Electricity market their subsidiaries; and London Electricity published London Lights magazine, and was then contested by the DPR, for offering tickets to Chessington World of Adventure (MW January 31).

Last year, *Marketing Week* revealed that the gas and water companies are also breaching DPR guidelines. British Gas used its database for non-supply purposes – with a planned mailing of a Welcome Pack which included third party vouchers (*MW* June 14 1996).

Though the DPR only issued British Gas with a guideline – the first step in any enforcement action – three weeks ago, it is clear that the same rules have applied all along to gas and water, as the RECs.

Despite this, British Gas has mailed 19 million customers negative consent forms, telling them that mailings would be sent to them advertising products such as the Goldfish credit card (partly owned by British Gas) if they did not actively refuse, thus breaching DPR guidelines on fairness. Severn Trent Water mailed a booklet promoting washing machines and burglar alarms and Thames Water advertised home insurance and replacement windows.

British Gas received a preliminary notice warning of enforcement action, as did Southern Electric. Specific guidelines for the water companies have not been issued, but it is clear that these actions are, at the very least, against the spirit of the law. For British Gas and the RECs, the stonewalling by the DPR has become a major obstacle to becoming total energy providers. It is also affecting their ability to control costs.

Companies such as United Utilities and British Gas are understood to have plans in place to offer joint billings for all types of supply, enabling them to cut costs. DPR regulations outlaw joint billings of gas, water, electricity and telecoms – a move that could substantially reduce costs.

Though easing restrictions may allow the utilities to cut costs and sell more services, it could have a flipside. If British Gas is successful at getting the next government to lift the ban on data use, those retailers and service providers with much stronger brands, like BT, may reconsider their decision to stay out of the market.

All the indications are that the Labour Party is willing to listen, and is likely to respond to the utilities requests if elected. The DPR is also believed to be receptive. The windfall tax could yet have a silver lining for the utilities.

Direct Threat

New legislation brewing in Brussels puts the future of business directories in jeopardy. **DAVID REED** finds out why.

Here is how to carry out a very popular, relatively easy and surprisingly successful fraud. Identify a group of businesses which share a common trade and do not have highly developed marketing skills: hairdressers are a good example. Write inviting them to pay to be included in a directory of hair salons which will be widely circulated to potential customers. Pocket the money. Disappear without bothering to publish anything.

It is surprising how many companies have fallen for this ploy. A recently introduced twist is to affirm that failure to reply – even if it is to decline the invitation – constitutes acceptance under German law, leaving the target liable for the bill. While it is a deeply disreputable practice, it does reveal something about the nature of directories. There is a widespread belief that directories do exist on almost every business sector, even if companies in that sector have not seen it.

Indeed there are an incredible number of tightly-focused directories which are often the only source of information on that particular trade. This is a boon for business marketers, since the data is often endorsed by trade associations, giving the impression that they represent most of the market.

But if European legislation currently under consideration comes into effect, the directory may become an endangered species. And with the growth of electronic media, the process of compiling information in a paper format may in any case be obsolescent.

For the moment, directories are still used by many companies wanting to find out about suppliers and prospects, even in the marketing industry. "I have just filled out an entry for the Marketing Manager's Yearbook to promote our services. In filling it in, I have been thinking about the readership. Inevitably, it will be on other marketing managers' bookshelves as a source of reference," says Brenda Boardman, director of list broking and management at Lexicon Marketing Services.

But she also notes that the same information in the book will be rented out on tape and disk for direct marketing purposes. And it is this use which is likely to come under pressure from potential new legislation. For while the Data Protection Directive, which has been adopted and will pass into national law within three years, allowed legitimate use of personal data for direct marketing, at least two pending laws may make things much more difficult.

The first risk comes from the Telecommunications & Privacy (formerly known as the ISDN) Directive. Alastair Tempest, director general public affairs and self-regulation at FEDMA (the Federation of European Direct Marketing Associations), says Article 11 could cause problems. "It states that personal data contained in an electronic or printed directory and which is available to the public through Directory Enquiries should be limited to what is necessary to identify the subscriber, unless he or she has given unambiguous consent to publish."

Subscribers must be given the right to opt out of having their data used for direct marketing, to have their address published only in part, and to withhold information identifying their gender. The directive is currently self-contradictory – it says the service must be free of charge, but European member states may make a reasonable charge provided it does not act as a disincentive to register.

The real sting is in the tail of the article, as Tempest explains: "Member states may limit the implementation of the article to subscribers who are natural persons. It will be important that they do so, because the directive as a whole applies to businesses and consumers." This is an important development, since previous legislation has only applied to consumer data. The extension to include business information could drive directories – and any other formats – out of business.

Article 12 has further dramatic implications. "With regard to unsolicited calls, it requires member states to take appropriate measures to ensure for the purposes of direct marketing that they are not allowed without the consent of subscribers or in respect of subscribers who do not wish to receive them." That could mean harmonisation with the German law, which does not permit cold calling, or acceptance that a registration scheme like the Telephone and Fax Preferences Services is sufficient. This still has to be thrashed out in the directive.

Data owners and business marketers are keen to have this provision amended to reflect the different nature of business-to-business cold calling compared with business-to-consumer. "It would be pretty restrictive as far as automated calling and faxing is concerned. The point we are making is that for products like IT, where sales are made between enterprises, we don't feel the issue of privacy is key. We are looking to make a distinction between corporate and consumer use of data ," says Paul Evans, business development manager at EMAP Direct.

The argument that one company calling another is not as intrusive as when one company calls a consumer has merit. But it is countered by the direct marketing industry's own trend towards treating business targets like consumers. If this continues, then business people might fairly claim they should have the same rights to opt out of data use as the general public.

EMAP Direct currently markets a directory of the top 30,000 IT users which gives 127,000 points of contact. Evans says: "We are hoping to develop a database which includes personal attributes. We could see in a short space of time information on whether an executive plays golf, for example."

To justify this development he notes that, "a lot of IT sales are made on the golf course". His company is not alone in moving its database in this direction. At TDS Inform, which sells a range of business information including the Business Census (an enhanced database of virtually every business in the UK), managing director Gary Selby says: "We are confident of the fact that a business person is just a consumer at a work address."

He says that gaining a better understanding of the individual point of contact in a company helps business marketers to be more effective. But the key is still that the target represents the company, not his or herself, when it comes to making a decision.

With regard to the potential legislative threat, Selby says: "The fact that we have got an individual listed is largely irrelevant, so we don't have to be too concerned how consumer legislation is implemented on business. We will have to accept it."

Directories also face restrictions from yet another directive being considered by the European Commission. A Green Paper is due to be published on data privacy and publicly available data. One of its aims will be to define the public domain and how information in it may be used.

"In the original Data Protection Directive, one of the few good things was that it said public domain data could be used for correspondence purposes. We have interpreted that to mean it can be mailed or phoned. Under this proposal, it is going to be a question of whether you will be able to do anything," says Tempest.

The Northern European members of the Union tend to have very restricted use and access to public information.

In Sweden, any information held by the government has to be published and openly available to prevent it from using such data against its citizens.

For the same reasons, Germany has adopted an approach limiting the amount of data which the public sector may gather. Data may be in the public domain, but that does not mean the public can access it, as they are able to with the UK's Electoral Register. Again, these outlooks will have to be reconciled.

But there is a piece of European law which has at least cleared up one perpetual concern for directory publishers – the protection of their copyright.

"From time to time, our clients say, 'why can't we just get a directory and copy that information onto our database?'," says Boardman.

The perception is that since a directory has been published and is often to be found in public places, such as libraries or Business Link offices, it is also in the public domain. Marketers may be tempted to copy out names and addresses and use them without paying a royalty.

The Protection of Databases Directive has changed copyright law to prevent "unfair extraction" of this kind. Data owners have 15 years' protection before their information becomes freely available, by which time it is likely to be of little use. The courts have also taken a strict line, as in the Profords case which found the company had mixed Reed Directories and Yellow Pages information, without carrying out any "sweat of brow" enhancement.

The free availability of published information (or even electronically distributed data) means data owners have to take steps to monitor its use. "Seeding is seen as the best way of maintaining control over our copyright," says Angela Norton, marketing manager of reference services, at Dun & Bradstreet. "We place seed names in all our databases. If somebody buys it for a one-time use and uses it ten times, our seeds would receive those communications and we would know about it."

Large scale data theft is relatively rare, but there are grey areas. "If you rent a phone number with a person's surname and initial – if you ring up and get their full name, does that mean you have enhanced the data?" wonders Boardman. The bigger concern is just how much business information is going to be available to marketers once current planned legislation is passed.

If an individual within a business can opt out of receiving cold calls, what will be the impact on business marketing? Some directory publishers, like Yellow Pages, do not offer named contacts, so they are unlikely to suffer. But one outcome might simply be a return to less targeted marketing activity, which is likely to annoy business people even more. The lobbying is already underway. The number for the European Commission is in the telephone directory.

New data rules fail to smooth out flaws

Data protection legislation is about to change as the Government prepares to adapt existing law but other legislation, particularly regarding the utilities, may cause more, instead of less, confusion. **DAVID BENADY** reports

In the past year the Data Protection Registrar has investigated more than 100 companies, found 52 guilty and convicted them for breaching data laws. Companies have subsequently criticised the DPR, Elizabeth France, for misinterpreting existing data protection legislation.

But the situation is now about to change with publication of the Government's guidelines for adapting the existing law. The proposals fall short of a radical overhaul. But they do bring the UK's data protection legislation into line with the European directive on the subject which was first drafted in 1990 and represents the most major makeover of UK data protection law in 13 years.

The proposals clarify and strengthen certain consumer rights which have brought companies into conflict with the DPR. And formalise the use of "opt-outs" by companies in their mailers.

The UK Government's interpretation of the directive should become law by October 1998. Significantly it will take a second legal overhaul later in the year to clarify the position for the utilities whose sharing of database information has brought them into conflict with Elizabeth France.

Direct Marketing Association director of legal affairs Colin Fricker says: "There are some battles to come, though in most respects it seems the Government is taking a realistic line. Business can be comforted that the Government is not taking a hostile stance."

The new act will clarify certain thorny issues. The Data Protection Act 1984 made only vague reference as to how consumers should be protected from unwelcome mailings. It said the data had to be collected "fairly" so as not to mislead. The new Act will put into law the consumers' right to object to being sent circulars.

The proposals state: "In accordance with the first part of article 14b (of the European directive) the Government intends to provide for data subjects to be able to object free of charge to their personal data being used for direct marketing purposes (that is to opt out.)" This will not change the practice that many marketers have been involved in since 1984, which usually consists of sending a form with a box which the consumer ticks if they don't want to receive the mail-outs.

In the case of so-called "sensitive data", such as information about ethnic origin, voting patterns or sexual orientation, there must be an explicit consent or an "opt-in" – the consumer must say they do want to receive mail-outs before companies can target them.

The proposals continue: "The Government is still considering how best to give effect to the requirement for data subjects to be made aware of their right to object."

This is where the DMA will be trying to persuade the Home Office that the industry is best placed to inform consumers about their rights. Fricker says: "The data subject must know about the possibility of objecting to mailings being sent. We suggest that to inform subjects, we might take out notices in the press."

Ironically, the organisation which promotes the interests of the direct marketing industry is preparing to turn to above-the-line advertising to communicate with the public.

Another issue the DMA is discussing with the Home Office is the move to give consumers a legal right to request information about who is processing data about them and why.

So where does this leave some of the companies which have fallen foul of the Data Protection Registrar?

One company being investigated at the moment is Tesco after a number of complaints – ten to be exact – about the way it has targeted members of its Clubcard loyalty scheme with information about products from other companies.

The DPR insists that the new proposals would not change its view of this matter – Tesco did not tell Clubcard members they would be targeted with third-party mailings when they first signed up. Therefore, argues the DPR, it is only fair that members request specific information about other products, rather than sign an opt-out.

Tesco argues that as it offered members an opt-out, it is in the clear. The DPR says the European Directive – and thus the new Data Protection Act – still insists that information on individuals must be fairly and lawfully collected, as well as enshrining in law the right to be offered an opt-out.

Neither will the new regulations change the situation for the utility companies which are seeking to cross-sell other utility services – for example gas companies looking to sell electricity. The most high-profile row concerns British Gas sending mailers to its 19 million customers allowing them to opt out if they do not want information about other products, such as the Goldfish Credit Card which enables you to get money off your gas bill.

The DPR says it is in the terms of the Gas Act, which paved the way for gas privatisation, that British Gas cannot use data collected on customers when it was a state monopoly to push products other than gas, without a specific request (or opt-in) from the consumer. The DPR has put in place an "enforcement order" forbidding British Gas from using opt-out clauses. The utility is understood to be preparing to call for a DPR tribunal on the subject.

But this situation is not affected by the new data protection legislation, but rather the acts governing utilities.

President of the Board of Trade Margaret Beckett announced at the beginning of July that she would review regulations governing the utility industries "to ensure they deliver value, quality and choice to consumers". She says: "In short, it is time to take stock to see how the existing framework can be updated, modernised and refreshed."

British Gas and other utility companies are pushing the Government to ditch the requirement for them to have to use opt-ins. Liberalisation of data protection was on the agenda in a series of secret pre-election meetings (MW April 17) between the Labour Party and the utilities.

At the time it was believed that data protection was the quid pro quo for not opposing the windfall tax. The utilities are stumping up £5bn to the Government and they want something in return – the right to target existing consumers is a beginning.

Ironically, if they gain the right to request only opt-outs rather than opt-ins from the utilities review this will fly in the face of the DPR's view on what is a fair way of gaining information. It raises the prospect that Beckett's utilities legislation will allow the utilities to behave in a way that other companies cannot. Which can only add to the confusion which the new Data Protection guidelines are designed to erase.

ISSUES

1. **Why has the issue of data protection become so topical?**

2. **What are the legal implications of databases?**

3. **What are some of the current issues with regard to legislation on marketing databases?**

4. **What is your reaction to the EU directive on data protection?**

EXPLORATION OF ISSUES

1. The use of computers to gather, analyse and use information on customers and prospects has almost certainly contributed more to the growth of direct marketing than any other single factor, and possibly more than all other factors put together. It is this which allows the direct marketer to communicate on a one-to-one basis with a customer or prospect in a meaningful way.

This means that the database list is one of the direct marketer's single most important assets. It was widely reported that a former public utility company spent in the region of £100 million on its customer database system after privatisation.

Although accountants have been slow to recognise this, and database lists do not appear on balance sheets as an asset, the law does protect them. And it is only because database lists are protected by law that list brokers are able to recover the enormous sums of money required to gather the data by licensing them out to direct marketers.

However it is not only those who create databases

who are protected: so too are the individuals about whom data is collected. Consequently there is a complex interaction of different principles and laws.

2 Databases are protected by copyright, but there will be changes to this protection under forthcoming legislation and new database rights will be introduced. Most databases are protected by copyright, which makes it unlawful for anyone to copy a substantial part of the database without permission from the copyright owner.

It is important to realise that copyright does *not* protect the raw information – for example the names, addresses, ages and so on of the individuals included in the database. What copyright does protect is the database itself: the selection and structure of the data in it. Copyright only prevents people from copying the database. It does not prevent them from creating a similar or even identical one.

Computerised database lists receive even greater protection. With these it is not only telephoning or writing to the people on the list that infringes copyright. Merely loading the database list onto a computer infringes copyright unless the copyright owner has given permission.

3 The EU has issued directives that are likely to affect the operation of marketing databases and the law in this field is set to change. For example there is an EU directive on harmonising the protection of databases throughout the European Union. Under this directive, all member states must take steps to protect databases and they must do so by a combination of copyright and two new rights: the extraction right and the reutilisation right. The result will be that all computer database lists will be protected throughout the European Union for at least 15 years.

There are two ways in which these rights can be used. First, the rights owner can keep the database list to her or himself in order to obtain an advantage over her or his competitors. Alternatively, the rights owner can allow others to use the database upon payment of a fee. This permission is called a 'licence' and the rights owner may specify the purpose for which the database list can be used and how many times it can be used. If the user (known as the 'licensee') uses it for any other purpose, or on more occasions than is permitted, then that unauthorised use is unlawful.

Rights owners often insert traps into their database lists. For example they might often insert their own names and addresses to ensure that they receive a copy of every mailshot made using the list. This allows the rights owner to monitor usage of the list and to take legal action if the user breaches the terms of the licence or if someone is using an unlicensed copy of the list.

In practice, list brokers often bring together data that has been collected by other organisations so as to offer a more comprehensive service. The owners of the rights of the various lists often retain those rights and this leads to complex licensing, cross-licensing and sub-licensing arrangements. A consequence of this is that a database list will often contain trap addresses planted by more than one person as each of the rights owners attempts to monitor the usage of their own list.

The consequences of ignoring database rights can be very serious. Direct marketers who take a copy of a database list, either in the form of a photocopy or on disk, knowing that they do not have permission to do so commit a criminal offence. Their companies could be fined an unlimited amount and those responsible, as well as the directors and managers involved, could be prosecuted. If convicted they could be imprisoned for up to two years and be fined an unlimited amount. The courts are beginning to treat copyright infringement as seriously as theft, which in reality is what it is: the theft of someone else's work.

4 The individuals about whom direct marketers collect information have various legal rights, and they will soon have even more as new legislation is being introduced. The main legislation in this field is the Data Protection Act 1984. The purpose of this Act is to protect the rights of individuals when people such as direct marketers collect information about them and store or process it on computers. Under the Act, any direct marketing organisation that stores information about individuals on a computer must register with the Data Protection Registrar. It is a criminal offence to store or use personal information without being registered. The organisation must register various types of information, including:

- The type of personal information held.
- The sources from which it is obtained.
- The purposes for which it is used.
- To whom it might be disclosed.

Having registered with the Data Protection Registrar the organisation must comply with the data protection principles. Among other things, personal information must:

- Be obtained and processed fairly.
- Be adequate, relevant and not excessive in relation to the purpose for which it is held.
- Be accurate and up-to-date.

- Be held for no longer than is necessary for the purpose.
- Be adequately protected.

Perhaps the most troublesome of these for the direct marketer is the principle that personal information must be obtained and processed fairly and held for no longer than is necessary for the purpose.

Two services that help to deal with the use of database lists are the Mailing Preference Service and the Telephone Preference Service. These enable individuals to notify the service that they do not wish to receive unsolicited direct mail or unsolicited marketing telephone calls. There is no explicit legal requirement for direct marketers to make use of these services. However the British Codes of Advertising Practice and Sales Promotion and the Direct Marketing Association Code of Practice require that database lists are 'cleaned' by comparing them against the most recent version of the records held by these services and removing names and addresses as appropriate. This will obviously be taken into account by the data protection registrar when deciding whether or not information has been processed fairly.

It might not always be enough to use an opt-out mechanism, whereby people have to object to information about them being used for other purposes. In some circumstances it might be necessary to use an opt-*in* mechanism, so that the information is not used for other purposes unless the individual has specifically consented to this.

Direct marketers prefer to use an opt-out rather than an opt-in for the simple reason that – human nature being what it is – people often cannot be bothered to object. However it is for this very reason that at the data protection registrar is considering legal action against some of the privatised utility companies for the way they are using their databases.

The registrar's particular concern is that when these companies were state-owned they acquired vast amounts of information about their customers, who had no choice about where they obtained their gas, electricity and water and no choice about the information they were required to supply. The registrar believes that these companies should only use this information to market other goods and services if their customers have opted in, and that they are not processing information fairly if they rely on opt-out and the inertia of their customers.

5 The law in this area is due to change following the introduction of an EU directive on data protection. As with all directives, it is not in itself binding on direct marketers but the government must pass legislation to include it in UK law.

Direct marketers can only collect and process information on people if those individuals have given their clear consent. This will give people the right to object to the collection and processing of information on them unless the direct marketer can show that it is 'necessary' for the legitimate interests of the direct marketer or of any third party to whom the information is disclosed (such as the client). It will seriously hamper the activities of direct marketers if they have to obtain everybody's consent, so it has to be hoped that the latter justification will be applicable under UK law.

Unfortunately, the directive does not explain what is meant by 'necessary'. The usual meaning of 'necessary' is something that is essential. Although it may be highly desirable to process marketing information on computers, and indeed it may be impracticable to do it any other way, can it be said to be essential? We will have to wait to see how the directive is implemented in the UK and how the courts interpret it.

The directive introduced a specific provision with regard to direct marketing, but the government has two option on how the provision is implemented in UK law. The first option is that people must be given the legal right to prevent information on them from being used for direct marketing purposes. The effect of this would be to introduce a legal right equivalent to the Mailing Preference Service and the Telephone Preference Service. This is the least objectionable option as far as the direct marketing industry is concerned.

The second option is for the government to oblige direct marketers to notify each individual before using information on them for direct marketing purposes on behalf of a client, and before disclosing any of that information to anyone else. They would also have to tell those individuals that they have the right to object to that use or disclosure. This option would cause fewer problems for direct marketers working in-house because they would not have to notify people unless they intended to disclose the information outside the organisation. But it could be very expensive and an administrative nightmare for direct marketing agencies, which would be required to notify people of their rights.

If direct marketers wish to collect personal information from individuals they must tell them whether or not they are obliged to provide that information and any possible consequences of not providing it. They must also tell them of their right to see any information that is beeing held on them, and of their right to have it corrected if it is wrong. (Based on material provided by Paul Sampson for O'Malley *et al.*, 1999.)

3 Consumer Behaviour

Use of Psychological Peripheral Cues

KEY CONCEPTS

- Peripheral cues
- Subliminal messages
- In-store cues
- Use of colour, light, smell

Psychological Warfare

Consumers are becoming more sophisticated at spotting marketing techniques. So, marketers are resorting to new psychological techniques to sell them products.

HELEN JONES

Marketing, it is said, is a mixture of smoke and mirrors. This may explain why toy company Hasbro has employed the services of a shaman. You might wonder what a primitive Siberian religion, based on holy men communing with good and evil spirits, has to do with selling Sindy and Action Man, but Hasbro is taking it very seriously.

Although the company is tight-lipped about the process, marketing director Amanda Cutbill says: "We will explore all methods, traditional or new, to fully understand our brand."

It is part of an exploration in conjunction with brand specialist Wickens Tutt Southgate to identify the soul of the Hasbro brand.

As consumers become ever more sophisticated, and deconstruct the marketing messages they are sent, companies are attempting to focus on what it is about a brand that makes it sell. WH Smith is believed to be next for the magical treatment.

A host of other companies are also trying to identify what makes their brands tick, and DDG Brand Guardians is working with many of them. It creates sounds which are intended to represent the emotional qualities of a particular brand – whether it is a car or a mobile phone.

DDG director Jonathan Mercer says: "These are used internally to create a personality and a mood so that everyone in the marketing department knows, in an emotional sense, what the brand sounds like – although that sound is not intended to be a corporate jingle. If the company understands a brand, they are better able to understand why consumers will or will not buy it."

That companies are trying to get to the heart of their brands and use psychological techniques is an indication that consumers can no longer be manipulated in traditional ways.

Richard Zambuni, managing director of branding company CLK, says: "Consumers can decode the language of marketing and can see the intention that lies behind it. It is getting increasingly difficult to use tricks on the public, because they are very aware of what is going on."

Consumers, he asserts, know the language of packaging: white packs and stripes indicate diet products; purple, as used by Cadbury, is intended to convey luxury and indulgence (although consumers may not know that for centuries purple was associated with richness and the Catholic Church because it was such an expensive dye to produce.)

Consumers also know ready meals are photographed on small plates so they appear bigger – an illusion which is shattered as soon as you open the pack and realise you should have bought a pack intended for a family of four.

Behavioural Dynamics managing director Nigel Oakes says: "Tricks and so-called subconscious devices do not work. If something isn't 90 per cent right you can't make it better by using a bit of psychology."

His company, which launched in 1989, is a Swiss consortium funded by businesses which have invested £30m in examining behaviour and psychology and its impact on persuasion and communication.

The company is engaged in research with universities around the world and aims to offer competitive advantage to clients through the understanding and modification of human behaviour. "We are aiming to make behavioural dynamics the thing that revolutionises marketing. It's a different way of thinking, but it will take ten years to reach fruition," adds Oakes.

He dismisses a lot of psychological devices, "not because they are manipulative or covert, but because they don't work. They can only act as an add-on and then their impact may be minimal".

His scepticism is shared by Chris Pinnington, managing director of EURO RSCG Wnek Gosper and a former psychologist, says: "The idea brilliant psychologists sitting around developing tricks is nonsense. In reality, psychologists are used by advertising agencies to carry out research in a more objective way."

Tests carried out by Coca-Cola in the US hid subliminal messages in a cinema ad, alternatively flashing the words Coca-Cola and thirsty. "It failed dismally. Yes, sales increased during the test, but this was probably because they also turned the heating up. There are no conclusive experiments that show that sublimal messages work, says Oakes."

However, he says there are some psychological devices that can have an impact on consumers. The first and perhaps one of the most powerful is aroma. Smells are highly evocative. Whether it is the smell of cakes baking, or the smell of a particular type of disinfectant that reminds you of infant school, it produces an emotional, rather than a rational response.

David Goudge, a director of brand consultants The Brand Development Business, says: "There are stories that the makers of luxury cars spray both their showrooms and cars with an essence of leather in order to enhance the perception of luxury. You can see why that would work."

Behavioural Dynamics subsidiary Marketing Aromatics is examining the effect of smells on consumers, and has produced a number of corporate smells which 25 companies – who decline to be named, but are believed to include large department stores – are testing.

Oakes says smells can be used in an associative way. "For example, a travel agent may ask for help to sell more tickets. A solution could be to use a smell of coconuts or rum punch to produce an aroma reminiscent of holidays. This would get people thinking about exotic breaks, rather than the

cycling holiday in Wales they may have been thinking about when they first came into the shop."

But what would have a stronger effect, says Oakes, would be a 'behavioural' aroma such as the smell of airline fuel to remind consumers of the excitement of crossing the tarmac. However, he says that even if you could bottle it in a diluted form, it would take a brave marketing director to use it.

There are other problems with using smells, not least of which is pumping it around stores. "Sometimes it wafts around in a big cloud," says Oakes. However, he adds that gas giant The BOC Group has recently developed a system called Aroma Gas which ensures more even distribution.

Oakes says that while smell can be powerful in some environments, it is not suitable in all circumstances and can not work miracles. "There is too much snake oil associated with aromas at the moment and pumping round a lavender smell will not make a customer buy a dress. It is debatable whether in a high pressure environment such as a department store, any smell can put hassled shoppers at ease. It is likely to be a complete waste of money."

Other psychological tools can be more obviously successful. Stores have to be laid out in such a way that the consumer's brain can process the information it is given, says Oakes.

He maintains that the gestalt in a retail environment is absolutely critical. He cites Marks & Spencer as an example of getting it right. "In recent years it has introduced standalone sandwich shops within food halls where you can get all the components for a snack lunch – sandwiches, crisps, fruit and a drink etc. In the past you had to wander all round the food hall to get these items. Since they have been grouped together sales are claimed to have risen by 30 per cent."

This method of grouping products together is called consumer preference layout, and works just as well in traditional supermarkets. Oakes says that if fruit is all grouped together – fresh, tinned and dried – then sales increase because consumers think in terms of fruit rather than in terms of tins. "Using this layout method in tests, we have boosted sales by 15 to 20 per cent," he claims.

Lighting can also have a psychological impact – the brighter the lighting, the faster people move through the store. Red-toned lighting is used in areas for impulse purchases. For example, says Oakes, stationer Rymans uses red tones at the front of its stores for impulse buys such as pens and stationery. At the back of its stores, it uses blue tones because they create a relaxing environment in which consumers can make decisions on large purchases, such as computers.

But perhaps the most interesting psychology experiments carried out by Behavioural Dynamics and another of its subsidiaries – Retail Dynamics – are to do with sound.

While musak, store announcements and in the case of some Marks & Spencer's stores the broadcast of Sky News, can be extremely irritating, research indicates that shoppers find quiet stores intimidating. In such cases, Retail Dynamics can supply "white noise" – a dull hum like the noise of a fridge which is barely discernible but cuts out any feeling of awkwardness.

In an experiment at a Birmingham shopping centre, Retail Dynamics used sound to see if it could cut down on shoplifting. "We ran a simulated radio station with musak and announcements such as "if you lose a child, report to a security guard" or "if you want an application form for a competition ask a security guard".

"The subtle but endless references to security, and the fact we mentioned a BBC film crew would be covering 'a day in the life of a shopping centre' cut theft by 34 per cent."

Honest shoppers got a feeling of reassurance, and thieves got the message that the centre was crawling with security guards. "It was a very interesting test, but dangerously close to consumer manipulation, so we pulled out," says Oakes.

While many marketing directors may be sceptical about the impact of psychology on their businesses, Behavioural Dynamics is confident it can identify tricks which don't work and techniques that have measurable results.

Oakes says: "Imagine if we were to offer payment by results? It will really shake them up and will show the traditional marketing community we mean business. But we have to be very sure of what we are doing, and that is why we won't be ready to launch for a number of years."

ISSUES

(1) **Discuss how peripheral cues such as light, colour, smell and sound might influence customers in a retail environment.**

(2) **What is a subliminal message and what is your assessment of the use of this approach in marketing?**

(3) **Are the approaches discussed in the above article 'tricks' or 'techniques', dangerous 'manipulation' or legitimate 'marketing'?**

EXPLORATION OF ISSUES

(1) It can be argued that, on the one hand, the techniques described in the article above, such as the use of sound, smell and colour, are based on classical conditioning in which certain natural and unconditioned responses result from specific stimuli. For excample, long-haul holiday makers are familiar with the aroma of rum punch and palm trees, and respond favourably to those aromas, then the same favourable response should be elicited if a travel agency uses the same aroma in-store.

On the other hand, to what extent is this ubliminal? Take sound, for example. 'Mood music' might be about more than just 'mood' – it might influence behaviour without the consumer being aware of it. Adrian North and David Hargreaves of Leicester University, for example, has found that classical music prompted the purchase of more expensive wine in an off license, compared with when top 40 music was played. They also found that when confronted with a display of wines from different countries, consumers bought different wines according to the music being played. When the music was clearly French, French wine outsold German wine by 5:1. When German music was being played, German wine outsold French wine by 2:1. However only 2 per cent of buyers admitted (or were able to admit) that the music had affected their choice!

They also found that when different types of music were played in a cafeteria, sales were 14 per cent higher when classical music was played.

The tempo of music can govern the speed at which customers move through a store, so slightly more up-tempo music at closing time might encourage them to hurry to the check-out, while slower music at other times might encourage them to linger and perhaps spend more.

2 Subliminal messages are those which are not noticed at the conscious level but are designed to be taken in via the subconscious.

Many people believe that consumers are subconsciously or unconsciously influenced by 'subliminal' advertising. Subliminal advertising is supposed to exert an influence on behaviour without the consumer being aware of it. An example of subliminal advertising was the insertion of flash visual messages – 'Eat popcorn' and 'Drink Coca-Cola' – in a movie being shown in New Jersey.

These flashes were too short to be consciously observed. Another example was reported by Reuters in 1994, when red faced officials at the Walt Disney company had to answer the question 'Who undressed Jessica Rabbit?' Apparently three additional frames (depicting Jessica without her underwear) had been inserted into the laser disc version of the film 'Who Framed Roger Rabbit?' At the normal 24 frames per second playback this wasn't noticeable but when viewed frame by frame it was. But who has laser discs these days anyway! Subliminal images can also be inserted in photographs in a scrambled or hidden way, for example the word sex in ice cubes in a glass of whisky.

The argument is that these hidden flashes or pictures are unconsciously observed, processed and, without any cognitive defence or screening by the superego, transmitted to the mind of consumers. Recent research, however, does not support this view, but if subliminal advertising does work, it is questionable whether it would be allowed. A subliminal message encouraging us to buy a particular brand of baked beans would, if it worked, be bad enough, but what about the implications of a subliminal 'vote for me' at election time? If this method works then clearly it is very powerful, and even though the experiments described proved inconclusive, subliminal messages have been banned them in most countries.

3 Whether the approaches discussed in the article represent dangerous manipulation or legitimate marketing is really a matter of opinion, but the discussion this has provoked is usually valuable and has produced additional insight. We shall not produce a list of specific suggestions here because of the subjective nature of the issue.

Demographic Profiling

- Profiling
- Segmentation
- Demographics
- Social grade
- Family life cycle/life stage

No longer simply a case of ABC

Tried and trusted, the ABC1 system of consumer classification has served the industry for more than 40 years. But is it time the furnace men and coopers were replaced by Maggies and Telly Addicts?

MEG CARTER

Classifying consumers by media consumption rather than their profession and social standing has been described as a step towards John Major's dream of a classless society. But in fact the traditional ABC1 social gradings have been outdated for some time.

Computer technology has enabled different companies to incorporate and adapt a range of consumer research data, tailoring groupings to individual advertisers' needs. Now Carat Research has launched another system – known as Media Graphics – but are social demographics finally a thing of the past?

Carat Research director Colin Macleod believes not. For all its faults, the ABC1 classification system is familiar and well-understood across the industry. However, he hopes Media Graphics will become a viable, standard alternative.

Media Graphics is based on TGI data. The system classifies people by the types of newspapers and magazines they read and television they watch. This illustrates their attitudes and lifestyle – a better indicator of the products they are likely to consume and the activities they pursue, Carat believes.

According to Media Graphics, nine per cent of the UK population are Broadsheet Browsers – reading a lot of quality newspapers and viewing little ITV – Media Graphics group M1. M2 are Media Hermits, 13 per cent of the population, who read few newspapers and view little TV. M3, or Maggies, read many women's magazines but few newspapers (16 per cent). M4 are Telly Addicts (20 ber cent) – who watch some ITV but read little.

Heavy media consumers are classified as Media Junkies or M5 (15 per cent), Tabloids not Telly – M6 (nine

per cent) and Popular Masses, M7, representing 18 per cent of the UK population.

"Media Graphics works not only because people choose their media to fit in with their attitudes and lifestyles, but also because what they read or watch helps develop these attitudes and give ideas on how to live their lives," says Carat Research managing director Phil Gullen.

To demonstrate the ease and effectiveness of the system, Carat cites examples including draught lager drinkers (51 per cent fall into the Tabloids not Telly and Popular Masses categories – these people are 88 per cent more likely to consume draught lager than the average adult drinker). Marks & Spencer shoppers (50 per cent fall into groups Broadsheet Browsers, Maggies and Media Junkies, who are 22 per cent more likely to shop there) and hired video watchers (56 per cent are Media Junkies, Tabloids not Telly and Popular Masses – 32 per cent more likely to view).

The advantage of Media Graphics to the advertiser is that it is both selective and practical, says Gullen. A product used by Maggies would advertise in women's magazines, another used by Telly Addicts would use ITV and Popular Masses would be targeted via The Sun. 'It is very simple and a much more direct approach than with social class,' he adds.

The ABC1 system was devised after the Second World War and was first used by research company RSL, in postwar national readership surveys. Based on professions, some of its classifications appear archaic. But it has been updated a number of times. These include a reclassification in 1992 of head of household – now known as chief income earners – "the person with the largest income, whether from employment, pension, state benefits, investments or any other sources".

Top of the pile is grade A, the upper middle classes comprising higher managerial, administrative or professional people. Grade B is the middle classes - intermediate managers, administrative and professional employees. C1 covers lower middle classes, C2 skilled working classes, D working classes and E "those at lowest levels of subsistence".

Different professions and occupations are sorted within these bands. A number are – or will soon be – obsolete, others undoubtedly require updating, from professional furnace men (D), to coopers, hoop makers and benders (C2), stevedores (C2) to clerks, cashiers and office machine operators (C1). While the likes of ministers of the crown are banded A, and authors, journalists and creatives ABC1, the grading for sportsmen and women depends on their success.

Moves are afoot to redefine social gradings across the Continent. An EC 'Euro Barometer' has attempted to do just this, and is now being used for a number of pan-European EC initiatives, although is yet to be adopted on a wider scale. Classifications are based on ownership of consumer durables rather than income, because of the disparity in earnings between different countries.

Pym Cornish, a non executive board director of RSL and former director and deputy chairman, is currently writing a book on social grading. Although a number of companies have attempted alternative grading systems since the ABC1 system was introduced in the Forties, none have become industry standard, he says.

One, devised by Cornish, was launched in 1980. "Sagacity" was based on the concept of the life cycle. People were grouped into dependents (still living with their parents), independents (supporting themselves), family stagers, empty nesters and the retired.

"Sagacity interlaced this with social grades giving a total of 12 classifications which cross referred people's stage in the life cycle with broad social gradings," he says. Lifestyle offered an improvement on classification by age because some people in their 20s could still be living at home – a dependent rather than an independent.

The system has proved to be successful, although it has been adopted most extensively within higher education, he adds.

However, as different companies now access and manipulate different data by computer to identify their own target groups, the days of the industry-standard classification system could be numbered. But whether social gradings will ever become obsolete is open to question.

According to one research company source: "Analyse the characteristics of different groups and you see obvious differences. The ABC1 system must still have some relevance."

Cornish agrees. "I believe something like it will always exist," he says. "It changes its meaning over a lifetime because it is based on occupations, and over time occupations change their meaning and existence."

As some occupations – notably those associated with computing – have evolved, others, such as clerical work, are decreasing, while automation has made others obsolete. "The whole structure of society is constantly changing slowly," Cornish adds. "But I think the broad concept of hierarchy, from As to Es at the bottom, will more or less remain."

ISSUES

1. **What is social grade and why has it been so popular among marketers for so long ?**

2. **Why did marketers start to question the value of social grade?**

3. **What is life stage, or family life cycle, and how useful might it be for segmenting and targeting markets?**

EXPLORATION OF ISSUES

1 Marketers have long adhered to the basic principle of social stratification but have avoided researching possible segments on the basis of social class in any true sociological sense. This would involve a rather complicated assessment of income, wealth, power and skill. So instead, in the UK and many other European countries, social grade is used, determined in the UK by the occupation of the household's chief income earner, resulting in a sixfold classification: A, B, C1, C2, D and E. Many commercial market research programmes have found significant differences in buying behaviour between the various social grades. The occupational basis for social grade in the UK are shown in Table 3.1, and examples of social grade's indicatory power are provided in Table 3.2.

The traditional justification for the continued use of social grade is twofold. First, it is simple to research. All that is required is for data to be analysed according to the occupation of the 'chief income earner in the household', previously 'the occupation of the head of the household'. Second, social grade appears to be a reasonably good indicator of buying behaviour, and the profile of UK voters has remained remarkably stable over time (Table 3.3).

2 During the 1980s in particular, a number of signifi-

Table 3.1 Social grade in the UK

Social grade	Social status	Head of household's occupation	Percentage
A	Upper middle class	High managerial, administrative, or professional	2.7
B	Middle class	Intermediate managerial, administrative or professional	15.2
C1	Lower middle class	Supervisory, clerical, junior managerial or administrative	24.1
C2	Skilled working class	Skilled manual workers	17.8
D	Working class	Semi- and unskilled manual workers	17.8
E	Lowest levels of subsistence	State pensioners, widows, casual or lowest-grade workers	13

Source: JICNARS 1991

Table 3.2 The indicatory power of social grade, indices of usage (national average = 100)

	Toothpaste	Tea	Baked beans
A,B	140	78	89
C1	119	90	95
C2	123	108	128
D,E	52	103	40

Source: Market Research Society 1981

cant criticisms of the use of social grade were made. There are inevitable anomalies in its use, for example nearly a third of those earning over £21 000 are C2DE and half those earning £15–£21 000 are C2DE. Thus the formerly strong correlations between social grade and income have weakened. Some of those in C2, such as highly skilled manual workers, now earn more than some middle managers in group B.

O'Brien and Ford (1988) found that of 400 respondents in earlier surveys who were reinterviewed to confirm their social grade, 41 per cent had been put in the wrong group and this is afurther indication of inadequacy of the system.

However, if we were to integrate the above demographic variables and discover that those most interested in our product or service are predominately, say, AB males, aged 45–54, we would have a combination of some of the most used segmentation variables of recent decades. Inferring the activities, interests, opinions and indeed buying behaviour of segments like this, or of others such as C1 females aged 18–24 or C2 males aged 25–34, is quite simple and can probably be done in a

Table 3.3 Voting stability over time, UK electorate, 1983 – 1997

	Conservatives				Labour				Liberal/Democrats			
	1983	1987	1992	1997	1983	1987	1992	1997	1983	1987	1992	1997
A,B	60	57	56	41	10	14	20	31	28	26	22	22
C1	51	51	52	37	20	21	25	37	28	26	19	18
C2	40	40	38	27	32	36	41	50	26	22	17	16
D,E	33	30	30	21	41	48	50	59	24	20	15	13

Source: Sunday Times, 12 April 1992, 'The Polls' HTTP://www.mori.com/ge-1997.htrr

Table 3.4   UK family lifecycle

Lifecycle stage	Percentage of households
Bachelor	1.7
Newly married couples	3.8
Full nest 1 (with preschool children)	14.6
Full nest 1 (lone parent)	1.5
Middle aged, no children (aged 35–44)	1.5
Full nest 2 (school-aged children)	2.1
Full nest 2 (lone parents)	2.4
Launching families (with non-dependent children)	7.8
Launching families (lone parent)	1.8
Empty nest 1 (childless, aged 45–60)	11.6
Empty nest 2 (retired)	11.7
Solitary survivor (under 65)	3.3
Solitary survivor (retired)	17.4

NB   This totals 81.2 per cent because only these groups can be determined from the current UK census
Source: Lawson, 1988

couple of minutes, showing the power of stereotypes but also revealing the probable inaccuracies of inference alone.

3 The family lifecycle concept relates to interests and buying behaviour changing over time due to the progression from single person to newly married, married with children, married with children who no longer live in the parental home ('empty nest') and finally to solitary survivor. Some product categories, for example life assurance, are predominantly chosen by the husband, while other categories, for example food and children's clothing, are 'wife dominated', and yet others, such as choice of holiday and housing, are based on joint decision making that sometimes includes the children. Buying needs, values and behaviour differ in the various stages. An updated lifecycle model for the UK is presented in Table 3.4.

A recent promotional campaign by Barclays Bank depicted the life stages of their customers, by showing a young single man, then a couple with a family and then an older couple whose children had left home, and suggested that the bank offered financial service products to suit all individuals as they progress through these stages.

The concepts here have been extended and applied in practical market analysis programmes such as Sagacity, which combines an abbreviated version of the family lifecycle with income and occupation. The result is twelve categories based on life stage, irrespective of whether or not both partners are working, and on blue-collar or white-collar occupations:

1   Dependent
   1.1 White collar
   1.2 Blue collar
2   Pre-family
   2.1 White collar
   2.2 Blue collar
3   Family
   3.1 Better off
      3.1.1   White collar
      3.1.2   Blue collar
   3.2 Worse off
      3.2.1   White collar
      3.2.2   Blue collar
4   Empty nest
   4.1 Better off
      4.1.1   White collar
      4.1.2   Blue collar
   4.2 Worse off
      4.2.1   White collar
      4.2.2   Blue collar
Source: Research Services Ltd 1980

It is perhaps a significant indicator of the end of marketing's love affair with social grade that from 1988 Granada TV replaced social grade as one of the profiling characteristics in its audience research with family lifecycle (they call it life stage).

Lifestyle Profiles

- Consumer profiling
- Market segmentation
- Targeting
- Databases
- Psychographics

The data game

The lifestyle data industry is coming into its own – with new players developing and expanding the business.

DAVID REED

The lifestyle data industry has gone through something of a revolution in recent years. From being divided between three companies – CMT, ICD and NDL – the market is now shared with CCN's Chorus, Consumer Survey's Lifestyle Focus, The Daily Telegraph and others. That such companies should consider it worthwhile investing the significant sums required to build a lifestyle database suggests they view data as something very valuable indeed.

According to David Grafton, managing director of Equifax Europe's Decision Solutions, the reason is that lifestyle data gives important extra insight into consumers. "The simple geodemographic code is like the ECU of prediction. It is useful, but to drive modelled solutions, it is individual data that provides the power."

To have value for marketers, lifestyle databases need to reach a critical mass. CSL has managed a significant feat in building a file of 3 million names since it launched last June. That allows it to be a player, but to win clients, the data needs to have something special to offer. Managing director Bob Hayward claims: "We have a different proposition to all the others. We opt people in to receiving information."

The mailings for the Lifestyle Focus surveys carry an overt explanation that the purpose of the exercise is to allow marketers to target direct mail at responders. Hayward notes there is an element of risk in asking people to opt into being mailed in this way, since historically response rates have been lower than for an opt-out approach. "When you treat UK consumers like adults, you have to hope they will react as such. Response rates for clients are bearing that out," he says.

This may in part be a factor of the recency of the data – new names on file tend to respond better than older ones. In part, this is what has helped to bring in the new players. Traditional lists have undergone a cycle of slow replenishment because of the sluggish economy. Hayward accepts that good response rates for clients mailing to CSL data may be because of this freshness, or even because of the nature of the offers being made, "but there is also evidence it is because of the opt-in".

At NDL, group marketing manager Lynn Cooper believes clients can benefit not just from the new sources, but from the fact that existing ones are expanding. "I believe there is a growing pool of individuals answering surveys," she says. In the ten years it has been trading, NDL has amassed 23 million survey responses, giving a mailing file of about 11 million.

One criticism of lifestyle data has always been that each source has a slant towards certain consumer segments. This usually reflects the way in which the data has been captured. In NDL's case, the surveys have been inserted with the product registration cards in brown and white goods. While there is still a large pool of manufacturers to be tapped, Cooper notes that other sources such as travel companies, telecoms and fmcg are now being explored.

"The challenge as technology develops is finding new ways of reaching people to get them to fill in a form," agrees Roger Williams, NDL's head of marketing. He notes that new media opportunities, such as the Internet, may prove viable, but in the medium term, continued growth in the data available suggests there is no real crisis.

Among the new players, however, there has been a concerted effort to try and introduce data on individuals who are not currently covered by other surveys. At CCN, this led to a link-up with EMAP to run lifestyle surveys in its 90 consumer titles. Associate director of CCN Marketing Services, Jim Hodgkins, says: "Every lifestyle company knows which titles work for inserts and which lists to mail for surveys. Clients want fresh data – EMAP lets us get to new groups."

If its Chorus database can pull in significant volumes from EMAP's 10 million readers, it will give the company a useful marketing hook. If the pool of data subjects is being expanded by such initiatives, so too is the range of clients to whom suppliers can sell their data. "On the upside, there has been consistent growth in fmcg demand over the past three years ," says Martin Kiersnowski, surveys director at ICD.

He notes that many brands are sponsoring questions on surveys about use of competing brands. Companies like Procter & Gamble, Imperial Tobacco, Guinness and Premier Beverages have all taken the exclusive rights for a year on answers by consumers about their brand repertoire. This information on specific buying behaviour remains the strongest element of lifestyle data.

"There is very little interest in atti-tudinal questions. Clients want specific information on potential buyers or competitors' buyers. There is less interest in attitudinal stuff than four or five years ago," says Kiersnowski. This view is echoed at CMT, which runs the National Shoppers' Survey and markets a lifestyle database called BehaviourBank. Its managing director, Mark Patron, says: "We do not tend to get too involved in attitudinal questions over and above those we already ask, such as reasons for purchase. Those areas are very important – do you go on price, promotion and brand or do you rotate products?"

He notes that the power of the grocery multiples and electrical goods chains has helped to stimulate the market for lifestyle data. Manufacturers need more than ever to be able to understand what share of customer they have and what is stimulating purchase. "It has made manufacturers raise their game in terms of the use of information," says Patron.

The geodemographic profile providers have also had to respond to the recent upsurge in interest in lifestyle data. Not that they are necessarily losing out. As Greg Bradford, managing director of CACI, notes: "Our base is in Census data and that is still very much needed, for example, in retail planning." He emphasises that the advantage geodemographics still has over lifestyle is that it is based on data on every individual in the country – the closest lifestyle can get is one in two households from the MIC database formed by pooling CMT and NDL's surveys.

But rather than continue the divisive marketing battle between the two camps, CACI is among a number of suppliers which have launched systems that draw on both sets of data. CensusLifestyle combines CACI's Acorn geodemographics with lifestyle data licensed from ICD. "You can use Census data to take the bias out of the lifestyle data and then model up to cover the whole country," says Bradford. One new product to flow from this fusion of data is PayCheck, which allows marketers to predict likely income for every postcode, something which has always been difficult to achieve in the UK.

The willingness of lifestyle data owners to licence their data for use in this way is bringing about significant changes to the marketplace. Linked products that draw on the strengths of both elements are likely to become more common. But the changes are not limited to just these geo-lifestyle products.

In a move likely to expand use of targeting and profiling beyond the home market of direct marketing and store planning, some suppliers are now combining market research products with lifestyle and Census information.

Taylor Nelson AGB is marketing SmartBase, which "bridges the gap between market research and database marketing", according to David Sneesby, marketing director of Taylor Nelson AGB's marketing services division. "Whereas the two disciplines seem to have gone on quite separately and independently of each other, this is a positive step forward." He notes that inferred behaviour is not as robust as actual data and that where lifestyle sources have been deficient is in showing what consumers actually buy.

By licensing data on 13 million households from MIC and linking it to the AGB SuperPanel, SmartBase combines both breadth and depth of information. One reason this has not been done in the past is the sheer difficulty of linking the two. Emphasising that the market research information continues to be held by Taylor Nelson under strict data protection and Market Research Society rules, Greg Ward, development director of Taylor Nelson AGB, says: "We have a process called T-Groups.

"If you see the potential universe of all consumers as a cube, MIC has a thin slice across the top and we have a thin slice downwards. Where those two lines cross, it creates a smaller cube. SmartBase is about enabling clients to use that little cube to extrapolate out to the entire cube," he says. The process is robust because MIC has information on 60 per cent of households, and has a match to 7,000 of the households on the SuperPanel.

A similarly complex process has been used by Equifax Europe to build its Dimensions database, which incorporates census, lifestyle, market research from MORI, and other data sources. "For marketing purposes, you want a combination of different characteristics on customers and prospects," says David Grafton, managing director of Equifax's Decision Solutions division.

"The only way to get that is to make use of the different databases available. The problem is, you have to go to all the different suppliers of data and buy them piecemeal, then you have to match them at a common level of geography," he says. Within most companies, each of the different data sets

is probably in use by separate departments in isolation.

With the trend towards centralisation of information into data warehouses, companies want to be able to get the whole picture. At the same time, data users want to retain the predictive power of the data sets they are familiar with. While the third-party products which have already fused these sources are one answer, this corporate trend may also be favouring external suppliers who are not committed to any one source in advance.

At The Database Group, sales director Neal Muranyi suggests that companies which can process client data, and also cherry-pick the best third-party information, are well placed in the current market. "Each of the data sources has something good, but none is right for everybody. If you look at client data, it will have a certain bias. If you apply geodemographic and lifestyle data, then run a Chaid analysis, you can create a customer segmentation that is balanced," he

says.

He believes that the underlying trend is towards this combined approach, which he calls "biographics". With so many suppliers now offering multiple choice solutions to targeting and profiling problems, marketers are not short of ways to improve their results. What may be harder is for them to understand what each system offers, how it is constructed, and what slant the data may have.

But Hodgkins counsels caution before assuming the rules have changed for good. "You may not get as much predictive value as you are being sold as getting," he says. Indeed, the products now being marketed may be in advance of the market's ability to understand them. Hodgkins adds: "The main use is still for direct mail, rather than market analysis, and users still judge by response rates. They don't understand how you write the model or what's in the selection criteria."

Facts of life

MARTIN CROFT looks at how lifestyle databases have developed in their short history, and where they are heading now.

Nearly ten years ago, I interviewed the marketing director of a major bank who was bursting with pride over his new computer system. With the evangelical fervour of a man who had just discovered the wonders of information technology, he told me in hushed tones that the bank could now find the answer to its biggest unsolved question: how many customers it had.

Yes, it was only in the late Eighties that Britain's banks installed computer systems that identified customers by name. Until then, all they knew was how many separate accounts there were – but they had no idea how

those accounts related to actual consumers.

If the marketing director in question thought being able to count his customers was revolutionary, imagine how he must have felt when he first came across a lifestyle database.

Lifestyle databases exploded onto the British scene in the late Eighties promising – and delivering – revolutionary new ways to reach customers.

Using information collated from millions of consumer surveys, the big lifestyle database companies have managed to put together information on pastimes, employment, car purchasing habits, favourite brands, sports – and so the list goes on.

Lifestyle databases were the esoteric marketing superweapon of the time. They offered UK marketers previously unheard of targeting ability, which would allow them to mail selectively those sections of the community which were more likely to buy their products. A sports shoe company, for example, could identify households where people played sports: a breakfast cereal manufacturer could identify kitchens where its products were consumed.

Furthermore, if developed, marketers could use lifestyle data to segment and profile their own existing customer records, identify the high spenders, and then go out and look for other consumers who had similar behaviour patterns.

But marketing technology has moved on over the past ten years, and lifestyle segmentation and profiling has become humdrum and run-of-the-mill – even commoditised.

The new catchphrase tripping off the tongues of marketing gurus is one-to-one marketing. This is using detailed knowledge of individual consumer's habits, drawn from the marketer's own database of existing customers, to tailor products and services directly to each one – so they spend more with you. Why bother wasting money on acquiring new customers when it is so much cheaper to milk the ones you already have?

Jon Epstein, a director of customer-driven marketing consultancy Results R Us, argues: "The only role for lifestyle data is prospecting for new customers, and this is only viable if the source of business with existing customers has dried up, or the data on them has not been collected. It costs 50 times more to acquire a new customer than it does to sell to an existing one at the right time. Direct marketing to known customers on the basis of accurate information about their buying needs will dramatically increase profitability."

Epstein accepts that lifestyle databases still have something to offer, saying: "Don't get me wrong – I'm not claiming they're dead as a dodo."

But he believes that marketers should look first at the behavioural data they already have in their transaction and contact databases, before going to the lifestyle companies.

He adds: "What someone did has got to be more powerful than how they replied to a questionnaire to a third party."

Epstein bases his observations on research undertaken by himself and Glen Peters of Price Waterhouse, with over 150 senior marketing professionals at the Marketing Forum in the autumn of 1996. He argues that marketing professionals should know that effective marketing is not just about delivering the right products and services at the right price, but also delivering to customers who are ready and who want to buy them.

He says: "Achieving this demands that customers are treated individually, and not as stereotypes defined by ageing and aggregated geographic or lifestyle data. This research demonstrates an overwhelming recognition that customer-driven marketing is central to improving business performance. No longer can customers be treated generically. Rather, marketing must address customers individually according both to their needs and to their value to the business."

But Epstein admits: "The same research also proves that few businesses will adopt the approach which their marketers know to be right." Indeed, a straw poll he conducted recently among representatives of major lifestyle and geodemographic data providers at a recent DMA seminar suggests that the suppliers themselves believe 70 per cent of marketers are failing to use data properly.

Marc O'Regan, head of data consultancy at direct marketing agency Barraclough Hall Woolston Gray, argues that lifestyle databases have become far richer and more useful over the past decade, and that marketers have a long way to go before wringing the last drop of usefulness out of them.

He adds: "Lifestyle data has been an invaluable tool to help us understand customers and prospects better, and target more effectively. The volume of respondents, the richness of data held on them and the sophistication of the ways in which the data is exploited have grown tremendously. My first contact with lifestyle data in 1987 involved intuitive selections that delivered relatively small universes – a far cry from using the latest techniques, such as Chaid or regression models, which can sift through millions of records to find the right consumers."

And O'Regan argues that the lifestyle database market has room to grow. He observes: "While rental of lists from the lifestyle databases is now a routine aspect of database marketing, the data-tagging market – where lifestyle data is matched to client database records using a name and address match – is less mature." He admits, though, that "there is a difficulty facing marketers in assessing the incremental value added by lifestyle data".

Dawn Orr, sales director of NDL, probably the biggest lifestyle database company operating in the UK, rejects the idea that lifestyle databases have had their day. She says: "Lifestyle data, once an information source used almost exclusively for customer acquisition through consumer list rental, is now rapidly broadening its remit in the market."

She cites two factors to support her argument. Firstly, sheer mass. Lifestyle database companies have now collected so much information on UK households that it can be used "for a whole range of other strategic marketing applications". NDL and sister company CMT, which are now both owned by the Dutch publishing group VNU, have between them information on nearly three-quarters of the UK's households.

Secondly, even those companies which want to be one-to-one driven need the services of lifestyle databases, she claims. "In the bid to cross-sell, up-sell and retain customers in the battle for increased market share, organisations are having to become ever more sophisticated in their approach to database development, customer analysis and predictive modelling. Up-to-date, relevant customer/market data is the common currency driving important advances in these areas. As a result, lifestyle data is increasingly in demand by organisations for a whole range of applications."

David Cheek, marketing director of The Computing Group, says that lifestyle databases still have a role to play, either "as cold list sources for specific information such as age, interest in bingo and so on, which you can combine with similar information to provide a profile", or "to add colour to a database".

Cheek explains this second point: "A customer database usually holds simple transactional data, but lifestyle data can give you much more. When you start matching different clusters, you can put in additional information like age. With even more specific data from sponsored questions, you can add details such as the person's favourite food, his intention to buy a conservatory or whether he has wedding plans."

Maria Dooley, list sales manager of list broker Lexicon Marketing services, strongly believes that lifestyle databases are still a vital element in marketing programmes. She says: "As independent list brokers, we believe all six lifestyle databases should be considered by our clients. First of all, they offer clients 'universe' potential which is not always available from other files, and secondly the companies which own them offer data tagging and profiling services.

"Profiling helps the client understand more about his/her customer database, while tagging makes the client more valuable, allowing more personalised mailings which should increase the response."

Epstein accepts all of these arguments in favour of lifestyle databases: but he still believes that there is little use in clients going to relatively expensive suppliers of lifestyle information if they are going to continue to ignore their own data sources.

Marketers, as far as he is concerned, are scandalously wasteful of their own resources, and seem to be more concerned about investing money in the pursuit of those consumers who fail to respond to their wiles than in rewarding those who have.

"The problem is," Epstein says, "that marketers have become ignorant or lazy. They think they have to send all their customers questionnaires, or buy data from lifestyle databases. I challenge the idea that if they buy data and overlay it, they'll understand their customers better. What they should do is look at their own records collected through the sales of their products – they will have a huge amount of transactional and behavioural information." And that information, he says, is always going to be more relevant than what someone who may never have bought one of their products says on a survey.

But even today, Epstein laments: "Ultimately, most companies still can't tell you who has responded from a particular direct mail campaign, and they usually have no idea how they acquired those customers they do have."

It sounds as if relatively little has actually changed since the days when banks knew exactly how many accounts they had, but no idea how many customers – let alone where they lived or what they did at weekends.

ISSUES

1. **To what extent does lifestyle data provide what demographics do not?**

2. **Are 1990s lifestyle databases developed in the same way as lifestyle research of the 1970s and 1980s ?**

3. **What are the implications of the merging of profiling databases and what effect on profiling techniques might transactional data have ?**

EXPLORATION OF ISSUES

1 For a long time organisations relied mainly on demographic market profiling, and even today some still rely on little more. Demographic variables were used by marketers for several decades, but there is now much criticism of some of these variables and other, non-demographic approaches are in widespread use.

Demographics merely profile consumers. Any relationship with actual buying behaviour tends to be based on correlation and inference than anything more directly causal. For example there may be a strong correlation between the buying of beer and social grade, but the link is not to do with occupational type but also an inferred lifestyle that different occupations often engender.

Also, the demographic profiles reported in commercial market reports such as MINTEL are usually based on very few characteristics, for example age, gender and occupation. Lifestyle surveys provide profiles based on what consumers say interests them. They tick boxes to express interest in a vast range of hobbies, products and services – perhaps hundreds – and this data is matched with names and addresses.

We are now obtaining more useful data because, firstly, it is about what consumers say interests them, rather than being mere profiling. Secondly, the vast range of interests covered provides more profiling bases than demographics ever could. Thirdly, the cross-tabulation of interests can reveal opportunities for cross-selling. This sort of profile can help determine appropriate product/service features, and facilitates an advertising message that is congruent with the segment's lifestyle.

A problem with the current system is that although lifestyle companies claim high response rates and boast of multi-million respondent lifestyle databases (even a lifestyle census has been claimed) they are based on self-selected samples.

2 Life style, as a variant within 'psychographics' emerged during the 1980s. At that time lifestyle surveys were typically based on respondents being presented with a series of statements such as the following (taken from the lifestyle statements used in the Target Group Index annual research programme):

- I buy clothes for comfort, not for style.
- Once I find a brand I like, I tend to stick to it.
- I always buy British whenever I can.
- I dress to please myself.
- My family rarely sits down to meal together at home.
- I enjoy eating foreign food.
- I like to do a lot when I am on holiday.

All answers are graded according to the five-point Likert scale: definitely agree, tend to agree, neither agree nor disagree, tend to disagree, definitely disagree, not applicable.

An example will demonstrate the approach. In the 1980s in the United States, Levi Strauss launched a new product development programme for a range of up-market men's suits (BBC 1984). The associated market research programme revolved around an attempt to dis-

Table 3.5 Taylor Nelson's Applied Futures

Lifestyle category	Characterised by	Percentage of population
Belonger	Places great store in home, family, country, the establishment etc.	19
Survivor	Disposed towards identification with groups and bows to authority. Self-expression and creativity are irrelevant.	16
Experimentalist	Attracted to all that is new and different, always looking for new ideas, items and experiences.	12
Conspicuous consumer	Energy is directed towards the consumer dream via material possessions. Takes cues from reference groups, is non-critical of advertisers and is a follower of fashion.	18
Social resister	Seeks to maintain the *status quo* with regard to self, family and society. Suppresses self in favour of duty and moral obligation.	15
Self-explorer	Self-aware and self-concerned. Self-expression important.	14
Aimless	Uninvolved and alienated. Aggressive towards the system and resentful of its failure to provide employment.	6

Source: Taylor Nelson, 1987

cover 'lifestyles'. This was concerned with investigating activities, interests and opinions, sometimes referred to as AIO analysis.

The lifestyle approach usually involves presenting respondents with a series of statements and asking for their degree of agreement with each (Likert scale). Such lifestyle data is then cluster analysed to produce respondent groupings that are relatively homogeneous within each group but heterogeneous between clusters in terms of activities, interests and opinions. Each cluster is then allocated a somewhat glib title. In its lifestyle research programme in the United States, for example, Levi Strauss used this type of research to identify the main clothing segments: the 'classic independent', the 'mainstream traditionalist', the 'price shopper', the 'trendy casual' and so on. This sort of profile helps determine appropriate product/service features and an advertising message that is congruent with the segment's lifestyle.

A UK lifestyle typology, called Taylor Nelson's Applied Futures, is outlined in Table 3.5.

Sampling for lifestyle research is based on the more traditional random or quota approaches and this is one way in which it differs from more recent lifestyle research methods, which tend to rely on self-completed questionnaires inserted in newspapers and magazines or attched to warranty cards. The Likert scale approach is not so prevalent; instead respondents tick only those interests, activities and products that apply to them.

As stated above, one problem with the current system is that it is based on a self-selected sample. There can also be a fair degree of respondent bias in that all interests are not necessarily revealed and consumers can play games with marketers by ticking things at random just to get a free gift for participating.

3 During the 1980s lifestyle approaches and geodemograpics tended to be conducted in parallel, but in the 1990s they began to merge. As lifestyle databases expanded to cover millions of individual consumer records they were used as another layer of data in the ever-growing marketing database, and they now overlay the census-based data of geodemographics.

Geodemographics provide sophisticated profiles of consumers based on dozens of census and other variables, and in this sense are more useful than the relatively monolithic demographics of old. However they are just another way of profiling and do not explain much about buying behaviour, which again has to be inferred.

The addition of lifestyle data means that the buying interests of consumers can be linked with detailed profiles. This aids targeting via the media and, because of postcode links, via direct mail.

As powerful a tool as the merged geodemographics and lifestyle data appearsto be, it is being threatened by a new wave of data – transactional data. Capturing data at the point of purchase allows marketers to accumulate personalised data not only on the type of people the customers are, but also on what they actually buy.

Such behavioural data is considered by many to be even more valuable than other types of data and can overcome the respondent bias mentioned above. By combining it with geodemographics and lifestyle profiles, marketers can build up sophisticated models of buying patterns in different market segments (themselves based on highly refined, often in-house models of buying segments).

Marketing to the Over 50s

- Age segmentation
- Marketing to the over-50s

Time pundits

How do you categorise third-age consumers? Well, they're all over 50. Except there's much more to it than that. Now, the most agile of marketers have used the latest census to draw up finely honed profiles of this diverse group and the results are full of surprises.

BARBARA CUMMINS

It's no longer fashionable to be a teenager. The new darlings of the marketing world are the over-50s, or third agers, because they are the ones with the money. But they are discerning spenders, and it is not just a question of going out and grabbing share – this market needs to be handled with care, and profiles need to be pinpoint accurate.

The wiliest publishers are already climbing onto the bandwagon with dedicated magazine launches. Of these, Chic – pitched at 40-year-old women – has undoubtedly received the most attention. Managing director of consultancy 3rd Age Marketing Danielle Barr thinks its suggestive rather than obvious angle is the main reason for its success. "Older people are sophisticated consumers and any approach should be made with subtlety. Chic is Cosmopolitan taken on to the next stage," she says.

By contrast, The Oldie, – Richard Ingrams' tongue-in-cheek look at third-age living – is blatant in its targeting of older readers. And Mature Tymes – a free monthly tabloid distributed through retail outlets such as B&Q – reads like a local paper for the over-60s.

The emergence of such magazines demontstrates that marketers are waking up to the opportunities provided by older readers. But other journals traditionally take a campaigning rather than money-making stance. 050 magazine is produced by the Association of Retired Persons and is a far cry from the slick Chic: an advertorial from the rather staid Heather Valley mail-order collection is the only fashion spread in the magazine – and it looks outdated.

Active Life – a bi-monthly magazine published by Aspen Specialist Media on behalf of the Post Office – has a similar feel with a focus on health, money and travel. It was created after the Post Office realised the potential of ready-made access to an older customer base. Initially, no demand was identified for the product, but the publishers point to high take-up as indication that it has been well-received.

"We measure its success by how quickly the magazines disappear and by the response we get to competitions. We are receiving between 35,000 and 40,000 postcards in response to various items in every issue," says deputy managing director Malcolm Preston Of the 300,000-strong circulation, 70,000 are sent to subscribers and the remainder is available in large post offices.

The three veterans of the industry are Choice, Yours and Saga. Saga is an offshoot of the holiday company; Yours was originally the magazine of Help the Aged and, like Choice, has been going for more than 20 years. EMAP bought Choice and Saga in the late Eighties and revamped both. Ad director Cathy Torpey points out that EMAP has formulated a clear profile of each title's readers. Choice is for 55 to 65-year-old ABC1 couples and Yours is for over 65-year-old state pensioners.

"Everyone sees huge potential in the market and launch into it without perceiving how specialist the different age bands are," says Torpey. "We have a specific age band in mind, but to be honest, we are moving towards more of a focus on life stage than age, especially as fewer companies insist on compulsory retirement these days."

The gardening press is also good at attracting older people – its core readership – without dwelling on their age. And in radio, Classic FM has won similar success by capitalising on a mature audience without patronising them as past-it oldies.

The diversity of the third-age market presents marketers with a great challenge. The effort and resources which are currently poured into marketing to youth will have to be redirected. and more sophisticated research and marketing techniques are going to be required if the potential of third agers is to be realised.

Profiling the 50-plus market, and identifying distinct patterns of purchasing behaviour. attitudes and lifestyle is the obvious starting point. The over-50s are not a homogeneous group. and marketing strategies which stuff members of this age-group into the same pigeon hole are likely to miss out.

Leo Burnett's deputy media director Mel Varley says: "If you're going to look at the over50s, you have to be aware that you've got three or four generations in there. You can't talk about them as one group."

The latest census has provided invaluable information about this elusive group. CDMS Marketing Services, which produces Super Profiles, has used census-based geodemographics to identify two groups. Marketing manager Tracy Weir explains that these groups termed the "thriving greys" and "senior citizens" – didn't exist before Super Profiles was redeveloped using new census data. "We classify geographic areas," she says. "The nearest we got to a 50-plus profile before was 'older suburbia'. Now we have two distinct groups."

The thriving greys, as defined by Super Profiles. are aged 50 upwards, fairly. prosperous, likely to own their home – a semi or detached house – and have an active lifestyle. They represent the second-most affluent group of British adults, and make up 11 per cent of' the population. The senior citizens. as might be expected. are more elderly, retired and less affluent. They have more passive recreational pur-

suits, save for a rainy day, and many are older women living alone.

"Customers are using these profiles more and more," says Weir. "For example. the Post Office Active Life Club – for the over 55s – is using the profiles to target consumers." Travel agencies and mail-order companies are also showing an interest.

Geodemographics alone is not sufficient, however, to produce anything but the broadest categorisation of the over-50s. Profiling in terms of attitude, and overlaying the resulting groupings with geodemographic data is potentially much more revealing.

TGI identified five significant groups in 1993 after conducting cluster analysis by attitude and behaviour. The context of the research was shopping, and 3rd Age Marketing's Barr point the resulting profiles only examples of the types which can be identified. "They may vary," she says, "according to the context of The research – the product area, for example."

The first group identified by TGI were "astute cosmopolitans", who constitute just over 19 per cent of the 50 to 75 age group and, as their name suggests. are discerning shoppers with a strong sense of style. By contrast, the "temperate xenophobes", who make up 20.4 per cent of 50 to 75-year olds tend to be unwilling to go abroad, eat foreign food Or be a little adventurous in their lifestyles.

TGI, and also make up 20.4 per cent of the 50 to 75 age group. A further 19 per cent of third agers fell into the "outgoing funlovers" group, and the largest group, making up 21.4 per cent of the 50 to 75 age group, were dubbed "apathetic spenders". These people use credit cards to buy things they can't afford, and don't like parting with cash.

Whereas TGI has analysed lifestyle to come up with its groupings, The Research Business has used lifestage to identify five groups among the over-50s. Says Beth Salmon, director of The

Research Business: "Young people pass through various stages of development, and there is a mirror pattern among older groups."

Paired "depth" interviews with over-50-year-old consumers resulted in the groupings, two of which are characterised by an optimistic attitude to life, sophistication in terms of consuming habits and the fact that "they are still making the same sort of choices as younger people".

The first of these groups are the "emptying nesters", whose children have left home, but not necessarily for good. They have a lot more freedom and spending power than previously, and have similar attitudes to the "empty nesters/pre-retirement" group, who may still be working, may have grandchildren and may still plan to move house. "Retired empty nesters" are the third group identified by The Research Business. They are likely to have stopped work, but are physically active, and are likely to arrange their lives around grandchildren.

The "retired" group, meanwhile, are predominately older women living alone. They are physically active but, says Salmon, "more inward-looking. They are not so likely to go abroad and, although they may play bowls, they will have given up downhill skiing!" Finally, the "elderly" group are physically infirm, although they may be mentally active, and likely to be living in retirement housing.

As for the marketing applications of these more sensitive profiles, it seems that to date these have been limited. Salmon comments that attempts to use profiles of this group tend to be in the traditional areas, which are aimed specifically at the over-50s, such as cruises, health products, and specially designed financial products such as special motor insurance policies.

Barr notes a similar phenomenon Financial services companies have shown an interest, she says, but on the whole there have bven few attempts to use the 50-plus profiles which are available. "Marketers are still using stereotypes, and a patronising voice in their portrayal of the over-.50s," she says. "They are not in tune with them."

Barr believes, however, that it is only a matter of time before marketers' attitudes change, to come more into line with the reality that third agers include groups of active, sophisticated and demanding consumers.

"There is a time lag, with any, change in society, before advertisers begin to reflect that change," she says. "As far as marketing to the third age is concerned, we are in the middle of that time lag."

ISSUES

1 **Should marketers bother with the over 50s?**

2 **How can marketers target the over 50s?**

3 **In tactical terms, how might the over 50s be targeted?**

EXPLORATION OF ISSUES

1 The over 50s are clearly different from the group marketers have traditionally targeted. For a start they are physically different – age has caught up and may be manifested in wrinkles, thinning hair and sagging everything! From a marketing perspective people with these physical characteristics are worth targeting with anti-wrinkle cream, hair restorer, health products and even plastic surgery. But the over 50s have become even more interesting to marketers than these more obvious factors suggest.

The generation called the 'baby boomers' – those born in the years following the return of soldiers after the Second World War – have become a very important target for marketers. In the 1960s they were involved in a massive social revolution that changed music, fashions, political thought and social attitudes forever. They grew up in the period when the term 'teenager' first came into use. Unlike previous generations they were not 'small adults' who wore similar clothes to their parents. This generation wanted their own culture, fashions and music. Furthermore they rejected the social values of their parents, often violently in street demonstrations – remember the events in Paris in 1967, at Kent State University in 1968 and in Trafalgar Square in 1969. Nothing like this had happened among previous genera-

tions of teenagers/20 somethings. Indeed a popular motto in the 1960s was 'never trust anyone over 30'!

Coupled with their desire for ownership of their own thoughts and lives, the baby boomers were the most affluent (generally) of any 'youth market' to date and were able to engage in the consumer market. Marketers responded with a fashion and music offering the like of which had never been seen before.

This generation is now turning 50 and millions more will do so in the first couple of decades of the new millennium. They are a very large, consumer-literate group and make an extremely attractive target for marketers. In the United States it has been estimated (*USA Today*, 1996) that in 2001 one baby boomer will turn 50 every 6.8 seconds!

Not all the over 50s are baby boomers of course, and those 60 plus are from other generations with lifestyles and attitudes of their own. Taken as a whole, the over 50s are in what has been termed the 'third age'. They represented about a third of the UK population in the late 1990s and numbered some 18 million. By 2020 they will represent about a half of the UK population.

2 It would be a big mistake to lump all over 50s together. There are various submarkets here. One factor

to consider is whether they are in work or retired, in all its various forms. One of the greatest social/economic changes since about 1980 has been a widespread increase in early retirement as organisations downsize/rationalise their workforces/cut costs and so on. In many organisations, as soon as one reaches the age of 50 there is a fair chance of being targeted for early retirement, so it is not enough to talk of the over 50s employment status has to be considered as well. Many of these early-retireds will find new employment – perhaps several small jobs, perhaps totally new careers. For some it is the opportunity to do what they have always wanted to do. For others it can mean the scrap heap, with a severely restricted income and little hope for the future.

In general, however, the baby boomers are quite wealthy in terms of inheritance from their parents, who bought their houses when house prices were low and lived a much less materialistic life style. As a result their estates can be significant and this wealth is cascading down to the new over 50 market.

So in summary, the over 50s present the marketer with a series of segmentation questions, not just one.

3 Research into the over 50s has revealed several characteristics. For a start, although they may not like to be portrayed as 'old' they would see through attempts to portray them as 'young', so caution is needed. There has certainly been a move towards the employment of more mature models and stereotypes in marketing to these older age groups and this is generally to be welcomed.

Second, the over 50s tend to have definite likes and dislikes and are more inclined to reject irrelevant marketing offerings than is the case with their younger and slightly more expansive counterparts.

Third, not surprisingly many are concerned about their 'sagging everything' and their health, so there is an obvious market for health and anti-ageing products and services.

Finally, many are responsive to discounts and special offers, as contained, for example, in B&Qs *Mature Tymes* for the older customer (coupled, it should be noted, with a policy of employing the over 50s as staff).

One area of interest, especially to direct marketers, is the reaction of the over 50s to being targeted individually. There is evidence to suggest that in general the over 50s do not like direct mail or telesales.

There are also spending differences between those in their 50s, 60s and above. Those in their 60s generally prefer to use cash and are rather cautious consumers. Those over 70 are perhaps even further along this continuum.

There has certainly been an explosion of magazine titles aimed at various over 50 groups, demonstrating that the market is not homogeneous and that the various groups can be reached. Profiling in this sector is not merely based on age – social grade and geodemographics are also being used and there is a trend towards overlaying this with attitudinal research. An example of this comes from the 1993 analysis by the TGI, (as described in the article above), which found, based on shopping attitudes and behaviour, that 'astute cosmopolitans', who constituted about 19 per cent of the 50–75 year olds, were discerning consumers. There were also 'temperate xenophobes' (20 per cent of 50–75 year olds), who were less likely to go abroad or eat 'foreign food'. The 'thrifty traditionalists' made up 20 per cent and a further 19 per cent were 'outgoing funlovers'! The largest group comprised the 'apathetic spenders' (21 per cent), who used credit cards to extend their purchasing power beyond what they could really afford.

Hence it is important not to generalise when targeting the over 50s and to take into account the very real differences between the subgroups when designing tactics for marketing campaigns.

Pester Power

KEY CONCEPTS

- 'Pester power'
- Family influences
- Demographic segmentation

Kids take control of the trolleys

Research carried out by The Children's Channel has shown that children greatly influence their parents when it comes to buying the weekly groceries, but some of the findings were surprisingly unpredictable.

MEG CARTER

Children could be the new saviours of the brand in the mounting battle against own-label, because, according to new research conducted for sat-ellite broadcaster The Children's Channel, there is a heavy and increased bias towards branded goods when children accompany parents shopping. This reinforces the view that what appeals most to children are instantly recognisable, extensively advertised products.

The findings coincide with an increased debate about advert-ising aimed at children. Last week, the Advertising Association published a report that discredited previous research criticising advertising to children and the AA itself received flak from health campaigners, who accused the organisation of attempting to protect "vested interests" (*MW* October 28). And three weeks ago, the Independent Television Commission published new guidelines on food-product and slimming advertising to children and adolescents (*MW* October 21).

But The Children's Channel research also questions the accuracy of the well-worn phrase "pester power". While children's influence is invariably portrayed as negative – encouraging parents to spend more and buy more sweet and sugary products – the research shows that in fact the value of expenditure often remains virtually unchanged. The difference lies in which products are bought and how many of these are, in fact, healthy.

Particularly surprising is the increase in toothbrushes, mouthwashes and health-conscious products bought when children accompany parents to the supermarket, not least in the light of mounting concern about child tooth decay because of increased sugar consumption.

But what will concern some brand owners is the number of household brand names which actually suffer when children are present. Sales of major cereals and soft drinks are among those adversely affected.

Earlier this year The Children's Channel commissioned research company HPI to analyse more than 2,200 family supermarket bills from 450 households over a two-month period. This covered shopping trips when children were present as well as when they were not. All of those surveyed were of C1 or C2 demographic groups, subscribed to The Children's Channel and had offspring aged between two and 13 years. All sometimes shopped alone and sometimes with their children.

The results indicate that fathers spend up to 13 per cent more when shopping with their children. By contrast, mothers spend less: they increase their spend by an average £5 per trip when *alone*. While "pester power" is in evidence, mothers, it seems, are far more resistant, although they quickly balance the budget by dropping normal items from the shopping list to make room for unusual products bought at a child's request.

When the data was analysed by

product category, it became evident that parents accompanied by children buy more tea and less coffee; more cola and less fruit juice and mineral water; more white bread than brown bread. More surprisingly, however, they also buy more non-chocolate cakes and fewer chocolate cakes, more shower gels, shampoos and conditioner and less soap.

Not surprisingly, sales of kids' favourites such as ice-cream, burgers, fish fingers and chips increase when kids are present. But items bought less frequently also include breakfast cereals, chocolate products, chewing gum and brown sauce.

Looking at cold drinks only, the data shows that own-brand colas and own-brand fruit carbonates are losers when children are present. But so too are Ribena, Tizer and Lucozade. While sales of Coke and Tango go up, sales of Pepsi Cola and Pepsi Max rise more significantly. Among squash purchases, own-label dominate, although Robinsons Squash and Robinsons Ready To Drink buck this trend. Sparkling apple juice is also a popular choice when children are present.

In the hot drinks sector, Brooke Bond PG Tips and Tetley Tea are brand winners, as are Kenco Coffee and Cadbury's Chocolate Drinks.

However, own-brand teas and all other coffee brands – notably Nescafé, Gold Blend and Maxwell House – lose out.

When toothcare products are analysed in isolation, it is clear that sales of mouthwash, toothbrushes, Macleans and own-label toothpaste increase with children present. But sales of all toothpaste, Colgate, Signal and Aquafresh in particular, diminish.

"These findings show that children influence what you buy, but not the amount you spend," says Children's Channel sales director David Harrison. "We knew children influenced parental shopping behaviour, but we didn't know in what way." The findings, he adds, are the first based on quantitative research into "pester power".

"The results will open up questions, and will not please everyone," he believes. "But we have taken time to check certain areas, to validate the data and, where only small movements have taken place, assess just how accurate this is."

Children are becoming an increasingly important retail force. The number of under-15s will grow by ten per cent this decade, according to a recent report by flavourings manufacturer Borthwicks. And by 1998, this age group will have a disposable income from pocket money of £9bn a year.

Previous studies support the powerful pressure children can apply when shopping. According to a Henley Centre report published last autumn, 12 to 16-year-olds influence 75 per cent of UK parents when they shop for clothes, buy or rent videos, have a day out, or visit a travel agent to choose a holiday.

However the same report claimed that with virtually no knowledge of the historical development of brands, the perceived two-tier structure of lower quality, cheaper own-label products and higher quality, premium-priced brands just does not exist. To children, it claimed, all products are brands.

The latest findings will be used by The Children's Channel to develop its advertising business. Although available as part of the Sky Multi-Channels subscription package, between 25 and 30 per cent of its income is from advertising and the channel is working to expand this.

Fmcg remains a major area for Harrison, but he says that it is also important to develop other categories, notably household products and other items targeted at adults – housewives in particular. Only 58 per cent of The Children's Channel's audience is made up of children.

ISSUES

1. What is 'pester power' and how important is it for marketers?

2. How does pester power combine with other influences within the family decision making unit?

3. What ethical issues arise there for marketers with regard to pester power?

EXPLORATION OF ISSUES

1 How many times do those who shop with their children leave a supermarket or other store with items they would not have bought if their children had not been with them? Just watch what happens as they go around the store. Children will pick up various items, sometimes asking nicely for them, sometimes screaming if they don't get them and sometimes surreptitiously putting them in the basket – especially at the supermarket checkout. Their power to influence is highly visible.

Some marketers target their advertising at a slightly older age group so that the 'trickle down' effect operates – younger children see the product being used by their elders and want to follow their lead. By the time it has trickled down to them the older ones have been enticed by the next craze.

The concept of 'brand' probably begins to be understood by children when they reach five or six. Parents are targeted with a 'sensible' message and kids with a more persuasive one – this can be related to Freudian psychology and the balance between the id and the superego, the response of children being more id, tempered by the superego reponse of their parents. When a product is deemed 'naughty but nice', the ego can more easily rationalise the purchase as logical.

With children of about seven or eight, parental influence is less constraining and the children develop their own notion of acceptable brands – TV advertisments and the current favourites of older children being the main influences. Parents might be inclined to buy their children products that help their development but are often persuaded to buy things that add to their children's street credibility – the 'right' brand.

When children reach primary school age, school friends often become more important product influencers than parents. Observation and word of mouth are very important in determining children's preferences.

Many marketers have taken this on board and have started to get into schools via various sponsorship and 'educational' ventures. Schools badly need help with their finances but some teachers are uncomfortable with this way of getting to the children's market. Sponsorship is clearly a sales route here, but as the Labour government found in Autumn 1997 with the controversy over the sponsorship of Formula 1 racing by a tobacco company, it can be a minefield!

Any viewing of commercial TV programmes for children will confirm the proliferation of commercials aimed at children. Younger children may merely treat these as entertainment, but as they grow, brand and image become salient in their minds as a result of associative learning processes and vicarious learning by seeing others use a product.

2 As well as direct consumption by children, we are also concerned here with the role of children in determining more adult purchases – which car the parents will buy, where to go on holiday and so on.

The family is a decision-making unit and there are different roles for each member. There will be deciders, influencers, buyers, users and gatekeepers (holders of information), and different members may play each of these roles at different times – including children. Children are increasingly influencing the choice of houshold durables, clothes, TV, video, cars and holidays as well as more conventional purchases such as sweets.

Many parents have succumbed to youth culture and look to their children for what is 'hip' to buy. A BBC Money Programme survey in October 1997 found that 72 per cent of parents admitted that £20 of their weekly spending was influenced by their children, 22 per cent thought that up to £50 of their weekly spending was the result of pester power and 4 per cent thought that up to £100 of their weekly spending was based on this! This would amount to £5 billion a year if averaged across the UK.

3 Clearly pester power does raise ethical issues. By definition children have not fully matured, yet they are heavily targeted, sometimes in subtle ways by marketers who wish to instil brand preferences.

Although there is evidence to suggest that brand loyalty is not as stable as it used to be – we now switch more regularly in many product markets – once a brand has become a clear favourite it may well remain within the repertoire of acceptable brands for a considerable period.

Consider the effect of heavy branding campaigns targeted at children in the United States – there are stories of ten year olds mugging and even killing for the 'right' brand of trainers.

Most UK marketing trade bodies outlaw practices that exploit minors. However there are often ways of getting around this, for example the Direct Marketing Association has a clause in its code of conduct that implies that direct appeals are acceptable if a product is 'affordable' and of 'interest' to children. Well this can be liberally interpreted, surely? The DMA, does, however, ban the use of lists of under 14s unless there is parental consent. Having said this, in the lead-up to Christmas 1997 Lego promoted its kindergarten brick, Duplo, with a £5m campaign through direct mail, plus advertisements in magazines sent to mothers. This is a preschool market.

Most consumer organisations across Europe are increasingly concerned about marketing to children – what do you think?

Gender Segmentation

KEY CONCEPTS

- Gender segmentation
- Marketing to women
- Sexist advertising

The good, the bad and the sexist

Despite what you may see in a typical ad, real-life women are out there wrestling with real issues, not simply worrying themselves to death about the performance of their soap powder or sanitary towel. Having said that, there is a healthy selection of the sublime to go with the ridiculous, and the downright offensive.

BARBARA NOKES

If you accept that the way we advertise to women should be viewed against the prevailing culture, you must agree that these have been a very interesting couple of months.

Lorena Bobbit was in court for slicing off the penis of the husband she claimed had sexually abused her for years. She got 45 days in an insane asylum and this headline in The Sun: "WILLY-CHOP WIFE GOES FREE".

In some Gateway stores, gingerbread men became gingerbread persons. Meanwhile, Tim Yeo enjoyed a three-hour lunch at Langan's with his mistress on the same day that his wife vowed to stand by him, and Marie-Claire published interviews with five women who pay men for sex.

One survey showed seven out of ten UK mothers have jobs outside the home, while another confirmed women really are safer drivers than men.

Women in real life are clearly wrestling with some real issues. Which is why the ads I object to most are not the outrageous ones, such as Lowe Howard-Spink's Vauxhall Supermodels series for the Corsa, questionable though I know some women find them. I despair more of the ones that behave as if the product and the woman's relationship to it is a matter of life and death. Most soap powders are guilty of this.

So is Claire Rayner and her sanitary towels with wings. As I've said somewhere before, periods are a bloody nuisance, not a woman's *raison d'être*. Advertising for sanpro would be wise to reflect that.

Interestingly, the J Walter Thompson Oxo commercials that I've loved for years have begun to grate a little, particularly when Mum appears on tenterhooks about whether or not the family will eat her shepherd's pie. Let them eat cake, I say.

The BSB Dorland Kenco commercials are much more my cup of coffee. As my office is next to that of Bruce Haines, I sometimes answer his phone and callers invariably assume I am his secretary. So, when the Colombian coffee-grower remarks that he'd better clear the order with the boss and Cheri Lunghi points out with satisfaction, that he just has, I'm cheering.

Still on a reliability strategy the TV ad for the VW Golf, through BMP DDB Needham, is great stuff. It manages to project the just-divorced woman in its witty commercial as a bit tough a bit vulnerable but ultimately optimistic about her future. On the other hand, the VW Vento ad featuring Kimberly-Anne of the rippling muscles strikes me – and interestingly, my 15-year old daughter – as quite repellent. Maybe it's something to do with making a woman look strong in a macho way.

And most women must love the Prudential ad by WCRS with the couple on the couch, talking to camera. He's planning a safe life enjoying the garden and going out once in a while; she wants to stuff the garden and go out every night. One of the added attractions of this ad is that the woman is not conventionally pretty.

It's not only nice for women to think naughty thoughts in ads, it's nice for women to be naughty, too. When her unsuspecting husband calls up her mobile phone at her boyfriend's flat, Joanna Lumley, in another BMP ad, pretends to be at the British Gas showroom.

At first glance, GGT's longrunning Cadbury's Flake advertising would not appear to go down particularly well with women. But I'm wrong. According to research, the one where the young woman is sitting in a window seat sucking on her Flake while the phone rings away scores well with women. Apparently, women assume it is her significant other trying to get through while she's indulging herself.

An article like this can't be complete without reference to the ads that are sexy and ads that are sexist. Sexy ads show men and, women enjoying themselves and each other. Bartle Bogle Hegarty's marvellous Häagen-Dazs campaign is an excellent example.

So is TBWA/Holmes Knight Ritchie's very funny press ad for Gossard's Wonderbra (before Playtex claimed the brand), with a laughing woman and the line: "Say goodbye to your feet". More recently Lansdown Conquest's commercial for the Rafaella bra, in which the woman wearing it carries the (uncomplaining) man off to bed, strikes the right chord.

Sexist ads, however, show or refer to women as powerless objects to be used by and for the gratification of men. The Marr Associates ad for Linn Hi-fi runs off with the prize here.

Does it matter if a brand's advertising is sexist? I think it does. Years ago, I bought a turbodriven vacuum cleaner. Two weeks later I opened a magazine and was confronted by this headline: "AT LAST A TURBO FOR WOMEN DRIVERS". I haven't bought this brand since.

The guardians of brands in agencies and client companies should know that all they've heard about women being deeply unforgiving of slights is true.

Calvin Klein makes 'offensive' ads pay

The designer has pulled its controversial ads, but not before earning worldwide publicity, reports **JON REES**

Calvin Klein has joined the canon of advertisers accused of flouting moral codes. Its entry in the misdemeanours dictionary will be filed under "P" for pornography somewhere between "A" for Aids (Benetton) and "T" for transvestism (Levi's).

But now that the fashion designer has bowed to pressure and withdrawn its controversial jeans advertising campaign – amid accusations that it was peddling child pornography – some commentators say the company should have stuck to its guns.

The TV and press campaign was produced by the company's in-house advertising unit, CRK Advertising, and featured pubescent-looking models in various states of undress. All were almost wearing something from the CK denim range.

There are two striking things about the poster campaign: one is the youth of the models – though supermodel Kate Moss's career, in particular with Calvin Klein perfume brand

Obsession, has blunted that impact. The other is the washed-out, listless, joyless poses in which they are presented. This, combined with the tawdry backroom settings, speaks irresistibly of child pornography, claim groups as diverse as the American Family Association and The Guardian newspaper.

The TV ads provoke a stronger reaction: same models, same setting but this time with the addition of an off-camera contribution from the "director". He says, "Nice body, do you work out?" and similar comments to the young male and female models as they take off various articles of Calvin Klein clothing. The scene is suffused with awkwardness and embarrassment and the overall impression is of exploitation, not fashion.

Following a furore on both sides of the Atlantic – the campaign didn't even break in the UK although it was scheduled to air across Europe on MTV – the company took a full page ad in The New York Times withdrawing the campaign, which it claims has been misunderstood.

In a separate statement, it said: "The whole point of this campaign is that people, regular people from anywhere have glamour inside of them which is tied to their independence."

The American Family Association is still trying to force the US attorney general to launch a federal child pornography investigation into Calvin Klein on the grounds that the ads "sexually exploit what appear to be children by exhibiting them in a lascivious manner".

Tony Kaye, who directed the shelved Guinness ad featuring a gay couple, says the withdrawal of the Calvin Klein campaign was a triumph only for hypocrisy.

"It's totally fresh and represents kids in the way they are. The only people that are objecting to it are old and out of touch. I think that's a sad indication of how the world is, that people can look at it and see filth," he says.

Certainly those who have seen only the posters tend to be less concerned than those who have seen the full campaign.

Mark Blenkinsop, marketing manager for Europe at jeans company Pepe, which itself ran a controversial campaign based on teenage angst and suicide earlier this year, saw little to cause offence in the poster work.

"The style of the pictures was a little close to the bone but it did not offend me. If the setting had been a little more glamorous, I don't think there would have been any problem. It looks to me like the ads draw on the work of underground photographers from the Sixties," he says.

Stockist Harrods also failed to be outraged by the poster work. "I think it was unnecessary to withdraw them," says a spokesman.

Critics of Calvin Klein say that despite the withdrawal, the campaign had more than done its job. It resulted in the company's name and product being splashed across the world's leading newspapers and magazines as well as hitting the screens of some of the highest-rated TV shows.

Ads for other jeans brands have come close to the edge, but according to one agency source who works on a "youth" brand, this one steps firmly over the line.

"The Versace jeans ad features two supermodels in white high heels, jeans and no tops and no one says a word. The defining thing about the CK ads is the age of the models."

The other jeans ad best-known for it obvious use of controversial sexual imagery is Levi's "taxi" ad, created by Bartle Bogle Hegarty. This features a cab driver lasciviously eyeing a girl in the rear view mirror and then being disconcerted when "she" turns out to be a "he".

One agency source says: "The difference was that the character in the Levi's ad triumphed over the taxi driver. He was also evidently an adult. And transvestism has a long history of acceptable humour surrounding it. In comparison, the 'feel' of the CK campaign was dirty, grimy, trashy – and humourless."

Whatever Calvin Klein's intentions for the campaign, the ads have been consigned to the dustbin, attracting reams of publicity in the process. Many suspect that is what they were designed to do in the first place.

Who sits in the driving seat?

The diffuse nature of car ownership means that manufacturers must find out much more about who their customers are and what they want.

JOHN CLEMENS

There is not much to choose between one car and another these days. They are similarly priced within their ranges, they are all more or less reliable and offer similar equipment. Yet car manufacturers spent £116m on advertising last year in an attempt to persuade people that this is not the case, that there really is a difference between the Renault Clio, the Nissan Micra and the Vauxhall Corsa.

Advertising plays a crucial role in brand and model choice by building image and promoting real and apparent differences in price and finance. Getting the image of a model right in brand advertising is of course important. But manufacturers also need carefully to target their potential consumers using direct marketing techniques, and for this reason an accurate picture of who their consumers are is essential.

Last year, 851,000 of the ten top models were sold, bought by 3.5 per cent of households. The above-the-line ad spend for these ten models was just less than £150 for each car sold. TV and newspapers were used extensively, demonstrating that mass media advertising is essential to compete effectively in the market, even though the number of buyers in any one year is very small compared with most markets.

Car ownership is highly fragmented. Last year, just one in eight of the 1.5 million Ford Fiestas on the road was bought new. A large proportion of the Fiestas, the UK's most popular model, are either used cars or form part of company fleets.

For car manufacturers, the diffuse nature of car ownership can cause a headache. The new car buyer is their main advertising target. But although this is the case, particularly in the small car market, all drivers need to be influenced as resale values, and the used-car market for any model, affect new purchases and the speed at which the replacement market moves.

In such a complex market it is essential for manufacturers to understand and know their valuable but numerically small markets. About one in ten women drivers owns a Fiesta, compared with one in 30 men drivers. It is by far the most popular women's car.

This female bias holds true for all Fiestas, though it is much less marked in the new, privately bought Fiesta market. In this sub-group, slightly less than 60 per cent are women, compared with close to 70 per cent of all Fiesta drivers. So despite the female bias, advertising has to take careful account of the male drivers of new, privately bought Fiestas.

In addition, the new privately bought Fiesta attracts the over-65s: about one in three buyers of new Fiestas are over 65, compared with just one in eight of all Fiesta drivers.

This kind of age profile is, of course, not peculiar to Fiestas, it is true for most new private buyers of smaller cars. Many new cars are bought as retirement cars, probably purchased with the cash part of pensioners' carefully saved pensions. Care again needs to be taken to appeal to this market, at the same time as attracting young used-car buyers of Fiestas.

Financing and price are naturally very relevant in the new private car market. New private Fiesta buyers are much more prone to use hire-purchase and personal leasing than the market overall; used-car buyers are more likely to use personal loans.

Personal leasing is now growing for private purchases, and according to our data it already accounts for some six per cent of new private Fiesta purchases. Manufacturers need to know what kind of people these are, why they decide to use leasing and how leasing varies by model and by manufacturer.

In addition, more and more models are sold to individuals and not to households. More than one in four car-owning homes now have two cars, and in some market sectors as many as one in ten homes have three cars.

This is true of middle-aged homes, homes in which there are likely to be three or more drivers – two parents and one or two teenagers. Which car is the privately bought one: is it the main car, or is it a company car? Is it the second car, the one used more often by the wife (even these days, when most women work, company cars still tend to be a male preserve), or is it the car bought for all the family to use, a fun vehicle?

This is the ultimate fragmented market, in which small groups of buyers account for very large expenditures. It is a market that can make great use of new forms of marketing, database selling, relationship marketing and one-to-one marketing, where each mailing and offer is geared to an individual's make-up.

The cars may be more or less the same, but last year's buyers had 851,000 different reasons for choosing the models they did. Manufacturers need to know exactly what these reasons are.

Bare-faced cheek of a naked butt

The viewing public – unmoved at the sight of a motorway pile-up – would go into shock if shown a male buttock in an add.

IAIN MURRAY

The recent survey on nudity in advertising showed once again the impossibility of the satirist's task.

In his novel The Tin Men, Michael Frayn describes how, at the William Morris Institute of Automation Research, computers are programmed to carry out menial tasks such as writing newspapers and saying prayers. Research is a necessary part of the programme, hence the crash survey to establish newspaper readers' preferences.

Among the findings were that people were not interested in reading about road crashes unless there were at least ten dead.

"A road crash with ten dead, the majority felt, was slightly less interesting than a rail crash with one dead, unless it still had piquant details – the ten dead turning out to be five still virginal honeymoon couples, for example, or pedestrians mown down by the local JP on his way home from a hunt ball. A rail crash was always entertaining, with or without children's toys still lying pathetically among the wreckage."

Just how easily the bizarre inventions of a comic novelist's mind are translated into everyday life was shown by the Independent Television Commission's research. The study conducted by the Qualitative Consultancy on behalf of the quango discovered that while a single female nipple under the shower is tolerable, a bare male bottom is not.

When a man is glimpsed with "legs spreading", as in swimming shots, it causes still greater offence. "Men had a particular problem with images of nude men," says Wendy Hayward, a member of the research team. "Perhaps there was some homo-erotic problem lurking there." Or then again, in the case of men who prefer their naked humans to be female, perhaps not.

Among the other findings were that while over-the-shoulder shots of single breasts were regarded as largely acceptable, scenes of full frontal female nudity were considered beyond the pale for advertising at any time of day.

You have only to step back from this survey to appreciate its exquisite absurdity. In a Britain beset by all manner of seemingly intractable problems, from juvenile crime to drug abuse, there are a few cosy havens in which a selected sample of inhabitants are gently questioned about nipples.

"If shown an over-the-shoulder shot of a single breast, as opposed to an under-the-thigh depiction of a full complement, would you be offended (a) hugely, (b) fairly hugely, (c) not much, or (d) don't know?

Which of the following is, in your opinion beyond the pale: (a) a single naked female buttock, (b) a pair of male clothed buttocks, legs spread (c) two small breasts, wet, (d) a male bottom, hairy?

Of course, there's no pleasing some folk. Had the researchers quizzed Ms Peggy Alexander, of the Green Party, they would have found that she prefers naked people to be imperfect.

In an example of how even the most impeccably politically correct movement may be deemed politically incorrect, Ms Alexander excoriates an animal rights group for using a naked supermodel in an advertising poster.

A campaign on behalf of People for the Ethical Treatment of Animals (Peta) shows the blonde German model, Nadja Auermann, seated decorously in the half-light and wearing only lipstick and blusher. Beside her is the slogan: "I'd rather go naked than wear fur."

"This advertising campaign shows that women can only make protests by showing their breasts," splutters Ms Alexander, even though care has been taken to conceal the Auermann breast beneath the Auermann arm. "It says it is okay to show your body as long as you are thin and six feet tall. Peta should also include images of overweight and short people."

I should be surprised if a survey such as that conducted by the Qualitative Consultancy were to find public opinion behind Ms Alexander. A population that draws the line at a single comely nipple is unlikely to endorse the depiction of a deeply pendulous breast whose downward progress is arrested by a protuberant belly atop a squat pair of legs.

There is, after all, such a thing as aesthetics. The Greek sculptors of old could have put Peggy right on this one.

In any case, there may not be as many overweight people as previously thought. The Government's view that obesity is fast reaching epidemic proportions is supported by allegations that we are a nation of idle slobs.

But – wonderful things, surveys – according to research on behalf of Volvo UK, we are in fact a people brimful of energy. The study found 60 per cent of the general public "following an active lifestyle and many looking for more adventurous pursuits".

Cycling, mountain bike riding, fell walking and mountain climbing are popular pursuits, with many demonstrating an interest in snow boarding and water sports. More than half those surveyed say that taking part in this type of action activity makes them feel "more alive".

Should the ITC wish to take its interest in nudity further, it might be an idea to investigate the attitudes of cyclists and fell walkers. As a working hypothesis it might be the case that, being more alive, they are more tolerant, even exuberant, about nipples and buttocks. In which case there would be implications for the advertising of bicycle clips and the works of A Wainwright.

ISSUES

1. **When is advertising sexist ?**

2. **Have there been changes over time, in marketing to women ?**

3. **Are there any corresponding issues associated with marketing to men?**

EXPLORATION OF ISSUES

1. This is another of those 'matter of opinion' questions. However class discussion or assignment work often reveals similar themes, and some different and insightful perceptions usually emerge as well.

One argument is that sex appeals ads are not necessarily sexist. Used in a relevant context both men and women can respond positively. Famous Club 18–30 advertisements such as 'Beaver Espania' and 'One Swallow Doesn't make a Summer' might reflect one of the main motivations of both sexes for taking such a holiday. However the advertisements attracted many complaints because the choice of media outlets was broader than it perhaps should have been and they reached non-target markets as well. This is a borderline issue – were they sexist irrespective of where they appeared? A less controversial example is the Haagan Daz yoghurt advertisement showing a couple erotically eating Haagen Daz – or was this also sexist?

One test might be to judge whether either sex is in any way demeaned. If there is clear evidence of exploitation or if the image is out of context, then it is sexist. A lot of French advertising has been attacked in the UK as being sexist because scantily clad women in suggestive, erotic or subservient poses have been featured in advertisements for products and services as remote from these images as chutney and even advertising space itself!

2. The historical examples of advertisements aimed at women described in the article by Nokes demonstrate how far we have generally come in marketing to women, but they also reveal a few instances where there has been little change.

Until the late 1970s and early 1980s there were – for advertisers – perhaps only two main female stereotypes: the mother and the mistress. The former was typified by a washing powder commercial in which the mother was shown, in slow motion, wrapping her child in a soft, newly washed towel. The 'mistress' stereotype was manifest in the overt sexuality, yet subservience, of the women being portrayed.

Indeed, in the mid 1970s advertising copywriters asserted that these were the two stereotypes to which most women of the time aspired. They defended their position by suggesting that if they had got it wrong, then women would soon let them know by not buying the product. One of the authors of the present book remembers that at the time some of the large multinational companies with their own advertising and copywriting staff would recruit new copywriters not from among students on the marketing courses he and his peers were teaching, but from among Oxbridge graduates – and Oxford 'English' graduates at that! Perhaps whatever mindsets such people possessed were taken into their work.

In the early 1980s, however, things began to change. More women were moving into the workforce and becoming financially and attitudinally more independent. The rising divorce rate meant that both sexes were having to fend for themselves rather more. Both trends were reflected in buying behaviour, so marketers had to target them differently. The cosy family stereotype of two adults and 2.4 children had become far less indicative of the UK population.

Initially the change in advertising approach was erratic. One hotel chain portrayed a 'career woman' with the caption 'I've finally found an hotel that treats me like a man'. Perhaps the right thinking, but what about the execution? Thereafter other advertisers started to depict the more independent career woman. The power dressing of the 1980s was one source of inspiration, but more recently we have seen a blending of this approach with more sexual images – do the Wonderbra advertisements demonstrate female assertiveness and independence, or are they just sexist?

Independence appears to be an important theme as the market has become much more individualistic over the years and women are demonstrating a greater sense of self-identity. Other branches of the media reflect this, including films, for example Catwoman partnering Batman to save Gotham City and Sigourney Weaver's strong role in Aliens. An illustration of the greater financial independence of many women is that one in ten Ford Fiesta drivers is female, compared with one in thirty men.

Another consideration concerns fitness. An increasing number of women are participating in sports and fitness activities and are bombarded by images of amazing slimness and fitness, to which they may or may not aspire, but the approach has brought distress to those who try but fail to achieve the body images presented to them. Is this approach sexist? The 'mother' image is still around. Many advertisements for washing powder and cleaning products still suggest the woman's place is in the home.

Having said this, studies consistently show that although there have been some changes in terms of democracy in the household, few men do the cleaning or ironing. Is this partly a result of advertising approaches or is advertising an accurate mirror of society? The 'Oxo' campaign is another one that still adheres to the 'happy families' stereotype, with 'mum' serving up wonderful meals for the rest of her family.

It is also clear that the 'mistress' image is still blatantly employed. One advertisement for a lawnmower depicts a young, scantily clad woman in chains on a lawn! This was This was shown in the 1990s, although the style was more akin to the 1970s. At least this was banned by the ASA, but there are numerous other examples of the use of mother/mistress/career/independently assertive stereotypes in advertising.

To reinforce the proposition that we have moved forward, though, an advertisement dating from around 1900 portrays a woman wearing what is, to all intents and purposes, a mask over her face. The copy refers to Dr Batt's patented device to prevent one's wife from smoking in public. The subtext mentions that it would also be suitable for wives who talk too much! So perhaps we can conclude that 'all things are relative'.

(3) With regard to marketing to men, in 1997 the Advertising Standards Authority upheld complaints about a Lee Jeans poster showing a woman in jeans resting her stilettoed foot on the a naked man's bottom. The copy read 'put the boot in'. The advertisement was defended on the basis that it reflected the prevailing mood of 'girl power'. This is a clear example of the tables being turned! What do you think?

Any change in the societal role of one gender is bound to affect the other because the balance is dynamic. The 1990s were heralded as the caring, sharing decade. Early examples of how this was reflected in advertising included an Audi commercial showing a father driving carefully to attend his child's birth.

Similar forces have affected men's lives as those which have affected women. High divorce rates mean that many more men have to care for themselves – do their own shopping, cooking, cleaning and so on. They are taking more care with their appearance and buying more grooming products. The extensive range of men's style magazines is a reflection of their interest in this area. It was only a decade or so ago that men's magazines meant soft porn!

Even some advertisements for cleaning products are depicting men. However a Persil advertisement showing a teenager trying to wash his shirt for an important night out depicts him as incompetent, spilling the washing powder as he tries to read the instructions on the side of the packet. Is this sexist?

New male stereotypes are emerging as men reshape their self-image and display their individualism. The 1990s saw a Levi commercial starring a transvestite in a New York taxi and gay images are becoming more common as marketers target the 'pink pound'.

In 1997 the gay market was estimated to be worth around £7 million and to be composed of relatively affluent trend setters with few dependants, and therefore a significant disposable income. The *Gay Times* (1998) estimated that the average gay household brought in £36 000 a year – much more than the average straight family. It is also much easier to reach the gay market than in the past because of the greater variety of gay magazines, the Internet and now advertisements on mainstream TV at appropriate times.

4 Marketing Research and Information

Survey Research

KEY CONCEPTS

- Marketing research
- Survey research
- Group discussions

Flaw poll

A petfood ad claims that eight out of ten owners who expressed a preference, said their cats preferred it. But if the growing band of market research critics are to be believed, you might as well ask the cats. Are surveys a valuable source of information, or an imprecise discipline that tells marketers what they want to hear?

CHRIS BOULDING

Market research would support original sin. From a representative survey taken in the garden of Eden, it seems half the population definitely supports taking a bite of the forbidden fruit, and the other half doesn't know. Conclusion: most consumers are in favour of greater apple consumption; probably target females.

This is what Adam, the world's first puzzled decision maker, wanted to know, and what his research told him. Alas the decision taken was wrong. It involved relocation, a substantial decrease in personal shelf life and heavy marking down on the divine balance sheet.

Is all market research rubbish, or are we asking the wrong questions?

Some 50 years ago, Ford launched a new brand of car called the Edsel, named after Henry Ford's son. After a huge programme of research, examining every curve and feature of the brand, success was shown to be inevitable. The launch flopped, partly because no one had bothered to ask the public what they thought of the car as a whole.

More recent history is littered with the carcasses of failed new product launches – all of which have been thoroughly researched. "If market research is so good, why do so many of these products fail?" asks one brand consultant.

Market research consultant John Wigzell identifies at least one recurrent flaw. Sometimes the real purpose of doing research is to prove we are right. "If there is large-scale investment in a project – emotional as well as financial – marketers want to demonstrate to their masters on the board that it will not be lost," he says.

Large research companies naturally disagree. In their view, market research finds questions not answers. Louise Southcott, strategic brand development head of NOP Research Group, the third-largest market research company in the UK, says: "Research can be ideal for identifying what the questions and issues are, especially when dealing with an unknown, such as new product development."

In July, the Daily Mirror used a large survey to demonstrate to its own satisfaction that Prince Charles should never be king. A study of reader attitudes the day after Jonathan Dimbleby's documentary on the Prince of Wales "proved" that 32 per cent of Britons regarded him as unfit to reign, against a simpering 61 per cent who thought him worthy. The conclusion – somewhat elliptical – was that this was a vote of no confidence.

Robert Bean, chairman of the start-up agency Bean M.C. and former marketing director of BT, remembers a marketing director who would make up his mind, think for a moment and then commission some "findings" to back up his decision. The problem for such people is that research is only used when they have already made the decision.

Bean believes one of the malaises of British management is the notion that there is a need to control the outcome of research and only investigate those areas of the decision-making process that present straightforward evidence. "We're in danger of valuing most that which we can measure best," says Bean.

If a type of consumer can't be defined within ordinary research categories, he or she may be seen as less valuable to the marketer. George Michaelides, a partner in new strategic media company Michaelides & Bednash, cites "sensual enthusiasts" as an example. Media research, whether BARB or NRS, doesn't have a category for this group, making it harder to reach through conventional media.

The quality and depth of ordinary research is pitiful, according to Michaelides. He compares the rather weary system of audit panels used by BARB, or even by the TGI, with the far more detailed and project-specific information within other large indus-

tries. "We devote billions to media expenditure, but hardly anything to research."

By the time most research emerges it is out of date, fuelling a "rear view mirror" approach to marketing – a term defined by Anita Roddick, a self-proclaimed debunker of the art.

The large surveys like TGI give programmes such as Blind Date and Spitting Image huge "preference to view" indices, reflecting the public's historic affection for the programmes. "In fact, if you talk to people now, they will say both have gone off the boil, and they switch off or do something else when they come on," says Michaelides.

The picture that emerges is of a confused and imprecise discipline that panders to the paranoid "give me figures" yell of the marketing director. But it gets worse. Quite a lot of research also uses these figures to predict the future.

The 1992 election was a disaster for research prediction. All the polling companies bar one predicted a "hung parliament" days before the event, and got it wrong. "What we can never do is predict with certainty what the British electorate will do," says MORI chairman Bob Worcester. The polling companies claim their figures represented the voting intentions of the British public accurately (within their permitted margins of error), but they were foiled by a late swing to the Tories.

A two-year investigation by the Market Research Society exonerates them. One has to bear in mind the effect of the polls themselves on voting, as well as floating voters' natural desire to claim they will vote against the government in power. But the fact remains that research is a bad base for accurate prediction – even over a few days – if the mood of the population is constantly shifting. Uncertainty is surely the one defining element in consumer behaviour.

The days of quantitative research are numbered, according to some mar-

keters. But advertising, design and branding specialists at least have their own species of research at the "touchy-feely" end of the market.

Qualitative research – in the form of group discussions or focus groups – was invented in the Sixties precisely to get around the rather sterile world of statistics. But who really wants to know that if your name is Margaret, your partner is more likely to be a John than anything else? Such population data analysis is experiencing a rebirth, as computer power exceeds its usefulness.

It certainly tells marketers very little about their brands. The trouble with qualitative research is that it only gives marketers another person's experience. For instance, a recent extensive survey by Research International on Teenagers of the World tells us that "close friends provide close companionship and fun, understanding, empathy and advice". It also provides us with revealing quotes direct from the lips of teenagers around the world, such as: "Hair is important, it makes a great difference to your looks".

Some agencies say it's hardly surprising you get such banal results when focus groups operate as they do. MBA planning director Mark Tomblin thinks such groups tend to homogenise both the product and the advertising. "It actually screens out and knocks off all the edges – the things that make a product stick to you like a burr on a jumper," he says .

Launch a washing powder with a pack sporting a day-glo orange against bluey-green and people in research will say it's not like their ordinary powder. That is the reason to create it, says Tomblin.

Part of the problem with these "seven housewives and a bowl of peanuts" groups is that many of the participants are fakes. Tomblin claims that many of the carefully targeted "respondents" are either friends of the moderator or semi-professional extras who play the research circuit for the money (£20 or £30 cash-in-hand for a 90-minute session). "It's a fraud, and more widespread than the industry believes or wants to believe," says Tomblin. "What is the point in having a discussion with eight people who are acting?"

He is a great believer in what he calls the Japanese approach: launch the product first and research it after-wards. As he points out, inside Japan, car manufacturers create many models that never make it to the UK on the principle that the only research that matters is the reaction of buyers.

It has worked before, most famous-ly with Akio Morito's launch of the Walkman in the face of prophecies of doom from market researchers. Such parables are gold dust to creatives, who have spent years research-bashing to safeguard their little creative mas-terpieces. GGT creative director Tim Mellors says that if research had ruled, neither the Heineken ads nor the BT Maureen Lipman campaign would have seen the light of day.

So much research is a "will o' the wisp". But "what else have we got?" is obviously the wrong question to ask, according to Robert Bean.

ISSUES

1. What forms of interviewing are used in market research?

2. What are the characteristics of postal surveys and do you agree with the cynical views expressed in the above clipping?

3. What are the characteristics of telephone surveys and do you agree with the cynical views expressed in the clipping?

4. What are the characteristics of personal surveys and do you agree with the cynical views expressed in the clipping?

5. What are the characteristics of group discussion and do you agree with the cynical views expressed in the clipping?

6. What are the characteristics of good marketing research?

7. What can organisations do to improve outside research quality?

EXPLORATION OF ISSUES

1. Various interview techniques are used in research surveys, and a distinction is usually made between per-sonal, telephone and postal interviews. Further distinc-tions can be made between structured and unstructured interviews, and the personal interview can be of an in-depth or group type. New technology allows another kind of interviewing, where the computer provides a vehicle for asking questions and collecting responses, in some cases using the Internet.

2. Postal questionnaire studies have the obvious advantage over personal interviews of being able to cover a very large geographic area, usually with little increase in postal costs. The main characteristic of postal

surveys is the absence of an interviewer, which eliminates interviewer bias but at the same time provides little scope for respondents to query the meaning of the questions. The lack of personal contact also means that when a questionnaire is sent to an address, there is no guarantee that the respondent is the addressee, since the questionnaire may be completed by another member of the family or organisation.

On the positive side, when a survey requires the respondent to consult with others, or with filed information, the postal survey provides the necessary time and freedom, and another bonus of there being no interviewer is that some respondents may be less inhibited about answering certain questions. On the other hand, without an interviewer, misunderstood questions cannot be explained, open questions cannot be probed, and non-verbal communication by the respondents (facial expressions, intonation and the like) cannot be observed.

However, the single most significant problem with most postal surveys is the low level of response – it is all too easy for selected respondents to ignore a postal questionnaire. Without a carefully constructed covering letter, emphasising such factors as how useful (and confidential) the respondent's replies will be, or without a reminder, the response rate can be as low as single figures. Even when stamped addressed envelopes are enclosed the response rate may be so low as to be unrepresentative of the selected sample. The point is, of course, that non-response may not be a random factor – the characteristics of those who do respond may be significantly different from the characteristics of those who do not respond – a factor for which survey results should be tested whenever possible.

Despite the above problems, postal surveys are used extensively, perhaps because they represent an acceptable compromise between reliability and validity on the one hand and cost considerations on the other.

Postal questionnaires are widely used by direct marketers, generally because they can be included with planned mailings to customers – promotional mailings, utility bills, bank statements and so on – but thought must be given to the length of the questionnaire. A variation on the postal questionnaire is the 'inserted' questionnaire. Self-completion lifestyle surveys have become an established component of contemporary marketing. these questionnaires are usually inserted in newspapers or magazines or attached to warranty details on new purchases, where the consumer is asked to post the completed form.

3 Although telephone interviews are not used as much as other interviewing approaches and are less popular than in the UK than they are in the United States, they are becoming more important and merit consideration in research design, as long as the sampling can be restricted to those with telephones. Indeed the Market Research Society (1994), in a major report, confirms that most telephone interviewing is just as appropriate as personal interviewing but much more convenient because of the easier, cheaper and more comfortable access to respondents – no waiting in cold and wet streets for the 'right' people to come along when a quota sample is being used, no more futile multiple call-backs to an address when the sample design is random and the interviewing is face to face.

As in the case of postal surveys, there is also a geographical advantage, although this is less pronounced than with postal questionnaires because of long-distance telephone rates, time-related call charges and the impossibility in many cases of making use of cheap rate times (phoning companies at the weekend or in the evenings promises little success).

Telephone interviews are often appropriate for industrial or organisational surveys because most companies have telephones and the chance of contacting someone in an organisation during office hours is reasonably good – although it may be more difficult to contact the person who is most relevant.

Once the problem of getting past the organisational switchboard is overcome, telephone interviewing can be the quickest of all the interviewing methods because the interview is conducted from the researcher's desk, so no fieldwork travel is involved, and the replies are immediate.

Telephone interviewing can also be used in consumer markets. For example, BT conducts some 13 500 telephone interviews a month. Interviewees are chosen from those customers who have asked for a service or fault repair, or made a request or complaint.

There can also be a misuse of the telephone for bogus 'research' purposes. Consider the car exhaust and tyre company that made telephone contact with its customers on the basis that they had been recorded in the database as having purchased new tyres/battery or exhaust systems in the last month. The questioning commenced with satisfaction with the service, according to a five-point scale and with no request for further feedback. Soon, however, the questions moved on to cover aspects of car insurance such as renewal dates. The research was clearly an attempt to cross-sell another service because when customers tried to provide reasons for their dissatisfaction, the questioner was very reluctant to pursue this and admitted there was no provision to record such information.

There are many applications for new information technology in marketing research. For example a questionnaire can be stored on a computer and as the interviewer goes through the interview over the telephone, the computer can select and display appropriate questions for each respondent, and the replies can be keyed directly into the computer, for immediate analysis. This is now common place and is referred to as computer assisted telephone interviewing (CATI).

Clearly, however, some questions cannot be asked over the telephone, such as those which require the respondent to look at a product or package, and telephone interviews are of necessity restricted to questions that are capable of being answered instantly. On the other hand the telephone can sometimes hide the existence of a questionnaire, and the interview can seem more like a conversation to the respondent, who is thus more relaxed and less inhibited.

The more sophisticated interactive TV technology allows questions to be sent down the line to households possessing such a system. The questions are displayed on TV sets and the answers keyed in via a keypad or a home computer keyboard and sent back along the line to the researcher for analysis. Such systems are as yet in their infancy, but already tested and used is a compromise between the above approaches, involving the use of a computer visual display unit to present a self-completion questionnaire. The future is likely to see the Internet being used more as an interviewing vehicle. Appropriate respondents can be identified through records of their web-browsing or other lists. They can be 'e-mailed' questionnaires and any responses can be analysed rapidly because the data will be communicated on-line in an already coded form.

4 The distinguishing feature of personal interviewing is, of course, face-to-face communication between respondent and interviewer, which poses problems of bias and error as well as offering flexibility and control. However it is the fieldwork cost that constitutes the main disadvantage of this type of data collection. In fact the sample design employed is of some importance here, because different fieldwork problems occur with different sampling methods. For example, with a quota sample the interviewer has to select respondents who possess the required characteristics, while with random sampling the interviewer must contact a specific person or address.

The presence of an interviewer provides the opportunity for varying degrees of structure. For instance questions might be open-ended to allow the respondent to answer in hisor her own words, without the constraint of predetermined optional answers, and the interviewer can ask the respondent to expand on a point, using various probing techniques. Unstructured interviews are more like conversations because there is no set sequence of preworded questions. Such as in-depth interviews are examples of qualitative as opposed to quantitative research.

5 Group discussions (or focus groups) are generally unstructured and qualitative. Several respondents (about six to ten in number) are brought together, perhaps for a coffee morning in the home of one of the respondents, and the interviewer guides the discussion through relevant topics, leaving most of the talking to the members of the group. This method is widely used to pretest advertisements. While the cost per respondent may be high because of the degree of skill required by the interviewer and the time that a group discussion takes, group discussions may still prove cost effective relative to large-scale sample surveys.

In the late 1990s the cost of a group discussion could exceed £3000, including screening participants for relevant characterises, devising the interview schedule, paying the participants, organising an appropriate venue, recording and transcribing events and analysing the results. Since groups revolve around the sociology of group dynamics, the interviewer, as group moderator, must possess the social skills to deal with respondents who emerge as group dominators and who can adopt the roles with which moderators must deal: the competing moderator, the compiler, the rationaliser, the conscience, the choir, the rebel, the super ego and the pseudo-specialist. A number of criticisms of group discussions have to be acknowledged, including that the method can be used to provide evidence in support of preconceptions, and that it relies heavily on the moderator's interpretation.

6 We can pinpoint seven characteristics of good marketing research.

Scientific method.   Effective marketing research uses the principles of the scientific method – careful observation, formulation of hypotheses, prediction and testing. Statistical analyses test the hypotheses.

Research creativity.   At its best, marketing research can lead to the devlopment of innovative ways of solving problems, for example video diaries.

Multiple methods. Good marketing researchers shy away from overreliance on any one method and adapt the method to the problem, rather than the other way round. They also recognise that multiple sources provide better information.

Interdependence of models and data. Good marketing researchers recognise that data are interpreted from underlying models. These models guide the type of information sought and, therefore, should be made as explicit as possible.

Value and cost of information. Good marketing researchers estimate the value of information against its cost. Value–cost considerations help the marketing research department to determine which research projects to conduct, which research designs to use and whether to gather additional information after the initial results are in. Research costs are usually easy to determine, but the value of research is harder to quantify. The value depends on the reliability and validity of the research findings and management's willingness to accept and act on those findings.

Health scepticism. Good marketing researchers show a health scepticism towards glib assumptions by managers about how a market works.

Ethical marketing. Good marketing research benefits both the sponsoring company and its customers. Through marketing research, companies learn more about consumers' needs and are able to supply more satisfying products and services. However marketing research also has the potential to harm or annoy consumers. Many consumers see marketing research as an intrusion into their privacy or construe it as an attempt to sell them something. Indeed many research studies appear to be little more than vehicles for pitching the sponsor's products. Increasing consumer resentment at such self-serving research has caused major problems for the research industry, including lower survey response rates in recent years.

7 Organisations can do a number of things to improve outside research quality, including the following:

- Increase their involvement at the decision making level, especially during the early stages of the research.
- Use suppliers with qualified personnel.
- Review the suppliers' data validation procedures.
- Conduct frequent evaluations and individual assessments of suppliers.
- Use more than one supplier.
- Obtain several proposals for each research project.
- Ask the suppliers' views on the implications of the research findings.
- Become involved in the specification of the tabulation (data analysis).
- Consult other outside agencies about the reputation of the agencies under consideration.

Technology in Market Research

Time runs out on the meter

Beset by financial woes and member disagreements, BARB has shelved plans for electronic metering and opted for the cheaper, paper-diary service.

TORIN DOUGLAS

It was a hectic weekend for the UK's top research firms, particularly BMRB International. Monday was the deadline to tender for one of the country's largest survey contracts and executives were hard at work putting together their submissions. What made it more onerous for BMRB was that it was having to compete against itself, using two entirely different research methods.

The contract in question is BARB's Audience Reaction Service – which produces the Appreciation Indices that measure how much viewers enjoyed a programme. It's a continuous survey, requiring a Television Opinion Panel of up to 3,000 adults and 1,000 children, each recording his or her views of the programmes watched. The results are an important measure of a programme's quality, as distinct from its popularity and, used properly, they can also play a role in a channel's scheduling.

At the moment the panel members fill in a paper diary, which they return each week by post. But BARB has just begun testing a different method, using electronic meters like those used for the main BARB survey, which measures the size and composition of audiences. The meters report their findings each day automatically via the telephone. BARB has commissioned a pilot survey in 200 homes, conducted jointly by BMRB International and Mediametrics, a firm which specialises in electronic research technology.

A press release last year trumpeted that this study would pave the way for the world's first electronic measurement of how people react to television programmes. The output will provide the BBC and the ITV firms with the world's most sophisticated system for evaluating viewers' opinions on programme quality.'

The pilot service began this month, yet, before it has produced any data,

BARB seems to have rejected its findings. For the technique specified for the new Audience Reaction Service is the old paper-diary method.

One observer described the turn of events as "fascinating and astonishing". Another said: "It's become a farce."

It's also become a race against time. For BARB only told research companies of its change of heart on December 23, just in time for the nation's annual ten-day shutdown. If those tendering had worked throughout the festive-season, they would have had fewer than four weeks to prepare their plans. Those that only woke up to the opportunity on January 4 would have had 12 days.

The deadline for tenders is tight because the new system has to be up and running by August 1. The BBC, which has run the survey until now, will cease to do so at the end of July. It was felt, by BARB and the BBC itself, no longer "appropriate" for a broadcaster to carry out the research. The Corporation sees the Audience Reaction Service as a measure of its accountability, in the run-up to the renewal of its Charter.

What makes time even tighter is that the broadcasting organisations which control the contract have yet to decide what form the survey should take, how much it should cost and how much each of them is prepared to pay.

(So what's gone wrong? It seems a combination of equipment teething problems and a change of heart by some of the service's users means there is no longer the time or the money to go ahead with a full-scale, all-singing, all-dancing meter system.

BARB's chief executive Bob Hulks says: "The electronic system is looking good but it's started late and it's costing more than we thought. The industry cannot wait for the full pilot survey results because the new system has to be in place by August. Time has run out."

All this is true. Richard Silman, a BMRB director, says production of the equipment took longer than expected and the BARB committee wanted to test different ways of registering audience reaction, such as asking viewers to rate programmes on a scale of nought to ten, instead of one to six, as at the moment.

Installation of the meters began in mid-November, instead of October,

and the three-month pilot has only just begun. BMRB reckons that to have a full service up and running by August, it would have to get the go-ahead from BARB by the end of January, with only one month's data ready.

But there is another problem. One of the survey's biggest sponsors, the Independent Television Commission, no longer wants to pay for the service, even though it has helped fund the electronic pilot project. Since it accounts for around a quarter of the budget, this has left a substantial hole in the funding at a time when other participants are also questioning the amount they should pay.

The current service is funded by the BBC, the ITC, the ITV Association, Channel 4 and S4C, the Welsh Fourth Channel. The specification published on December 23 for the new Audience Reaction Service does not mention that one of these is pulling out. But the ITC has said it will not be subscribing to the Audience Reaction Service from this summer.

There are two problems says a spokesperson: "It wouldn't be sufficiently relevant to our duties under the Broadcasting, Act. And there will be a narrower range of data, because the national sample isn't big enough to give us sufficiently robust data on regional programmes in most of the ITV regions."

In law, the ITC is no longer the broadcaster but the regulator, and it now seems to believe it is the job of the

ITV firms – not itself – to commission this type of research. The ITC will presumably rely on the firms to inform it whether their programmes are appreciated by their audience, in the hope they tell the truth and are not unduly selective. But had the data been the sort the ITC wanted, it might have taken a different view of its duties.

The real problem is that, as currently conceived, the new Audience Reaction Service will be national, covering the network programmes, and won't give reliable data for regional programmes. Since the network schedule is no longer the responsibility of the individual firms', they can really only be judged on their regional output, plus any contributions the Network Centre lets them make nationally.

What is in no doubt is that tha ITC's withdrawal creates a huge and damaging hole in the Audience Reaction Service business plan. It is hardly realistic to expect the ITV firms to make up the difference in the funding. Indeed, some at ITV say they should pay no more for the service than their direct competitor, Channel 4. And the BBC will not be keen to pay any extra.

Hence the decision to put the already-delayed electronic system on ice and call for the cheaper, paper-diary service. But whether even that can be achieved on time must be in some doubt.

ISSUES

1 What is a consumer panel and what is its role in marketing research?

2 What methods are used to collect data in panel research and what are the implications for accuracy?

3 What other examples are there of technological developments in marketing research and how might they affect research?

4 What are the implications of technological developments for market research?

EXPLORATION OF ISSUES

1 A consumer panel has nothing to do with group discussions, but is a form of *continuous research* on the buying and other behaviour of the same respondents over time. Households are recruited to the panel and provide information on their purchases in specific or general product categories, and on their media habits – such as viewing television, listening to the radio and reading newspapers.

Households are commonly selected on the basis of random sampling (using electoral registers and/or geodemographic lists and multistage sampling of the type discussed shortly) rather than quota sampling. The major problem with panels is the high withdrawal rate among panel members due to boredom, moving house and so on. As many as 40 per cent after the first interview. Clearly their replacements should be as representative as possible, however recruitment problems and the need to offer members some form of inducement or payment means that the panel is in constant danger of being unrepresentative. Furthermore, new members sometimes change their behaviour after recruitment, so it might be appropriate to exclude the findings from these households for a time until their behaviour reverts to normal.

The basic procedure of the panel system is for operators to compile reports for example on consumer profiles, matching behaviour with names, addresses and aspects of buying behaviour, such as stores used, brands preferred, times of purchase and so on) and sell these to their clients. The latter can thus monitor their competitors' direct marketing efforts as well as their own, with

the additional advantage that time series information is built up, allowing the identification of trends and changes over time.

Direct marketers are now linking panel data with other databases to add richness to their data. It has been found, for example, that in lifestyle and other surveys some consumers exaggerate certain buying patterns, but panel data, being a record of actual buying, can be used to weight some of these responses. A specific example concerns cat food – one elderly lady in a state of confusion bought eighty cans of cat food a week for several weeks, and this somewhat distorted the panel results!

A panel in which one of the authors was a participant provides a good example of another use of panels. HTV is a 'split' region, there being HTV Wales and HTV West. The panel was set up in South Wales, where households tune in to one or other of the transmitters. The panel was funded in association with retailers and split-run experiments were possible, with different versions of the same advertisement being broadcast via the different transmitters. The results could be tracked through analysis of viewing and subsequent purchases via shopping baskets being scanned at home and by tracking responses to the commercial. This particular panellist may not have been a very good one because of lack of dedication to the scanning task, but the household concerned was able to receive both HTV Wales and HTV West, and occasional 'channel hopping' did indeed reveal different versions of some commercials being transmitted at the same time.

This example demonstrates a practical way of sending

out alternative commercials to different, but matched, audiences and being able to record the effects in terms of the shopping basket.

2 The reporting of consumer behaviour used to be by means of a diary (which is still used in some cases) that was completed by the respondents and either posted to the research agency concerned or collected by a researcher. For example the radio stations listened to by a panel for media studies would be noted on a preprinted chart for each day of the week, and a grocery panel would record the brands, pack sizes, prices paid and stores used for the product categories being studied. In a sense, this method is a variation of a self-completion questionnaire.

The Royal Mail has just such a panel to study the receipt of different types of mail from a variety of sources, including of course direct marketers.

However it is increasingly the case that panels do not involve any form of interviewing. Some, for example, have a special audit bin, into which the packaging from products is placed for a researcher to monitor. Meters that record data on television viewing are commonly used used today to measure, for example, exposure to commercials. These link the TV with a phone line and overnight the research agency is able to download data on which TV channels were tuned into and for how long. The problem of determining whether people were actually watching at the time has also been addressed, though only partially. People meters allow each member of the household to press a coded button (even visitors can be coded) whenever they leave and enter the room.

Another piece of equipment that is often provided to panel members is a hand-held barcode reader. The panel members are asked to scan all their groceries, key in the price of every item, and scan a barcode on a card to indicate from which store it was purchased and whether it was on special offer. They may also be asked to scan a barcode on a card to indicate which newspapers and magazines were read that day and to which radio stations they had listened.

One of the authors was a panel member, and although it is far from scientific to base conclusions on a sample of one – indeed oneself – the reader will no doubt question the likelihood of *everybody* in that household pressing their button on the people meter *always* when they left or entered the room.

With regard to the barcode reader mentioned above – the reader might wonder whether those who are willing and able to perform all these tasks *daily* are really representative of the population.

3 The following further examples of technological developments in marketing research.

Interactive TV. In addition to its 'narrowcasting' role, cable-based systems (cable TV, Internet) can be used in an interactive way to conduct surveys, with respondents using their TV keypads to give precoded responses to questions appearing on their screens.

MRT (market research terminals). These are hand held recorders and in effect act as electronic clipboards. Interviewers previously needed a different questionnaire for each respondent and the recorded answers then had to be coded and typed into a computer statistical package. The electronic clipboard allows each respondent's replies to be entered already coded and stored for later downloading to the main analysis computer.

Laser scanning. This allows the barcodes on packaging to be read at the checkout, which not only provides a quick way of processing sales, but can also be linked to stock-level databases in order to update them automatically as purchases are made. A specific marketing research application here is the Retail audit – rather than researchers conducting regular physical stock checks in stores in the audit sample, sales records for specific brands and pack sizes in the categories being researched can be stored for each day's trading and, if desired, downloaded to the research agency's computer overnight via a telephone link with the store's computer. This provides rapid and accurate statistics. The contract for compiling record charts used to be held by the BMRB, but the old system of physically filling in a diary and posting this to BMRB lost out to Gallup's newer technology, based on the above type of system.

Improved instruments. Examples include meters to monitor the TV channels watched by households in TV audience research consumer panels; the psychogalvanometer, which measures physical responses that are a manifestation of emotional responses and has been used as part of advertising pretests; the eye camera, which traces the path the eye takes over a preset space onto which photos of advertisements, shelf displays and so on are projected; and the tachistoscope, which flashes pictures (for example of advertisements, packaging designs, alternative logotypes and so on) for a fraction of a second – this can help identify which designs, colour combinations and typefaces are more readily observed and understood.

Video synthesised posters for pre-testing. Before the advent of video technology it was not possible convincingly to simulate the testing of a poster in an actual high street location before the campaign was launched. Now it is possible to video a high street scene – one with a billboard site, of course – and then superimpose the test poster on the billboard in the film. The poster does not 'fall off the edge' of the billboard frame and appears most convincingly to be present in the high street in question. This enables pretesting questioning in a much more realistic simulation of reality than was previously possible.

CATI (Computer Assisted Telephoning Interviewing). This requires interviewers to watch their VD's while questioning respondents. The questionnaire is displayed on the screen and as responses are given a predetermined code is typed in by the interviewer, thus avoiding the time delays and errors associated with coding and entering data after the interviews. After each entry the next appropriate question appears on the screen on the basis of which answer has just been given – that is, there is automatic 'routing' through the questionnaire, thus avoiding sequencing errors.

Telemarketing. One of the newest additions to the portfolio of market research techniques is telemarketing, described as a 'marketing communication system which utilises telecommunications technology and trained personnel to conduct planned, measurable marketing activities directed at target groups of consumers' (Voorhees and Coppett, 1983). It is a quick and cost-effective way of gathering research data, on either an *ad hoc* or a continuous basis, on present and future markets. This method gives greater control over research activities by eliminating outside agencies.

Saris and Pijper (1986) initially developed this interview procedure to improve response measurement of personal interviews by using continuous scales, correcting random error measurement and checking answer consistency, but they postulate future applications with regards to face-to-face interviews. The extent of controls, coding and punching could be reduced in large-scale surveys, and data could be automatically stored in an analysable form. Likewise products could be tested along with advertising effectiveness evaluation. Random samples of the population could be issued with a product, or shown an advertising concept by means of digital photography, then questioned about their reactions. Furthermore, the results of pilot studies could be more easily incorporated into the survey, and at greater speed.

Computer geodemographic databases. These link national census data with, for example, the postcode system, databases on bad debt and so on and make it possible to identify specific types of household and contact samples of these by name and address. Market research

conducted in this way provides new insights and allows better targeted advertising, promotional and merchandising activities (Whitehead 1992). Database manipulation along these lines already exists in the form of Acorn (produced by CACI), Pin (pinpoint identified neighbourhoods) and Geoplan (produced by Market Profiles).

The Geoplan mapping system enables manufacturers, retailers and advertising agencies to convert the results of national survey research and their own databases into marketing maps. The resulting maps, for example can identify current product penetration, potential target markets for products and services, sites for new outlets and media coverage of identified target audiences. Colour-coded 'hot spots' of locations of 'best prospect' customer can be shown and indeed any data which is postcoded can be mapped. Thus customer files, purchase lists, direct mail respondents, promotions entrants and so on can all be mapped on the Geoplan postcode sector boundary file. National surveys that utilise any of the geodemographic systems can be linked by that system to postcode sectors. Demographic manipulation such as this permits the size of local markets to be quantified with a precision that was previously impossible, and the size and distribution of retail competitors can then be used to build a more complete picture of the marketplace.

Developments in IT have led to the proliferation of increasingly sophisticated marketing databases and geodemographic market segmentation systems. Computer-based decision support systems and simulation models will soon be used to evaluate marketing programmes prior to real-world introductions, and data bases and evaluation systems will be integrated into larger, more useful information systems. New systems are needed that can link data bases together in ways that vastly increase their value to management decision making. Expert systems and knowledge-based systems will be used to devise competitive marketing strategies.

4 Overall, technological change will continue to have a profound effect on marketing and marketing research in three main ways. First, it will contribute directly to new product development programmes because new products often result from technological change. Second, new ways of conducting marketing research are likely to emerge. Third, technology may change life styles and therefore market behaviour, and marketing research will have to respond by measuring different behaviours, interests and concerns.

Personalised Consumer Information

KEY CONCEPTS

- The social environment
- Personalised information
- Relationship marketing
- Database marketing
- Privacy

Tapping a valuable commodity

As more companies adopt database marketing techniques to tailor their goods and services to consumer needs, so, in turn, consumer information will become more valuable. **ALAN MITCHELL** predicts.

A condescending smile comes over his face and patiently he presses his internal "explain for the thousandth time" button. And out it comes, again. Complaints against junk mail are falling not rising; the improved targeting that extra information creates means less junk mail and more appropriate messages; millions delight in pouring out their innermost secrets to companies – just look at the astonishing success of the lifestyle databases; and so on. There's hardly a direct marketer who avoids this knee-jerk response to what they obviously pigeonhole as "the media's privacy question".

Everything they say is true. But it's not the whole truth. Direct marketers may have won the first argument. But they haven't won the war. Fear of Big Brother is still there, but it is just part of the information age cocktail. And though it is bound to return as the industry ventures down the path of database integration, it is not what the war is about. Last week, at the Direct Marketing Association's tenth anniversary seminar, the Henley Centre unveiled its Dataculture report – a dataculture being "a culture of information exchange between companies and their customers in return for specific benefits to the customer". The foundations of such a culture have been laid, it says. There is "a healthy and encouraging environment in which database marketing, properly conducted, can flourish".

The key question is what that "proper conduct" will consist of. Most consumers, the report says, have a pragmatic approach to revealing personal details, the crucial factors being that they want to feel in control, they want the data exchange to be relevant to the product or service that's being sold, and they want to see the benefits of that data exchange.

These are eminently sensible objectives. But they could be a graveyard for marketers, for two reasons. First, mismatched expectations. It's very easy for a company to take the theoretical standpoint that the more it knows about its customers the better it can shape its offers to them. But how does my answering this questionnaire deliver me an immediate, palpable benefit that I value?

Likewise relevance. From the marketer's point of view, all the usual suspects (income, age, occupation, *etc*) are "relevant" to building profiles of key market segments. But many consumers don't agree.

Conceivably both these issues could be tackled by education. But the third issue – control – cannot. That is about power. And, as Calyx UK managing director Mark Patron pointed out at the seminar, just as the focus of information power shifted from manufacturer to retailer in the Eighties, so now it is moving towards the consumer. Saturated markets are buyers' markets, and the information revolution is giving buyers ever more access to ever more information about sellers.

So far consumers have not wielded their new power. But just as they have become ad literate, so they're becoming data literate too.

Indeed, the education process that is needed to allay naive fears will drive home the simple truths that lie at the heart of the information economy. That, increasingly, it's information and not things like coal or steel that are its core raw material. And that every purchase transaction also involves a parallel exchange of data which carries its own value: information is an asset in its own right – don't just give it away.

Net result? Data-literate consumers will require increasing control over which marketer gets what information for what purposes – a demand which goes way beyond the current blanket choice of either totally "opting in" or totally "opting out". And the prime reason for seeking this control is not fear of Big Brother but the realisation that privacy creates information scarcity and scarcity enhances your bargaining position.

List renters don't give away their data free. They hire on a 'once-only' use basis and require premiums for anything more. If list renters do that, why shouldn't consumers? Rising information literacy has an inevitable side effect: the idea that consumers should be the rightful and beneficial owners of information about themselves – not marketers. And that they should be free to give it or sell it as they wish, for the highest price.

When Tesco offers one per cent off, it is not only doing a promotion. It is beginning to pay consumers for data. And who says one per cent is a good enough price? Certainly its top five per cent customers could probably charge a lot more. It's conceivable that in future elite "customer clubs" could emerge for this very purpose. How long before some info-entrepreneur organises one?

If that sounds far-fetched, try something a bit more down-to-earth: marketers will have to develop new brands and brand positionings to cater for different customer clusters who have different attitudes to information sharing and who want different sorts of relationship with different companies (equal partner, teacher, guardian, servant). And "how I will handle your information" and "what benefits you will get by telling me about yourself" will become an increasingly overt differentiating factor.

Commenting on the Henley report last week, DMA chief executive Colin Lloyd predicted "the price of one-to-one relationships will go up as consumers get more demanding". That's a good candidate for understatement of the decade.

ISSUES

1 **What issues are involved in the debate on privacy and how might they affect the development of relationship marketing?**

2 **What does the issue of 'control' mean for consumers and marketers?**

EXPLORATION OF ISSUES

1 The question of privacy embodies a number of distinct issues (tempered by the consumer's sense of control in the exchange process), including information privacy, physical privacy and accuracy. These issues may well reduce the utility of direct and database marketing in building, maintaining and enhancing customer relations. Likely outcomes include reduction of trust, dilution of commitment and respect, and unwillingness to participate in a relationship. The link between privacy concerns and the associated difficulties in establishing relationships with consumers is illustrated in Figure 4.1. In the centre of the diagram are the integral elements of relationships, while the outer circles represent consumers' privacy concerns, which are affected by the more perva-

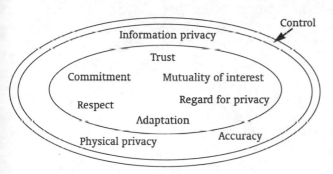

Figure 4.1   Privacy and relational elements

Source: Lisa O'Malley, Maurice Patterson and Martin Evans, 'Intimacy or Intrusion? The Privacy Dilemma for Relationship Marketing in Consumer Markets', *Journal of Marketing Management, Vol. 13, no. 6*

sive 'control' issue. Abuses in these areas may create a barrier to the development of meaningful relationships with consumers.

Essentially, as privacy concerns grow it will become increasingly difficult to foster the integral elements of a relationship. Thus the current reliance on direct and database technology to facilitate relationship development is exacerbating privacy concerns, and this must be resolved if the potential for relationship marketing in consumer markets is to be realised.

(2) Consumers' perceived loss of control in the exchange process has been identified as a key factor in eliciting other concerns. When consumers provide personal information they do not always understand the full implications of doing so. Nor do they have any control over how their personal information is utilised and managed. This manifests itself in what is generally termed 'invasion of privacy'. The widespread availability of consumer data on the open market is a particular concern.

In terms of role theory, consumers and service providers adhere closely to a well-defined script when they interact. In the past marketers requested only that sought information which was required to process a specific transaction, and consumers willingly provided such information as part of their predefined script. However as marketers moved towards relationship building their thirst for new (and often sensitive) information increased, and as a result many consumers are now experiencing role dissonance.

There is debate at present about the possibility of consumers charging marketers for use of their personal details. This would shift control towards consumers and allow them to sell only those details they feel comfortable about revealing – perhaps for specific purposes in particular product categories, or even just for the use of a specific marketer.

Biographics

New model army

Gone are the days of the 'straightforward' marketing database – now companies need systems which offer sophisticated functions to fulfil complicated requirements. **DAVID REED** finds out which solutions today's technology can provide.

The range of activities carried out by direct marketers – profiling, regression analysis, customer loyalty programmes – has become extremely diverse and highly specialised. At the same time, the underlying technology has become critical to success.

From the initial goal of simply having a marketing database, the issues have become harder to resolve as the use of that database has increased. In particular, the database is having to interact with a broader range of departments within client companies than it was originally designed for.

As marketing initiates a dialogue with customers, the customer service department needs to access details when an individual phones in. Similarly, the billings department needs to ensure the way it records transactional data is compatible with the marketing records structure.

This is creating as many technological problems as there have been solutions. "The common thread is that you get problems if what you specify attempts to cover more than one functional area. If it is for customer service, the system is not going to be easy to use for other areas," says Hector Vass, technical director at marketing services agency Lovell Vass Boddey.

He says that moving systems from the original department into other areas is causing problems for many marketing databases. Typically, clients are finding problems with the speed of processing data. "Some people talk about wanting more speed because they have set up their system erroneously if they want quick access. If you are running a relational database on a mailing machine, you've got speed problems," Vass says.

Marketing databases often represent the "great white hope" for a company in terms of improving business performance. But this image is increasingly becoming tarnished as problems arise. Hardly surprising – the market is saturated with software packages and crowded with suppliers offering solutions that often reflect their own need for a return on investment in hardware rather than their clients' real needs.

Just keeping up with technological change is hard enough. The risk for many clients now looking for a marketing database, says Vass, is that many of the existing models were developed in the Seventies for financial services or mail order operations.

"Companies such as American Express were successful in their day in the way they built their database. But people are just repeating that and it is not relevant, for example, to fmcg companies. Amex would not do the same again because marketing has become more complex," he says.

For this reason, an increasing number of companies are outsourcing their databases. Using a supplier who has already developed a system and who carries the expense of development is both simpler and more flexible. What is becoming noticeable is that the computer bureaux themselves are also moving away from a fixed, packaged approach, looking instead at holding a blueprint which is then built using bought-in packages for each client.

"There is no 'black box' solution," says Mark Gregory, managing director of PCL Marketing Services. "If your objectives are to improve margins, to retain a greater percentage of customers – for example, in the telecoms industry – or to improve response, that tends to bring specific requirements."

The breadth of activities now relying on IT support is revealed in a survey by Gallup on behalf of PCL. It found that in addition to database management, which was the most widely automated function, IT is now used for sales lead tracking (75 per cent of the sample), customer/prospect profiling and telemarketing (both 65 per cent), sales territory planning (63 per cent) and campaign management (60 per cent).

At mailing and fulfilment house Mailcom, database management has grown out of a simple process – holding a mailing file – into a powerful service which can capture response and run analyses. "We can offer a set of analytical tools to be applied to customer data, to simply segment or to cross-tab response to different media," explains account director Jonathan Ellis.

Like PCL, his company does not package its solution, preferring to put together the resources to fit each client. What each direct marketer is really buying is the expertise in analysing data which can then support decision-making. "We have a set of criteria or techniques that we can apply across all their data. The interpretation then depends on the client," he says.

One issue for marketers has been the ability to interface with data sources from elsewhere in their company. In the retail sector, this has been especially problematic. Transactional data captured at point of sale is potentially the most valuable information

for marketing. But the sheer volume involved demands a mainframe computer.

With most marketing databases operating on a PC platform, extracting the relevant information can be complex and expensive. The Database Group believes it can now offer a solution, following its recent joint venture deal with Olivetti, via its UK subsidiary Syntax Processing.

"Retailers have been frustrated for years because they had no way of using transactional data. Now Tesco is doing it and everybody realises the system doesn't have to be that big. Entry level costs of EPOS are reasonable – a few pounds per week for a simple terminal," says Neal Muranyi, sales director at The Database Group.

"The Olivetti deal has given us a leg up. You can get transactional data through EPOS and we feed off that," he says.

Even without transactional data, the size of many marketing databases can easily reach thousands, or even millions, of records. Given that the strategic objectives require this information to be available, the problem becomes one of how to manage this volume of data and still gain access to it at reasonable speed.

At TDS Marketing Services, managing director Adrian Gregory says: "We are finding clients have huge amounts of customer data that is either inaccurate, or the sheer volume of it means they can't make sense of it. So we developed a suite of applications using the power of massive parallel processing. It enables us to crunch huge volumes of data."

The Mar-Kit system is based on a White Cross Systems client-server and has four modules. Auditor analyses the database to identify which fields are populated and where any weaknesses are to be found. Interrogator allows for fast analysis to generate counts of the records which match the selection criteria.

The most powerful module is

HeatSeeker, which Gregory describes as a "data-mining tool". Using a decision-tree process and taking advantage of the speed of the parallel processing, it allows marketers to follow "train of thought" analysis of their customer base to tease out the key characteristics of the most valuable customer segments, for example. List Generator then generates the file to be acted on.

If high-speed processing of high-volume raw data delivers a critical benefit to marketers, another new technology is also providing a solution to the problem of incomplete or inaccurate data. "Neural computing is the natural progression – it is another tool to get an edge," says Nick Ryman-Tubb, chief executive of Neural Technologies.

"The majority of our clients are companies with poor data, disparate databases, customer names all over the place, or who are even throwing data away. They are looking at neural computing because it is the most tolerant of poor data," he says.

There are two ways of using neural networks. The current most-used approach is supervised neural computing. The system is fed historical data, for example on known responders and purchasers, which forms the outcome the system has to emulate. Other data is used as the input on which it is to base its predictions. The system is then "trained" to analyse the input data until it produces outcomes of its own accord which match those which have already been achieved.

Companies such as Britvic have used neural networks in this way to forecast sales of new soft drinks like Apple Tango, while advertising agencies such as McCann-Erickson are applying it to the optimisation of media schedules.

Ryman-Tubb says this method is very powerful for inferring "what if?" results, such as price elasticity. The other, cutting-edge, way of using neural networks is where there are no clear inputs or outputs, just a mass of data. The system groups data sets that seem to have a relationship and comes up with clusters.

"You will see a number of prominent groups sticking out which you know are right from instinct. Very often there are also groupings you hadn't realised, for example, an older age group among your customers which you hadn't considered before," he says.

While these powerful technologies are making it ever easier for marketers to take advantage of the powerful data residing in their files, without having to learn specialised computing skills, they are also being used to maximise the value of even the simplest data tasks.

Address management has generally only been considered as a necessary procedure to ensure that a mailing file can obtain full Mailsort discount by being properly postcoded. But Printronic International has recognised that there is considerable value

to the marketer in the information contained in each record.

Where multiple files are being deduplicated and matched, that process can provide significant insights into the target profile. "Data matching is the key because it bridges sources. If you have a list with a name and address, a database with name, address and other information, then external data sets like the Census, postcode or lifestyle, you can match them all together onto one record and start to make a picture of a person's life," says Nick Di Talamo, sales director of Printronic International.

He claims that work with Britannia Music Club has added £12m to the bottom line over three years for an investment of £90,000. At First Direct, the software has allowed the bank to build three-dimensional models of its customers which analyse the database by response, conversion and value. This is only feasible if the data sources can be matched to each other with

total confidence.

"We have been able to demonstrate increases in response," says Di Talamo. "We can show a clear cost-benefit analysis. If it doesn't work, so what? But if it does, it makes such a difference."

No wonder that marketers are becoming excited at what technology is offering them. Unlocking the power of data sources, whether through the ability to link up transactional and customer records, to profile the entire file, or to hand the project over in its entirety to a supplier, gives them the chance to make a big impact on their companies' revenues.

But despite the undeniable potential of these systems, marketers also need to be aware that using them is not just a matter of automating an existing process. As Vass warns: "If you are going to put in a database, it doesn't do anything itself and it eats money. You also need to change the way you do marketing – that's what will achieve the benefits."

Knowledge is power

For years, researchers used one of two sources, the lifestyle questionnaire or the Census. Now that technology has pushed the boundaries of information gathering, is targeting more flexible – or more complicated asks **DAVID REED**?

"The road to success is paved with information." So says Brian Woolf of US consultancy the Retail Strategy Centre. If this is true, then marketers may well feel they have stubbed their toe on a few loose pavings in the past. Data that did not live up to expectations has let down many a campaign.

The sheer number of paving stones now being laid threatens to turn the information road into a four-lane superhighway.

Choice about targeting methods used to be restricted to the principal geodemographic clustering systems, supplied by CACI, CCN and CDMS. Variables from the Census are used to pick out targets from the Electoral Roll by their postcode.

Next came the launch of lifestyle questionnaires, led by CMT, ICD and NDL, which began to assemble high-volume (3 million-plus) files of data on individuals who had given answers to more than 150 questions on their pur-

chasing behaviour and intentions. For years, these two approaches clashed, one side arguing that Census data was not responsive enough because it was not about "real" individual answers, the other that lifestyle data was too thinly spread to support robust profiling into target groups.

The first hybrid could be said to have been Define, launched by Infolink and now owned by Equifax Europe. It introduced a wide range of non-Census sources into its classification system, which also has the widest number of possible segments, at about 350. The lifestyle databases then reached critical mass, with the Lifestyle Census (a linking of NDL and CMT's databases) claiming to cover half of all households.

In the past year, even more systems have come into play: CACI's Census Lifestyle, which classifies groups using geodemographic and lifestyle data; three new lifestyle databases from CCN, Consumer Surveys and The Daily Telegraph; and Psyche, an overlay to CCN's Mosaic system that allows users to target by social value groups.

Anybody feeling left in the slow lane by this acceleration of information systems should not feel too bad. With so many choices, recognising which will be the most effective has never been harder. Bill Portlock, planning director at WWAV Rapp Collins, is fortunate in having a client "who wanted to undertake a lot of analysis using external data sources".

He pulled in all the rival systems, and compared them head-to-head, using them interactively within a Chaid analysis structure. "A combination of a couple of sources worked best," he notes, but adds that this "is not necessarily the way forward in every case."

Suppliers believe the investment in the systems will pay dividends when it comes to client service. It is this that is driving the fresh investment. "We can put our clients in touch with people who want to hear and who can offer optimum response rates," says Bob Hayward, managing director of Consumer Surveys, which markets new-entrant, the Lifestyle Focus database.

He cites motor insurance specialist RL Insurance, which used the file for a mailing in August inviting respondents to call for a quotation as an example. Response was 9.8 per cent, with conversion to sale of new policies of 13 per cent. For the client, the higher cost

of this data source paid off compared with its previous files, which yielded responses between 5.5 per cent and ten per cent and conversion of ten to 13 per cent.

At this direct, return-on-investment level, marketers will have to continue to test each source until they find which works best. This is one reason why the recognition of targeting's importance is rising, says Susan Squires, marketing director of Capscan, which markets Cenario, a CD-Rom Census data system.

"In part, it is because there are more about; in part, it is because there is now more expertise and knowledge. But if you can find the magic key that does discriminate your customer base against your competitor's, that is an advantage," she says. Squires has a ready counter-argument to the point of view, expressed here by Portlock, but to be heard across the DM industry, that "when you get to the stage of having massive coverage by lifestyle lists, there will be less need for Census demographics".

Instead of tossing aside the classifications that have up to now been marketed off the shelf, Squires believes that digging into the core Census information may yet yield valuable targeting clues.

"There can be something underlying geodemographics that may give users what they want. Different users have had a measure of success with this data and they are not willing to give it up yet," she says.

But suppliers who have historically based their business on profiling customers through Census variables, have obviously felt the lifestyle companies snapping at their heels. All offer hybrid targeting, with a mix-and-match approach to data sources allowing far greater flexibility than ever before.

They have even started to look at offering new dimensions in what their systems will tell marketers about customers and prospects. With these developments come two new concepts

adding to the traffic on the information road – psychographics and biographics.

Psyche, a joint venture between CCN and Synergy Consulting, is the best example. It offers what it calls values-driven segmentation, by providing an attitudinal overlay to the Mosaic geodemographic classification. Seven social value groups are identified: self-explorers, experimentalists, conspicuous consumers, belongers, social resisters, survivors, and aimless.

Developed in the US more than 30 years ago, work on a UK version began in the Seventies. The groups are based on the premise that "people have a set of values, beliefs and motivations that are relatively consistent and that underpin everything they do," explains director of Synergy Consulting Peter Cardwell.

"These values and motivations then form as attitudes and lifestyles, which in turn manifest as behaviour," he adds. This much has long been recognised by marketers, who have used research to identify the values that trigger purchase. What has not been possible until now has been linking those types back to targeting systems, allowing companies to find out where those value groups live, what else they do and so on.

The new system solves this by overlaying the social value groups on Mosaic target groups. Peter Mouncey, general manager of group marketing services at the Automobile Association, is one of the first to test the system. The AA had already moved from Acorn to Mosaic as a "second-generation" targeting approach. "We are now moving on to see whether there is added value in social value groups which could provide an extra dimension in our targeting," he says.

The AA was in the process of test launching a new member service in one TV region. Responses to the commercial were analysed using Psyche to reveal which groups had reacted favourably to the concept. "We also looked to see how we might develop more effective messages. The appeal of the service was not to the group we had expected, because it conflicted with the values that group would take an interest in. Instead, responders were seeing through the message to a better way of doing things," says Mouncey.

Folding psychographics back into the planning process from response data is an important step forward for direct marketing. Too often, the analyses available have been most effective in identifying targets that were the same as existing customers. Problems arise when the people who have already bought were influenced by factors other than the direct marketing, such as price, or were not the demographic the company wanted to appeal to.

Another missing link is being put into place through what Les O'Reilly, chairman of The Database Group, calls "biographics". A persistent criticism of lifestyle data suggests that it only delivers claimed purchasing activity. With the increased availability of transactional data, not least through retailer loyalty schemes, real purchase behaviour can be identified.

"In the past, we found companies were promoting to niche ranges, based on lifestyle or geodemographic information. That was useful and allowed companies to target people they thought they wanted. But few companies could supply the bridge to customers who actually came into the shop, what they bought and where," says O'Reilly.

With so many ways of looking at customer data, and so many external data sources on offer, it might seem that direct marketing has no excuse for failing to work effectively. In fact, there is probably an increased risk of "crash and burn" in a campaign by using the wrong sources.

Certain sectors have already found that it is possible to over-profile data and end up with a diminishing return from declining numbers of customers. Fundraisers have been trying to get out of just that trap in the past couple of years.

Avoiding that problem requires a combination of informed marketers and suppliers that do not push just one system. The obvious flexibility now being shown by data owners suggests at least one side of this equation has been solved. As O'Reilly puts it: "You can get a lot of data, little information and no intelligence. We're here to guide clients through."

Scores on the doors

Companies running door-drops are being offered smaller and smaller target groups. Are they really necessary? asks **DAVID REED**

If you believe marketers, the only people who buy their products are in the ABC1 social classes. Yet for some companies, the C2D segment can be critical to sales volume, especially in low-price retailing.

Even within the upper classes there are huge variations in buying behaviour. The drivers of a BMW and a Volvo may both be ABs, but they are clearly pursuing different lifestyles. And when it comes to driving to the shops, relying on socio-demographics alone will run into problems. One of the drivers may have to cross a major motorway junction – and therefore enter a completely different drivetime

area – in order to reach the nearest outlet.

Geography remains one of the most defining elements in marketing, especially in retail and packaged goods. In media terms, door-to-door also remains the most geography-dependent distribution method. That is why 90 per cent of the material dropped through letterboxes is produced by retailers or packaged-goods companies looking to drive sales, according to Andrew Burgess, media director at Tri-Direct. "Door-to-door is flexible and quick. You can get a leaflet out in reaction to last week's offer or a short-term sales promotion," he says.

Not surprisingly, geographical information systems (GIS) are playing an increasing role in the planning and targeting of door- drops. By taking the postal geography, which marketers now rely on, into a mapping system it is possible to make better judgments about how to reach target markets.

"People now want to put a geographical dimension into their existing databases," agrees Chris Green- wood, director of Kingswood Consultancy. His company markets GeoConcept, a PC-based GIS which is rivalling MapInfo as the industry standard (and has just overtaken it in sales in France).

The software attaches to external databases and allows users to interrogate their information. This can be particularly useful when trying to refine the media schedule for a leaflet distribution around a retail chain. "With catchment area analysis, if you can express the relationships between customer characteristics, we can model them. That can be highly predictive for site analysis," he says.

GIS is making its way onto the individual marketer's desktop alongside the marketing database and analysis system. It can be a major advantage to work with the same tools and in the same format as other departments in the same company. Property, distribution and sales people have long been working primarily with geographical, rather than customer data. If marketers can bring the two together, communications become more efficient and easier to justify.

That is why the major distribution companies have invested in targeting systems and GIS. In particular, there has been a lot of emphasis on taking the level of coverage which can be bought in the door-to-door medium down below postcode sector level. On average, a sector contains 2,500 households. At Circular Distributors (CD) the MicroTargeting system can build distribution plans at levels of about 700 households.

"A number of clients were saying if we could get down to smaller units, they would be quite interested. On the back of that research, we decided to throw away our current postcode sector solution and rethink the distribution process," says CD managing director Nick Wells. By examining the geography and geodemographics of each delivery person's round, CD has been able to bring detailed analysis into play when defining door-drops.

Cross tabulations to Target Group Index's, Mosaic's, Acorn's or AGB Superpanel's data can be run and then translated into a media schedule with less wastage. In a test distribution by Black & Decker, which ran three control groups at different geographical levels, micro-sectors proved the most cost-effective despite the premium charged. Wells notes that financial services have shown a lot of interest, but adds: "It is not the panacea for everybody's targeting needs."

At the Mediaforce Group, which has recently taken over MRM Distribution and merged it with The Leaflet Company, CACI's InSite system – a staple of retail site location – is in use. Mark Young, managing director of The Leaflet Company, says it's vital to be able to examine the geographical issues of the medium. "People look at the demographics, but they don't think about where people go to buy the products," he says.

Young says most targeting is done at postcode sector level, which is accurate enough to reveal how door-drops should be bought around different outlets. "Take SupaSnaps, for example. Each outlet may have a completely different offer, with one shop in the high street and another in the suburbs. Door-to-door is the only medium where you could cost-effectively deliver different messages for both to 20,000 homes," he says.

But do clients really need to target door-drops with this level of accuracy? Is there in fact a contradiction between the inherent nature of the medium and the move to lower levels of geography through GIS? According to Tri-Direct's Burgess: "It comes to a point where the unit cost of delivering below postcode sector level can make it less effective to use door-to-door. Compared with the response rates you would achieve through direct mail, it is not as good."

Efficient targeting is an honourable goal, he says, especially to remove sectors in which few potential customers live. But by reducing total volumes through using smaller target units, the cost per item increases as a result of the delivery premium and the loss of economies of scale in printing. Since door-drops are inherently less effective than direct mail, the return on investment might not make sense.

"It is a simple equation that is geography-led. If you want to target households, you can buy them at lower cost as names on the Electoral Register," he says. Young agrees: "I believe what is happening is that people are trying to convert door-to-door into direct mail. Is door-to-door built for this? No."

However, he does accept that some door-dropped items may be worth using tighter targeting on. Samples which can cost 25p or more each, for example, could be more cost-effectively distributed with less wastage. On leaflets printed at a penny each, however, the return is unlikely to be sufficient.

What may become more relevant, and may give GIS its "killer application" in the medium, is measuring the efficiency of distribution within each postcode sector. It is a fact of life that none of the distributors achieves 100 per cent delivery, but some are worse than others.

The companies themselves, and the planners and buyers who specialise in them, have been slowly building up data on which sectors have the best and worst record. Improving effectiveness by maximising reach within the most efficiently-delivered sectors may be © the way forward. At Royal Mail, the debate about geography has a slightly different flavour. Although it only sells distribution at sector level, it has two advantages over the other national distributors. Firstly, it can offer every home in the UK, because leaflets are delivered by regular postal workers. And secondly, the geography which underlies all marketing data is the one invented by the Post Office. That means there is no slippage between a schedule defined on the basis of geodemographics and the on-the-ground areas corresponding to the delivery list.

It has chosen a targeting system

that gives more flexibility without taking the geography down to household level. "We use Cenario, which Royal Mail jointly developed with Capscan," says Andrew Kershaw, marketing manager of unaddressed mail. "With most of the other systems, data is clustered and you are given the housing type. With Cenario, you have the raw data. You can select against sex, age, household type, or any of the 50 questions asked on the Census."

He believes that what is important is providing efficient delivery combined with a system that allows clients to import any characteristics which matter to them. "For example, the issue in mail order is propensity to purchase by mail. Unless you have got something that allows that to be looked at, it could be a problem."

So should door-to-door be trying to embrace GIS, or is it a step too far? For Burgess, who plans and buys about 250 million items annually, using geographical systems at postcode sector level is sensible. But taking them below that level runs against the inherent value of door-to-door. "The media itself can not deliver the level of targeting that is expected of it. That is where it falls down," he says.

At Kingswood, Greenwood has seen many different industry sectors struggling to define what is the appropriate level of geography to work at.

He recalls an oil company worrying about five minutes' difference in drive-times for an oil depot in Spain, when its economic forecasts for the next ten years were accurate to plus or minus ten per cent.

"The trick is to get the geographical scale to match the potential business benefit," he says. "In my experience, people try to buy better geography than the underlying business issues require. That is because if you can produce a map it gives the whole thing credibility," he says. Clients using door-to-door may want to consider whether they really do need to count target letterboxes in tens, rather than thousands.

ISSUES

1. **Why has transactional data become available and what help can it provide for marketers?**

2. **What are biographics?**

3. **What is a GIS and how can it help the marketer?**

EXPLORATION OF ISSUES

1. The installation of point-of-sale (POS) computers was the first step in making transactional data available. Widespread acceptance by retailers has resulted in smaller, faster and more reliable electronic point of sale (EPoS) terminals. Closely allied to this progress has been the development of product codes that are standardised between manufacturers, distributors and retailers. European article numbers (EAN) are compatible with universal product codes (UPC) in the United States. This implies that any retailer with an EPoS system can access information. More importantly this can be downloaded daily to gain rich market information.

The increasing trend towards category management is manifested in the sharing of data by retailer and manufacturer, and some of this is transmitted automatically via EDI. However this can sometimes go wrong, for example one person was repeatedly woken up by what turned out to be telephone calls from a Coca Cola machine to its supplier! In another case an elderly woman was rung up throughout the night by a public lavatory in a park in Leicester because it had developed a fault!

The marketing advantages of barcodes (EAN/UPC) in retailing include the ability to record who buys what. Products can be matched with customers via credit and debit (switch) card numbers, and retailers are therefore able to match special offers with individual customers.

ASDA, the UK supermarket group, is using the US

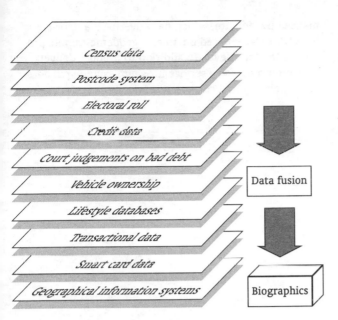

Figure 4.2   Layers of database marketing

Cataling system to analyse customers' shopping baskets at the checkout and generate on-the-spot offers tailored to them. Other retailers are capturing transactional data at point of sale via loyalty card schemes – for example Tesco, Safeway and Sainsbury. By autumn 1998 Tesco had analysed its customer database and identified 60 000 different segments, each of which were targeted differently. Tesco's aim at that time was to be literally one-to-one eventually.

An implication is that it easy for special offers on products suitable for, say, a shopper's child's birthday to be made at the right time, and for shoppers' new purchases to be added to the bank of information on their previous purchases. Hence the amount and quality of information grows – and so does the relationship with individual customers.

The next development is likely to be the use of 'smart' cards, upon which can be stored vast amounts of cardholder information, ranging from age and date of birth to previous purchases and even medical records.

In the progression from profile data to transactional data, profiling has moved through demographics, geodemographics and various forms of psychographics to the most recent version of life style data. With reference to transactional data, inspection of a loyalty scheme database may reveal that 'Mrs Brown' shops once per week, usually on a Friday, has a baby (she buys nappies), spends £90 per week on average and usually buys two bottles of gin a week. By knowing what individual customers buy, the retailer can target them with relevant

offers and the custoumers save money in the process. If a relationship develops, the retailer is moving from the more expensive 'acquisition' to the much cheaper 'retention' of its customers – several writers advocate this in times of low industry growth.

2   Now that transactional data is at the heart of many databases, overlaid with a multitude of profile data, we are perhaps moving into the era of biographics – the fusion of profile and transaction data (Figure 4.2).

Indeed, as stated in the 'Model Army' clipping, 'data matching is the key because it bridges sources'; the ability to combine names, addresses, purchasing behaviour and lifestyles in one database record allows companies to build up a picture of someone's life. Database linking occurs at two levels. First, at the industry level census data, geodemographics and lifestyle data can build up a broad picture of the population that is ideal for segmentation purposes. Second, at the individual company level matching this data to credit history, actual purchasing behaviour, media response and the recency, frequency and monetary (RFM) value of purchases can potentially describe a person's life, hence 'biographics'.

3   Geographic information systems (GIS) which are specifically designed to access, manage and link geographical data and reveal the spatial patterns inherent in many sets of data, provide an important framework for dealing with geographic information. Since postcode data is widely used in database management, GISs can clearly make an important contribution. Furthermore, advanced statistical techniques such as logistic regression and discriminant analysis, as well as neural networks and so on, have enhanced marketers' ability to optimise customer response by using internal database information.

It is often very useful to be able to picture, geographically, what database information tells us. The keys to this are addresses and postcodes because geographical information systems allow any linked database to produce map overlays, such as with the MapInfo system.

Another application of GIS-linked data concerns the siting of posters for direct responses, based on the profile of the neighbourhood or even through traffic. A related software solution is offered by The Data Consultancy which calculates drive time 'isochrones' (the distance one can drive in a given time along roads) from a postcode point in order, for example, to profile the catchment area of a retail outlet.

GIS databases can even target newspaper rounds. This usually involves about 150–200 households and links transactional data with lifestyle, geodemographics and panel data to provide a very accurate picture of individual buying patterns. The newspaper round – or milk round – can be used for door drops or direct mail as well as for local catchment area analysis. This has been for- malised by Unigate, which has advertised a door-step delivery service based on Mosaic geodemographic pro- files at the local level. In addition to product delivery they offer a delivery service for samples and vouchers and a delivery and collection service for questionnaires.

Part 2
Issues in Marketing Programmes

Introduction

Marketing programmes are concerned with getting the right product to market at the right time and place. The traditional elements of the marketing mix are therefore relevant here and these form the subject matter of Part 2. *Marketing Week* clippings are used to explore contemporary issues with regard to products, prices, distribution and promotion in a variety of markets, including business-to-business and international.

Chapter 5 is concerned with contemporary product issues, including the changing nature of new product development and a variety of topical issues to do with packaging and branding, such as brand equity, the role of packaging in branding, global packaging, retrospective branding, niche branding and the extent to which a brand might be diversified.

Pricing policy is explored in Chapter 6, while a number of aspects of distribution and retailing are discussed in Chapter 7. For example the changing balance of power in distribution channels has great significance not only for manufacturer–retailer relations but also for the strategic and operational understanding of consumers. One development to emerge from this has been the loyalty scheme, which is offered by both manufacturers and retailers. The implications of this development are explored with the help of several clippings.

Related to the way in which loyalty schemes operate is the incredible rise of the database (Chapter 9), and again clippings are used to delve into the nature and implications of the marketing database in terms of understanding customers and targeting them, increasingly via direct routes.

Marketing via the Internet is of great interest at present, and this too is explored in Chapter 9 through a number of clippings that approach the topic from various angles, together with coverage of interactive marketing.

Appeals to fear in advertising are discussed, as is the nature of public relations in the context of ethical issues and poor measurement methods.

We also discuss the increasing use of 'characters' in advertising and sponsorship and draw from opinion leadership theory to explain how this operates.

5 Product Policies

New Product Development (NPD)

KEY CONCEPTS

- New product development
- Category management
- Innovation strategy

Unilever's NPD blues

Faced with mounting competition in mature markets, Unilever has changed its tactics and opted for a high-profile, high-risk 'accelerator' strategy. But, as the launch of Persil Power and Liptonice has shown, the company is struggling to justify the cost of new product development. **SEAN BRIERLEY** reports

To the City, Unilever is fighting fit. While the rest of the world languished in sick-beds suffering from recessionary flu, the packaged goods giant didn't even sneeze. Despite last year's obvious European hiccups, it maintained worldwide profits at a hefty £2.6bn. Its growth prospects couldn't be better.

Yet this rosy global picture hides a deeper malaise. Van Den Bergh Foods marketing director Simon Turner says: "Unilever has to respond to specific threats in mature markets, particularly Europe and the US." He says the cumulative factors of a squeeze from retailers, changing consumer tastes, own-label penetration and price competition are familiar to most marketers.

However, one brand consultant, who has worked with Unilever in the past, cites other reasons for its change in strategy: "Unilever had been consistently beaten in new product development by its rivals in the late Eighties, especially in the concentrated detergent sector. It was a case of change or watch the brands die".

Ever since Lever Brothers bought Pears in 1909, the company has traditionally responded to competitive threats through conventional, low-risk means. Over the past three years, the company has bought 72 businesses worldwide, including Colmans' food interests, which it purchased from Reckitt last month.

More critically, Unilever has also developed a high-profile, high-risk strategy of taking short-cuts to innovation, and forging links with other companies.

It managed to launch the Power range of detergents across Europe within eight weeks as part of what was known as "Operation Clover".

The now legendary venture was a disaster of epic proportions. The Power detergents' "accelerator" formula was found to be defective. Not only did the company waste about £100m on their launch but it cost an additional £57m to wind them down. Lever's brands suffered disastrous sales losses. It particular, it caused millions of pounds worth of damage to the Persil and Omo brands across Europe.

Procter & Gamble's Ariel is now

the market leader in the UK for the first time ever.

At about the same time, Unilever subsidiary Brooke Bond responded to price competition and declining tea sales by announcing the joint launch, with PepsiCo, of US tea-based soft drink Liptonice.

Last month – a year after its launch – the UK version had to be completely reformulated, repositioned and repackaged for a relaunch. Smith New Court analyst Tim Potter says: "It is arguable whether it is a long-term prospect in the UK."

Both launches are high profile indications of the failure of Unilever's npd strategy.

In the past ten years its annual research and development spend has almost doubled. And over the past five years Unilever has been involved in an exhaustive programme of restructuring and rebuilding to respond to the crisis in its core mature markets.

Five years ago, Unilever also introduced a system of regional and product category management to facilitate a rapid response to changes across its markets. It began to allow products to be speedily developed and adapted in each country.

Regional innovation centres have been opened to enable the rapid introduction of new products. They range from hair product centres for Chinese hair in South-East Asia, to health margarine in Bedford.

Turner says one consequence of the new direction is a shift in culture within Unilever: "Innovation managers have become more significant within the company than brand managers." The centres are intended to bring research and development, brand management, advertising and promotion teams together to speed up the process.

Potter says: "The strategy enables Unilever to switch successful brands rapidly across markets, such as Ragu and Chicken Tonight."

So far the system has had a number of successes, as with I Can't Believe It's Not Butter and Chicken Tonight, brought in from the US, and Jif Mousse Cleaner from Japan.

Unilever has also been moving into new areas. Ten years ago personal products represented five per cent of the group's operating profit. By 1994 it had risen to 19 per cent. The company has extended its interests into what appear to be un-Unilever areas, such as luxury personal care. It bought Calvin Klein and Elizabeth Arden in 1989.

Unilever's response to pressure in mature markets has been to move into developing and emerging regions. The East European, Latin American, Indian and Chinese markets have pre-occupied Unilever in recent years. It has spent $200m (£126m) in China to form eight joint ventures, such as that with the Shanghai Soap Company, and set up ice cream factories in Beijing and Shanghai.

Such moves have gradually transformed the character of the company. Europe, as a percentage of Unilever's turnover, has dropped from 62 per cent to 53 per cent, whereas the rest of the world (everywhere outside Europe and the US) has increased from 19 per cent to 27 per cent.

But such solutions have created new problems. In addition to the cost of the reforms, the need to shorten the development time for new products has multiplied expenditure. Rather than drip-feeding established brands with constant advertising and promotional support, it is having to spend millions of pounds more to launch new products.

Advertising and promotional costs have risen enormously since 1988 (see table, page 41). Potter says Unilever's advertising and promotion to sales ratios will not see an improvement on 11 per cent over the next two years.

To compound matters, many of Unilever's companies are engaged in intense price competition, which has squeezed margins still further.

Marketing costs will remain high if Unilever continues with its policy of bringing products rapidly to market and if, as is likely, competition remains intense. The firm is increasingly having to restructure to make the savings which will then fund advertising and promotions.

Its promotional spend has also increased because of the addition of a number of premium personal product companies to its portfolio.

In 1994, £1.7bn of the total £3.7bn Unilever advertising and promotion budget was spent on media advertising. The company has tried to claw back some money through reviewing advertising and media arrangements and negotiating knock-down deals with media owners. However, this strategy conflicts with Unilever's need to improve its creative work.

One source close to the company's helm says its top executives blame poor advertising executions for a lack of sales success. At the same time as Liptonice's relaunch, Unilever switched creative work from Ogilvy & Mather to J Walter Thompson.

But it is understood that there is a more fundamental change in strategy taking place. Top Unilever executives are believed to be considering a Coca-Cola style switch of brands out of its four roster agencies – O&M, JWT, McCann-Erickson and Lintas – and into creative hot shops. "They are planning to use the roster agencies as media buying networks and to outsource the creative work," says the source.

A recent example of this was the switch of Elida Gibbs' Lynx brand in the UK from SP Lintas to Bartle Bogle Hegarty, last week. Lintas' media independent, Initiative, retained the media buying, but BBH was awarded the creative work. "We are likely to see many more developments like these over the next six months," says the source.

Potter says these increases in R&D, advertising and promotional expenditure have constantly forced Unilever to rationalise its business operations. In 15 years, it has cut its UK staff from 100,000 to 25,000. In February 1994, it announced that 7,500 jobs were to be cut worldwide. And, more recently, Brooke Bond and Van den Bergh were merged to cut costs. It is likely that further rationalisation will take place.

The jury is also out on new products such as Chicken Tonight, which are claimed to be examples of the success of the company's new strategy. Chicken Tonight is suffering severe competition in its home market, the US, and has not proved to be the long-term success in the UK that was expected. The much-vaunted Calvin Klein's cK one fragrance still has to prove its worth in the US.

Van den Bergh's much-acclaimed I Can't Believe It's Not Butter lost market share in the UK last year to butter brands. It had to be relaunched last month with a new flavour and marketing campaign.

And despite the new "accelerator" innovation strategy, its historic problem of being beaten to market has not gone away.

In food, Kraft Jacobs Suchard beat Unilever into the UK yogurt margarine market last month with the launch of Vitalite Touch of Yogurt.

And Unilever has been slow to launch into the frozen yogurt market. Grand Metropolitan subsidiary Häagen-Dazs launched a frozen yogurt in France in 1991 and then rolled it out across Europe.

Back in January 1993, Unilever signed a second joint venture deal with Europe's biggest yogurt maker, French-owned BSN, to develop a range of frozen yogurts across Europe. But so far Societé Yaourt et Glace has only launched a yogurt and ice cream dessert, called Yolka, in Spain and France. Yolka came out last year at about the same time as Persil Power and Liptonice. Plans to roll experimental yogurt ice cream, Yolka, into

Germany, Italy and the UK, appear to have been frozen.

At first glance, it might appear that Unilever is reversing its strategy. But Unilever chairman Sir Michael Perry said last month that the Persil Power disaster had not undermined the company's resolve to continue with its "accelerator" strategy. "We have reviewed our internal processes and, across the board, have taken the lessons to heart. One thing has not changed. Our commitment to innovate and produce innovative and superior technologies is as resolute as ever," he said.

If this is the case, Unilever will need very deep pockets to accommodate future difficulties. One Unilever roster agency source says: "There are undoubtedly more Persil Powers and Liptonices on the horizon. Unilever's pride has been damaged and the men at the top are hell-bent on proving their strategy is right."

ISSUES

1. **What is the traditional approach to the NPD process?**

2. **What is category management and what are its implications for marketing?**

3. **How might the points made by Brierley in his article change the traditional NPD model?**

EXPLORATION OF ISSUES

1. Generating ideas for new products, or for modifications to existing ones, is the traditional first stage in the NPD process and the subsequent stages are designed to screen those ideas in order to identify which are most likely to be successful. Typically, many ideas emerge from stage 1, perhaps in excess of 100.

Ideas that are deemed incompatible with the organisation's aims or resources are eliminated in the screening stage. The remaining ideas are then subjected to 'business analysis', which includes estimating market demand, costs and profit forecasts. At the screening and analysis stages, ideas are not converted into product form but various tests are conducted to determine whether conversion would be a wise move. These tests are referred to as concept tests.

If a product idea survives concept testing, it might be made up into a prototype and enter the development stage. Here its various components are tested, for example its package, colour, smell, shape and so on. Placement tests are often conducted, whereby samples of the product (and often different versions of it) are presented to respondents for a 'real' trial in the home. Different versions can be presented via comparative tests in which the test version might be lined up against the current market leader and the various characteristics of each are compared.

Finally, before full-scale launch the product might be evaluated in some scaled-down version of the intended market, perhaps in one ITV region. If the results obtained in the test market are favourable, then a national launch might follow.

2 With regard to category management, the concept of managing 'categories' rather than specific brands involv cooperation between manufacturer and retailer in the development of, say, a washing powder. So rather than salespeople trying to sell the manufacturer's brand to the retailer, an alliance is formed to develop the entire product category.

There is scope for sharing consumer and market data, especially when manufacturers and retailers are both developing consumer databases, often as a result of loyalty schemes. In 1997 the consortium Jigsaw investigated the possibility of linking data from Unilever, Bass, Kimberley Clark and Heinz.

3 The main implications here are in terms of the speed of the NPD process and the integration of marketing and technological NPD drivers. One of the most damaging 'gaps' is the marketing–technology void, as was clearly demonstrated by the Sinclair C5 venture. In the Unilever case, that organisation attempted to launch on the basis of a technology-driven NPD process, and now probably needs greater integration with customer service and image/communications aspects as well. Product ideas that arise from a customer problem and a specific technology to solve it are more likely to succeed, and this is the basis of the 'dual drive' NPD approach suggested by C. Merle Crawford (1991).

Packaging as a Marketing Tool

KEY CONCEPTS

- Packaging
- Design
- Brand names
- Brand value analysis
- Brand equity
- Branding and pack harmonisation

The personal touch

As the public becomes increasingly design literate, packaging design needs to talk to potential customers. Even in 'difficult' product categories such as sanpro and condoms, packs are no longer afraid to declare their contents.

MARY LEWIS

A new, up-front stance is emerging in packaging design as consumers become better informed and more confident about their choices.

This is particularly true of product categories such as sanpro and contraception. Products that once hid shyly behind their brand names or coy, confusing concepts are moving to centre stage.

The driving force is two-fold. First, san-pro products now have all kinds of gizmos, absorbencies, shapes and surfaces. Clarity of information and choice is paramount. Second, consumers are demonstrating a new pragmatism. Now visually literate, they know when they are being sold to.

It used to be a lot easier as a consumer to ask the shop assistant for Lil-lets rather than a box of tampons – or for Durex instead of a packet of condoms. Brand names offered discretion. But packaging is no longer afraid to declare its contents.

Lil-lets' relaunched packaging throws caution to the wind. Brewer Riddiford, designers of both the old and the new Lil-lets packs, has helped the brand to do a complete about turn. The old pack was beautifully bashful: once the cellophane was removed, the brand name disappeared. The consumer was left with a smart, unmarked blue box. Discretion was the brand's point of difference.

Today there can be no doubt about the contents of these bright-blue packs. The cellophane has gone and Lil-lets is emblazoned across the front of the pack. With plentiful information about innovative tampon developments, there's nothing shy about this packaging. It is confident and straightforward.

That's not the case with Durex. Its packaging, designed by Pea Green Boat, looks like it has walked straight out of the Seventies, with an attitude to match. The branding is strong, but the product names are as uninformative as Mills & Boon imagery. What is Elite? – posh sex? In contrast to Mates, Durex is coy to the point of embarrassment.

The new Mates, designed by Blue Marlin, has grown up. The brash red and white pack of the Eighties has become sleek silver. Confusing symbols have gone and a diagram of the product itself now appears. Clearly, condoms are no longer taboo. But the copy and coding lack confidence. We know what the product looks like, but will consumers want it? If one product is Ultra Safe then what are the others – high risk?

The problems are not confined to

"difficult" products. In the crowded haircare market, Organics has claimed a patch of territory. Designed by Mike Cassidy & Associates, the strident colour and upfront product benefits shown on the pack declare that it is a no nonsense brand.

But compare it to Finesse. The packaging features the original US bottle and graphics and appears to have no unique proposition or benefit. With nothing intelligent to say, designers are hard-pushed to create anything but a bland pack.

Lil-lets, Mates and Organics may have intelligent pack designs, but do they go far enough? Lil-lets is courageous, but where does the brand's point of difference lie? Meanwhile, Mates is yet to declare openly that some of the products are aimed at homosexuals. The Organics design may be distinctive but it misses a trick. Today's women want the lot. The brand proposition hits the mark, but where's the emotional appeal?

However, the innovation which has been introduced points to a new kind of designer: pragmatic, bold and intelligent.

ISSUES

1. In recent times, packaging has become a potent marketing tool. Well-designed packages can provide convenience value for the consumer and promotional value for the product. What factors have contributed to packaging's growing use as a marketing tool?

2. Comment on the most common criticisms of packaging.

3. Define 'brand stimulus development' and comment on its implementation process.

4. Discuss the concept of brand equity.

5. How can brand identity be used as a major asset in a product differentiation strategy?

6. Discuss some of the key current and future developments in packaging.

EXPLORATION OF ISSUES

1. Various factors have contributed to packaging's growing use as a marketing tool.

Self-service. An increasing number of products are sold on a self-service basis in supermarkets and discount houses. In an average supermarket that stocks 15 000 items, the typical shopper passes by some 300 items per minute. Given that 53 per cent of all purchases are made on impulse, effective packaging serves as a 'five-second commercial'. The package of a product must perform many of the sales tasks: it must attract attention, describe the product's features, create consumer confidence and make a favourable overall impression.

Consumer affluence. Rising consumer affluence means that consumers are willing to pay a little more for the convenience, appearance, dependability, or prestige of better packages.

Company and brand images. Companies are recognising the power of well-designed packages to provide instant recognition of the company or brand. The Campbell Soup Company estimates that the average shopper sees its familiar red and white can 76 times a year.

Innovation opportunity. Innovative packaging can bring large benefits to consumers and profits to producers. Toothpaste pump dispensers have captured 12 per cent of the toothpaste market because many consumers find them more convenient and less messy. The first companies to put their soft drinks in ring-pull cans and their liquid sprays in aerosol tins attracted many new customers.

2 Recent decades have brought a number of improvements in packaging. However some packaging problems have yet to be resolved.

Some packages suffer from functional problems in that they simply do not work well. The packaging for flour and sugar is extremely poor, although one flour manufacturer has introduced carton packaging. Both grocers and consumers are only too aware that these packages leak and are easily torn. Can anyone open and close a bag of flour without spilling at least a little? Packages such as biscuit tins, milk cartons with fold-out spouts and potato crisp bags are frequently difficult to open. The traditional containers for products such as ketchup and salad dressing make the products inconvenient to use. Have you ever asked yourself why, when thumping the bottom of a ketchup bottle, the producer didn't put the ketchup in a mayonnaise jar? Certain types of packaging are being questioned in connection with recyclability and biodegradability. For example throw-away bottles require considerably more resources to produce than do reusable glass bottles. Furthermore, although many steps have been taken to make packaging safer, critics still focus on safety issues. Containers with sharp edges and easily broken glass bottles are sometimes viewed as a threat to safety. Certain types of plastic packaging and aerosol containers represent possible health hazards.

At times, packaging is accused of being deceptive. Package shape, graphic design and certain colours may be used to make a product appear larger than it actually is. The inconsistent use of certain size designations – such as 'giant', 'economy', 'family", 'king' and 'super' – can certainly lead to customer confusion. Although customers prefer attractive, effective and convenient packaging, the cost of such packaging is high. For some products, such as cosmetics, the cost of the packaging is higher than the cost of the product itself.

3 'Brand stimulus development' refers to the development of materials designed to help consumers express and explore core brand values. These might include a range of picture boards covering different personality types, moods or situations; a series of exercises featuring questions such as, 'if this brand were an animal/car/country, what would it be?'; or a selection of music excerpts or fictitious headlines. After the preparation of this research material, research is conducted among consumer. The interpretation of the research findings is aimed at identifying the core brand values and how these are expressed and understood by consumers in order to decide on future brand development.

Some design companies use a patented system for their pack redesign analysis. Strategic branding consultancy Interbrand calls its methodology 'logo value'. These consultants normally divide all the features of an existing pack design into elements that are (1) inviolable, should only be changed after the most careful consideration or can tolerate substantial change, and (2) relatively inconsequential in visual terms, but required for statutory, marketing or distribution reasons. The most crucial task is clearly to identify the 'inviolable' features and ensure that they feature appropriately in the redesigned packaging so that the changeover from old to new pack is smooth and all existing visual equity is retained.

4 Brands vary in the amount of power and value they have in the marketplace. At one extreme are brands that are unknown by most buyers in the marketplace. Then there are brands for which buyers have a fairly high degree of brand awareness (measured either by brand recall or recognition). Beyond this are brands that have a high degree of brand acceptability in that most customers are not averse to buying them. Then there are brands that enjoy a high degree of brand preference – these will be selected over others. Finally, there are brands that command a high degree of brand loyalty. A powerful brand is said to have high brand equity. The higher the brand equity, the higher the brand loyalty, name awareness, perceived quality, strong brand associations and other assets such as patents, trade marks and channel relationships. The point is that a brand is an asset insofar as it can be sold or bought for a price. Certain companies are basing their growth on acquiring and building rich brand portfolios. Nestlé has acquired Rowntree (UK), Carnation (US), Stouffer (US), Buitoni-Perugina (Italy) and Perrier (France), making it the world's largest food company. When Grand Metropolitan bought Heublein, it added $800 million to its assets to reflect the value of Smirnoff and other names.

Measuring the equity of a brand name is somewhat arbitrary. There are different approaches, including basing it on the price premium, the stock value, the brand replacement value and so on. For example, one measure of brand equity value is the price premium the brand commands multiplied by the extra volume it covers over what an average brand would command.

The world's top ten brand superpowers, according to Interbrand, are (in rank order) Coca-Cola, Kellogg's, McDonald's, Kodak, Marlboro, IBM, American Express, Sony, Mercedes Benz and Nescafé.

High brand equity provides the manufacturer with a number of competitive advantages: reduced marketing costs because of the high level of consumer brand awareness and loyalty; greater leverage when bargaining with distributors and retailers since customers will expect them to carry the brand; the opportunity to charge a higher price than that for competing products because of higher perceived quality; the easy launch of brand extensions since the brand name carries high credibility; and above all, some defence against fierce price competition.

As an asset, a brand name needs to be carefully managed so that its brand equity does not depreciate. This requires maintaining or improving brand awareness, the perceived quality and functionality of the brand, positive brand associations and so on. These require continuous R & D investment, skilful advertising, excellent trade and consumer service, and other measures. Some companies, for example Canada Dry and Colgate-Palmolive, have appointed 'brand equity managers' to guard the brand's image, associations and quality, and prevent short-term tactical actions from damaging the brand.

Companies such as Proctor & Gamble, Caterpillar, IBM and Sony have achieved outstanding company brand strengths, as measured by the number of product markets where the company is the brand leader or coleader. Brands can be seen as outlasting a company's specific products and facilities. Brands can also be seen as the major enduring asset of a company. Yet every powerful brand really represents a set of loyal customers. Therefore the fundamental asset underlying brand equity is *customer equity*. This suggests that the proper focus of marketing planning should be extending loyal customer lifetime value, with brand management serving as a major marketing tool.

Concerning brand identity, in addition to product attribute and customer benefit associations, brands can gain a strategic position by association with:

- Product class (Carnation Instant Breakfast is a breakfast food).

- Product user (Miller is for the blue-collar, heavy beer drinker).
- Lifestyle and feelings (the Pepsi generation).
- Personality (Harley is a macho male and a free spirit).

5 A key and enduring business asset is identity – the associations attached to a company and its brands. Brand association is anything that is directly or indirectly linked in memory to a brand. The most common association is that of product attributes or customer benefits.

In addition to product attribute and customer benefit associations, brands can gain a strategic position by association with use or application, product class, product user, lifestyle and feelings, personality, and symbol. A brand's associations are assets that can allow differentiation, provide reasons to buy, instil confidence and trust, influence feelings towards a product and experience of its use, and provide the basis for brand extensions. All of these create a sustainable advantage.

Associations can provide an important basis for differentiation, especially in product classes where it is difficult to distinguish objectively between various brands. A differentiating association can be a sustainable advantage, and a strong position is not easily overcome by competitors. The competitive advantage can be substantial when the association is based on intangible perceived value such as with health foods. It is difficult for competitors to demonstrate superiority over or even parity with such an attribute.

Many brand associations involve product attributes or customer benefits that provide a specific reason to buy and use a brand. They represent a basis for purchase decisions and brand loyalty.

Some associations influence purchase decisions by ascribing credibility and confidence to a brand. Other associations stimulate positive feelings that are then transferred to a brand and to its use experience. the associations and their companion feelings then become linked to the brand.

Associations can create positive feelings during the use experience, serving to transform a product into something different from what it might otherwise be. An association can provide the basis for an extension.

6 Packaging is becoming an increasingly important aspect of marketing strategy as companies see packaging as a way to attracting customers to new and existing brands. For existing brands, there is a growing tendency to repackage; that is, to redesign the existing package or container. Redesigns are seen as a potentially cost-effective way to boost sales.

There are two opposite trends in packaging. One involves reducing the package size. Possible future examples include self-destructing and shrinking packages. The opposite trend is to increase the size.

A significant issue facing marketers is the environmental impact of packaging. Concern is growing about the harmful effects of plastic packaging on animals and humans. Sea animals and birds mistake discarded plastic packaging, foam, beads, and bags for food, which results in blockage of their digestive tracts, while some plastic-based foam packing has been found to be harmful to the earth's ozone layer. Because today's plastic packaging can remain intact for up to four centuries, packaging producers are putting millions of pounds into research on biodegradable plastic packaging.

Many developments and innovations in packaging are looming on the horizon, including 'talking' packages, self-destructing packages and 3-D packages. All manner of technological wonders, including advanced holograms and 3-D images will change the face of packaging. For example holograms could be particularly popular for liquor, coffee and cosmetic products. Some companies are trying to incorporate voice chips into their packages. For example tapping different spots on a food package would activate the voice to describe vitamin content, fat content and cooking directions. Pharmaceutical companies will probably be the first to use the 'chatty' packages in their search for ways to protect themselves from lawsuits.

With more companies marketing their goods globally, packaging will bear fewer words and more universally understood symbols and pictures. Also, because of environmental concerns there will be self-destructing packages made from time-programmed polymers that turn the containers into a harmless powder.

In order to maximise space in recycling storage areas, companies may turn to the incredible shrinking package, for example plastic bottles could take a bellows-type form so that they decrease in size as the contents are consumed. The tremendous improvement in scanning technology means that UPC codes could be reduced to the size of a pinhead. Packaging will be more visually interesting in the next decade, and emphasis will be on personality and identity.

'Smart' packages will be emerging soon. For example microwavable foods will come in packages that the oven can 'read'. The hungry consumer will not have to do a thing except pop it in the microwave.

As a result of environmental concerns, there will be greater use of alternative materials for packages. Companies will cut back on inks with metallic elements and use more recycled materials, although it might be more difficult to produce the brilliant colours and clean looks that have the most shelf impact. Still, companies will continue to press brand image. The physical dimensions of packages will change. Instead of being the same old square box, the package shape will become so unique that the consumer will be able to identify the product instantly.

Finally, packaging must be balanced with economics. Scent strips may make sense for fragrance marketers, but how cost-effective would aroma packaging be for a cracker manufacturer?

Brand Extension

Testing out Virgin territory

Following airline success and a less fruitful foray into radio, will Richard Branson's plans to delve into other, diverse sectors be a licence to fail?

NICK HIGHAM

Forgive me if this column mentions Richard Branson for the second time in a fortnight, but he becomes ever more interesting as he adds marketing wizard to his portfolio of media monickers.

What's more, I should have been in Dublin last Friday interviewing him at the Commercial Radio Conference. I apologise for my absence.

I wasn't there because I'd decided to fly from London City Airport, for reasons which seemed perfectly sound at the time (close to home, never tried it before) and because the London to Dublin route is operated by a company called, appropriately, Virgin Atlantic City Jet.

But the plane, due to take off at 9.30am, never left the ground. It seems London City Airport only has two fire engines and both had broken down. And the rules for airports are clear: no fire cover, no flights.

A bus to Stansted was offered. We would be airborne "by 11.30am". Even allowing for an hour's flight and a half-hour taxi-ride from Dublin airport to city centre, we would be cutting it fine for a lunch appointment with the bearded one scheduled for 1pm, assuming there would be no further hitches.

The decision to abandon the trip and spend the last day of half term at home was made easier by the news that Branson had announced he'd be happy to take questions from the floor.

This was despite the fact that his aides had earlier insisted that a question-and-answer free-for-all was out of the question – on the grounds that radio forms a relatively small part of the Branson empire and he was alarmed at the prospect of being quizzed about it in any detail.

I've no doubt that in the event he was pressed hard to justify Virgin 1215's decision to apply for an FM licence for London.

Is it simply that national commercial radio is a new phenomenon? Or is there some more fundamental problem which may prevent the new commercial stations ever proving as popular as local commercial radio?

I would also have asked about ventures like Virgin Atlantic's London to Dublin service. This is not operated by Branson's airline, but by an independent company, City Jet, which has effectively bought a franchise on the Virgin name.

Increasingly, Virgin is expanding through such deals. Virgin cola, produced by a joint venture company in which Virgin and the Canadian Cott Corporation are equal partners, is the exception that proves the rule.

The Virgin PC and Virgin Vodka are both licensing arrangements in which somebody else shoulders the financial risk of manufacture and marketing, paying Virgin for the right to use its name.

This is brand extension by proxy, and the attractions (if you have as strong a brand name as Virgin) are obvious. So too are the risks. Last Friday's local difficulties at London City weren't the fault of City Jet. But what if they had been? Virgin gets negative publicity but isn't actually to blame. The brand name can suffer for reasons beyond the brand owner's control.

It is also a way of doing business at odds with Branson's usual approach.

In the early years of Virgin Records, Branson insisted on setting up subsidiaries in overseas territories rather than entering licensing arrangements with established record companies, reasoning that he got to reap more of the rewards of success.

Similarly, he has, until recently, insisted on keeping the control of his empire in his own hands or those of trusted lieutenants, even buying the company back after mistakenly taking it public in 1986.

The reversal of his previous policy, implied by his willingness to licence others to exploit the Virgin name, is almost as surprising as his current penchant for highly regulated business sectors like airlines and the media.

Richard Branson used to be a classic entrepreneur who liked to build businesses organically in areas like retailing, records and condoms, where you didn't need a licence to get started.

Then in 1984 he bludgeoned the Civil Aviation Authority into giving him a licence to fly the London to New York route. In the past ten years he has made a succession of licence applications to expand the airline, and has tried to break into new sectors.

He has been less than successful. His applications for ITV licences underestimated the stringency of the Independent Television Commission's selection process.

His application to run the National Lottery appears to have been a much more substantial and credible document, even though Branson came late to the application process. But he failed because it offered less to the Government's fund for good causes than Camelot's winning bid.

Branson's mistake had been to siphon off some of the proceeds to his own charitable foundation. When Peter Davis, the director-general of Oflot, refused to take this into account, Branson appeared mighty miffed, but the tight rules under which Davis was operating did not allow him that flexibility.

It is no coincidence that his successes in winning media licences have been in radio, where the Radio Authority operates a more relaxed regime than either the ITC or Oflot.

It makes the question of what Branson does next all the more intriguing. There appears to be no scope for a second Virgin radio station. Perhaps he should have a go at the unregulated business of magazine publishing, now that the débâcle of his 1981 rival to Time Out, entitled Event, is long past. Perhaps he should even try newspapers.

However, the lure of the cash-flow (if not the margins) to be had from fast-moving consumer goods may well shift the balance of the Virgin group inexorably towards the supermarket and away from the high-profile activities with which it has been identified in the past.

Or, perhaps Branson should go into politics, to become Britain's own Silvio Berlusconi.

I really must find an opportunity to ask him some time.

Nick Higham is BBC TV's media correspondent.

ISSUES

(1) Comment on some key advantages and risks associated with a brand extension strategy.

(2) Devise a framework for joint venture analysis.

(3) Name some of the advantages and disadvantages may arise if a company establishes a manufacturing licensing contract.

EXPLORATION OF ISSUES

1 A company may decide to use an existing brand name to launch a product in a new category. Brand extension offers a number of advantages. A well-regarded brand name gives the new product instant recognition and earlier acceptance. It enables the company to enter new product categories more easily and instantly establish a conviction of the new product's high quality. Brand extension saves the considerable advertising expenditure that would normally be required to familiarise consumers with a new brand name.

Like line extension, brand extension also involves risks. The new product might disappoint buyers and damage their respect for the company's other products. The brand name may be inappropriate for the new product – consider buying Black & Decker grooming aids, or Boeing cologne. The brand name may lose its special positioning in the consumer's mind through overextension. Brand dilution occurs when consumers no longer associate a brand with a specific product or very similar products. Competitors benefit from brand dilution. Transferring an existing brand name to a new category requires great care. Companies that are tempted to transfer their brand name must research how well the brand's associations fit the new product. The best result would be the brand name boosting the sales of both the new product and the existing product. An acceptable result would be the new product selling well without affecting the sales of the existing product. The worst result would be the new product failing and damaging the sales of the existing product.

2 See Figure 5.1

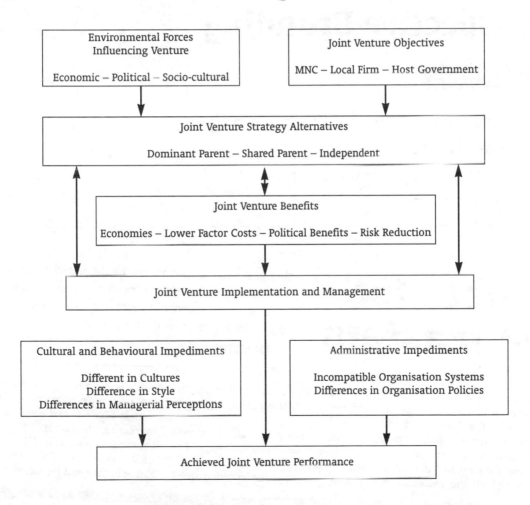

Figure 5.1

(3) Listed below are some of the advantages and disadvantages of establishing a manufacturing licensing contract.

Advantages

- Little capital required.
- Immediate access to market knowledge.
- Quicker start-up with fewer problems.
- Market entry at low risk.
- Opportunity to form a partnership or buy out a local manufacturer.
- Transfer of manufacturing responsibilities.
- Reduction in tariff barriers.
- Expansion capability into new markets.
- Increased resources from innovation.

Disadvantages

- Loss of control over manufacturing process.
- Difficult to control product quality.
- Loss of potential profits on sales.
- Sales might be under-reported by licensee.
- Disagreement might arise in terms of marketing effort.
- After expiration of contract, may have potential competitor.
- Contract may only reflect current market conditions.
- Difficult to find licensee with necessary technical experience and skills.
- Conflict of territory between licensees.
- Risk leakage of technology through licensee.

Retrospective Branding

KEY CONCEPTS

- Retrospective campaigns – lazy marketing
- Global marketing
- Brand archaeology – brand heritage
- Brand performance

Respect for past masters

Retrospective campaigns may be dismissed by some as lazy marketing. But when a brand has built a valuable heritage over a number of years, perhaps it is only smart to plunder the reserves of strategic wisdom

ALAN MITCHELL

One of the best ads around is a poster: a black and white silhouette of a bottle and the words, "Quick. Name a soft drink". Within seconds any Western consumer will recognise the shape of the Coca-Cola bottle and all the associations: the red label, the fizz on the tongue, the taste, the refreshment, will come streaming back.

The resulting thought is almost involuntary: yes, indeed, Coke is The Real Thing.

Until recently, the contour shape bottle was a relic from Coke's marketing past. Five years ago Coca-Cola wouldn't have talked about the critical marketing dimension of shape and package, admits Gavin Darby, president of Coca-Cola North-west Europe. "We had forgotten it. We had moved away from it," he says. "Now we are moving back to it, very, very fast."

Indeed "activating" the contour bottle design was Coca-Cola's number-one global marketing priority last year. And, judging by its latest annual report, even Coke marketers have been astonished by the results: a 23 per cent sales increase in Japan among participating bottlers, 30 per cent up in Spain and, in parts of the US, up 90 per cent.

Coca-Cola is not alone in returning to its marketing history. Pepsi has revived its taste challenge while Colgate recently reintroduced the ring of confidence in its TV advertising. Pedigree has been running Pal commercials with snippets from 40 years of TV advertising and Jaguar has rekindled our memories of its beautiful old cars with an ad showing a little boy's dream of driving one coming true many years later. Kellogg is meanwhile rescuing Cornflakes from the image graveyard, while some companies have actually disinterred the remains of dead brands and tried to relaunch them. Fancy some Hai Karate?

But what's behind all this retro marketing? Partly, it's just fashion and nostalgia. Some marketers are simply riding on the back of a retro trend led by clothes designers who have recreated looks from the Fifties, Sixties and Seventies.

A few may even be so lost for ideas that reviving the dead is the best they can think of. Similarly agency creatives, who are always on the lookout for something new, have recognised that raiding the imagery of the past can be a novelty in its own right.

But there's something more to the retro phenomenon than mere ephemera: a handful of switched-on marketers are realising that their forbears often knew a thing or two about marketing. Instead of dismissing them as old-fashioned, perhaps we should sit at their feet and learn.

When modern retailers talk about selling leisure and the shopping experience, you could be forgiven for thinking they were new ideas. Yet old-fashioned department stores with their roof gardens, fashion shows, musical performances, libraries and reading rooms had it all.

Likewise, sassy marketing consultants have realised that downsized, delayered clients are often sitting on a stockpile of unused wisdom but are simply too busy, or arrogant, to get at it. Increasingly, the first thing market researchers, new product development experts, and brand strategists do nowadays is ask to see the old files – if they haven't already been discarded. Often, all they need to know is lying there. The information was used once or twice and then discarded, its true value unrecognised.

It's hard to pin a definition on this approach. It has been named brand archaeology, but the dry, dusty implications of such a term fail to do justice to the concept. It's not even simply a matter of rediscovering brands' heritage. For this conjures up sentimental feelings when, in fact, it is all about exploiting raw marketing power – in this case, the power of time.

Time is the one thing that you and your competitors can never have again. And how it is used – or not used – can be crucial. Ad campaigns and brands may die, for example, but the memories we have of them often stay fresh in our minds, mingling with all the other encounters that for some reason we take with us through our lives.

Such memories can be extraordinarily powerful, releasing a host of associations and emotions, even blurring the distinction between distant past and present in our minds. It's a theme that Proust found rich and complex enough to spend a lifetime exploring through his novels. And only now is it perhaps beginning to be explored by marketers.

At a simple level, retro marketing may be just a fancy way of exploiting the extraordinary levels of recognition and familiarity that brands with long-term, consistent marketing campaigns can create. As Charles Wrench, client services director at Colgate agency Young & Rubicam points out, years after it was dropped, Colgate's ring of confidence is still the best-recalled advertising property of the category, bringing with it strong feelings of affection and trust. In an era of rapid TV inflation, instant recognisability is a godsend. "Why not harness the power that people freely give you?" he asks.

But that's just a start. The crucial point is that, like a mature garden, the place that older brands can establish for themselves in consumers' minds can't be replicated overnight. The depth, the richness, the time, the pleasing overall shape – it's all a product of time, of years of careful nurturing.

Newcomers, including retail brands, may be able to imitate, match, or even excel in other aspects of brand performance and imagery. But this particular attribute is beyond their reach. It is the product of history and competitors can't touch it.

A spokesman for Pedigree Petfoods says its retro ad – sparked by Pal's 40th birthday – reminds consumers that it's been serving their pets for 40 years, unlike many other brands on the market.

Most older brands probably have a far greater stockpile of marketing power buried in their history than is realised. But a youth and novelty-obsessed marketing culture means that brand managers and agencies are always seeking new, greener pastures rather than developing the gardens they've already got. And it's only when these great time-based assets are allowed to become stale, devalued or forgotten that the field is laid wide open for new competitors.

ISSUES

1. **What is brand archaeology?**

2. **How does consumer memory affect brand heritage?**

3. **How can a company monitor brand value and judge brand management performance?**

EXPLORATION OF ISSUES

1. Marketing consultants and advertising agency staff have realised that downsized, delayered clients are often sitting on a stockpile of wisdom but are simply too busy or too arrogant to get at it. Increasingly, the first thing that marketing researchers, new product development experts and brand strategists do nowadays is ask to see the old files – if they have not already been discarded.

Often, all they need to know is lying there. The information was used once or twice and then discarded, its true value unrecognised. It is hard to pin a definition on this approach. It has been named brand archaeology, but the dry, dusty implications of such a term fail to do justice to the concept. It is not even simply a matter of rediscovering a brand's heritage. For this conjures up sentimental feelings when in fact it is all about exploiting raw marketing power – in this case the power of time. Time is the one thing that you and your competitors can never have again. And how it is used or not used can be crucial.

2. Advertising campaigns and brands may die, but the memories we have of them often stay fresh in our minds, combining with all the other encounters that, for some reason, we take with us through our lives. Such memories can be extraordinarily powerful, releasing a host of associations and emotions, even blurring the distinction between distant past and present in our minds. It is a theme that only now is perhaps beginning to be explored by marketers.

At a simple level, retro-marketing may be just a fancy way of exploiting the extraordinary levels of recognition and familiarity that brands with long-term consistent marketing campaigns can create. For example Colgate's Ring of Confidence is still the best recalled advertising property of the category, bringing with it strong feelings of affection and trust. In an era of rapid TV inflation, instant recognisability is a godsend. But that is just a start. The crucial point is that, like a mature garden, the place older brands can establish for themselves in consumers' minds cannot be replicated overnight. The depth, the richness, the time, the pleasing overall shape – it is all a product of time, of years of careful marketing.

3. At present, few companies gather sufficient information to monitor brand value and judge brand management performance. However, there is a rapidly developing tendency to do so. More and more companies are bypassing the external reporting controversy to concentrate on internal brand evaluation and monitoring systems. Such systems not only directly affect marketing managers, but in many cases are driven by them. The development of a sophisticated brand value management system will inform the process of portfolio management and budget allocation.

The implications for marketing are significant. In addition to statistical measures of brand performance such as market share, distribution penetration and share of voice, such systems report detailed brand profitability data. They permit sensitivity analysis, allowing marketers to evaluate the consequences of price and margin changes, alternative trade policies and different promotional strategies. Advertising budgets and management reworked systems are being directly linked to them. Thus the process of brand management is more analytical and consistent.

They highlight the fact that marketing expenditure is not a discretionary budget line. Once brands are formally treated as fixed assets, albeit intangible ones, maintenance expenditure, tracked by brand value monitoring systems, will become essential.

Valuing brands and defining branded profits are vital activities for marketers and should not be cast in the 'too hard' basket.

Most marketers fully endorse the view that brands are identifiable, separable and extremely potent corporate assets that need professional management, consistent investment and maintenance. But left entirely to accountants, the way they are reported may not reflect these realities.

Niche Branding

Time to shed a little tier or two

Nestlé's announcement that it is to axe a number of second tier brand names highlights the huge cost of maintaining ad spend. But while a 'great brand cull' is on the agenda, huge opportunities exist for a new range of genuine niche brands.

ALAN MITCHELL

People have been batting on about the demise of third and fourth-line grocery brands for as long as I can remember, but there have been few examples as dramatic as last Friday's restructuring announcement by Nestlé. In one fell swoop it has exited all its canning businesses. A significant swathe of brands are being chopped, mostly from the Crosse & Blackwell range. They include tomato ketchup, salad cream, baked beans, pastas and canned soups.

Some may dismiss this decision as an isolated case. After all, few categories face the same crushing combination of adverse factors: changing consumer preferences, severe overcapacity and new competition from international players such as Italian tomato canners. But that misses the point. Every brand that's axed in the coming cull will have its special circumstances, and how many aren't competing in a context of chronic overcapacity and intensifying competition from low-cost producers from abroad?

But why should the "great brand cull" be starting now, just when we are supposed to be leaving recession behind us? Because of a combination of factors.

First, media inflation. Almost forgotten during the recession, it's now staging a comeback – forcing companies with bloated brand portfolios to ask hard questions about how many of their precious offspring they can really afford to keep.

Recent research by the marketing consultancy Added Value illustrates the agonies brand managers can face. It reveals that the typical marketing (advertising and below-the-line) cost of being a "big" (top 70) brand is nearly £8m – a sum that accounts for a high proportion of lesser brands' total sales.

A company like Kellogg can afford to invest £61m in advertising its range of 16 brands – giving each one a respectable critical mass. Meanwhile, firms like Heinz, with a total advertising spend of £15m to spread across 20-plus product categories – such as baked beans, soups, baby foods, ketchups and Weight Watchers – are left panting. Its average of £800,000 a category just isn't credible, hence Heinz's celebrated decision to go below the line.

A quick glance at Nestlé's brimming UK brand portfolio (which spans the bountiful Rowntree, Findus, Nescaf,, Chambourcy, Crosse & Blackwell and Carnation stables, as well as Buitoni, Dufrais, Friskies, Foxes, Libbys, Gales, Sarsons and Sun Pat) suggests that it is facing similar pressures.

Secondly, a radical reassessment of the Eighties fashion for brand extensions is underway. OK, some marketers did agonise about the risk of diluting and confusing core brand values. (Until the axe fell last week Crosse & Blackwell endorsed pickles, cold sauces, ketchups, salad creams, soups and baked beans. What exactly are its brand values? What does the brand name bring to the party?) But few ever looked beyond market share arguments to the broader considerations.

Retailers, for a start, don't like cluttering their shelves with scores of me-toos. Branded goods companies should be adding value, not cost (the more stock keeping units there are, the more expensive it gets). They should be making life simpler for consumers, not confusing them with a "plethora of product variants". And they should help them in their choices, not try to manipulate them, as Andrew Dixon, a Tesco marketing controller, told marketers at a Marketing Forum session last month. Me-toos (which most range extensions are), he added ominously, do have a place in retailers' minds as a "profit opportunity" – because manufacturers are forced to offer very fat margins just to keep their product on the shelves.

Further, any analysis of the true cost of producing range extensions shows that most cost more money than they make. A recent study by PA Consulting teased out these costs by looking at such things as the time and money spent researching and developing new formulations, packaging and promotions, factory stoppage time and extra storage and distribution costs. Its conclusion? On average, among the unnamed food companies investigated about half of their products produced 150 per cent of final profits, while the other half gobbled up 50 per cent (to leave the 100 per cent final total). Simply rationalising a brand portfolio, PA concluded, could be the cleverest and quickest way to turn a quick buck.

But perhaps the most urgent pressure on brands comes from another, totally different direction – retail competition. Figures produced by Verdict managing director Richard Hyman at a Marketing Society event earlier this year sum it all up. From the Sixties onwards, he pointed out, the expansion of the grocery multiples took place at the expense of independents. Until 1980 UK grocery shopping space was actually falling. But between 1980 and 1990 it jumped from 380m sq ft to 450m sq ft, just when cannibalisation of sales from the corner shop was coming to an end.

The crazy rush to add excess capacity to excess capacity hasn't stopped. Instead, as discounters establish themselves (discount shopping space was up 22 per cent in 1993 alone) the pressure on retailer prices and margins is becoming acute. That pressure is being passed back up the chain to suppliers – undermining the viability of once healthy, second tier brands.

These three factors – media and marketing costs, the quest to root out expensive complexity and the developing crisis in grocery retailing – all suggest that Nestlé's announcement will be the first of many. One implication is that over the next few years the real tests of marketing skill (and the real displays of ingenuity) may not be from among the well resourced, headline grabbing "power brands" but from smaller brands that no longer have the muscle to play the marketing game by its old rules, or that see advantages in the gaps created by big firms clearing the weak and sickly from the brand undergrowth.

Indeed, be warned. As the inexorable logic of size and power sweeps over all things commercial, all the social and political trends suggest that consumers are yearning for the opposite – the warmth that local identity or cultural roots provide. Consumers may be buying "power brands" but they are also searching for community and identity.

Of course, in the real world they'll have both. But perhaps the ironic result of a second tier brand bloodbath will be the huge opportunities it opens up for a new raft of genuine niche brands.

ISSUES

ISSUES

1 What are the reasons behind the new trend referred to as 'brand cull'?

2 Comment on the development of 'power brands' and niche brands as well as the demise of 'half-hearted' brands.

3 How can meaningful brand innovation be achieved?

EXPLORATION OF ISSUES

1 One of the main reasons for 'brand cull' is the huge cost of advertising. There is also a crushing combination of adverse factors: changing consumer preferences, severe and chronic overcapacity and new and intensifying competition from international players (low-cost producers).

Almost forgotten during the recessions, media inflation is now staging a comeback – forcing companies with bloated brand portfolios to ask hard questions about how many of their precious offspring they can really afford to keep. Furthermore, a radical re-assessment of the 1980s fashion for brand extensions is underway. Some marketers did agonise about the risk of diluting and confusing core brand values, but what exactly are a company's brand values? What does the brand name bring to the party? But few have looked beyond market share arguments to the broader considerations.

For a start, retailers do not like cluttering their shelves with scores of me-toos. Branded goods companies should be adding value, not cost (the more stock-keeping units there are, the more expensive it gets). They should be making life simpler for consumers, not confusing them with a 'plethora of product variants'. They should help them in their choices, not try to manipulate them. Me-toos (which most range extensions are) do have a place in retailers' minds as a 'profit opportunity', because manufacturers are forced to offer very fat margins just to keep their product on the shelves.

Furthermore, any analysis of the true cost of producing range extensions shows that most cost more money than they make (for example the time and money spent on researching and developing new formulations, packaging and promotions, factory stoppage time, extra storage and distribution costs all have to be taken into account).

Conclusion? Rationalising a brand portfolio could be the cleverest and quickest way to turn a quick buck.

But perhaps the most urgent pressure on brand stems from another, totally different direction – retail competition. From the 1960s onwards the expansion of grocery multiples took place at the expense of independents. The crazy rush to add excess capacity to excess capacity has not stopped. Instead, as discounters establish themselves, the pressure on retailer prices and margins is becoming acute. That pressure is being passed back up the chain to suppliers, undermining the viability of once healthy, second-tier brands.

These three factors – media and marketing costs, the quest to root out expensive complexity and the developing crisis in grocery retailing – also suggest that an extensive 'brand cull' is about to start. Examples can already be seen at Nestlé, Unilever, Procter and Gamble and Grand Met.

2 With regard to the development of 'power brands' and niche brands and the demise of 'half-hearted' brands, one implication of this is that over the next few years the real test of marketing skill may not relate to well-resourced, headline-grabbing 'power brands' but smaller brands that no longer have the muscle to play the marketing game by its old rules, or to take advantage of the gaps created by big firms clearing the weak and sickly from the brand undergrowth.

As the inexorable logic of size and power sweeps across all things commercial, all the social and political trends suggest that consumers are yearning for the opposite – the warmth that local identity or cultural roots provide. Consumers may be buying 'power brands' but they are also searching for community and identity.

Of course, in the real world they will have both, but perhaps the ironic result of a second-tier brand blood-bath will be the huge opportunities it opens up for a new raft of genuine niche brands.

'Half-hearted' brand strategies are one of the reasons why some manufacturers have been pushed to the edge. The real brand split today is between real brands, – Mars, Kellogg's, Sainsbury's and Marks and Spencer's – and pseudo-brands – products that fail to provide real product benefits or value for money, or fail to get the production, research and development or promotional support they need. They are not brands, they fall into the category of 'manufacturer label'.

Recent research findings (London Business School, 1996) reveal that better-performing companies (in terms of sales) stress the development of strong brands in their planning activities. Brands are assets that need to be nurtured and many have a long-term payoff, particularly those in highly competitive marketplaces. The delivery and method of delivery of brand information is fast becoming their only product differential. Communication has become the product! The most important ingredient is not the brand name, but what lies behind it. Pretty pictures and lofty slogans won't help. Buyers want to know what you stand for.

3 Meaningful brand innovation has been replaced by operational brand finessing. The stretching process extends the brand core too far so that brand values are no longer coherent. First, there is the brand, its ability to offer consumers a clear and distinctive performance. Which brands are doing this nowadays? Think of a brand campaign that seems to be consistently putting this foot forward. Yes, there are a few, but not many come from the multinational powerhouses, with heritage brands and cultures that still dominate the marketing world. Second, put at its simplest, today few advertising agencies offer strategic brand counselling, some are endeavouring to put together a high-quality range of communications for the decade ahead, and to integrate them in such a way that the clients, as well as the constituent companies, can all gain from a stronger final entity.

Given that the key issue is the effective management of brands by committed and expert marketing teams, you can expect to see the aspirations of tomorrow's companies fulfilled by new, dedicated and highly professional companies, not all of whom will remain under the banner of advertising.

6 Pricing Policy

Low Pricing

KEY CONCEPTS

- Every day low pricing (EDLP)
- Pricing policies
- Category EDLP
- Price elasticity

Every day low pricing is a high-risk strategy

Research shows the latest US export – EDLP – has not travelled well, says **ANDREW SCOTT**.

Recent moves to import the US policy of every day low pricing (EDLP) into the UK have sent shock waves through the retail sector. The theory behind the strategy is that by keeping prices constantly low, without resorting to a confusing array of price promotions, sales will increase over time, and so will profits.

But EDLP has had a rocky time in the UK. When retail giant Kingfisher adopted it across its chains Comet, Woolworths, B&Q and Superdrug, the experiment was a failure, and City observers dubbed it "Every Day Low Profits". Kingfisher soon dropped the policy.

A series of studies by Information Resources Inc in the US has shown that pure EDLP may not be in the best interests of retailers or manufacturers. In short, it doesn't always work.

In the studies, the performances of up to 63 product categories were monitored in retail chains with EDLP pricing policies, chains with heavy price promotions and also within different stores in one group where EDLP, Hi-Lo and control groups were set up for 16 weeks. The product categories monitored included butter, beer, carbonated beverages, cereals, household cleaners and shampoo.

Whichever way the studies were run, the results were similar. A ten per cent category price decrease in an EDLP environment resulted in a mere three per cent sales volume increase, while a ten per cent price increase in a Hi-Lo promotional environment only led to a three per cent sales decrease.

Most seriously, because of the low consumer response to changes in every day price there were also large differences in profitability. An EDLP policy reduced profits by 18 per cent, whereas Hi-Lo pricing increased profits by 15 per cent.

One possible reason for the failure of consumers to respond to EDLP is confusion created by heavy promotional activity in store.

Although EDLP store prices were on average nine per cent below Hi-Lo stores, they were still promoting as much as Hi-Lo stores (26 per cent of volume sold with some sort of merchandising support in EDLP stores and 24 per cent in Hi-Lo stores).

Because of the lower everyday pricing, the gap between everyday pricing and promotional offers was much smaller than in Hi-Lo operations, making the impact of the promotion much less obvious.

This was compounded by the fact that EDLP stores relied on displays to highlight their promotions, whereas Hi-Lo stores focused more on high impact feature activity. Basically consumers were conditioned to the greater impact of promotions in Hi-Lo stores.

Obviously, over a longer period of time and if the EDLP policy is advertised, the image of lower pricing can contribute to a more noticeable impact on traffic and sales volume, provided that other elements such as service, stock convenience and choice are right.

Discounters like Wal-Mart in the US have been successful through a consistent chain-wide policy of EDLP which includes advertising that its prices are "always the lowest".

However, most retailers have adopted EDLP on a more limited level, sometimes labelled Category EDLP, where prices of certain categories, such as soft drinks or disposable nappies, are reduced in an effort to increase traffic in the hope that store-wide sales will benefit.

The indication is that the lower prices in these cases simply do not bring new customers to the store fast enough to compensate for the lower profit margins. Basically a ten per cent price cut needs a 39 per cent volume uplift to break even. That means a third more customers or a third larger average shopping spend.

In some circumstances this can be achieved. For example, if a store is new, there is potential to increase traffic levels and if the store has a high proportion of secondary shoppers they can potentially be encouraged to buy across more categories. This was accomplished by Somerfield in 1994 with a price campaign that was highly effective in increasing average consumer spend per store visit.

The only other way to make Category EDLP effective is to limit price cutting to the few high-price elastic product categories where EDLP is actually more effective than Hi-Lo pricing.

With low and medium elasticity products such as sugar, bread and toilet paper, practically all the products, respond better to Hi-Lo pricing. It is only among the very elastic categories that EDLP has more of an impact and these product areas are therefore the only ones where a consistent EDLP policy makes financial sense in the long term.

Of course, studies like these cannot provide all the answers. If the experiment had been continued for a couple of years and advertising had been included, consumer response to EDLP may have been greater.

In real life though, repositioning on an EDLP platform is risky and expensive and there are many factors more important than price in determining a consumer's choice of store.

ISSUES

1 Explain the concept of everyday low pricing (EDLP).

2 Discuss issues related to category EDLP.

3 Why are retailers adopting EDLP?

EXPLORATION OF ISSUES

1 An important type of value pricing is everyday low pricing (EDLP), whereby retailers consistently charge low prices with no temporary price discounts, such as in ASDA superstores. These constant prices eliminate week-to-week price uncertainty and can be contrasted with the 'high-low' pricing of promotion-orientated competitors. In high-low pricing, the retailer charges higher prices on an everyday basis but runs frequent promotions in which prices are temporarily lowered below the EDLP level.

The high-low strategy evolved during the early 1970s in response to rising inflation. When commodity prices began to drop, food manufacturers did not lower their inflated prices but instead offered deals to retailers on certain products. These discounts were then passed on to consumers, who were able to compare prices between shops. But in recent years, high-low pricing has given way to EDLP at such widely differing venues as General Motors car dealerships and up-market department stores. But the king of EDLP is surely Wal-Mart in the United States, which practically defined the term. Apart from a few sale items every month, Wal-Mart promises everyday low prices on major brands. 'It's not a short-term strategy', says one Wal-Mart executive. 'You have to be willing to make a commitment to it, and you have to be able to operate with lower ratios of expense than everybody else.'

2 Category EDLP is the name given to a policy where the prices of products in certain categories, such as soft drinks or disposable nappies, are reduced in an effort to increase traffic in the hope that store-wide sales will rise. However the indication is that these lower prices simply do not bring enough new customers to the store to compensate for the lower profit margins. Basically, a 10 per cent price cut needs a 39 per cent increase in sales volume in order to break even. That means a third more customers or a third larger average shopping spend.

In some circumstances this can be achieved. For example if a store is new, the potential exists to increase traffic levels, and if the store has a large proportion of secondary shoppers, they can be encouraged to buy across more categories. This was accomplished in 1994 by Somerfield, whose price campaign was highly effective in increasing average consumer spend per store visit.

The only other way to make category EDLP effective is to limit price cutting to the few high-priced, elastic product categories where EDLP is actually more effective than high-low pricing. Products with low and medium elasticity, for example sugar, bread and toilet paper, practically all respond better to high-low pricing. It is only among the very elastic categories that EDLP has more of an impact, and these product areas are therefore the only ones where a consistent EDLP policy makes financial sense in the long term.

3 Retailers adopt EDLP for a number of reasons, the most important of which is that sales and promotions are costly and erode consumer confidence in the credibility of everyday shelf prices. Consumers also have less time and patience for such time-honoured traditions as watching for supermarket specials and clipping coupons to put into voluminous coupon files.

EDLP does not guarantee success, however. Sears' EDLP initiative failed when it was launched in 1989 because the store did not reduce costs to cushion it against the inevitable drop in business that would occur while consumers waited to see what was up. Wal-Mart has been able to stick to its EDLP policy because its expenses are only 15 per cent of sales; Sears, in contrast, spends 29 per cent of sales on administrative, occupancy and other costs. Finally, Sears also failed to make sure that its everyday low prices were actually lower than those of its competitors, and it continued to advertise sales so that the low prices lost credibility with customers.

7 Distribution

Channel Relationships

Grabbing a piece of the transaction

These days, the retailer, or middleman, has it good: ownership of the customer relationship, and the facility to cream off a profit at the end of a complex supply chain. Now the information revolution has opened the way for the manufacturer to control distribution channels. **ALAN MITCHELL** asks where this leaves marketers

If marketing is still a matter of getting the product, price or promotion right, then over the coming decade, the most important area of innovation will surely be where the transaction takes place. During the Seventies and Eighties we witnessed an often spectacular battle between opposing models of enterprise – public versus private. Over the coming decades that may be replaced by an equally vast and complex struggle, this time between "supplier" and "middleman".

The prize will be "ownership" of the customer relationship, and the site of the battle will be the distribution chain.

It is quite easy to see why. In most categories and most industries, between 30 per cent and 40 per cent of the final consumer price is accounted for by the retailer's, or middleman's, take. Suppliers could live with this situation when there was nothing they could do about it, the middleman was not using his position to leverage his way into "ownership" of the customer relationship and the middleman was not claiming an increasing proportion of the total supply chain profits for himself.

Now, many suppliers are beginning to realise that they may, at last, have the means to turn the tables on retailer power.

Multimedia developments have paved the way for a formidable combination of forces. Telecoms, cable, computer hardware, software and media companies now see enormous revenue-earning potential in multimedia and its home-shopping applications. In addition, existing distribution companies, such as the Royal Mail and Post Office, mail-order companies and logistics companies, are realising that their businesses could experience exponential growth if home delivery (or greater local delivery) really took off.

In many industries innovative players are already proving that established distribution networks are not cast in stone. First Direct and Direct Line have blown apart traditional financial services distribution – and cost – structures. Direct selling of holidays and computers is growing apace. Car companies such as Daewoo are successfully eliminating dealer networks.

Now one of the world's biggest consumer electronics companies – which must remain unnamed – has made a multibillion-pound strategic decision: over the coming decade it will eliminate the middleman, developing its own "showcase" stores and a parallel direct distribution system. The common factor is disintermediation, whether it's of middlemen businesses or physical places or both.

There are, of course, plenty of sceptics. At the recent Marketing Forum, Verdict director Deborah Grant dismissed speculation that virtual reality-based, home-shopping systems would ever be able to bypass existing retailers. Home shopping will double its market share, she predicted. But only from a paltry four to eight per cent. And, she estimates, it will take 15 years to do so. "Shops are a tried and tested means of bringing consumers and products together," she declared. "Shopping from home will never dominate retailing."

There are many good reasons for this. Massive infrastructure investments are needed to create new physical distribution systems that are both convenient and cost-effective. The mass penetration of affordable, easy-to-use interactive media (apart from the telephone) is a long way off. There remain serious question marks over the emergence of secure payment mechanisms.

In addition, techno-enthusiasts ignore the social and psychological aspects of shopping. Meeting people, going out, and using your full range of senses to shop – seeing the flesh on the meat, feeling the quality of the cloth, will remain crucial. After all, if remote shopping was going to be such a big new idea, mail order and off-page selling would have taken off a long time ago.

Yet the sceptics may be missing the point. They take for granted the very thing that is now being thrown into doubt: the shop as a unique bundle of numerous processes.

The modern retailer provides a combination of factors – a product showcase, a place for making payments, a distribution point, an opportunity for a social or leisure experience, to name a few. The big question is whether it is ripe for unbundling, and if so, how it could be rebundled into a new, commercially viable combination.

Why not, for instance, go to a fashion show (which is a product showcase plus a social occasion) but order and pay from home? Or why not have showcase and payment at one place and delivery to another – as is already the case with most white goods shopping?

As soon as the possibilities of unbundling and rebundling are considered, the potential permutations are vast. Perhaps this is why so many corporations are taking such a lively interest in once-marginal subjects such as pizza-style home delivery operations, vending machines and petrol station retailing, as well as the multimedia kiosk and the Internet.

The key issue is not the place where consumers shop but from whom they shop. Who owns the transaction and the information it generates? In what way, and to what extent, can existing links in the distribution chain be eliminated or reconstructed in such a way that it adds value for consumers as well as cutting costs?

Retailers and other middlemen are, of course, acutely aware of such potential reform. After all, there's no reason why they too cannot use any of the new technologies to enhance what they offer.

This is where marketing skills will be so crucial. The winners in the coming struggle will not necessarily be those with the greatest technical advantages, but those who are best at the marketing mix: who can construct the most attractive packages of price, choice, convenience, service, interest and excitement as each stage of the distribution revolution as it unfolds.

The question for the future is, are existing marketing departments the best place to find the unbundling and packaging skills companies now need?

Matsushita plans own network to bypass high-street retailers

Matsushita, the Japanese consumer electronics giant which owns the Panasonic and Technics brand, is believed to be planning a network of retail outlets in the UK to bypass established retailers such as Dixons and Comet.

It would follow in the footsteps of rivals such as Sony, which has built a chain of 90 stores throughout the UK selling Sony products exclusively. The stores are run on a franchise basis.

There are already two dedicated Panasonic shops in the UK, which are owned by the retailer.

Earlier this month Matsushita announced it would open a chain of 3,000 retail outlets in China to sell only its own products. The company's success in Japan is largely because of a network of 20,000 "corner shops" selling its products exclusively.

"Panasonic has been discussing this idea for at least two years," says one source. "But nothing has happened yet. It believes this is a good idea but that it will be difficult to implement."

A quest for successful relations

Faced with the threat of retailer relationship marketing, major companies are retreating cloak and dagger-style to the drawing board in an attempt to discover a formula which will pull in the customers – and retain their loyalty.

ALAN MITCHELL

There's one story that you will be unlikely to read about in the pages of the marketing press. Yet it is probably the most important marketing story of the moment. Like the cold war powers during the nuclear arms race, more and more major companies are retreating behind closed doors to rethink their marketing weaponry from scratch.

To be sure, the normal rough and tumble is taking place: this ad campaign, that new product launch. Meanwhile, future organisational structures, communications budgets and priorities, supply and distribution chains and brand strategies are all being taken back to the drawing board as senior executives realise the rise in retailer power and changes in IT and media are fundamental and irreversible. Tweaking traditional formulae is no longer enough. A new formula must be found. But no one is sure what it will look like.

Vast sums are being spent in the quest for this new holy grail. According to some sources, P&G has recently invested £100m developing its UK consumer databases. Neither the figure nor the activity is possible to verify. The confidentiality clauses surrounding the exercise make the CIA and the KGB look like paragons of openness. But here's one possible picture. P&G has realised that the UK has effectively become the guinea pig for a new order in marketing worldwide. What's happened in the UK – with retailers' access to superior information sources and increasing ability to "own" the customer relationship – means that retailers now have guns while suppliers are stuck with the bow and arrow. As retailers in other countries catch on, some way of spiking those guns must be found, fast.

Consumer databases potentially offer three ways of doing so. First, they allow suppliers to fight information with information. While retailers now often know more about manufacturers' performance than manufacturers' themselves, they have precious little detailed insight into how well their rivals are doing, category by category, catchment area by catchment area. Manufacturer databases, as opposed to store-based databases, can help provide that detail.

Second, the database is the germ of an alternative means of communicating with consumers which not only bypasses retailers and expensive TV companies but also has the added advantage of being covert.

Third – and this is where the real advantages begin to bear fruit – it provides the foundations for alternative distribution arrangements. Direct delivery of Ariel is not a commercial starter. But an enterprise offering the whole P&G range, perhaps in alliance with non-competing drinks, clothes and home products companies operating through a range of new outlets, including home delivery, may well become viable over the next decade. (Significantly, Unilever is said to be centralising its consumer data sources from its various company fiefdoms.)

But the core issue is "ownership" of the customer. There has been widespread scepticism about database marketers' ability to deliver cost effective and appropriate communications programmes that go beyond direct advertising to relationship building.

Sure it's difficult, but the numbers aren't as crazy as they seem at first sight. As the Buitoni Club's marketing manager Duncan MacCallum points out, 40 to 60 per cent of the populace are not interested in a category like Italian food, and most brands would be happy to have a 20 per cent share of those who are. By concentrating on 10 to 20 per cent of the most valuable of those customers a starting point of 21 million households quickly dwindles to about half a million – and that's becoming manageable.

Likewise, if you divide the 5 million names on Tesco's Club Card database between its 519 stores, it averages out at something like 10,000 per store. Not only is it feasible for each store manager to be charged with building a relationship with the 500 or thousand most valuable customers in each catchment area, the potential implications for all of Tesco's marketing are enormous.

Some intriguing questions follow. First, as the Tesco example shows, are retailers winning the relationship marketing race? Not in all categories. For the past few years, for example, Imperial Tobacco has been monopolising lifestyle questionnaires to build a multimillion-strong database on smokers and their brands.

Second, who is best placed to exploit databases and relationships? Again, not necessarily the retailer. As Pedigree Petfoods faces Sainsbury's forthcoming launch of Paws its need to rethink is obvious. Already it sends birthday cards to Sheba and Caesar buyers' pets. Why not extend the relationship to offer a total pet care service? This could take in everything from taking the hassle out of pet food shopping through direct delivery, through to dietary and veterinary advice, to clubs for different breeds, to pet-sitting services for holiday makers or burial services for the bereaved, and so on. Pedigree could become not only *the* authority on pets, but also *the* funnel for pet-related services and transactions.

Third, what becomes of brands in a world such as this? Brands first came into their own after the industrial revolution when buyers no longer knew who was baking their bread or making their candles and the need for trust grew. When the customer is in ongoing contact with the maker how does that change branding and brand management? US consultant Regis McKenna suggests that the brand "becomes an ongoing dialogue, the interactive experience of buying and using the product".

Fourth, what will the long-term social effects of such initiatives be? It has often been argued that mass marketing was a democratising, equalising force. As the guru of mass customisation, Joseph Pines, points out mass marketing's goal was "developing, producing, marketing, and delivering goods and services at prices low enough that nearly everyone could afford them". Relationship marketing, on the other hand, is about treating your most valuable customers better than the rest. Could marketing become anti-democratic and divisive?

There may be more to the concept of "owning the customer relationship" than meets the eye. And until a few of the major companies feel they've got some of the answers, we can expect the current climate of paranoid secrecy to continue.

ISSUES

1 **What is the background to the manufacture–retailer power struggle?**

2 **What is the role of loyalty relationship schemes in the balance of power between manufacturer and retailer?**

3 **How can a company conduct an analysis of distribution systems?**

4 Outline the key facets of a channel conflict management strategy.

5 Do you agree with the statement 'shopping from home will never dominate traditional retailing'? Why?

6 Discuss the key issues in the increasingly important area of channel conflict.

7 Elaborate on the benefits and costs of vertical integration.

8 Comment on the franchising system as a widely used distribution control strategy.

EXPLORATION OF ISSUES

1 One of the most notable trends since the mid 1960s in terms of distribution channels is the rise of the multiples and the corresponding decline of independent retailers. In the 'nation of shopkeepers' era, before self-service and the abolition of resale price maintenance, retailers operated on a neighbourhood basis, serving customers individually and getting to know them. Despite this, it was manufacturers who held the balance of power in distribution channels. It was they who developed the brands and controlled the advertising and pricing (through resale price maintenance). Retailers, despite their lack of control over brand marketing programmes, formed an enviable relationship with their customers – there was a personal link analogous to pub locals being greeted by the publican by name and their favourite tipple appearing in a personalised glass without even having to place an order.

The power balance shifted when the abolition of resale price maintenance allowed retailers to discount their prices. This in turn led to buying groups who negotiated cost reductions based on bulk buying, which meant that price discounts could be passed on to their customers. As buying groups became larger and ever more powerful and small retailers who could not match their prices went out of business, an unstoppable cycle was set in motion. Retailers became less staff intensive as a result of cost-cutting self-service methods, and with their buying power and resulting price advantage they were even able to undercut wholesaler prices. This process distanced the retailer from consumers until EPOS systems allowed them to be very clear about which lines sold and which didn't. Such information enabled retailers virtually to dictate to manufacturers what products should be produced and at what price. The emergence of retailer own

brands was one result, and this corresponded with a decline in manufacturer brands in many fmcg markets and to a relative decline in manufacturer control and power within distribution channels.

2 The battle among retailers for market share in 1995 manifested itself most strongly in loyalty schemes. These are usually card based, whether magstripe (Tesco), credit card based (GM) or smart card based (Shell) (Croft, 1995). Such loyalty schemes appear to be so attractive to the marketing industry that they are even being used within the industry itself, for example RSL now has a loyalty card for the clients of its Capibus Client Care omnibus survey!

Some consumers are loyal in that they deliberately choose one brand over another and continue, to purchase that brand over time. The loyalty scheme not only has the potential to attract customers but also to retain them, and if this potential is realised, loyalty schemes can become a significant part of traditional sales promotion discounting approaches. For example, in addition to consumers benefiting from cheaper shopping (in the sense of 'customer-specific pricing' rather than scatter gun discounts), they can also provide the retailer with a great deal of information about the buying habits of individual customers. This information can be used to extend tempting offers via direct marketing mechanisms, at point of sale or direct to the household. Tesco, for example, has already announced that it is shifting the emphasis of its £30m advertising and marketing budget from above-the-line to direct marketing, and that Clubcard data on its customers will be used to target them more carefully.

Manufacturers have been using databases and direct

marketing to try to get closer to the consumer, especially since the multiple retailers have shifted the power balance in their own favour. The retailer loyalty scheme may be a way for retailers to maintain and enhance their position. Indeed it has been suggested that the battlefield for loyalty building is the shop floor, regardless of how worried manufacturers are about the growing popularity of retailers' own brands.

3 Any analysis of distribution systems should include the following questions:

- What are the trends?
- Which channels are growing in importance?
- Which new channels have emerged or are likely to?
- Who has the power in the channel and how is that likely to shift?

Access to an effective and efficient distribution channel is often a key factor in success. Channel alternatives can vary in several ways. One is the degree of directness. Some companies – for example Daewoo, Direct Line and many industrial businesses – sell directly through their own sales force. Other companies sell primarily through mail order. Others, such as Radio Shack and several shoe firms, sell through their own retail stores. Still other firms sell directly to retailers, through distributors or other intermediaries, or use a combination of channels. The firms closest to the end user have the most control over marketing and usually assume the highest risk.

Sometimes the creation of a new channel form can lead to a sustainable competitive advantage. Thus it is useful to consider not only existing channels but also potential ones. An analysis of likely or emerging changes in distribution channels can be important to understanding a market and its key success factors. The emergence of home shopping and, the growth of convenience food retailing in petrol stations, speciality catalogue retailing and warehouse clubs are trends that have strategic importance to companies affected by the channels concerned.

Related to customer power in market profitability analysis is channel power. In industries without strong brand names, such as furniture, retailers usually have a relatively high degree of power and can hold down the price paid to manufacturers. The enhanced power of supermarkets, due in large part to the explosion of transaction information and the importance of promotions, has altered the way in which packaged goods are marketed. The influence that Procter and Gamble and other packaged goods firms once had over promotions, stock-

ing and display decisions has significantly reduced. The ability of pharmacists to substitute generic drugs has altered the power balance in that industry.

4 Channel conflict management strategies are designed to resolve conflict among channel members by devising a solution that is acceptable to all concerned so that they can cooperate to make it work.

1. Bargaining: a) Both parties adopt give-and-take attitude. b) Bottom line is favourable enough for both parties to induce them to accept the terms of the bargain.
2. Boundary: a) Nomination of an employee to act as diplomat. b) Diplomat is fully briefed on the situation and provided with leverages with which to negotiate. c) Both parties are willing to negotiate.
3. Interpenetration: a) Frequent formal interactions with the other party to develop an appreciation of each other's perspective. b) Willingness to interact to solve problems.
4. Superorganisational: A mental third part is brought into the conflict to resolve the matter by means of a) conciliation, b) mediation, or c) arbitration (compulsory or arbitrary).

Expected results: 1) Elimination of snags in the channel. 2) Results that are mutually beneficial to the parties involved. 3) Need for management time and effort. 4) increased costs. 5) Costs incurred by both parties in the form of concessions.

5 There are many good reasons why home shopping is not set to replace traditional shopping. Massive investment is required to create new physical distribution systems that are both convenient and cost effective. The mass availability of affordable, easy-to-use interactive media (apart from the telephone) is a long way off, and there remain serious question marks over the possibility of secure payment mechanisms.

In addition, techno-enthusiasts ignore the social and psychological aspects of shopping. Meeting people, going out and using your full range of senses to shop – seeing the flesh on the meat, feeling the quality of the cloth – will remain crucial. After all, if remote shopping had been set to burgeon, mail order and off-page selling would have taken off a long time ago.

Yet sceptics take for granted the very thing that is now being thrown into doubt: the shop as a unique bundle of numerous processes. The modern retailer provides a combination of factors – a product showcase, a place for making payments, a distribution point, an opportunity for a social or leisure experience, to name a few. The big question is whether it is ripe for unbundling and if so, how it could be rebundled into a new, commercially viable combination.

6   Although all channel members work towards the same general goal – distributing products profitably and efficiently – they sometimes disagree about the best methods for attaining this goal. Each channel member wants to maximise its own profits while maintaining as much control as possible. However, if this self-interest creates misunderstanding about role expectations, the end result is frustration and conflict for the whole channel. For individual organisations to function together in a single social system, each channel member must clearly communicate and understand role expectations. Communication difficulties are a potential form of channel conflict and can lead to frustration, misunderstanding and ill-coordinated strategies.

Channel conflict often arises when a given channel member does not conduct itself in the manner expected by the other members. If members do not fulfil their roles – for example, if producers fail to deliver products on time or the producers' pricing policies lead to a cut in the margins of downstream channel members – conflict may ensue.

Channel conflicts also arise when dealers overemphasise competing products or diversify into product lines that are traditionally handled by other, more specialised intermediaries. In some cases conflict develops because producers strive to increase efficiency by circumventing intermediaries, as is happening in marketing channels for microcomputer software and video games. Many software-only stores are establishing direct relationships with software producers, bypassing wholesale distributors altogether. Consequently suspicion and mistrust are heightening in software marketing channels.

Although there is no single method of resolving conflict, an atmosphere of cooperation can be reestablished if two conditions are met. First, the role of each channel member must be specified. To minimise misunderstanding, all members must meet unambiguous, agreed upon performance levels. Second, channel members must institute certain channel coordination measures, a task that requires leadership and the benevolent exercise of control. In order to prevent channel conflict, producers or other channel members could supply competing resellers with different brands, allocate markets among resellers, define direct sales policies to clarify potential conflict over large accounts, negotiate territorial issues between regional distributors and reward certain resellers for the importance of their role in distributing to others.

7   Vertical integration represents a potential growth direction. Forward vertical integration occurs when a company moves downstream with respect to product flow, such as a manufacturer buying a retail chain. A good way of investigating whether vertical integration should be considered and how it should be evaluated is to look at the possible benefits and costs:

Benefits
- *Operating economies.*   Economies of scale are possible: to the extent that a larger operation is more efficient, economies will be observed.
- *Access to demand.*   Forward integration could be motivated by a concern about product outlets.
- *Control of the product system.*   It may become necessary to integrate vertically in order to gain sufficient control over a product and maintain the integrity of a differentiation strategy. Vertical integration may be the only way to ensure that the desired quality is achieved.
- *Entry into a profitable business area.*   A vertical integration decision can be motivated simply by an attractive profit potential. Thus a chain of retail stores may simply be an attractive business investment and the fact that it now is an outlet for a firm's products may be a relatively minor consideration. Too often this rationale is faulty and is accompanied by an inadequate understanding of the consumers and competitors in the new market and of what it takes to be successful there. The attractiveness of a new source of sales makes it easy to minimise the difficulties.

Costs
- *Operating costs.*   Vertical integration has the potential to create operating costs that may outweigh the operating economies. The added complexity and coordination required might put a strain on the management system.
- *The risk inherent in increased commitment to a market.* Vertical integration tends to rerquire increased commitment to and investment in a certain market. If that market is healthy, then integration may enhance profits; if the market turns down, integration may cause profits to fall. Integration also raises exit barriers. If the business becomes weak, the investment made in integration will inhibit consideration of exiting.

- *Reduced flexibility.* Vertical integration usually means that a company is committed to an in-house customer. A decision to enter retailing may be regretted if customer preferences dictate that another channel will become dominant. There is often a trade-off between flexibility and commitment. Increased commitment can lead to higher profits but is also associated with a reduction in the ability to adapt to changing circumstances.

ALTERNATIVES TO INTEGRATION

Several alternatives to integration exist, such as long-term contracts, exclusive dealing agreements, asset ownership, joint ventures, strategic alliances and franchising. Exclusive dealing arrangements that link a manufacturer and a retail chain or distributor can lead to information transfer, strategy coordination and transaction and distribution efficiency. Although most of these alternatives involve difficulties, especially as circumstances and power relations change over time, they also provide many of the advantages of integration with few of the disadvantages. They should be considered before integration is pursued.

According to one study, although net profit as a percentage of sales does increase with vertical integration, the return on investment (ROI) does not. The increase in investment that accompanies vertical integration counters any increase in profit.

8 Once considered upstarts among independent business owners, franchisers now command 35 per cent of retail sales in the United States and experts expect that figure to increase to 50 per cent by the turn of the century. This is not hard to believe in a society where it's nearly impossible to stroll down a city street or drive on a suburban thoroughfare without seeing a McDonald's or a 7-Eleven. One of the best known and successful franchisers, McDonald's, now has 14 000 outlets world wide and racks up more than 23 billion in systemwide sales.

How does a franchising system work? The individual franchises are a tightly knit group of enterprises whose systematic operations are planned, directed and controlled by the operation's innovator, called a franchiser. Generally, franchises are distinguished by three characteristics:

- The franchiser owns a trademark or service mark and licenses it to franchisees in return for royalty payments.
- The franchisee is required to pay for the right to be a

part of the system. Yet this initial fee is only a small part of the total amount that franchisees invest when they sign a franchising contract. Start-up costs include rental and lease of equipment and fixtures, and sometimes a regular license fee. McDonald's franchisees may invest as much as $600 000 in initial start-up costs. The franchisee then pays the McDonald's franchiser a service fee and a rental charge that equal 11.5 per cent of the franchisee's sales volume.

- The franchiser provides its franchisees with a marketing and operations system for doing business. McDonald's requires franchisees to attend its 'Hamburger University' in Oak Brook Illinois for three weeks to learn how to manage the business. The franchisees must adhere to certain procedures when buying supplies. The most forward-looking franchisers also look to their franchisees for advice and ideas on how the business can be better run.

In the best cases, business format franchising is mutually beneficial to both franchiser and franchisee. Among the benefits reaped by franchisers are the ability to cover a territory in little more than the time it takes for a franchisee to sign a contract, the motivation and hard work of employees who are entrepreneurs rather than 'hired hands', the franchisee's familiarity with local communities and conditions, and enormous purchasing power (consider the purchase order that Holiday Inn is likely to make for bed sheets, for instance). Franchisees benefit from buying into a proven business with a well-known and accepted brand name. Franchisees also find it easier to borrow money from financial institutions and receive ongoing support in areas ranging from marketing and advertising to site selection and staffing.

However, as a result of the franchise explosion in recent years, many types of franchisers are looking at an increasingly saturated domestic market. Furthermore, there will typically be a conflict between the franchisers, who benefit from growth, and the franchisees, who benefit only when they can earn a decent living. Some new options that may deliver growth to the franchiser and earnings to the franchisee are:

- Strategic alliances with major outside corporations: an example is that between film company Fuji USA and Moto Photo, a one-book photo developer. Fuji Moto Photo franchisees enjoyed Fuji's brand name recognition and advertising reach.
- Expansion abroad: fast-food franchisers have become very popular throughout the world. Today

McDonald's has 4700 overseas restaurants, including a 700-seat restaurant in Moscow. Domino's (pizza) has been operating in Japan with 106 restaurants and continued sales of £170 million. Part of its success can be attributed to adapting Domino's' product to the Japanese market, where presentation is everything.

Retailing

KEY CONCEPTS

- Retail alliances
- Marketing intelligence systems
- Joint buying power and marketing synergies
- Own-label products
- International branding

Going shopping, European style

As scope for growth in the UK diminishes, more retailers are forming alliances with their foreign counterparts in the hope of both improving their operating expertise and widening product lines.

CLAIRE MURPHY

Retailers grabbed the headlines last week. Tesco announced it had bought into Hungarian supermarket chain Global, and Sainsbury's is to enter a "co-operation" agreement with three European food retailers (*MW* March 25).

Sainsbury's partners are French chain Docks de France, Delhaize of Belgium and Italian group Esselunga. The deal came to light as Sainsbury's announced it was to open a discount off-licence inside the Docks de France-owned Mammouth hypermarket at Calais.

Tesco's move involves buying 45 per cent of Global when it is floated in mid-April. The company already owns northern France retail chain Catteau, but Tesco says that this investment will give it a stake in a developing market.

Both Samsbury's and Tesco are well behind Safeway owner Argyll – it formed the European Retail Alliance (ERA) with French group Casino and Dutch retailer Ahold three years ago. The ERA was later changed into Associated Marketing Services (AMS) when eight other retailers, all from different countries, joined.

The deal gained much publicity when it was drawn up, and more when Casino began stocking Safeway own-label products last year. Safeway has used the alliance to source French wines more easily. It also claims some Casino own-label products have been sold in Safeway, but only in selected stores.

However, observers question how much real benefit the deal has been to each of the players. The 20-odd Safeway. products that went into Casino stores in the south of France were introduced with great enthusiasm, but there has not been a great deal else to shout about, "says Freddie George, European food retail analyst with Paribas.

Richard Hyman, of retail specialist Verdict, agrees: "I'm beginning to wonder if these alliances are rather more lowkey than first thought," he says, referring to the experience of the Safeway/Casino/Ahold deal.

Sainsbury's is certainly used to alliances with other retailers, even foreign ones. Its DIY arm Homebase is 25 per cent owned by Belgian retailer GIB (oddly, a competitor to Delhaize, one of its new partners on the grocery side) and Savacentre was set up with the help of BhS.

But the new deal has been lauded by observers as something quite different for the number-one retailer. "I believe this represents quite a significant step for Sainsbury's," comments Paribas George

"Until six months ago it was professing no interest in the rest of Europe. This move could be the first step for it into something much bigger," he adds.

Hyman is convinced that retail collaborations, whether ownership-based or simple cooperation agreements, are on the increase. "It is fairly clear that growth opportunities in British retail are now limited. Scope for significant corporate growth has diminished even in the past year

"So retailers have two options. They can either stay in their home countries and diversify product ranges, or stick with food and extend overseas. An overseas alliance is a relatively low-risk way, to do the latter," says Hyman.

Most observers agree that there are two major areas where Sainsbury's and its three new European partners can reap benefits from their alliance, First,

they can swap intelligence on matters including computing, distribution, marketing and logistics.

This will probably be of most use to Sainsbury's foreign partners as it is generally recognised that British retailers are far ahead in terms of supply and distribution systems. However, Sainsbury's should be able to pick up operating expertise from the foreign retailers.

The second main area of shared interest is in sourcing products. Any kind of crossborder link opens up a retailer to a wealth of new product opportunities. This is particularly important at a time when consumers are becoming increasingly interested in foreign food products.

Potentially of more importance, they can use their joint buying power to cut the costs of their own-label goods. Safeway claims it has not embarked on this course at all, but analysts reckon this has to be the biggest advantage of such an alliance.

George explains: "For generic products, such as salt and sugar, the retailers can get together to negotiate much better prices than they could ever do on an individual basis.

"There is then the possibility, that

the products could be manufactured at one place in Europe, perhaps even packaged similarly, and then have an overlay added with the individual retailer's name on it."

David Stoddart, food retail analyst at Société Genérale Straüss Turnbull, agrees this is likely to be high on Sainsbury's priorities. It does not, he says, constitute a restrictive practice as the retailers do not compete against one another for the same consumers.

For Sainsbury's (and Tesco) this could be a major leap forward in the battle against discounters. If they can offer impressively reduced prices on a selection of generic products they could remove many consumers' reasons for shopping at discounters at all.

This, of course, is what Sainsbury's "Essential for theEssentials" campaign has been about, allowing products such as an own-label medium sliced loaf to be sold for 29p (Kwik Save's "No Frills" bread is priced at 25p).

The link-up with European retailers can only improve this effort, allowing Sainsbury's to compete on price with the discounters, while still providing its quality guarantee.

ISSUES

1. What is the strategic rationale for forming alliances?

2. List the key 'push' and 'pull' factors influencing retail internalisation.

3. Comment on some of the potential problems with alliances that do not involve ownership.

EXPLORATION OF ISSUES

1 The introduction of the Single European Market has fostered a surge in joint ventures among European companies, but other forms of strategic alliance have also grown dramatically in the struggle to gain competitive advantage in an increasingly global market.

Recent research on strategic alliances is dominated by joint ventures and mergers; however, there is also much to be said about marketing agreements and acquisitions when looking at corporate competitive edge.

To comprehend what strategic alliances are, we need a reasonably robust definition to encompass what has become a very broad international corporate term. Strategic alliances can be seen as hybrids, and there are five main types of intercompany agreement:

- *Mergers*: the unification of two or more organisations into one entity.
- *Acquisitions*: the purchase of one organisation by another, enabling one buyer to assume control over the other.
- *Licence agreements*: the purchase of the right to use an asset for a set time. These offer rapid access to new technology and product innovations.
- *Supplier arrangements* (of which partnering is one specific example): contracts for the sale of one firm's output to another.
- *Joint ventures*: these result in the creation of a new organisation that is formally independent of the parents; control over and responsibility for the venture varies greatly from case to case.

All these points warrant different levels of organisational commitment from the purchasing or alliance-forming organisations; for instance a merger can stretch management to the limit as it is forced to grapple with building up a new organisational structure, merging the two businesses and developing a single corporate direction and culture, to name but a few tasks. As the Single European Market becomes consolidated, so merger and acquisition activity has increased in the EU as companies position themselves to take advantage of or defend themselves against the consequences of the Single European Act.

2 Many retailers see international activity as an important part of their business, and for some, it represents a significant proportion of their total turnover. For example just over 70 per cent of the turnover of Delhaize

Table 7.1 Push and pull factors influencing retail internationalisation

Push factors	Pull factors
Economic instability	Economic stability
Low market growth	High market growth
High operating costs	Underdeveloped retail structure
Poor operating environment	Favourable operating environment
Need for economies of scale	Large market
Hostile competition	Innovative retail culture
Mature domestic market	Investment potential
Small domestic market	Niche opportunities
Format saturation	Company owned facilities/operations
Restrictive regulatory environment	Relaxed regulatory environment
Consumer credit restrictions	Positive social environment
Political instability	Political stability

le Lion, the Belgian food retailer, comes from international business, whilst for Tenglemann and Ahold the figure is between 50 per cent and 60 per cent. The reasons for internationalisation are many and varied. Some are 'push' factors, arising from conditions within the domestic marketing environment that leave the retailer little choice but to internationalise, while others are 'pull' factors – favourable conditions within foreign markets that make them attractive to the retailer. Table 7.1 summarises these push and pull factors

Retailers also form looser international alliances, based on contracts and agreements rather than on total or coownership. These are often geared towards the streamlining of purchasing and logistics rather than direct involvement or interference in each other's retailing operations.

3 There are a few potential problems with alliances that do not involve ownership. While joint buying power may bring about lower purchase prices, that power cannot be used to maximum effect unless the retailers can threaten the supplier with delisting in all the alliance members' stores. Such unanimity might be difficult to achieve. There might also be cultural differences. Products that might be popular and acceptable in one country might not be wanted in another, thus limiting the buying scope of the alliance. Finally, membership of an alliance might hinder a retailer's ability to expand into its partners' domestic markets, or eventually to take

over a partner. Nevertheless the number of such alliances is increasing, not just in food and grocery retailing, but in electrical DIY tools and toys, among many other sectors.

Retail Loyalty

KEY CONCEPTS

- Customer loyalty
- Relationship marketing
- Database marketing
- Volume segmentation
- Sales promotion

Few benefits on the cards

Loyalty schemes have now become an essential 'me-too' marketing tool, with everyone from Tesco and Sainsbury's to British Gas viewing them as the best way to keep customers faithful. But most companies fail to recognise that the costs involved could outweigh short-term advantage.

DAVID BENADY AND SEAN BRIERLEY

Loyalty is the late 20th century marketer's Holy Grail. A thing that many pursue but which few will ever find. Yet the reward for the finder is so great that there is no shortage of corporate knights willing to risk all to uncover the secret of how to keep consumers faithful.

However, there are growing signs that the knights may be looking in the wrong place. That the loyalty bubble is, if not ready to burst, certainly showing signs of deflating. And that the central plank of many loyalty schemes – the card – represents a long-term financial commitment that far outweighs any short- or long-term benefit.

The ostensible commercial logic is simple and compelling. If you get the consumer early, provide the quality of service and product they want, then you get them for life. A theory fatally flawed by growing evidence that consumers remain promiscuous and cynical about the offers – not surprising when faced with such a plethora of offers.

In the past two years the list of companies launching loyalty cards reads like a Who's Who of retailers, manufacturers and utility companies ranging from Tesco, Sainsbury's, Safeway, Budgens, and BhS, to General Motors and British Gas. Others including Marks & Spencer, Esso and Shell have been in the mar-

ket much longer.

Boots is testing a card called Advantage in East Anglia but delaying a full launch to assess the success of the Tesco and Sainsbury's ventures. Even Asda, which has resisted the temptation to launch a scheme without any apparent damage being done to its profits, is about to launch its own loyalty card and a co-branded payment card with the Midland Bank (*MW* June 28).

The grocery retailers' entry into financial loyalty is a blatant attempt to attract promiscuous customers. Many are having to improve their offers by moving into financial services to tieup consumer's cash.

Last year Procter & Gamble conducted research into retail buying habits which showed that the trend towards "repertoire" buying – buying a number of brands in the same product category, rather than a single brand – has moved into grocery retail. It could be argued that shoppers are now becoming as disloyal to the stores they shop in, as to the brands they buy.

But the theory behind loyalty cards suggests that they enable brand owners to get closer to, and better understand, their customers via the detailed information identifying shoppers and their needs. They can then be targeted with tailored promotions. But in practice this is expensive and difficult to organise.

The opportunities for retailers to use the information to target customers is enormous. They can track individual customers' buying habits and encourage them to spend more on certain lines. But this is not happening. In many cases, it has taken longer than expected to develop the necessary technology. And card issuers have yet to decide whether to motivate those who are not buying certain products to buy them, or to encourage those who are already buying to buy more.

The loyalty card is essential to the process. It provides the psychological reassurance of being tangible – something consumers can put in their wallet. But the oversupply of cards threatens to neutralise the benefit for all but a few.

From day one there has been an almost blind acceptance that loyalty equals customer retention equals cost effectiveness equals a good idea. But there is a growing sense that things are getting dangerously out of control.

"The supermarkets have rushed into these schemes without thinking through all the implications," says one marketing director, involved in a major loyalty programme. "If they start a discounting war and begin adding on costs in order to compete it will all backfire.

"I do not think that many have thought through what will happen when their competitors have the same schemes running. Everything is far too short term and tactical. Some haven't even thought through how they can quit the programme.

"Major supermarkets' loyalty card schemes are a short-term tactical gimmick, they are not part of a strategic vision. They have become too obsessed by their performance in the City rather than by thinking through how they can fully service customer needs.

"The financial (loyalty) schemes are another example of this, they have not been done because the supermarkets want to add services for customers, they are simply short-term bribes aimed at restricting consumer choice by holding their cash. It cannot last as a long-term loyalty proposition."

This assessment echoes the views of many others who see the frenetic attempts of the past two years to resolve one problem – growing competition – simply creating another, a potential financial timebomb.

Sainsbury's is said to be demanding a four per cent increase in sales from its stores to pay for the running of its Reward Card, launched three weeks ago. For Tesco, the Clubcard cost £10m to launch, with another £50m in money-off vouchers for the seven million cardholders. The chain said that the cost of launching the card would re-quire a rise in like-for-like sales of between 1.5 and two per cent, which works out at about £50m a year.

This is despite the fact that Tesco scored a notable success by being the first major supermarket to break into what David Sainsbury disparagingly called "electronic Green Shield Stamps," in February 1995. Others, later into the market, including Sainsbury's and Safeway with its Added Bonus Card, will have to pay more to catch up.

Tesco's advantage appears to have been erased. The launch of a financial services version, Clubcard Plus, was an attempt to keep ahead of the crowd. With most of the other grocery retailers launching their own schemes, Tesco's one per cent discount was not enough to keep consumers loyal. The aim now is to lock in consumer's cash as well.

But the rush into financial loyalty opens up a whole new raft of problems. What happens when they have to turn down half the applications for credit, which the banks do? What does this do for loyalty?

Many store chains also appear to be less aware of the risks associated with bad debt and fraud than the banks. Tesco carries the liability for Clubcard Plus, not its financial partner NatWest. The average high-street bank loses between £200m and £300m each year on bad debt.

Then too, the rush to get customer money also provides a longer term strategic problem. Mike Leys, director of loyalty marketing consultancy Ad'Ventures International, says: "Everybody is competing for wallet space. Storecards, budget cards, debit cards, credit cards are all in competition. It means that Mastercard is not only competing against Visa and Amex but also against Tesco's Clubcard Plus, Marks & Spencer's Charge Card, Dixons, British Gas and the bank debit cards for share of wallet space."

The consequence, says Leys, is that consumers will select a primary card for everyday use and one other card which builds in greater loyalty. The store or company offering the greatest incentive for use, which carry points and added benefits rather than simply a cheaper annual percentage rate (APR) will win out.

The main problem is that financial loyalty will go down the same route as the discount loyalty schemes, and everyone will run their own financial banking operations to lock in consumer cash. Each will offer better and better terms which again makes the process very expensive.

But as one insider says: "It's not so much a question of looking at the advantages of having a card, but looking at the disadvantages of not having one." Company finance chiefs will also have been wise to calculate the cost of getting out of a scheme both in financial and loss of loyalty terms.

"The problem is that if all of the retailers are offering cards with simple discount schemes, the stores will enter into a discount spiral," says Leys. If a card issuer offers a one per cent discount then a rival offers two per cent it will very quickly become difficult to withdraw from the market yet very expensive to stay in.

At the same time industry figures have started to question the contribution the Clubcard has made in propelling Tesco into the number one market share position in UK grocery retailing.

Sainsbury marketing director Kevin McCarten, accepting his bias, says: "Clubcard has been given a bit more credibility than it has deserved, not because we are negative about it, but most people underestimate the causes of Tesco's performance. Many factors contribute to its relative success and our relatively disappointing results. The issue is more complex. Asda has

not had a card and has done very well."

Indeed, last week Asda announced a 24 per cent increase in its annual profits to £305m. This in a year when its major rivals have all been eulogising the benefits of loyalty cards.

Archie Norman, chief executive of the chain, says: "This has been the year of the loyalty card. But we would rather give customers value for money today than the opportunity to get a one per cent discount in three months time if they spend enough.

"We believe these cards represent one of a variety of options available to market the brand. The cost effectiveness of database marketing remains unproven, although its time will come."

But some industry insiders claim that Norman is being economical with the truth and that Asda will launch its Club Card, which is now being tested in 18 stores, next month. The chain is also on the verge of signing a deal with Midland Bank for a co-branded payment card.

This discloses how Asda is being pressured into launching a card – apparently reluctantly – in an attempt to keep up with its rivals. If Asda follows the pack it will seriously undermine the chain's public view that keep-

ing prices low is better than launching a costly loyalty device.

Ironically, one advantage for the supermarkets is that by shifting shoppers' attention away from prices – the number one concern in grocery retailing in the early Nineties – they can allow prices to drift up.

As one analyst says: "Loyalty desensitises the price issue." With food price inflation at Tesco running at double the Retail Price Index, this could be the case. But the chain insists that the higher prices are made up of rapidly increasing raw material costs on paper and – oddly – potatoes.

It would be ironic if the running of a loyalty scheme were added to that list of rising raw material costs. But it is conceivable. There are undoubtedly opportunities in having your own loyalty card and access to consumer data but many companies appear to have gone down the road without investigating all the eventualities. The number of "me-too" cards make the introduction of more a waste of time.

It will only be the companies with the deepest pockets that can survive in this environment and inevitably they will have to ask themselves whether knowing that somebody buys more of brand x, over own-label y, justifies the colossal spend.

Benefit system

Fulfilment is often viewed as the unglamorous end of loyalty programmes, but there is nothing that turns off consumers more than receiving goods they deem unworthy of their hard-earned 'points'. **DAVID REED** reports

How much would it take to ensure you always buy your petrol from Shell rather than Texaco? Or do your DIY shopping at Homebase rather than B&Q? The answer might not be easy to define

purely in cash terms, but it is clear that consumers do become more loyal if given the right rewards.

Yet while customer loyalty has become the marketing paradigm of the Nineties, delivering the physical

benefits remains as grittily difficult as it was in the Eighties (and probably every other decade).

Fulfilment is the unglamorous end of the process – sheds full of products and mailsacks bulging with orders. But get it wrong and the customers who should have been filled with warm feelings about your company can end up harbouring cold resentment.

That handsome carriage clock, sent as a thank you, looks less appealing after an hour's journey to the local sorting office (because it was too large to fit through the letterbox) or when broken into pieces because the packaging was too flimsy.

Ensuring that the benefits of a loyalty scheme have the right impact should start with the selection of what is on offer. According to Barbara Barsa, vice president of Membership Rewards at American Express. "Cardholders say that what we offer is special as they perceive it as a reward. We try to keep the programme simple while offering choice – big brochures may be interest ing, but they are also confusing."

Amex has steered clear of merchandise in favour of more aspirational premiums – restaurant meals, hotel stays, free flights. It has also taken the view that these should be completely free when cardholders redeem.

"The Amex brand stands for trustworthiness and reliability. As a result, we have had very strong principles in the scheme about being up-front with customers. We try not to have conditions on rewards at all. We are keeping their status free, whereas other programmes get launched as free, then realise the level of commitment that means and move to self-liquidating," says Barsa.

How much work customers have to do to achieve rewards in a scheme is always a critical issue. Set the thresholds too low, and the client becomes over-committed while also eroding the value of the programme in influencing purchase. Set it too high and customers become disillusioned and disloyal.

Terry McCarthy, managing director of Product Plus International, notes: "Consumers always weigh up whether

or not they will be able to make enough purchases – and earn enough points – to be able to obtain the reward." He says that schemes need to recognise this in the level of redemption needed, because it also allows the different segments of the customer base to benefit.

"When it comes to selecting premium products, clients should always consider a two-tier gift structure. The first level of gifts should be set at a lower level in terms of product value and purchase requirement. Higher-value aspirational products can be aimed at higher-spending customers who recognise that they will be able to achieve these gifts by making a little extra effort," he says.

However this issue is resolved, a scheme will rapidly fail if the technology supporting it does not recognise who has genuinely achieved a reward point and who has not. (Assuming that the link has been made between purchase and benefit, which is not always the case.)

"People start with a marketing database, build in a couple of fields and call them 'points collection', and think that equals a loyalty system," says Nicholas Turner, business unit executive responsible for loyalty schemes at Acxiom. "It isn't. How do you respond, for example, to queries about points balances?"

He notes that in discussing how to build customer loyalty, many marketers overlook the fact that, to have real impact on this area of behaviour, a scheme has to become part of customer service. That means access to operators who can interrogate data and provide immediate answers.

It also means building an operational system, not a maintainance or analysis database, says Acxiom managing director Jerry Ellis. "When you are concerned with the individual – the customer – you need the characteristics in a system of reliability, 100 per cent data integrity and immediate response."

None of these can be achieved by extending the marketing database, since this is usually built on aggregate data where accuracy is not paramount and processing does not have to be immediate, or by working on an existing operational system.

"Marketers say you don't need two systems because the data is all there already. But when you push the button to respond to a customer query, it locks out your operational access for five minutes," he warns.

One of the mistakes being made by companies entering the loyalty programme arena is to avoid duplicating systems and data. Ellis believes some marketers even view this as in some way wrong, preferring to keep one integral database. But the varying needs of each part of the business prevent such an approach being effective. And if the technology does not allow the company to answer customer queries about their status in a scheme, then it is certainly not helping to build loyalty.

The sheer volume of data which gets amassed in loyalty schemes can bring the best-laid plans to their knees if consideration has not been given to what to do with the information. "The tendency is to ignore what needs to be done to run a scheme and the amount of information that is collected," says John Merry, development director of The Database Group.

"If you have 10,000 customers a week, that seems like 10,000 records. But if they each buy 40 items at different prices every week, you get phenomenal amounts of data that you can't deal with," he says.

Decisions need to be made at the outset about the level of detail needed and whether information can be aggregated.

Does a retailer need to know if a customer bought a carrot or a potato, for example, or is the point of interest that a purchase was made in the grocery department? "You have to pre-screen rather than take everything and sort it out later, because you will come unstuck later," says Merry.

If the right type of benefits have been chosen and the right technology put in place to run a scheme, then all that is left is to fulfil redemption orders. But it is here that some of the worst difficulties can arise. One of the perennial problems for promotional handling houses is stock levels.

"Because of cost, they are always kept to a minimum. Beforehand you have to guess at redemption levels per item, but consumers are very fickle. It often doesn't run to expectations," says Jan Morris, managing director of Mail Marketing (Scotland).

This fear of being left with overstock, with its attendant problems of storage and disposal costs, often leads to understocking.

What then happens is that items run out and delay letters have to be sent out. With delivery times on many premiums running into weeks, or even months, this turns a reward into a broken promise. Even if sufficient stock has been ordered in good time, problems await the unwary client.

"Packaging is difficult. Handling houses are often pressed into costing it out before they have seen an item, even buying packaging before the items arrive because orders are coming in," says Morris.

Some problems can be easily avoided by asking obvious questions – if a product is to be fulfilled in units of four, the premium supplier can ship them to the handling house pre-packed in those numbers. But if it is not asked, it may deliver them in packs of six or 12, requiring costly repackaging.

There are few problems in running loyalty schemes that cannot be resolved and that have not been encountered before.

The difficulties tend to arise when advice is not sought from those who have already had experience, especially technology and handling suppliers. As long as loyalty remains at the top of the agenda, the risk will be high that well-laid plans will founder for lack of a small amount of consultancy. As one supplier warns, running loyalty programmes is like "walking on quicksand".

This year's model

A new study splits consumers into four groups – switchers, habituals, variety seekers and loyals – creating the 'Diamond of Loyalty', a model to determine and, more importantly, influence customer behaviour. **DAVID LAZARUS** explains.

There can be little doubt in the minds of most marketers that the focus for the Nineties is on customer loyalty. Much is written about defining loyalty and devising schemes to encourage it. Less, perhaps, has been available on how to uncover just how many buyers of a product or brand can really be described as loyal, or how others, who may not yet fit into this category, can genuinely be motivated to change their purchasing behaviour.

Fingerhut Associates has uncovered some interesting research from the Cranfield School of Management, which is now making this analysis easier and so has practical implications for brand managers in the development and management of their brands.

Few would disagree that, tradition-ally, retailers have worked with manufacturers to market their products to the consumer. More recently, however, the retailer has begun to force the manufacturer to accede more to the retailer's requirements in return for the lead to the consumer. This has meant that brand issues and relationship marketing which go beyond the store interface need to be developed, so the brand manufacturer can reform relationships with the consumer, while still ensuring that they work in partnership with the multiples.

Marketers have long been familiar with the "ladder of loyalty" concept, climbing from trial, through repeat purchasing, to brand loyalty.

However, through its research, Cranfield has developed a model to "emotionalise" the relationship between consumer and brand in order to answer the key question of how to categorise brand loyalty. The result is the "Diamond of Loyalty".

This outlines the relationships between consumers and the brands they purchase in a matrix describing the type of products they buy against the association of each of the four groups by marrying attitude and behaviour.

• Switchers have a high purchasing repertoire but low involvement with an individual brand. They purchase the type of product frequently but are not loyal to any particular brand and are generally highly influenced by price.
• Habituals have low involvement and a narrow purchasing repertoire. They purchase a particular product or

brand out of habit and may switch if their interest is aroused.

• Variety seekers love the product and probably buy a lot of it, but are not committed to only one particular brand, preferring to vary their choice.

• Finally, the truly loyal consumers have a narrow purchasing repertoire from a particular category and a high involvement with that individual brand.

Cranfield is extending this research to uncover which outside influences and techniques can be used to change the buying patterns of consumers displaying these purchasing styles. It argues that more research is needed by most manufacturers to establish just where their brand equity lies within the Diamond of Loyalty. This could be used to establish market share of loyals, variety seekers and so on. It would form the basis for setting market share targets based on loyalty types rather than aggregate sales.

Dr Simon Knox, head of the Institute for Advanced Research in Marketing at Cranfield, comments: "Across product categories, the composition of loyals, variety seekers and so on will vary, since the purchasing behaviour of an individual is likely to vary category by category.

"For instance, in the cereal market there are a large number of variety seekers, while newspapers are bought primarily as a loyal purchase. It remains an open question whether or not the deep price cuts that newspaper proprietors are currently engaged in is

an appropriate strategy for developing 'loyals' or encouraging 'swit-chers'. There may be more effective marketing strategies which could be deployed to build market share cost effectively, particularly among habitual newspaper purchasers. For instance, widening distribution channels and sampling points in city centres and on commuting trains could be more cost-effective in the long run."

Therefore, to use the diamond to improve loyalty for a brand, it is essential that manufacturers look at their own brands and determine what the profile of its loyalty diamond looks like, and then to contrast this with the loyalty diamond for its competitors.

This is a vital role that can be played by the promotional marketing consultancy. By taking a step back from the brief to consider the strategy and background of brands, it is often possible to develop strategies which indicate that a totally different approach is warranted.

Cranfield has been using this model to develop appropriate strategies for clients' brand marketing. Once the initial concept has been grasped, clients will be keen to look at the wider implications of brand relationships with consumers, and formulate a strategy which creates changes in brand purchasing behaviour, reducing switching.

In a recent study for a wine retailer with a chain of stores in the London area, the management was keen to explore the extent of portfolio purchasing of its customers.

The results showed that both

switchers and habituals – all low involvement customers – make up about half the customers but contribute under a third of in-store expenditure.

More interestingly, from a management point of view, was the retailer's remaining customer base, which made up two-thirds of all store purchases. These were loyals and variety seekers, with both groups expressing a real interest in the brands of wine they buy, whether proprietary or from the store's own-label selection.

Since both loyals and variety seekers have a real interest in the purchasing process, but seek different purchasing outcomes, management can develop separate point of-sale material and promotional schemes that capture the imagination of both groups. By aiming to increase frequency of purchase of loyals, and portfolio purchasing of variety seekers, using differential sales promotion techniques, cost efficiencies and selective market share gains across priority customer types can be achieved.

Cranfield's research has already involved a number of companies in the packaged goods and retail sectors. Together with Fingerhut Associates, the University is seeking new partners to extend the project and establish a research programme.

Certainly, the results produced so far have proved very exciting and, with the extension that would come with the next stages of the project, current thinking on patterns of consumer loyalty will be significantly extended.

ISSUES

1 What is 'loyalty'?

2 What are the advantages and disadvantages of loyalty schemes for customers and marketers?

3 What is the relevance of 'volume segmentation' in the operation of loyalty schemes?

EXPLORATION OF ISSUES

1 Loyalty should go beyond regular purchasing. Dick and Basu 1994, in their conceptualisation of the loyalty phenomenon, argue that 'relative attitudes' are also important. That is, loyalty depends not only on a positive attitude towards the store or brand, but on differentiated attitudes towards the alternatives. In other words if a consumer is positive about store A but not very positiveabout stores B and C, then the consumer might indeed develop loyalty towards A. On the other hand, if there are fairly similar positive attitudes towards A, B and C there is unlikely to be real loyalty. In this case the consumer might patronise a particular store regularly due to factors such as convenience and familiarity rather than commitment.

This analysis is useful because it explains why apparent loyalty (at least regular patronage) might not be true loyalty. It also contributes to our understanding of why some consumers exhibit aspects of real loyalty without having a particularly strong positive attitude towards a certain store. In the latter case the argument would be that a positive but weak attitude towards A might be accentuated by an even weaker attitude towards B and C.

Dick and Basu describe a situation in which relative attitude is low (little to choose between the alternatives) but is also characterised by high store patronage – they describe this as 'spurious loyalty' (Table 7.2). Alternatively, where there is low patronage but a strongly differentiated and positive attitude towards A, this is 'latent loyalty'. Expected high patronage in this case might be inhibited by coshoppers' preferences, for example.

When it comes to real loyalty, Dick and Basu see this as where there is both high patronage and a positive attitude towards the store that is not matched by a similarly

Table 7.2   Dick and Basu Loyalty Model

Repeat patronage

	High ⟷ Low	
High Relative attitude **Low**	Loyalty	Latent loyalty
	Spurious loyalty	No loyalty

Source: Dick and Basu (1994).

positive attitude towards alternative stores.

Some consumers are loyal because they deliberately choose one brand over another and continue to purchase that brand over time. The loyalty scheme not only has the potential to attract customers but also to retain them, and if this potential is realised, theloyalty scheme can become a significant part of traditional sales promotion discounting approaches. For example, in addition to consumers benefiting from cheaper shopping (in the sense of 'customer-specific pricing' rather than scatter gun discounts), they can also provide the retailer with a great deal of information about individual customers. This information can be used to extend tempting offers via direct marketing mechanisms, at point of sale or direct to the household.

This will be reinforced by linking it to customer data from a variety of sources, known as data matching. The ability to put names, addresses, purchasing habits and lifestyles all together on one record allows companies to build up a picture of someone's life. The retailer can match this data to credit history, actual purchasing behaviour, media response and the recency, frequency and monetary (RFM) value of purchases.

Loyalty scheme data, then, can be combined with a variety of data from a large number of sources, including geodemographic and life style databases. The next phase of this development involves the use of 'smart' cards, upon which can be stored vast amounts of cardholder information, ranging from age and date of birth to previous purchases and medical records.

2 Most retail loyalty schemes operate on the basis of customers receiving discounts in exchange for spending. Thus the first advantage to customers is cheaper shopping. There are variations in the way schemes provide this: some offer a percentage off at the time of purchase, others involve the accumulation of points until the customer reaches a certain threshold, whereupon discounts are triggered or money-off coupons mailed out.

Because retailers have access to their customers' actual purchasing records, another advantage to customers is that retailers can make more relevant offers – not generalised money-off coupons but coupons for products the customer is more likely to want.

On the other side of the coin, though, if customers have to spend relatively large sums to reach the threshold level, and even if spending is constantly discounted without an accumulated target being required, they might think that although a, say, 1 per cent discount is better than nothing, it isn't much. They may wonder why prices are not lower in the first place.

Another possible concern for some customers is the need for retailers knowing too much about them – their demographics, purchasing behaviour and so on information that is crucial to individualised targeting. Many people are not bothered about retailers knowing what they buy or who they are. Others are growing concerned about invasion of personal privacy. For example women who live on their own may not want anyone to know about this for reasons of personal security. There has been a reduction in trust of large corporations over recent decades – perhaps not rapid or dramatic, but significant. The more people within a corporation who have access to personal data, the greater the concern about individual privacy. The issue is not only that others know who we are and where we live, but also that we have just bought an expensive sound system or mountain bike. Indeed we don't even know whether that and other

personal data is being sold on to others – unknown others at that!

Marketers gain from knowledge of their customers. Such knowledge used to be the norm, decades ago, when the corner shopkeeper not only knew his or her customers by name, but also what they liked and disliked. As time went on a distance emerged between retailer and customer as self-service took the place of more personal contact. Now that we have the technology to record individual purchases against names and addresses via scanners and databases, it is again possible to discover what different people want and don't want. Much is made of this data when deciding on stocking policies at branch level and in targeting different segments with, for example, different store magazines. Some of these magazines are themselves based on analysis of transaction data to produce segmentation models, such as tailored versions of the family life cycle. Targeting can be via the post or at the checkout. Marketers are also able to share scanning data with manufacturers. This was unheard of several years ago, but now, with the introduction of category management retailers and manufacturers are beginning to cooperate more closely.

'Loyalty' has been heralded as something of a holy grail by marketers. One cautionary note, however, is that many of the schemes introduced to date are really no more than sophisticated sales promotion schemes. If customers hold multiple cards and shop at a number of stores– and take advantage of the discounts offered – then such promiscuous shopping is not creating real loyalty.

3 Volume segmentation is based on the premise of differentially targeting customers according to their levels of buying and their relative contribution to sales and profit. The loyalty concept has provoked much research and debate in this area in recent years, and a fairly widespread view is that a relatively small proportion of customers contribute the lion's share of company sales and profit. What the loyalty scheme is beginning to do is to identify the top X per cent of spenders and target these with particularly beneficial and attractive offers, thus rewarding the most loyal customers. Clearly, a counterargument here is that this is akin to 'preaching to the converted' – they are already loyal.

Another related issue is the cost of attracting new customers as opposed to keeping existing ones. The latter is substantially cheaper than the former, and this is another reason why organisations are heavily targeting regular, high-spending customers.

8 Marketing Communications

Selling

- 'The officeless office'
- 'Mobile communications' marketers
- Mobile salesforces

Homing in on the mobile

In the era of 'mobile communications', offices may become a thing of the past with users able to access databases, read e-mail and send or receive information at the touch of a PC button.

MARTIN CROFT

Ten years ago the buzz-phrase in information technology circles was "the paperless office". Now, it's the "officeless office".

The marketers of hi-tech electronic equipment are trying to convince us that soon we will be able to do away with four walls, a desk, a secretary, a dying pot plant and a coffee machine, and carry everything we need with us – just sling the computer with fax modem, cellular phone and slimline printer into the boot of the car and, hey presto, a portable office.

A BT survey published earlier this year concluded there are some 7.5 million "mobile people" in the UK. Of these, BT estimates that 2 million are teleworkers who have an office but work from home at least part of the time; 600,000 are one-man bands, or

small office home office (Soho) users; 1.7 million are "managers on the move"; and 3.3 million are field workers. It is these last two sectors that are the prime targets for the "mobile communications" marketers.

It is already possible to buy miniaturised versions of just about every piece of office equipment. The stumbling block, as ever, is price. The smaller and easier to carry a PC is, the heavier the price tag. But for most mobile communications applications, you don't need all the equipment you would expect to find in an average office. Often, all you want is a notebook computer.

A large number of companies have already equipped their mobile salesforces with notebook PCs that can be used to collect data. Insurance sales-

men, for example, often carry PCs with them: some go so far as to have special carrying cases with a small portable printer, since it is better to leave a prospect with printed policy details rather than posting them to arrive a few days later – the more time targets are given to change their minds, the more likely it is that they will.

Portable PCs are also useful for salesforces dealing with large ranges of stock items. The company's product catalogue can easily be loaded on to the computer so that individual items can be found quickly.

Another advantage of using portable PCs, of course, is that the information collected by the salesforce can be quickly and efficiently downloaded to the company's mainframe or minicomputer, without the time-consuming and error-creating business of having often illegible notes transcribed.

Nor is it necessary to wait until the end of the day, or the end of the week, to collate the salesforce's data: if the computers are linked together, the information can be transmitted to "base" using a mobile phone and GSM technology while the salesperson is still in the field.

Of course it has been possible to transmit information over conventional phone lines for many years, and doing so is still cheaper than using a cellular phone, although less convenient. At least, nowadays, most phones use a simple jack connection which the computer can be plugged into: downloading data over the phone ten years ago required an acoustic coupler, a large and somewhat clumsy device that fits over the handset of a phone.

One of the biggest users of portable PCs is BT. In March, its National Business Communications division signed up to buy 1,000 Apple PowerBooks for its Business Intelligence Toolkit for Sales project.

The BITS project relates to the increased need of the division's sales force to remotely access up-to-date corporate sales and account information and to provide a two-way communications link between head office and the mobile salesforce, BT says.

Frazer Hamilton, head of operations at National Business Communications, says: "Our main objective for the project is to keep the salesforce fully informed, remotely, with up-to-date critical information. It is of great benefit in terms of client service to BT's customers.

"The business justification for BITS was a direct payback through the improved efficiency and use of sales time, and the consequent increase in sales and reduction in costs. However, early analysis has revealed the intangible benefits of easier working methods and sales staff performing better in front of customers."

Sales information is downloaded from a relational database on the corporate VAX minicomputer to the sales staff's PowerBooks. The portable computers can be used to manage everything from billing and quote generation to sales forecasting. The information the salesforce collects is fed back to and reconciled with BT's corporate database automatically, whenever the user links up, even if it is only to check e-mail messages.

At the moment, the system uses modems and the public telephone network, but Apple has recently launched a GSM Connection Kit for the PowerBook, so it could just as easily be used over a cellular network.

Kevin Chapman, mobile solutions marketing manager for Apple UK, says the company sees the "professional manager on the move" as a major market for PowerBooks. "It's great to be able to go out on the road and show clients what you can do."

In fact, Apple and BT have formed a partnership to sell mobile data systems to customers. The BITS project, while obviously of benefit to BT itself, is also a demonstration to potential users of what the system can offer.

BT is not solely linked into Apple, however. Indeed, in August it placed what is believed to be the largest single order for IBM-compatible PCs, when it awarded Toshiba a £30m contract to supply an estimated 22,000 notebook computers – 70 per cent of BT's total notebook PC requirement – over the next three years.

According to Murray McKerlie, product marketing manager for notebook PCs at Toshiba, the BT order is intended mostly for the telecoms giant's engineers, who need to have constant access to the company's technical database.

McKerlie says Toshiba practises what it is trying to sell to its customers: "Our sales guys all run around with portable PCs. When they are out of the office, they can just set themselves up at home, or at a desk in a dealer-

ship. They can read their e-mail, or find out stock availability. Some of them don't even have to use phone lines, because they have built-in GSM adapters.

The Toshiba order from BT highlights the increasing blurring of the lines between "mobile communications" and plain computing. Most portable computers on the market offer users a certain level of communications ability, whether they will be using it or not.

The reason for this is simple – it's good marketing.

Basic desktop computers have become almost a commodity item so to preserve margins, computer manufacturers have to add features that customers will be prepared to pay more for. Portability is just such a feature.

To an extent, however, portability itself has become an expected part of many PCs. While some BT staff will undoubtedly be using the communications ability of the Toshiba notebooks, many will not. Rather, as with so many large organisations, it has become the norm for mid- and senior-level management to be issued with notebook PCs (and in some cases PowerBooks) for general office tasks.

Indeed, some computer companies have recognised the dual roles their products are often being asked to fill, and have created "docking systems" which allow notebooks to slot into larger desktop systems. In the office during the day, these systems look and perform just like desktop PCs with standard screens and links to printers, local area networks and so on. Come knocking off time, all the user has to do is pull the keyboard out of the system and it is transformed into a notebook PC.

While notebooks and laptops are being used to keep in contact with field salesforces, the vast majority of portable computers are being used for fairly basic office paperwork functions. Surveys show that portable computers are used at least half the time to perform general office administration tasks.

If notebooks are in danger of becoming as much commodity items as the desktop PC, the manufacturers have to come up with something else to preserve their margins. Hence the launch of the PDA – the Personal Digital Assistant – or handheld computer spurred on, in part, by the success of the Psion Organiser.

The Psion Organiser is itself used for many mobile salesforce tasks, with a variety of organisations loading catalogues and stock lists onto the system's cartridges.

But while the computing power of the Psion is not to be sniffed at, the size of its keyboard and screen somewhat limit its uses. Hence the launch of PDA systems such as the Apple Newton or, more recently, the Sharp Zaurus, which feature interfaces based on writing by hand on their screens, as well as the more traditional keyboard commands.

The Zaurus ZR-5000, launched in September, fits into a jacket pocket, Sharp claims, and yet still allows users to send and receive e-mails, send faxes using cellular or regular phones, access on-line bulletin boards and exchange information with local and remote PCs.

Rosemary Eccles, Soho marketing controller at Sharp, says: "With the increase in the number of mobile professionals, ease of communications and productivity out of the office are both very important."

Over the next few years, we are likely to see a number of smaller systems from competing computer manufacturers: the real limits on the size of computers, after all, depend on the uses to which they will be put, and tend to revolve around the size of the keyboard and screen. If these are not important, there is no reason why a computer the size of a calculator could not be developed.

Notebook computers, however, will continue to be made because there will still be the need for them, just as desktop PCs have not – yet – been superseded by notebooks.

ISSUES

1. **Discuss the implicit advantages of mobile salesforces and sales automation tools.**

2. **How would you assess the small office/home office (SOHO) trend, and what advice would you give to a company wanting to target this market?**

3. **Since we are truly in a digital era, define some new rules of selling.**

EXPLORATION OF ISSUES

1. A large number of companies have already equipped their salesforces with notebook PCs that can be used to collect data. Portable PCs are also useful for salesforces dealing with a large range of stock items. The company's product catalogue can easily be loaded onto the computer so that individual items can be found quickly. Another advantage of using portable PCs, of course, is that the information collected by the salesforce can be quickly and efficiently downloaded to the company's mainframe or minicomputer, without the time-consuming and error-creating business of transcribing often illegible notes.

Nor is it necessary to wait until the end of the day or the end of the week to collate the salesforce's data: if the computers are linked together, the information can be transmitted to 'base' using a mobile phone and GSM technology while the salesperson is still in the field.

There is an increased need for a company's salesforce in the field to access up-to-date corporate sales and account information and for there to be a two-way communications link between head office and the mobile salesforce. One main objective is to keep the salesforce fully informed, remotely, with up-to-date critical information. It is of great benefit to them in terms of service to customers.

The business justification is a direct payback through improved efficiency and use of sales time, and the consequent increase in sales and reduction in costs. There are also the intangible benefits of easier working methods and sales staff performing better in front of customers.

Sales information can be downloaded from a relational database on the corporate VAX minicomputer to the sales staff's powerbooks. The portable computers can be used to manage everything from billing and quote generation to sales forecasting. The information the salesforce collects is fed back to and automatically reconciled with the corporate database. Some computer organisers are used for mobile salesforce tasks, with a variety of organisations loading catalogues and stock lists onto the system's cartridges.

2 The late 1990s will be the age of the home user, with companies targeting a new market known as SOHO (small office/home office). Business-to-business marketers are battling for their share of the burgeoning SOHO market, a market where product functionality, reliability and immediate post-sales service are usually much more important than in large office settings. SOHO buyers can easily become a nightmare, but the SOHO market is the hottest business market of the day. Many savvy business marketers are cashing in and building profitable long-term business relationships in the SOHO segment. The best option is marketing to the SOHO market's unique needs:

- Recognise that relationship building and the long-term value of the customer define SOHO segment profitability.

- Design, upgrade and promote products to emphasise functional benefits and reliability, not glitz and technical virtuosity.
- Develop appropriate SOHO distribution.
- New channel structures are evolving as SOHO expands, so treat SOHO leads seriously.
- Maintain low-cost contact with your market, such as through newsletters, occasional mailings and trade show invitations to keep the relationship warm between buying cycles.
- SOHO buyers want companies that treat them well. Your promotion and direct selling should avoid the extremes of technobabble and consumer drivel.
- SOHO buyers are business people with serious needs. Put fast, efficient field service in place before you ship the product.

3 Interactive techniques in the digital era are levelling the playing field, changing customer expectations and modifying the rules of personal selling.

- Customers are better informed.
- Better qualified prospects are more likely to purchase.
- Salesperson can spend more time selling.
- Interactive techniques enable sales 'Davids' to compete with the 'Goliaths'.

On-line transactions:

- Interaction.
- Dialogue: real-time discussions.
- Research: decision making, information gathering.
- Service: information dissemination and discussion.
- Support.
- Lead acquisition.
- Sales/ordering.

Advertising: Fear Appeals

KEY CONCEPTS

- Shock ads
- Social responsibility
- Contemporary advertising

Why shock ads have their place

Are shock tactics in advertising a breach of social responsibility, or an exercise in freedom of speech? John Shannon believes that, handled correctly, they play an important role in ad culture. **JOHN SHANNON** is president of Grey International.

In the past few months, Calvin Klein's advertising has divided the industry between those who see the work as child pornography and those who interpret it as a legitimate attempt to grab headlines, while reinforcing the brand's contemporary appeal.

Whatever one's personal view of some of the images, commentators have raised important and sometimes complex questions about the nature of advertising shock tactics.

Given the level of concern that this campaign has caused, it is worth reminding ourselves that advertising that shocks is not a new phenomenon. Indeed, it can only be evaluated and judged within the context of its time, market and the social priorities of the country in which it runs.

If we look back to the Seventies, Saatchi & Saatchi's pregnant man image was deemed to be deeply shocking and provoked a storm of hostility. Today, it is regarded as powerful advertising that few would find unacceptable.

Equally, advertising that shocks one nation might pass unnoticed in another. The sort of sexual imagery that is commonplace in French advertising would cause a flood of protest in the UK or the United States. Yet the French tend to be more sensitive to any hint of child exploitation than, say, the Germans.

Turning to social priorities, in New York, where the public debate about street crime is at an all-time high, the recent Levi's "Nice Pants" poster campaign for Dockers jeans, which featured the actual product, was accused of inciting theft. When a similar technique was used by Levi's in the UK, it was generally well received.

One has only to look through the letters pages of the advertising press to see how difficult it is to discuss issues such as these without stirring up deep-rooted emotions.

It is important to remember, however, that advertisers enjoy the same right to freedom of speech as ordinary citizens. It is equally important that advertisers, like everybody else, accept the social responsibility and legal restrictions that this right implies.

But any decision to censor or ban their work should be taken after rational evaluation of content and context, not on the basis of subjective emotional reaction.

ISSUES

(1) Comment on the question of social responsibility in advertising.

(2) What are your views on Benetton's controversial advertising campaigns?

(3) Discuss the use of fear appeals in advertising.

EXPLORATION OF ISSUES

(1) Advertisers and their agencies must make sure that their 'creative' advertising does not overstep social and legal norms. Most marketers work hard at communicating openly and honestly with consumers, but abuses do occur and public policy makers have developed a substantial body of laws and regulations to govern advertising. For example companies must avoid false or deceptive advertising; advertisers must not make false claims and they must avoid false demonstrations.

It is also illegal to issue advertisements that have the capacity to deceive, even though no-one may actually be deceived. The problem is how to tell the difference between deception and 'puffery' – simple, acceptable exaggerations that are not intended to be believed.

To be socially responsible, advertisers must be careful not to offend any ethnic groups, racial minorities or special interest groups. Some companies have built advertising campaigns on a platform of social responsibility, for example the Body Shop. Another company that purports to do so is the Benetton Group, the Italian manufacturer and retailer of stylish apparel.

(2) Benetton's controversial billboard and print advertisements featured a number of dramatic photos: a dying AIDS patient with the words 'HIV Positive' stamped on his body, a Mafia hit victim with a relative's face reflected in a pool of blood and a blood-soaked uniform of a soldier in former Yugoslavia. The only copy in each advertisement was enclosed in a tiny box and read simply 'United Colors of Benetton'. Oliviero Toscani, the company's in-house creative director and photographer for the advertising campaign, has said that the point of the campaign was to raise social awareness, and that 'everyone uses emotion to sell a product. We want to show . . . human realities that we are aware of'.

However well-intentioned and attention grabbing the Benetton advertisements were, they received more condemnation than praise. In 1995 a German court ruled that three images used in the Benetton campaign, including that of child labour in Latin America, were exploitative and illegal. The German court's decision followed an earlier ruling on the 'HIV Positive' advertisement, when a French court ordered Benetton to pay $32 000 in damages to French people infected with that virus.

(3) Fear appeals in advertising use a heavily negative emotional beginning and have an emotional focus. The effect of fear (a negative emotion) is to distract an individual from mounting rational counter-arguments. The overall finding from many years of research on fear appeals is that the higher the fear level, the more difficult it is for the core brand image to be maintained.

Ethical Issues in Public Relations

KEY CONCEPTS

- Public relations
- Ethics
- Opinion formers

A question of wealth interest

The cash-for-questions inquiry has uncovered a level of sleaze that in some areas of business would be considered entirely respectable activity.

GEORGE PITCHER

Has anyone else noticed that the alleged going rate for asking a question in the Commons – £2,000 – is exactly the same as is required to pay off a prostitute, whom a sometime parliamentarian has never met, at a London railway station?

Which activity, I wonder, is more sleazy? The motives behind the two actions are probably interchangeable. Asking parliamentary questions in exchange for cash is, it can be argued, a form of prostitution, while giving money to a commercial lady one has not slept with might amount to a conflict of interest (think about it).

But it is important that we distinguish between different forms of sleaze because – unlike the examples I have so far cited – some are considered respectable and some not. Indeed, in some areas of commercial practice there are sleazy activities that are central to the conduct of what is considered entirely respectable business.

This is especially true in marketing functions. So we had better know what we condemn and what we endorse. And, if you will allow me to take some low moral ground, we had better know

which is which before we condemn wretched MPs caught by the wrath of a spurned Mohamed al-Fayed. In short, we might remove the payola plank from marketing's eye before we point to the mote in the political eye.

Let's cite some examples of sleaze from what we can broadly call the media and corporate hospitality industries, and ask whether we can reasonably be in the business of casting the first stones at politicians.

When The Guardian's story of cash-for-questions – not to mention visits to well-appointed Parisian hotels – broke there was understandable haste among MPs to register any interest they could remember. Clare Short even registered a small rug – not, I imagine, without a degree of irony.

The media were quick to record the stampede, as well they might be. But note a quieter, more orderly stampede – a corral as it were – in some corners of the media, particularly among the press. Wide-eyed recollections appear of some hospitality that al-Fayed had provided, and a declaration of terror by writers that they could have been so dangerously close to the manipulative publicity machine.

It usually appears as a "diary" piece under a self-mocking headline such as The Day I Got Taken By Fayed. There follows a whimsical piece about the extension of some lavish hospitality, that runs something like this: "I have no idea why I was asked/presumed it was a private invitation/was tempted to take along a big basket/pantechnicon/I didn't like the hideous silk ties/I didn't even use the mini-bar, ha, ha."

The real purpose of such pieces is, as with panicked MPs, to declare the piffling little interest so that they can get back to the business of the day, which might include investigating the hospitality extended to MPs.

This syndrome would amount to little more than a discourtesy to the host – honourable enough in journalistic terms – were it not to draw attention to the wider issue of corporate hospitality.

I remember, in 1987, being flown around the capitalist world for a week as part of a press and City corps inspection of Allied-Lyons' global installations. The Independent's noble correspondent was with us. He was the only hack whose paper was paying his way. The Independent has a policy of not accepting freebies, insisting on travelling steerage, and so on.

This latter austerity proved tricky in this instance. We were flying Concorde, chartered for the week. The cost of the trip, it was explained, would be more than covered by a 2p or 3p rise in the share price that would result from the consequent press and City research coverage. In fact the price fell away because the cream of British brewery analysis was out of the country all week, getting drunk.

But there was copious coverage of Allied-Lyons in the British press. I produced not a word. I would like to suggest that this was because I was so high-minded as to be appalled by this lineage-for-largesse arrangement. In fact, the reason was that the daily mob had filed so much there was nothing left for the Sunday paper I worked for.

And therein lies the point. Journalists – and to some degree the City analysts – were not producing material on Allied-Lyons through deference to their hosts, but rather because they were under pressure

from colleagues and bosses at home. If you're flying around the world on luxury aeroplanes, staying in five-star hotels – the argument goes – you can bloody well produce some work. It's peer pressure, not PR pressure.

Having said that, I have no idea what was spent on us on that trip. But I bet it was more than £2,000 a head. What price tame questions in the Commons, compared with tame questions at a press conference?

Now, there will be those who claim that there is no comparison to be made. MPs, after all, are elected, and we are entitled to trust that they are independent of commercial pressure in the representation of their constituents' interests.

Journalists and City analysts, by contrast, are not elected. But this line of reasoning would work rather better if journalists were not quite so fond of claiming independence from commercial interest. And, for that matter, if City analysts were not forever claiming that their share recommendations are entirely independent of their own

firms' corporate finance and fund management positions. Again, what price sleaze?

The fashion, travel and catering industries invest considerable marketing effort in promoting the idea that hospitality will be rewarded with a puff. And, while I'm at it, not a few senior journalists over the years have had their noses in the trough at the Ritz in Paris. We know where you live.

I am not necessarily suggesting that the media should declare its interests. Nor that marketing directors should reveal in the annual report when an advertising agency has entertained them at Wimbledon or Glyndebourne. Nor am I suggesting that sleaze is so widespread that it excuses the commercial enthusiasms of MPs. All I suggest is that we maintain a degree of perspective as we go after them.

One final thought on the Fayeds. Isn't it fortunate that House of Fraser was successfully floated off from Harrods before this business blew up? Never let facts spoil a good story.

ISSUES

1 **What is the conceptual underpinning for the targeting of politicians and journalists?**

2 **What ethical issues are involved?**

3 **How are PR activities measured and evaluated?**

EXPLORATION OF ISSUES

1 A major factor in speeding up the diffusion process is the use of opinion formers, and this applies regardless of organisational size. Politicians are often targeted in a sophisticated way – specialist PR lobbying agencies compile lists of all MPs and their interests, political and non-

political. An example was the campaign on behalf of the music industry to put a levy on blank tapes to allow for extra payments to artists and music companies to counteract the home recording of borrowed music onto blank tapes. MPs with an interest in music were selected – not cabinet ministers. The reason for this was that the former were more likely to have credibility in terms of music, and were therefore selected as opinion formers. The audio tape industry countered with a similar campaign to maintain the *status quo* (not the band!)

The same model is used in other markets – the multistep flow of communication model. In connection with the pharmaceutical market, for example, the approach was described by Rawlins (1984) in *The Lancet* in somewhat critical terms. He described how medics were being targeted by the pharmaceutical industry and classified as either conservatives or risk takers. Sales representatives were able to identify the more innovative medics by discussing prescribing habits with local pharmacists. This information was used to target the more innovative when a new drug was being launched. The opinion formers were then invited to various 'events', seminars, lunches and so on. The result was that a substantial proportion of these opinion formers started to prescribe the new drug. Their behaviour was observed by the less innovative and emulated, thus demonstrating the two-step flow of communication, the first step being to target opinion formers and the second step being the social communication from opinion formers to followers.

Similar methods are employed in the motor market, where PR people possess databases on motoring correspondents and categorise them in terms of credibility with the consumer. Some PR people recognise a pecking order among journalists, for example they may have a list of 1700 motoring journalists but select 600 of the 'top' journalists for some events and just six for other events. In 1996 selected journalists were taken to South Africa for the Nissan Primeria launch, where they road tested the new car, enjoyed the sunshine, food and hospitality and were given a 'press release'. The latter was not merely a list of technical specifications but was full of favourable adjectives – to what extent did these reappear in the 'road reports'?

2 With regard to ethical issues journalists probably rarely plagiarise press releases but some of the adjectives used in the releases may well appear in their reports. Having said this, there is clear evidence that press releases may be closely reproduced in the regional press, even 'scanned-in' as sent by the press office. The consumer will view these 'reports' as coming from a totally objective and independent source. The editor of one car magazine has admitted that advertisers put pressure on editors to do this. If a particularly discreditable report is published the advertiser may inform the editor that they

will advertise elsewhere for a while. Because magazines do not make their profits from the cover price, but from advertising revenue, the pressure can be very real.

Returning to the pharmaceutical market, Rawlins (1984) was critical of the industry for its approach and even lays a charge of possible corruption at the door of some medics in that they might have expected rewards in return for what might sometimes have been needless prescribing. To take this further, some years ago the anti-rheumatoid arthritis drug 'Flosint' was launched. The launch was based on selected medics being taken to Switzerland for a weekend 'conference', with plenty of food and drink and an all-expenses-paid trip on the Orient Express. Many returned to prescribe Flosint and they were copied by the followers, hence the approach was clearly effective in speeding up the diffusion rate. The final twist to this particular story was that within a few months of its launch Flosint was associated with several deaths and it was banned.

Budd (1997) argues that 'the truth becomes immaterial to the role of PR' and that the industry's 'adjustments' of the facts, coupled with the 'shredded credibility' of the media, merely reinforces the image-fixing stereotype of PR. The founding father of the PRNA believes that 'if we can raise the ethical standards of the profession it might help to improve corporate behaviour' (Manners, 1994).

On 24 August 1995 *The Times* was issued free, subsidised by Microsoft as part of its launch of Windows 95. Needless to say there were many Microsoft-originated reviews of the product and several pages of Microsoft-originated publicity material. The objectivity of reporting under such circumstances is highly questionable.

The question of 'freebies' has recently been tackled by the Inland Revenue, which requires, under self-assessment, journalists to declare the value of such benefits. According to one tax advisor, 'many companies and journalists are becoming extremely worried about exactly how these new rules will operate in practice' (Ferrar, 1997).

3 Most PR personnel would probably claim that they thoroughly measure the effectiveness of targeting journalists. However all measures appear to be in terms of 'inputs' – that is, advertising space taken, size and position of article and relative coverage. Few measure how consumers receive and perceive such articles. One of the most popular measurement approaches in the motor market is that bought in from CMS (Precise System), which combines several of the above variables to construct an effectiveness index. An index rating is even provided for each motoring journalist, by name, for dif-

ferent car models, at different times of the year and for different features the client is trying to communicate (performance, comfort, handling and so on).

An IPR (1995) survey of PR evaluation methods found that 41 per cent of respondents did not know if they offered value for money, 24 per cent said 'no' and only 28 per cent said 'yes'. At a related IPR 'evaluation event' the organiser commented that 'the level of sophistication and knowledge is quite low, people know they should be doing more of it but they know less than they think they do' (Crowe, 1995). Few go beyond 'input' measures such as degree of exposure, but a few are moving towards greater sophistication with a combination of measures, including volume of coverage, brand (or corporate) visibility, message delivery and strength, impact and target audience readership. As for output measures (monitoring effects amongst the target audience itself), these are few and far between and usually rely on *ad hoc* focus group research.

To reinforce these findings, a survey conducted in May 1995 by Westcombe Business Research (1995) found that measuring the volume of press and tv coverage was still the most used approach but 42 per cent of PR clients said that their PR effort was not very effectively evaluated.

In another study of PR evaluation methods, Watson (1996) found a lack of knowledge about communications effectiveness measurement methodology and this, together with lack of time or resources, meant that 'most judge their work without any independent criteria'.

Several leading PR evaluation companies met in June 1997 to draw up an industry guide to objective setting and evaluation. It is likely that the group will recommend a common unit of measurement, the 'media relations point' (MRP), which would be capable of comparison with advertising's gross rating point (GRP) and television ratings (TVR) (Rogers, 1997) – but are these just more sophisticated input measures?

Promotion and Opinion Leader and Formers

KEY CONCEPTS

- Promotion
- Use of opinion leaders and formers
- Brand characters

Personality trade

Truth is stranger than fiction, but in advertising it's often difficult to tell the two apart '! Beattie, for instance, took on such a life of her own that she became too big for BT's good. Are brand characters a vital marketing tool, or should they be consigned to history?

JANE URE SMITH

From Mr Kipling to Captain Birds Eye and the Milky Bar Kid, fictional characters are a recurrent marketing tool. But are they just outdated evocations of a bygone age or a vital part of communicating brand values?

Although. many fictional brand characters have a lengthy heritage, Phileas Fogg is a relative newcomer. He is the creation of a company which began life only in 1982. Derwent

Valley Foods' four founders drew up a list of more than 100 "travelling" characters, including Christopher Columbus and Marco Polo, but in the end they plumped for Fogg.

As a brand character, Fogg is his own man: he has more to do with Medomsley Road, Consett than with the Jules Verne original. "With all personalities" you have to pick the elements you can use to your advantage and gloss over those that don't fit the game plan," says Derwent Valley Foods marketing controller Phil Lynas.

Mr Kipling of Manor Bakeries started life in 1967. Uncle Ben, from Mars subsidiary Master Foods, dates back to 1949. Other fictional characters that have become synonymous with brand names have equally long pedigrees. Unilever's Captain Birds Eye set. sail in 1967; Spillers' Arthur, the impeccably mannered big white cat, became a brand name in his own right in 1992, but first prowled across our screens in a 1965 advertising campaign. And Nestlé's Milky bar Kid, now in his tenth incarnation, has been treating his friends since 1961.

Fictional characters are created to give products an emotional appeal above and beyond their on-screen qualities. "A character may be a patron or an authority such as Captain Birds Eye," says David Adams, director and co-founder of design consultants Tutssel St John Lambie Nairn. In other cases, they will epitomise the product benefits, in the way the Pilsbury Dough Boy does, or they may be synonymous with the style of a product, like the Michelin Man."

Characters can work in other ways, believes Irene Inskip, a director of brand development agency CLK. "They can be used to bring to life an inherently difficult or boring product, such as Scottish Widows or Mr Sheen," she says. They can also be used to create an imaginary world for kids. "The whole process becomes interesting when you can elicit adult appeal and child appeal, but that is a very difficult trick to pull off," she adds.

Both Captain Birds Eye and the Milky Bar Kid manage to appeal to both groups. For adults, Captain Birds Eye embodies responsibility and reliability; he's the expert seafarer who knows just where to look for the best fish. For children, he's an adventurer, who pacifies pirates and welcomes stowaways aboard. "For mums, he represents all that is best about quality fish, yet for kids he is still exciting," says Richard Hytner, chief executive at Still Price Lintas, which created the character and campaigns.

The Milkybar Kid works much the same way. "Mums like him because with his glasses he is ever so slightly vulnerable, he is a generous, clean-cut lad," says Hytner. "He's not too worhy, so for very young children he's a bit of a hero – like a brother."

But are characters a hell or hindrance for an agency to work with and do they stifle creativity? "It can be an albatross later unless you have given the character enough leeway," says Inskip. 'But if an agency has created a character which they know is usable for several years it will actually liberate creativity because it gives a focus and to consumers it all seems coherent."

Mr Kipling is a case in point. The early black-and-white advertising focused tightly on the product: cakes in the making. In later campaigns the camera has pulled back to scenarios where the shadowy figure of Mr Kipling plays bowls, goes fishing and entertains his grandchildren. But the character is unchanging: consumers absorb him as the epitome of Englishness, a country gentleman who bakes cakes in his large kitchen somewhere in the Home Counties. In research groups, consumers readily fill in all the missing details of his life. "The trick is that we don't specify too much." says Judy Harman, planning director at the brand's agency J Walter Thompson. "It is a bit like radio voices: everyone has their view of what Eddie Grundy of The Archers looks like," she says.

However, brand characters can restrict the range of products a company can market under that label. Mr Kipling is unlikely to start producing French pastries or Mississippi mud pie because they wouldn't fit in with his character.

What unites the majority of the longest-serving characters is the essentially conservative values they embody. Mr Kipling, for example, harks back to an era that never was, when urban trauma was absent and families united. "He stands for traditional British values," says Colin Tether, marketing director at Manor Bakeries. John Major's much disparaged Back to Basics is in a way back to Mr Kipling.

"The values that the Conservatives are actually after, the ones that Major has failed so dismally to communicate, are embodied in Mr Kipling.

"He conjures up a mythical era that is demonstrated in Edwardian costume drama, Agatha Christie and Jeeves and Wooster, with cucumber sandwiches and everybody having a jolly time," says Tether.

Similarly, Captain Birds Eye firmly rejects modernity in favour of life on a mythical high seas, where there's no dispute a platter offish fingers cAn't settle. Arthur's sofa is equally remote from the real world and no blood gets spilled around the Milkybar Kid. It is surely no accident that three of these characters were born in the late Sixties, when the civil rights movement was shaking the US, Paris was on the brink of insurrection and London students were occupying the LSE. The brands embodied a safe and cosy fantasy world rather than the reality of a turbulent period.

Fewer brand characters are created these days. If they are to do more than make appearances in advertising, then nurturing them costs money.

"Inevitably, it requires a sizeable, investment to build a character – at least half of your investment is going to go into building that personality," says Adams.

Characters come and go along with ad campaigns. Inskip is critical of the practice. "People ditch characters too fast now," she says.

"The temptation is to say 'well, we've had that character for two years, so let's do something else', when in fact to penetrate consumer consciousness, if the character is a good one, it takes at least five years. But it is a brave ad agency that continues with something for that long."

British Telecom, in the past, has used the Busby and Beattie characters in advertising and beyond. Its new campaign will involve a celebrity, the first since Maureen Lipman's Beattie campaign ended in 1992. Beattie was retired partly because Lipman wanted to stop, and partly because she no longer fitted the message the company wanted to convey.

But there was a third reason, which shows that characters can have their drawbacks: they can be so forceful that they take on a life of their own. "The campaign had become the Beattie campaign, rather than a commercial about Chargecard or calling at the weekend," says Robert Bean, head of advertising and media quality at BT. "You've got to be very careful how you use characters. We learned with Beattie that people were ignoring the message, – and we've applied that lesson to our new campaign."

Yabba dabba dough!

See the film, buy the T-shirt and the jewellery and the biscuits . . . Movie licensing is a risky business – fickle audiences ensure that films, and their promotional products, often have a short shelf life. The Flintstones, however, already has a worldwide following thanks to the classic cartoon series and can look forward to more commercial success than most.

MEG CARTER

Movie merchandising and licensing activity for The Flintstones, which opens in the UK this week, looks likely to scale new heights. But film licensing can be a high-risk, short-term activity. The stakes are high for Sugar Puffs, Hula Hoops and Tetley Tea – these are only a few of the brands hoping to cash in on Steven Spielberg's latest epic.

The Flintstones is not a typical movie licensing property. As a spin-off from the long-running TV cartoon series, which has a worldwide following, its heritage gives it a built-in advantage over "unknown" movie properties. The classic Flintstones cartoon series, which was first shown in 1960, already has a comprehensive licensing and merchandising programme. There are more than 90 licensees in the UK, for a range of products including toys, jewellery, food and clothing.

The licensing programme is handled by Copyright Promotions. Long-standing client Turner Home Entertainment bought the series creator Hanna Barbera two-and-a-half years ago. So the licensing activities around the movie have been carefully designed to complement existing work, says Copyright Promotions director of UK licensing Angela Farrugia.

"Live action and animation are two very different things; it would have been easy to confuse the two. We didn't want to flood the market," she explains. "Ours is a long-term business; we do not want to put out too much merchandise at once." As a result, only a limited number of UK product and promotional partners have been signed up for the film.

In the long term, regular BBC audiences of 5.9 million for repeats of the cartoon series will be more important to the continuing success of the licensing programme than the movie itself. "But tapping into the hype and promotional spend surrounding the film offers an attractive opportunity for blue-chip commercial partners," says Copyright Promotions marketing manager Simon Crowther. "It's a $65m (£43m) movie and a lot of people want to be associated with it."

The film's largest deal was struck with McDonald's in the US. The chain is identifiably, and lightheartedly, featured in the film as RocDonald's. The McDonald's deal covers 35 territories. And promotional support includes a "Happy Meal" campaign, branded boxes and a range of collectables.

Promotional partners in the UK include Lyons Tetley (on-pack promotion, give-away prizes and Flintstones-branded TV campaign), Quaker (on-pack and TV support), KP, The Sunday Times and UCI. The movie benefits from tapping into the marketing budgets of these promotional partners. Meanwhile, the combined value of TV exposure for Flintstones-related promotions is estimated at £7m.

Licensees producing film-branded merchandise have been limited in number. But products were on the market as the hype began, some two to three months before this week's UK premiere. Their shelf life is expected to last beyond the Flintstones' video release next spring, says Keith Isaac, managing director of MCA Merchandising, a division of the film's UK distributor.

The Flintstones is a highly licensable movie, Farrugia says. "It is a combination of elements that never happens – an exciting cartoon, Steven Spielberg, the actor John Goodman. All the ingredients are there for success, with minimal risk." It also appeals to both children and adults. The latter will be drawn to the film through nostalgia for the TV series.

Industry scepticism about the film's appeal before its US opening in May proved to be unfounded. The Flintstones set a record for the strongest movie opening, taking $34.5m (£23m) in its first weekend. And confidence is high that it will be successful in the UK.

"A good licensing property goes hand-in-hand with a box office hit," Isaac says. But, while word-of-mouth is important to generate excitement for the film and its merchandise, not every successful film lends itself to this type of commercial exploitation.

Jurassic Park is a conspicuous merchandising success. It generated $900m (£600m) at the box office worldwide, and even more through merchandising and licensing retail sales. Sales are flourishing thanks to children's continued interest in dinosaurs, says Isaac. And the film studio hopes an additional wave will be generated when the video is released in October.

In the Seventies, the Star Wars trilogy became the first, and largest, movie licensing programme. "Star Wars heralded the advent of collectable figures – the first big toy line," says Jackie Ferguson, managing director of licensing company Leisure Concepts International. And this programme is still running.

Interest in Star Wars is being regenerated in the run-up to the release of a video trilogy this autumn, and plans by the films' originator George Lucas to make further episodes in the science fiction saga.

"Unless a movie has hype, licensees won't get behind it because the lifespan of movie licence is a matter of months. It's short-lived, unlike TV series which have constant media exposure," says Ferguson.

At the other end of the scale are movies such as Hook and Dick Tracy. Both were much hyped before launch but regarded as box office and merchandising disappointments. "Perhaps these lacked the heritage to be successful in the UK market," says Farrugia. Isaac adds: "I don't think Dick Tracy worked because, really, it was a period piece."

A number of key factors make the difference between a marketing hit or flop. "First and foremost is the awareness in place for the product. If it is already a known quantity this is a major plus," says Ferguson.

Also important is a strong promotional budget. "Principles behind the movie play a big role; Disney or Spielberg are a big help," she adds.

Early logo and styles clearance is also vital. Ensuring the quality of merchandise is critical. Retailers must have the confidence to stock the product before anyone can tell how the film will perform. "We try to understand the dynamics of the business of our licensees, to help them to develop their product lines more effectively," says Crowther.

At least one year's advance notice is essential, according to Farrugia. A release date confirmed well in advance allows sufficient lead times to get products designed and stocked in time for the run-up to launch . "And we must know about marketing and promotional spends," she adds.

Existing and potential licensees are looking for the next big thing to hit the UK box office. Earlier this month in the US the latest Walt Disney animated feature, The Lion King, opened to huge box office receipts – $42m (£28m) in one weekend. And there was "tremendous word of mouth", according to press reports. Burger King, Nestlés, and Toys R Us are some of the companies running US tie-ins.

The strength of The Lion King lies in its appeal to both children and adults, Disney believes. There is evidence that audiences are returning for second viewings. Merchandise sales are predicted to exceed $1bn (£66m) later this year.

Copyright Promotions is working on a number of future movie releases. Among them is The Page Master, a live action/animation fantasy starring Macaulay Culkin and Whoopi Goldberg, where a small boy (live action) enters a magical animated fantasy world. It is due for Christmas release.

The movie Judge Dredd, due for release next year, is based on the comic strip of the same name.

Also on offer is The Shadow, which opens in the UK this autumn. The movie, starring Alec Baldwin and based on Orson Welles' radio series from the Thirties, has already been released in the US.

Ferguson is working on The Swan Princess, an animated feature which is due to be released in the spring, and based on Swan Lake. "Provided this movie is successful and we sign up animation rights (for a UK TV series) it will be a successful licensing venture here," she says. Some 12 licensees have signed up to be associated with the film.

Even so, movie licensing remains a risky, unpredictable business, despite the growing sophistication of the market. Cinema audiences remain very fickle. No sooner has one movie opened, than their interest and spending power shifts to the next one.

"Movies do have a short shelf life," believes Crowther. "But the key is to continue the momentum by developing strong licensed products to keep interest going."

And with Hollywood's growing interest in exploiting TV properties for the big screen – Scooby Doo and Dr Who are two movie projects that have been announced – licensing may soon be given an added boost.

Rather than gambling on an overnight sensation, licensees will be able to link with a familiar character or storyline (with an established following). They will be able to cash in on the hype surrounding a major movie opening and be confident that when the movie opening frenzy has subsided, the property will still have a life. Farrugia says: "A lot of money can be made by a lot of people, if the product is exploited well."

ISSUES

1. The use of 'personalities' is based on the concepts of opinion forming and opinion leading – explain these concepts.

2. Discuss the two-step and multi-step models of information flows.

3. How can opinion leaders/formers be 'simulated'?

EXPLORATION OF ISSUES

1. Information is often sought from, and provided by, those who are thought to possess special knowledge and expertise. From this a two-step approach to communications emerges:

sender → opinion leader → receiver

People who influence others are referred to as opinion leaders, and some have status conferred on them by their peer group. Recognition of their expertise, prowess or particular knowledge or skills enables these opinion leaders to guide and lead the thoughts of others in particular product areas. Opinion leaders normally rely on word-of-mouth communications to influence others, and often do so passively.

To illustrate the difference between the two types of influencer, an accountant with particular taxation skills may be an opinion former to his or her clients, and communications can be expected to be formal and direct. To his or her peers he or she may be an important advisory or influential person, and is thus an opinion leader.

Communications in these circumstances will be more informal and indirect (word-of-mouth).

2. The two-step model of communication has a number of strengths and weaknesses. Opinion formers and leaders are assumed to pass on positive information, but communication planners need to be sure that they will not reprocess and transmit the information in a negative manner and so reverse the intentions of the source of the message. Furthermore opinion leaders are not only notoriously difficult to identify, but it is also difficult to measure their influence on opinion followers. Opinion formers on the other hand, are more easily identified but potentially less effective than opinion leaders.

It is common promotional practice to direct promotional messages to opinion formers and leaders. The launch of Haagen Daz super premium ice cream in the UK was built around a campaign that targeted messages at key celebrities or 'brand ambassadors'. These people were encouraged to talk to others about the quality and exclusivity of the new product. Such individuals, therefore, speed up the process of diffusion using interpersonal communications to influence opinion followers, who seek their advice in an attempt to reduce perceived risk. This acceleration of the communication process of course depends on the ability to identify suitable influencers in the first place.

As for opinion leaders, an early experiment by Mancuso in 1969 demonstrates the potential influence they can exert. A pop record was produced, but not distributed widely. Sociometric research was then conducted in a number of university towns. This entailed asking individual students, in isolation from the rest of the group, which other members of the class he or she was most likely to consult when it came to music and buying records. This revealed a network of communication between students in the class. Some were mentioned by many of their fellow students, which suggested that they possessed a certain degree of credibility with regard to music and records, and could be regarded as opinion leaders. A copy of the pop record was mailed to each of the latter as a token of appreciation.

A copy of the record was also mailed to students in other universities to act as a control group. In this case the names were selected at random from class lists. Some might have been opinion leaders, but this would have been a matter of coincidence and fewer of them would have been opinion leaders than those selected sociometrically. The record was subsequently released in the towns where the experimental and control groups were situated. In those towns where the 'real' opinion leaders were selected, the record actually entered the charts, but in the control towns, where opinion leaders were not deliberately targeted, the record did not become popular.

This example demonstrates the potential benefits of targeting opinion leaders, but also the difficulty of attempting to identify real opinion leaders just by name and address.

The two-step model suggests that opinion leaders, and to a lesser extent opinion formers, only receive information from mass media sources. It is now accepted that this is an untenable concept. Opinion formers and leaders also receive information from opinion followers and other opinion formers and leaders. Messages are assimilated, reconstructed and transmitted back and forth between a wide variety of people. In other words a multistep model of communication is more appropriate.

3 It is sometimes possible to identify people who are likely to be opinion leaders and feature them in promotional campaigns, for example the use of Lulu and

Lorraine Chase to promote the Freemans mail order catalogue and the Great Universal catalogue respectively proved an extremely effective means of attracting the target audience.

Something to guard against in such circumstances is consumers remembering the personality but not your product or brand! A long-running campaign using Joan Collins and Lennard Rossiter to promote a brand of vermouth was well remembered for the personalities but the actual brand could not always be brought to mind.

Many films and television programmes involve 'product placement', where brands are displayed or mentioned in the film. In such cases viewers do not put up their cognitive defences to the same extent as they might if the same products were to appear in commercials. The manufacturers pay for the privilege of course.

A classic example concerns the James Bond films, where many products are mentioned or shown, often just once. The idea is that James Bond acts as an aspirational reference point for some of the audience, an opinion leader in effect, and if he wears a Seiko watch, shaves with a Philishave and drinks Bollenger champagne, then followers should do so as well. This is a classic example of a simulated opinion leader.

Another example is yet another fictional character, Roy of the Rovers. The comic named after this character was bought by Gola, the sportswear company, and whilst there was little advertising in this publication, the sporting hero, Roy, always wore Gola kit.

Some years ago the brewing industry decided to give lager a more masculine image. The idea was to present more macho images of men drinking lager and to associate, through sponsorship, lager with energetic and aggressive sports. All of this probably contributed to the rise of the 'lager lout', but it was certainly an effective campaign. The simulated opinion leadership approach was prohibited in that anything vaguely indicating a lager lout stereotype could not be used. One company went as far as to introduce a bear character who was only a stone's throw from being a lager lout – the advertisement was banned, illustrating the perceived effectiveness of such advertisements.

Radio programmes are sometimes used to convey messages. An example of this is the Russian radio soap 'House Seven, Entrance 4' which is partly funded by the EU 'Know How Fund' with the aim of disseminating advice on living in a market economy. Prime Minister Tony Blair even appeared on this programme in October 1997 as an opinion former conveying a message about the importance of education. Likewise the BBC's 'The Archers' has been used as an opinion former to convey messages about farming practice – indeed one of its original aims when launched after the Second World War was to educate farmers about new farming methods.

Another UK soap, Channel 4's 'Brookside', frequently portrays issues that have either been influenced by or worked through in conjunction with a sponsor of some kind. For example a recent storyline about euthanasia was prompted by a press release from the Morphine Information Service, demonstrating the multistep flow model. According to the show's producer, 'we cannot get away from the fact that people will have an interest in putting a message across in stories we want to do'. The makers of this particular programme are also working, at the time of writing, with the government on a storyline about adult literacy, and the makers of BBC's 'Eastenders' worked with the National Schizophrenia Fellowship on their story about schizophrenia. These are strong examples of how 'issues-led' PR can use simulated opinion formers.

When Sony introduced the Walkman in 1979 the company gave samples of the product to film stars and models, thus using them as opinion formers to show that there was a fashion side to the product as well as a functional application. As the company's PR manager stated, 'the most powerful way of telling someone that something is a good product is if someone who is credible tells you that it is'.

A more recent example was the marketing of the Tamagotchi (virtual pet) in the late 1990s. In Japan, teenagers were recruited to 'spread the word' to their friends about the new product – and even to form queues outside stores to simulate strong demand!

9 The 'New' Marketing

Database Analysis

KEY CONCEPTS

- Database marketing
- Relational databases
- Database analysis
- Data mining

Golden prospects

Now one of the top car manufacuturers in the UK, Citroën's commitment to strategic marketing has meant building up an extensive database on potential customers. So far the prospects look very good indeed.

JANE CHIPPERFIELD

This January, Citroën became the UK's fourth ranking car manufacturer – after Ford, Vauxhall and Rover – taking 6.5 per cent of the market. It had already been expanding rapidly, rising from a market share of 1.8 per cent to more than 4.5 per cent in just seven years.

According to Citroën direct marketing manager JimMather, direct marketing played an invaluable role in producing this growth. "While every element of the marketing mix has a part to play, direct marketing is a strong methodology to bring people to the product." And this year's multimillion-pound direct marketing budget shows that Citroën is committed to consolidating its customer loyalty and prospects being people who have contacted Citroën for information

But recent years have seen drastic changes in the company's use of direct marketing. Blanket Mailings have been replaced by highly targeted campaigns built from extensive databases. The result has been a much greater focus on customer loyalty.

"There have been three phases to our direct marketing," says Mather, "ad hoc, mass-mailings and more strategic marketing". Before 1987 it had been using mailings on a project basis, some of which were done in-house. These were fairly successful and encouraged them to look at how much direct marketing could deliver if it were to be planned on a larger scale.

In 1987 the full-service agency, MHA Carlson, was appointed and direct marketing became an integral part of Citroën's marketing programme. At this time it was sending about 2 million mailings a year to complement insert and press campaigns. The mail-shots were designed to build interest in the Citroën car and generate showroom visits and test-drives.

"Not only did we generate product-trial but also dealership-trial. It put the dealership on the map for the prospect. Between 1987 and 1991 there were about 220,000 test-drives directly linked to the mailings."

While Mather says the campaign was successful, he admits the costs were Significant. And this, combined with technological advances in targeting and more sophisticated competition, resulted in Citroën's switch to customer loyalty and prospect generation programmes in 1991.

All Citroën's mailing activity, is driven by its "Trident" database. MHA Carlson began developing a pilot database for both customers and prospects towards the end of 1991. Last July this activity was moved to GSI UK.

Growing rapidly, Trident now contains details on around 250,000 customers and 150,000 prospects. Information includes names, addresses, car change dates and replacement intentions as well as lifestyle details. Data is collected through various methods including point-of-sale, questionnaires and telemarketing. Mather explains: "We use this information to talk to our customers on a regular basis to find out how they are reacting to product and dealership."

They use their data bank for strategic purposes focusing particularly on customer car change dates. But it is also sifted for mailings on special events such as launches: "We mail the right people at the right time and tailor the message to give people what they want. At the end of the day we're in the business of selling cars and the way to do that is to give customers the information they want to receive."

Prospects are generated using above-the-line campaigns, often coupons. After profiling, some are sent questionnaires. Citroën claims a response rate of around 50 per cent – good by industry standards – and intends to increase prospect generation activity in the future.

Both prospects and customers receive Directions magazine, published by Ware Anthony Rust. A mixture of product and nonproduct articles, this is issued on a quarterly basis, but it can be published to coincide with particular events.

Although some competitors, such as Ford, do not believe in using maga-

zines because every recipient receives the same material regardless of their profile, Mather claims research shows Directions is well received.

These strategies are well designed to keep the customer loyal. Mather sees targeted direct mail as a service: "Customer loyalty is absolutely not a trendy fad. As products become more similar, manufacturers must look for areas of differentiation and customer service is one area of competitive advantage. Customer service is made up of many aspects, dealership and after-sales care for instance. Directions . magazine keeps customers entertained and informed. Mailing test-drive invitations and product information provides a service.

But creating customer loyalty is not simply about providing services. It is also about establishing a relationship. MHA Carlson business group director Jane Clinton explains: "Not only are we getting people down to the dealership to see the car, but we're building a relationship with both customers and prospects A tactical approach, which several car manufacturers adopt, generate a lot of short-term showroom traffic, but doesn't mean people are actually going to buy a car! Our strategic approach ensures that the conversion to sales figures are going to be a lot higher."

Most manufacturers know the value of cultivating repeat sales. Ford marketing communications manager Gavin Crabbe says; "If we can hold onto all those customers who bought a Ford car, .we wouldn't have to attract anyone else." Ford, like Citroën, concentrates on database building and targeted mailings – a change initiated seven years ago.

Renault is also developing extensive databases. Advertising and promotions manager Jonathan Wignall says: "Looking at the figures it's easier and cheaper to sell to existing customers. Products are always changing and if the customer is happy with a product, that is a good base upon

which to build for a new product launch."

MHA's Clinton believes targeting an existing customer gives a company a head-start in getting its literature read. "They're interested already, they're positive. They like to hear from Citroën."

Citroën also holds a database of around one million "suspects", dating back to 1991. These are used as a pool for tactical mailings and for selection into the prospect generation programme.

But targeted direct mail can only be as good as the information on which it is based. While some rivals, such as Ford, use the written word for checking data, Citroën uses telemarketing to ensure that database details are correct and up to date. This is carried out by Merit Direct, first contracted for Citroën's Xantia. launch last summer, This was the first time that Citroën had used direct response television and Merit handled more than 11,000 enquiries as a result. Renault, on the other hand, uses telemarketing for special projects such as test-drives. Last year it was used to push Renault products to the executive sector.

Although the main purpose of Citroën's telemarketing is to check data, it also provides details on customers' car-buying intentions. Mather sees telephone contact as yet another form of customer service: "In terms of thinking about the consumer and the reactions we get, research indicates that the customer finds it a very positive experience."

Mather is confident that, even in the short term, the prospect generation and customer loyalty programmes are working. The database holds a' small number of prospects and customers with whom Citroën deliberately avoids communicating in order to test their progress. Sales are tracked using this control group and Mather claims that the ratios are in his favour. But there is room for improvement.

"We have many targets still to

achieve. I guess 1994 is the year when we will establish our programmes' true potential. It's only now that we're seeing our efforts come to fruition."

Citroën is looking at neural profiling to improve ways of identifying potential customers for targeted marketing. As the car market fragments into sections such as four-wheel drive or leisure vehicles, direct marketing will play. a more critical role. Whereas television is directed at everyone, direct mail brings specific messages to specific people and profiling those people will become increasingly important.

Databases were vital to last week's launch of the Citroën ZX Estate. "The lower-medium estate sector is new territory for Citroën and we do not have an existing customer-bank to rely on," says Mather. "It is in situations such as this that our new datebases have proved invaluable. We have been able to select a significant number of "suspects", prospects and customers including current estate owners or saloon owners with estate interest, and despatch a mailing encouraging showroom visits."

Ultimately Citroën's database may change both in terms of its systems and its use. The company is now looking at integrating the database with other areas of the company, which it hopes will lead to opportunities to use it in divisions such as customer services.

Knowing me, knowing you

Having a database is one thing – knowing which one to buy and how to get the best out of it is a completely different matter. Systems that have been developed and nurtured over a period of years usually prove most useful.

JO-ANNE WALKER

During the late Eighties and early Nineties, developing a database was top priority for many companies. Now that anyone who is worth anything has one, the question is what to do with it.

Many practitioners say that in the rush to create a database, a lot of clients took a short cut and ended up with databases which are limited in scope and difficult to build on. Databases were built for the sake of having them, with little thought given to how they should and could be exploited.

But merely owning a database does not guarantee a competitive edge; it is a marketing tool like any other. Only when the data is converted into information through analysis, can any value be derived from it. A really successful implementation of the database should result in fundamental changes in a company's business – but this is rarely the case.

The problem seems to lie in being able to merge marketing expertise with the techno brains. The marketing people know their stuff and there are plenty of computer whizz-kids around, but there are very few people who are well schooled in both. And they are very expensive.

Ogilvy & Mather Direct Dataconsult head Nigel Howlett says that most clients know how to develop systems around accounting and sales procedures, but they come unstuck when they build more sophisticated models which in-volve marketing strategies.

"It's really a matter of education. Most database users are not aware of the potential of the database, and if they are, they are not sure how to go about ex-ploiting it," he says.

Howlett says there are a number of pitfalls facing database development but the biggest is the desire to build a database as quickly as possible. "When people grasp the opportunities, they get terribly excited and that translates into having a database as soon as possible and as a result short-cuts are taken," he says.

"Databases' weakness used to be that technology was being stretched against delivery. Technology is now much better and cheaper, but the problem is that marketers are not ableto define what they want rigorously.

"Marketers are trained to think laterally. But you can't brief systems developers and programmers in vague terms. The first step is for the company to agree at senior level what the objectives and business needs of having a database are. Unless these objectives are defined by the client, it is unlikely the systems people will come up with what you want," says Howlett.

Because the investment in databases is usually so high, adds Howlett, there is often the danger of overselling the concept at board level and subsequently being bumped along to get the job done quickly.

SJA Direct director Steven Jenkins believes that clients must stop thinking of a list of names and addresses as being the same as a database.

"When you add relevant information to it, a list becomes a database. A marketing database is relational in style and running a database is a lot more involved than keeping a mailing list clean. A database should imply something active, like taking on an employee. Clients tend to think of it as a black box that things come out of but nothing goes back in," he says.

"In the latter part of the Eighties and early Nineties, having a database was the in thing. What was generally developed at that stage was in-company data resulting in a general transaction database, which is completely unhelpful for marketing purposes.

"Databases were not set up in a relational format, which means clients could not identify customers with specific characteristics. Unless you can do that, all you have is account-based information," comments Jenkins.

He admits that databases involve high investment, but adds that "the value of a database enables you to start calculating real customer value. With a database you can capture how much your customers are giving you in terms of margins, loyalty, longevity etc."

Because of this high investment, says Jenkins, clients are tempted to write massive specifications for a database; in short, turning in a wish list to get their money's worth.

"It's not necessary to have a database that holds everything. In fact, the more data you hold, the more chance you have of making a mistake with it.

"Most people populate their database with internal information and data that they buy in. Unfortunately, because of the recession, the quality of the material you buy in has declined in recent years. Direct marketing activity has been lower and list brokers have not been able to keep their lists as clean as they might, so you end up with the garbage in/garbage out scenario," says Jenkins.

LBV managing director Chris Lovell says his agency haschosen to call databases information or knowledge bases to reflect their potential.

Lovell also claims, however, that a truly inter-relational database would be so expensive to develop that there is no real business reason for doing it.

"The key is using data more intelligently rather than concentrating on actually build-ing it. The existence of a database makes marketers think they don't have to do any more. But a database is like a pen or a piece of paper – it's the using of it that counts," adds Lovell.

He says that most clients' knowledge of databases "ranges from the sublime to the ridiculous".

"Marketers have not bothered to educate themselves in data areas. Either they have recruited someone in or used the in-houseIT function to develop it.

"Computers and databases started for financial reasons when accounts departments wanted a system to replace double-entry book keeping, followed by production departments. In those circumstances, computers solved a lot of problems.

"But the systems developed for accounting and production have tended to be used in marketing – and it just does not work. Computer people have tried to formalise and create a static environment for marketing to work in – because that's the way computers work. But marketing, rather than being static, is very fast moving," says Lovell.

In the end, it's those databases which have been developed and nurtured over a period of time that are going to prove most useful.

The Computing Group database director Dick Davies believes it takes at least three years to develop a sound database.

"You can't just build it and not feed it," he says.

"When a system is put together to fulfil an immediate need, it will inevitably screw up. A company has to look at its long-term marketing objectives and build a database that reflects the whole operation.

"A company must know from the start that the database is about really understanding who its clients are and that process will take a few years," says Davies.

Most people feel that the gap between the marketers and the technocrats needs to be bridged by the marketers.

O&M Direct Dataconsult's Howlett says: "You shouldn't let technical vendors write the brief. Because database marketing is relatively new and clients don't really know what they want, the danger is to give the technical vendors the task of writing the specifications.

"The client's needs then tend to reflect what the vendor is selling; and you can't expect systems people to suddenly understand marketing."

In the end, however, all the technical wizardry in the world will not ensure intelligent use of data.

According to Howlett, the system has to be built in such a way that clients will be able to understand their customers better.

"There are some companies which have spent millions of pounds on building a database and then do nothing but the most cursory forms of analysis," says Howlett.

"To understand what drives people to do the things they do, you have to do data modelling and build predictive, rather than just descriptive models.

"Many companies tend to stop at the descriptive stage, but still have no idea about what makes their customers behave the way they do," he adds.

ISSUES

1 What are relational databases and how do marketers employ them?

2 What useful information can come from a car dealer's database?

3 What is data mining and what types of analysis can be conducted with database data?

EXPLORATION OF ISSUES

1 A database is composed of a series of 'records'. Each record contains data about someone or something, for example a customer or potential customer. Each record is then further divided into 'fields', which store particular data items such as postcode, name, age, gender and so on. The reason why it is necessary to separate this 'field' data is because we may want to extract those in a particular age category or gender for analysis or targeting purposes. We therefore need to be able to identify those categories in a discrete way while taking care to avoid having too many data fields jumbled up together, as this would not allow us to be as selective as individual targeting requires.

Key word searches extract the relevant records, and without separation into fields the search time would be greater because all the data in the homogenised record would have to be searched. For example, all the individual field data were jumbled together and we wished to extract all those conforming to the category 'Hooray Henry' for the targeting of trendily styled, fluorescent yellow mobile phones, we might also extract everyone whose first name or surname is Henry..

There are 'flat file' and 'relational' databases. The flat file database only deals with one file at a time. Think of a CD mail order business. This business needs to be able to store a customer's order and update the stock records as the CDs are transferred from stock to customer. A flat file database is only able to deal with either the stock or the customer record at one time – they can't 'talk to each other'. However a relational database allows both records to communicate with each other. The catalogue code for the customer's order might be 3jrk89 and the relational database allows the stock level of this CD to be checked and updated as the sale is made. The customer record is also updated, so we now have a field containing purchased CDs against each customer, from which a pattern of music preference can be analysed, together with whatever other data is being stored – quantities purchased, time of year when orders are usually placed, profile characteristics, method of payment and so on.

The relational database allows a variety of links between different tables:

- One-to-one: each record in one table can be linked with one record on another.
- One-to-many: each record in one table can be linked with many records in another.
- Many-to-many: each record in one table can be linked with many records in another table and each record in that table can be linked with many records in the first table.

2 When a car is purchased, the dealer can gather data on the purchaser – name, address, telephone number, whether there is a credit agreement and information on the customer's financial and occupational circumstances. The dealer can send letters (perhaps backed up by telephone calls) asking about the new customer's evaluation of how well he or she was treated during the purchase process, thus potentially starting a relationship with that customer. Such satisfaction surveys can also be used to gather a little more information about the customer – perhaps lifestyle details, which could help with the targeting of relevant offers.

At regular intervals the customer could be sent a service reminder, and after several services the dealer would know the mileage that the customer normally covers, thus allowing the reminders to be more timely. The dealer could also send out a timely MoT reminder by checking the purchase date in the log book. At appropriate intervals the customer the customer could be sent news about new car launches and modifications, thereby providing an up-selling opportunity for the dealership. Wine and cheese evenings could be arranged for selected customers for appropriate launches. Cross-selling is also possible because the dealer could provide the customer with details of car alarm systems and other accessories.

The customer's partner is an important target as well – the second family car might be a used vehicle and targeting for cross- and up-selling can be conducted in a similar way. Likewise it would pay to know the birth dates of the couple's children so that they can be targeted when they reach the age of 17.

The customer's business address might be useful for targeting a potential fleet market.

An analysis of customer's addresses – perhaps even a geodemographic profile – can be helpful in defining catchment area and determining where potential customers might live. This can sometimes surprise dealers who previously thought they knew their market. Prospective customers in this catchment area could be sent invitations to attend launches or other events.

In addition the dealer now has a list that he or she can sell on to, for example, warranty or breakdown companies.

With regular contact a relationship might develop, and if customers are retained for several years the 'lifetime value' of their business can be quite significant – and much cheaper to achieve than the recruitment of new customers.

Such data can also be used to 'score' customers. Most types of data are scorable. For example previous campaigns might have been more successful when marketing to those with the title Mr than to Mrs or Ms, in which case we can give a quantitative weight to titles. Postcodes are especially useful because we can profile geodemographically and make a comparison with previous success/failure rates to score the geodemographic cluster, and the postcode itself, at different levels – for example, do we have more success in BS16 or BS20? By adding lifestyle and transactional data and scoring all those in our database on a weighted index that incorporates all these variables, we can produce very useful league tables for targeting purposes.

3 A number of techniques can be used to analyse the database. Data mining refers to digging around in databases in a relatively unstructured way with the aim of discovering links between customer behaviour and almost any variable that might be useful. There is a parallel here with environmental scanning in that the latter also has the wide brief of identifying anything in the marketing environment that might be relevant to the marketing operation.

Marketers have mined a variety of unusual or unexpected factors. For example some have examined consumers' individual biorhythms as predictors of their purchasing patterns; others have linked their transactional and profile data with meteorological databases to predict, perhaps months ahead, what demand there might be for ice cream or woolly sweaters (linked with specific names and addresses); and others have even analysed buying according to astrological star sign!

Our database data becomes 'information' when we identify the 'recency, frequency and monetary value' (RFM) of customer orders.

- Recency: knowing that people have purchased from us in the past is important but not sufficient; we are probably less interested in those who bought from us in 1984.
- Frequency: a one-off purchase may make a customer less attractive (depending, of course, on the product market in which we operate). So knowing how often customers buy from us is an important measure.
- Monetary value: small orders are usually less attractive than larger ones, so this is yet another measure of significance. Marketers are increasingly concentrating on their 'better' customers – those whose purchases have the highest monetary value (and frequency) – and are segmenting on the basis of 'volume'. This is more cost effective because they are concentrating on those who bring the greatest returns. Vilfredo Pareto's theory of income distribution has been transferred and borrowed by direct marketers to support the proposition that 80 per cent of sales come from just 20 per cent of customers – in many markets the ratio can be even more polarised, and 95:5 is not uncommon. The Pareto principle is oft quoted by direct marketers and is certainly relevant to this discussion of RFM analysis.

Clearly, because of the nature of the variables involved, RFM analysis requires transactional data to be tracked by the database, so an actual purchase history is needed.

In addition to identifying volume segments and best prospects, RFM information can contribute to the calculation of 'lifetime value' – another of the direct marketer's cornerstone measures.

'Lifetime' in this context is somewhat of an overstatement – it does not mean the lifetime of the customer, but rather the period in which she or he is a customer of your organisation, and this might be as little as three years. It would probably better to refer to 'longtime' value analysis, but we shall stay with the industry standard.

The concept of what a customer is worth to the organisation in sales and profit terms over a period of time is critical in direct marketing. To take an extreme example, if a car company is only concerned with acquiring customers and does nothing to retain them, there is a fair chance that each customer who buys one of their cars this year will buy another make next time – and the time after that and so on. The value of the sale might be £10 000, but subtracting acquisition costs, production and other costs could mean a net profit of a just a few pounds.

With a more dedicated retention programme the company could expect customers to buy one of their cars every third year for perhaps twelve years, and as they progress through their life stages they may be able to afford more expensive models. So, it being cheaper to retain customers than to acquire them in the first place, together with repeat buying and the prospect of up-selling over a period of time, the sales value of each customer could be as high as, £70 000 (£10 000 + £12 000 + £14 000 + £16 000 +£18 000) if the customer trades up to more expensive cars by £2000 each time.

Field Marketing

KEY CONCEPTS

- Field marketing
- Data capture
- Database marketing
- Retail micromarketing
- Outsourcing

Team spirit

Field marketing has moved on from the Seventies image of scantily clad women handing out snacks. It now provides services such as data capture, site visits and sales planning, through highly professional teams.

DAVID REED

Which of these two descriptions springs to mind when you think of field marketing? "Middle-aged, out of work actresses giving out coupons and girls wearing low-cut tops offering free drinks", or "the provision of a dedicated solus field sales team to achieve specific agreed tasks for one organisation".

If it is the former, then you are stuck in the Seventies. Field marketing has moved on to such a degree that it now encompasses sales promotion, database marketing, research, space and stock management, and mystery shoppers.

It even covers such hot topics as outsourced service support and retail micro-marketing.

The reason why it suffers from this erroneous image is partly the fault of the sector, which has not promoted itself very well, and partly intrinsic to the work it carries out. "When people are working for a field marketing company, they identify themselves not as being with that company, but as being with their client," explains Tony Stratton, chief executive officer of CPM Field Marketing, part of the Omnicom group.

Even retailers who are the focus of their attentions may not be aware that the representative who has just been discussing stock, point-of-sale support and customer profile does not work for Mars, Nestlé, Cadbury, Procter & Gamble, Gallaher or any of the raft of blue-chip clients using field marketers.

But this is increasingly the case, as manufacturers look for staff cutbacks. "One way is to keep highly skilled functions in-house and contract out the 75 or 80 per cent of traditional salesforce functions, which are skilled, but more maintenance-led," says Stratton.

Field marketing agencies are able to call on thousands of individuals, covering the whole country, who can make the necessary store visits. What these people are not are "an attractive woman and her 30 friends" who Alison Williams, chairman of the Field Marketing Association (FMA) and managing director of FDS, says typified the business just ten years ago.

Instead, the account managers overseeing the field force are likely to be "male, 45-plus, with significant careers in sales and marketing at blue-chip companies who, through recession or restructuring, are on the job market". These are the managers who will each have about eight field reps working for them, according to Mike Gardham, managing director of Milton Headcount, "so we don't lose control of a campaign".

Those reps are most likely to be women returning to work who are looking for jobs that are enjoyable, demanding, but which do not conflict with their domestic commitments. At CPM, Stratton says, "they will all be contracted people who are permanent employees with a contract, paid holidays and a pension scheme".

The distribution of brands which are often backed by millions of pounds worth of sales promotion and advertising support may rely on these people. As one example, Gardham points to the launch of the soft drink Rio. A month before the TV campaign broke, his company built distribution in CTNs, petrol forecourts and golf clubs within the London area. "That way, when the ads broke, consumers could find it at point of sale," he says.

Reassurance that these people are professionals is growing. And it has been given a significant boost with the formation of the FMA two years ago. "Our aim is to make sure people have the right qualifications and are properly trained to do the work," says Williams.

The FMA is currently conducting an audit of the field marketing sector to build both universal figures and penetration of membership. Its current estimate is that FMA members account for 75 to 80 per cent of a business worth between £100m and £120m.

Just as the people working in the industry have changed, so too have the tools at their disposal. Technology, in the form of telephones and computers, is changing the way that field marketing is carried out, just as it improves the efficiency with which campaigns are tackled.

"We are no longer looking at boxes on shelves and re-ordering, because information technology is doing that," says Wendy Sweeney, managing director of PPM. "We are providing feedback, monitoring and point-of-sale material." She notes that one area of controversy concerns whether field marketers can claim to provide market research information.

"It is not viewed as such by market research agencies, but we can give a valuable response. We take weighted samples, we know what is going on in retail outlets. We can give clients an idea of what they have to achieve," she says.

A notable feature of the service now provided by field marketers is the building and maintenance of databases. At Milton Headcount, for example, some 500,000 outbound phone calls and 250,000 site visits are made annually, each contributing data.

Capturing information on the outlets targeted by manufacturers allows sales efforts to be targeted more precisely. This kind of micro-marketing keeps waste down, says Gardham. "If a newsagent sells a lot of Vogue, it is also likely to sell a lot of indulgence chocolate bars. If it sells more male-oriented magazines and The Sun, it will stock cheaper chocolate and soft drinks," he claims.

The field marketing agency may even be delivering information which is central to the way companies manage their business and their revenue stream. The TPS Organisation specialises in working for publishers and wholesalers in the news-trade, such as BBC Worldwide and Marshall Cavendish.

It holds databases, for example, on 26,000 newsagents and every doctor's surgery. "They are sorted by postcode so we can identify the number of outlets in any postal area. We know where to employ merchandisers and where they shouldn't go. It is helpful for planning," says Paul Lovesy, sales director of TPS.

His company carries out a telephone poll of a panel of 500 newsagents in key centres such as Edinburgh, Newcastle, Manchester and Bristol, to monitor the sales of titles, especially new launches. "From that, publishers can predict national sales," he says.

Third-party distributors like Comag and UMD have used TPS for revenue calculations. Wholesalers pass on a percentage of sales to publishers based on projected revenues. Since publishers expect to be paid during the lifetime of an edition, the distributor has to make an educated guess, until the figure can be adjusted from the true sales. Bringing in a field marketing agency like TPS to audit CTNs keeps the level of error in payments down.

In addition to higher quality personnel and high performance technology, field marketing is also being changed by developments in retail. "As multiples, whether grocery, petrol, off-licences or CTNs become stronger and more disciplined, there is less opportunity for manufacturers to effect positive change for their brand," says Stratton.

Frequent calling on multiples is less efficient since stocking and merchandising in-store is likely to be decided centrally. Instead, the independent grocers, who are being squeezed hard by the multiples, "become a more interesting and attractive proposition because there is an opportunity to influence them", he says.

Gardham supports this point by noting that, out of a total of 34,100 independent grocers, supermarkets and convenience stores, the top 6,000 account for 18 per cent of shop distribution, but 68 per cent of sterling distribution.

Targeting field force efforts onto those outlets may have a significant impact on a brand's performance and return on investment.

The number of manufacturers who are able and willing to support a salesforce big enough to cover even just the top 6,000 such outlets is diminishing. But they need to ensure their products are being stocked, that displays are correctly positioned, that labels are facing outwards, and that special offers are being provided to customers.

The only logical way to service this need, in these circumstances, is to employ a field marketing operation. Indeed, some of the requirements of the sales department may only be achievable through outsourcing. Williams says that FDS recently car-ried out 10,000 site visits in four days for a client who was selling in a new promotion. The capacity to carry that level of visiting and that speed cannot be kept in-house.

David Hellier, financial director of DFDS Field Marketing, says: "Over the past six to 12 months we have grown our business very much on the back of that development among clients to outsource their field marketing. They are minimising their risk, in terms of part-time legislation, and tapping into a flexible resource that is greater than they could afford to employ themselves."

He adds that, while the retailers who are the subject of field marketers' attentions may feel wary of the contact passing to a third party, there is no reason for the relationship to diminish if it is handled professionally. And that sort of marketing expertise does not need to be dressed up in a short skirt.

ISSUES

1. **Assess the key trends in database marketing.**

2. **Why is field marketing being changed by retail developments?**

3. **Comment on the continuing increase in outsourcing.**

EXPLORATION OF ISSUES

1. There is an obsession with the size of the database, worries about the quality of data and genuine concern about the lack of relevant skills within companies to plan and, most importantly, analyse and use the information to add value to customers.

The database revolution is offering up information in such volume, detail and scope that, it is equivalent to the invention of the microscope or telescope. With the rise of data-led marketing, the analytical and experimental mind may be more in demand than the traditional 'creative' mind. Database marketing is moving into profiling, and a major challenge for marketing will be to mine the data held on their marketing databases to create information. This will involve the use of text and image databases, together with data mining tools, to identify patterns in seemingly unrelated data. The system will look at all the different sources of data and give positive matches that can be refined, using data mining techniques involving neural networks and large parallel array processors.

The combination of sales and marketing databases with other technologies can lead to startling improvements in sales and marketing productivity. The great challenge now is to compress information, deliver it in a brand-sympathetic manner and reduce uncertainty to avoid being relegated outside the consumer choice range. The compression of information and its use to reduce decision uncertainty might well have been one of the great marketing challenges of the next millennium.

2 As multiples, whether grocers, petrol stations or off-licences, become stronger and more disciplined, there is less opportunity for manufacturers to push their brands. Frequent calling on multiples is less efficient since stocking and merchandising is likely to be decided centrally. On the other hand, independent grocers, who are being squeezed hard by the multiples, have become a more interesting and attractive proposition because there is an opportunity to influence them. Targeting field force efforts onto these outlets can significantly boost a brand's performance and return on investment.

The number of manufacturers who are able and willing to support a salesforce that is large enough enough to cover even just the top 6000 such outlets is diminishing. But they need to ensure that their products are being stocked, that displays are correctly positioned, that labels are facing outwards and that special offers are being provided to customers.

3 Traditionally, companies owned and controlled most of the resources that entered their business. But this situation is changing. Companies are finding that some resources under their control are not performing as well as those that they could obtain from outside the company. Many companies today have decided to outsource less critical resources if they can be obtained at a better quality and/or lower cost from outside the organisation. They key, then, is to own and nurture the core resources and competences that make up the essence of the business.

Interactive Marketing

KEY CONCEPTS

- Interactive media/TV
- Direct response television
- Home shopping
- Video on demand
- Interactive in store units
- Technology of Interactivity
- Media strategy
- Consumers as 'editors'
- Customised brands

Narrower targets come into sight

As consumers become interactive, targeting needs to be more than just a shot in the dark.

GRAHAM BEDNASH

Let's stop worrying about the future and get better at using media more effectively today. Even without the technology of interactivity, the rules of mass-marketing and mass-media are already being challenged. It's time then to make media strategy more effective.

The consumers of tomorrow, we are told, will no longer be "passive recipients" of advertising. Instead they will take on the role of "editor" – an active, involved participator. Forget about couch-potatoes, we're talking couch commandos.

To stay competitive in the world of interactive technology, advertisers will have to change their whole approach because the very concept of mass-marketing and mass-media will become irrelevant.

Even though this technology is years away, the issues need to be dealt with today because successful companies are already customising their mass brands to meet the varying needs of different target markets.

Look at Ford. It sells 24 variants of the Escort; the Automobile Association has seven different customer groups for just one product.

And surely it's taken for granted that the days of passive consumerism are over. Consumers are already active editors of their media because we've experienced an explosion in media choice. Even without the technology, it's now harder than ever for advertisers to reach their target groups through mass-media with the accuracy and cost-effectiveness that brands need.

Brands have become customised. Media owners have customised their businesses. The opportunity now is for mass-media strategies to do the same, because greater accuracy and involvement from the customer is, and will remain, the way to get the best level of response from media investment.

Effective targeting in mass-media is about understanding exactly how different customer groups edit their media, how best to involve them in the message and how the brand values of the medium influence the message.

Because the traditional approach to identifying customer's media usage is more than 40 years old and rooted in mass-marketing, brands will need much better ways of understanding how their specific customers edit and involve themselves in their media to achieve the greatest accuracy and the best value.

This demands a new discipline – the media strategy specialist. Such specialists will understand any specific media experience and be able increase the effectiveness of a message by focusing on accuracy and customer involvement – whether that's encouraging the taping and the playback of a TV commercial, using familiar space sizes in a completely new way or exploiting the impact of emerging media like CD-Rom.

A high street in every home

The development of interactive media promises to radically change the way consumers buy goods. But as cable TV and computer technology create a new world order, will advertisers be able to keep up?

MEG CARTER

Interactive media will fundamentally change the role of media in marketing, and advertisers should start addressing this now. So says Mike Beeston, former media planning director at Saatchi & Saatchi, who has joined forces with radio promotions specialist Curtis Hoy to launch an agency specialising in interactive media.

Curtis Hoy Beeston interactive will address interactive media from the advertisers' point of view. Direct response television commercials and the home-shopping channel QVC are already established, but the launch of a whole tier of new interactive services enabling viewers to select exactly what they want to watch and when, is imminent.

Interactive media is the bringing together of existing media – including TV, radio and print – with new computer, cable TV and telephone technology. This "media revolution" is being championed by telecomms companies on the one hand and cable TV companies on the other.

In the UK, British Telecom is working with London Weekend Television, Pearson and Kingfisher to develop BT's Video On Demand service, which is due to be tested in Suffolk this spring. VOD means that entertainment is sent to households via telephone lines. Picture quality is similar to video, although not as sharp as broadcast television.

VOD subscribers will have a decoder and can effectively dial a movie, TV show or video from the VOD database. BT is also exploring the potential for expanding this technology to new home-shopping services.

Meanwhile, cable TV operators are working to extend the network of UK cable TV homes and develop a range of interactive services. According to the Cable Television Association £5bn is likely to be spent in reaching more than 6 million homes in the next six years.

Since 1991, when licensing rules were loosened, cable TV companies have been able to offer telephone services, competing head on with BT. And this is one reason why BT has been, keen to enter the VOD market, – despite being restricted in the entertainment services it can supply.

Internationally, the market is characterised by the merging and consolidating of major players as each vies for supremacy over delivery systems and the libraries of programming and other material that will be the staple of these new services.

Last Year Tele-Communications Inc (TCI) merged with US cable TV operator Bell Atlantic, in a $33m (£22m) deal. More recently, Viacom has been battling against QVC in the takeover fight for Paramount. In the subtext for each move lies a desire for control of new interactive media services.

Meanwhile, computer companies are keen to develop a starndard system to process this new generation of entertainment and information "programming". Microsoft is spending more than £30m a year and has assigned a team of 200 to research interactive TV, according to a recent report.

Yet for many bystanders in the UK – especially advertisers – such activity seems a long way from home. Few advertising agencies are actively exploring the possibilities, although Leo Burnett, J Walter Thompson and DFSD Bozell, are notable exceptions.

"Some agencies will be ahead of the game because of relationships with multinational clients in the US," says

Paul Woolmington, managing director of Bozell's 20/20 Media. "As advertisers will have access to consumers in a completely new way, they should consider the potential now, to learn how interactive can fit within their conventional marketing mix."

Which is exactly why CHBi has been set up. Joint managing director Mark Curtis explains: "People talk about a media revolution as if it were a forthcoming event. We believe that they will wake up to a new order and wonder what on earth happened." Service, rather than more choice, is key. And the value of this serivice will dictate whether or not consumers, and advertisers, will ultimately take up interactive. Consumers must recognise the difference interactive systems will make to their lives. "They will enable you to do something you were unable to do before, or do it quicker," says Beeston. "And this applies as much to the advertiser as to the consumer."

Consumer interest in buying and using the medium will be critical. So far the industry has not finalised an agreed format. But is there a danger that services will be launched too soon and confuse the market by using rival systems? "Major players are aware of the need to avoid another VHS:Betamax scenario," Beeston says. "But there is a [consumer] interest in new technology – there are already 11 million PC/games machines in the UK alone," he says.

If companies are going to exploit the opportunities fully, then they will need the combined strengths of traditional media planning, promotions and direct marketing. Some might view interactive as a below-the-line activity, others maintain it will be of fundamental importance to all means of communication through the line.

Interactive media will offer the supplier instant feedback on consumer tastes and needs, enabling tighter targeting. And it poses the question, will traditional programmes and advertising messages be sufficient or will new forms of communication be required?

JWT media director David Byles dismisses suggestions that the traditional commercial is doomed. "There will be high reach advertising-funded channels alongside hundreds of interactive services," he believes. JWT is already running tests overseas on behalf of a number of clients.

Interactive media in the UK is limited. Videotron is offering interactive services to 60,000 households in South London. Using technology pioneered by Videotron's Canadian parent, it offers viewers interactive games and TV shows including quizzes and sports coverage which allows viewers to pick their own camera shots. Last year Ford ran a campaign involving a traditional commercial followed by a choice of options: to see more technical information; to see press reviews of the car; and to see lists of local distributors.

Sears and Argos have developed interactive in-store units enabling consumers to receive more product information than is conventionally available.

"To date, such systems have been technology-led. We want to reverse that and target the marketing need," says Beeston. The cost of computer hardware is no longer a prohibiting factor. And companies getting in on the act now will be well positioned to extend these activities when new interactive channels are launched – enabling consumers to browse around a shop from their armchairs.

Byles adds: "The vision of a direct relationship with a consumer through TV is of immense importance. "While retailers may be moving in the right direction, in-store units are merely the stepping stone, he says. "More interesting is the way manufacturers with brands will use interactive to develop a direct relationship between brands and the consumer."

ISSUES

(1) **Comment on mass media versus the new one-to-one media.**

(2) **Discuss the notion that consumers are increasingly becoming 'editors'.**

(3) **How would you anticipate the new trends in the commercial message in light of the technology of interactivity?**

(4) **Discuss the impact of direct response television (DRTV) as a new area of direct marketing.**

5 **Mass media is going interactive through video-on-demand, TV shopping and so on. Comment on these new trends.**

6 **What about Digizimes (or e-zimes)? Have you heard of them? What is their role in advertising?**

EXPLORATION OF ISSUES

1 One-to-one media enable the marketer to communicate directly with individual customers instead of 'shouting' at them in groups. One-to-one media are individually addressable, two-way and inexpensive. They have the ability to create dialogue opportunities with customers and to create markets by bringing buyers and sellers together.

Before any marketing mix can influence a consumer, the consumer must first want to engage with the mix. Consumers engage with traditional mass media advertising to a lesser extent than with any other element of the marketing mix. The media objectives of reach and frequency do not reflect interactivity. This is a natural consequence of a mass media orientation, because consumers can do nothing to alter the content of an advertisement that is sent out to them irrespective of whether they want it or not. Most consumers are not affected by the bulk of advertising they passively receive.

2 The consumers of tomorrow will no longer be 'passive recipients' of advertising. Instead they will take on the role of 'editor' – an active, involved participant. Forget about couch potatoes, we are talking couch commandos. Consumers are already active editors of their media because they have experienced an explosion of media choice. Effective targeting in the mass media is about understanding how different customer groups edit the media, how best to involve them in the message and how the brand values of the medium influence the message. Brand managers will need much better ways of understanding how their specific customers edit and involve themselves in the media to achieve the greatest accuracy and the best value.

3 The nature of the commercial message will change as we move towards the multimedia world of mass communication. Four predictions:

- The message will become multidimensional with interactive advertising pods of product information that can be peeled like an onion.
- The message will move from an 'intrusive commercial' to an 'invited conversation'.
- The message will be less ephemeral and more embedded.
- The message will move from a 'glib' intangible style to a substantive, value-added, tangible style.

Once advertisers deposit their 'digital bits' on a network, they will no longer control how or what bits will be rendered. After deposit, consumers and computers will work with the digital bits to create the advertising experience.

4 DRTV advertising is still widely regarded as an underdeveloped marketing opportunity, but new categories of DRTV advertiser are rapidly emerging. Telecom and power companies, and even the healthcare sector, are singled out as areas for future growth – as are fast-moving consumer goods brands.

Two major marketing strategies are linked with the use of DRTV as a marketing tool: the so-called 'direct response' and 'brand response'.

- Direct response: in this case DRTV is used to generate business leads, meaning that the advertisements are expected to lead to a large number of orders by phone.
- Brand response: tries to generate a positive perception of the brand and thus focuses more on presenting the brand's attributes than on attracting a large number of sales.

It is not just the emphasis on brand perception or hard selling that generates differences in DRTV, there are also different presentation formats for TV use. There are home-shopping advertisements of limited duration that offer the possibility of ordering by phone. There are also so-called 'infomercials' which are programme-length advertisements, and video mail, where a particular retailer presents its wares, and interactive telemarketing, where the customer requests information and places his or her order directly on the TV screen.

Whatever reasons lie behind the growth of DRTV, the 1990s will undoubtedly be remembered as the decade in which interactivity came of age. The growing importance of DRTV has gone hand in hand with the massive launch of satellite and cable TV stations, making TV more significant medium than ever and, in particular, making cost-effective airtime available. The newly launched channels are also targeted at smaller and more specific market niches. More generally, in a time when competition is growing among advertisers on the one hand, and customers are becoming fed up with advertisements and the trend towards cocooning on the other, advertisers have to offer additional incentives to distinguish themselves from their competitors and elicit sales. Today the telephone even seems to be old-fashioned compared with interactive telemarketing, where the customer does not even have to use the phone.

There are two other trends that are influencing the use of DRTV: the outsourcing of activities by companies and their growing involvement in overseas operations. In this case outsourcing means that companies delegate some of their activities to telebureaux. Companies must seek integrated marketing solutions and DRTV is only one strand in an elaborate marketing prism. It is thought that DRTV will generate the highest rates of increase of all direct marketing sectors in the near future. The reasons for this, as already outlined earlier, are greater competition and the high degree of internationalisation, where DRTV is a useful tool and comparatively easy to use. These trends will probably go on and the marketing world seems to be taking that into account. DRTV will become more sophisticated in the near future – 'Sophisticated' in that it will deal with quality management-related services such as customer care lines, customer service response lines, loyalty building campaigns, customer satisfaction surveys and so on. DRTV is likely to become even more important in the coming decades, taking into account changing circumstances such as increased competition and 'fed-up' customers.

5 In the past, newspapers, TVs, computers, motion pictures and telephones were all part of separate industries. These distinctions are now blurring and we are entering a new and more challenging phase for business and the home consumer, as mass media go interactive through video-on-demand, TV shopping and so on.

Because a critical mass of adopters is needed before sufficient value is provided to the user to enable interactive mass media technology to take off, it is anticipated that the effect on consumers will be dramatic but gradual. For the majority of families, this will be a gradual process over the next ten or fifteen years and beyond. An important development over the next five years will be steady improvement of the user interface. Interactive media technological innovation is a dynamic process but it will take time to improve content, for companies to learn what customers want and for consumers to get a feel for what technology can do for them and how to use it.

However there is an opposing school of thought, led by Nicholas Negroponte, founder and director of MIT's Media Lab, which believes that interactive mass media will integrate into our lives very quickly, say within five to ten years.

Survey evidence suggests that early adopters who will drive the change to new media comprise families with children at home, families with a significant income and the well-educated. In the longer term, however, television and PCs should not be considered in isolation or even as distinct media technologies. Some commentators foresee a 'box with a screen' in every room, some used for viewing, others for shopping, home security, homework or chatting with friends. Recent alliances between media providers, computer hardware and software manufacturers and telecom companies make this a realistic prediction.

There are three main areas that, will spur the mass adoption of interactive media. First, entertainment is expected to be the main 'driver' behind the mass adoption of interactive media, with applications such as video-on-demand and services such as interactive gambling. Second, marketing communications – there is a common belief that the integration of interactive mass media into consumers' lives will be accompanied by a proliferation and fragmentation of TV channels, and a swing away from advertising-funded entertainment/information towards subscription. However, many media commentators see advertising as a major force in the conversion of interactive media from a fringe hobby into a mass business. For some advertisers, Web sites are provide an effective way of learning how potential customers might use an interactive system. Third, information services are increasingly being provided on-line via the Internet or on CD-ROM, and multimedia kiosks are beginning to appear at airports, train stations, theatres, cinemas, shopping malls and museums.

In contrast with other media, interactive communications provide the opportunity to conduct the sale and collect payment at the same time. It also has one other important advantage: memory. Thus individuals can automate their grocery shopping by storing a shopping list that is automatically called from memory each week.

One of the attractions of the Internet has been its low cost, but as business on the Net grows, we are likely to see the emergence of a charging mechanism. A major factor in keeping down the costs, therefore, will be the willingness and ability of advertisers to exploit this new medium.

6　With names like 'Blender', 'Trouble and Attitude' and 'Launch', the latest magazines are not on the news stands but are accessible only via on-line services or the Internet. Unlike print magazines, digizimes are relatively cheap to start up and operate. For instance, launching a glossy publication for men aged 18–34 in the late 1990s would require at least £6 million, while the digizime start-up cost is between £120 000 and £300 000. Still to be worked out, however, is the advertising equation. Most digizimes charge by the megabyte, although some appear to be experimenting with numbers just to determine what the market will bear.

Marketing on the Internet

KEY CONCEPTS

- Internet marketing
- Advertising on the Internet
- Branding on the Internet
- Interactive advertising

Holes in the net

Many retailers are struggling to attract consumers to their Internet sites, with new research valuing UK online shopping last year at only £1m. IBM has become the first big name to pull out, as traditional retailers reappraise the market. **ROGER BAIRD** questions whether the Net has a future as a retail tool.

The Internet, like the Encyclopedia Britannica, is full of facts and figures. The most revealing fact of all is the one Verdict Research retail analyst Richard Perkis gives for the value of UK online retailing on the Net in the past year. It totals only £1m. This compares with a £160bn total retail business in this country over the past 12 months.

The value of any medium in terms of business use is how many products it can sell. And despite years of ballyhoo, the Net has still to prove how much use it is to consumers.

IBM, for one, will be acutely aware of this. The computer giant is currently running a series of TV ads lauding the technology as a business and sales tool. One of the ads ends with a woman executive asking two in-house computer nerds: "Have any of you

guys tried to sell anything over this?" It is a question that should cause red faces among IBM directors, because last week the company announced that it is scrapping its online shopping mall World Avenue in July, less than a year after it launched.

In a carefully worded statement IBM says the site needs to be promoted and: "Such promotional activities are best handled by the retailers because they have the most in-depth knowledge of their respective customers and are the experts in drawing customer traffic to their stores."

This is an official way of saying the 17 sites in the mall, which included department stores like The Hudson Bay Company, Gottschalks, Health & Vitamin Express and the official Wimbledon tennis championship's merchandise site, were making precious little money.

The UK-based BarclaySquare site, run by Barclays Bank – which includes sites for Sainsbury's, Argos, and Toys R Us – suffers from much the same problem. Though both sites will not reveal sales figures, they are known to be poor despite substantial investment. The fact that Virgin Net will not be replacing its former marketing director Martin Keogh also indicates that traditional UK retailers are taking a hard look at what the Internet really offers.

As Perkis says: "In the early days of the Internet there were a lot of people who were saying a lot of silly things. They vastly overestimated the rate at which it would take off. Even now there is a long way to go. It's still appallingly unfriendly to use. The picture quality of products you are expected to buy needs to improve massively, for example."

In Perkis' view we will see neither hide nor hair of the much talked about online retailing revolution until consumers have Internet access in their homes rather than predominantly at work, as is the case at the moment. This will mean the Net coming into homes through the TV using set-top boxes, and a much higher take-up of computers in the home. Verdict Research believes that it will take another decade before the Net becomes a mass consumer medium.

However, there are plenty who fervently proclaim the opposite: that the Web revolution is just around the corner. Only this month Datamonitor predicted that by 2001 European online consumer sales would be worth £2bn. It added that seven per cent of all homes in Europe would shop online (the figure is currently less than half a per cent), and that there would be 15,000 online shops to choose from. The report also claims that the market in Europe will be worth £60m.

It is hard to see how this latter prediction can be achieved as Datamonitor concedes that the UK, Germany and Sweden are three of the continent's most "Internet-advanced countries", yet according to Verdict's figures, the UK market is worth about £1m a year. This is the problem with much of the research surrounding the Net: too much of it is based on predictions rather than accepted standards.

A revealing report by Mintel took the temperature of UK online retail companies and found the waters decidedly tepid. One retail project manager puts it frankly: "If you measure success on the Internet in terms of sales, then it is not successful, it is a waste of time."

A director of a mail order company summed up the view that many in this sector hold: "Given the limitations of the Internet in its present form, I think transaction will be limited. It will be more important for people with information products, such as travel insurance, rather than selling physical merchandise in the way that we do.

"It will also be used as an information source and will start to affect where people get their information from before they go to the shop. This is more important than the transaction at the moment."

BT estimates that only about 300,000 homes have a personal computer with Internet access. Many of the small number of people using the technology at the moment share a something-for-nothing, pioneering approach to the Web – not very encouraging for commerce.

A project co-ordinator of an online shopping unit adds: "Shopping is hindered by low use of the Internet in the home. People mainly use it at work and shopping figures pretty low on their agenda. I am convinced that most Internet surfing is done on other people's phone bills. Employers are going to get wise to this at some point."

If this project co-ordinator is right, he is effectively puncturing the argument that the Web will take off when people are offered free local calls, as they are in the US, since in the UK users can already use technology free of charge.

However, Perkis thinks it was a mistake for IBM to drop its World Avenue site. In his view it is worth enduring ten years of losses in order to find the pot of gold at the end of the rainbow.

For Andrew Warmsley, chairman of the Digital Marketing Group which represents the majority of the interactive arms of the top 20 advertising agencies, the biggest problem he comes across is companies going online without really knowing why they are doing so.

"Marketers still have to grasp the strategic nettle when it comes to the Web, otherwise all they are doing is playing with it. You could argue that the IBM site was a success because it has shown us that that particular business model probably will not work. There is still a lot to learn in this area," he adds.

Warmsley does not dispute the Verdict figures covering retail on the Net, but points out that there is sizeable under-reporting surrounding Internet commerce.

For instance, he says he booked his holiday to Greece on the Web, but reveals that he will not pay for his room until he turns up at the hotel. Is that, asks Warmsley, an Internet purchase or not?

Without trying to sound overly mischievous it sounds as if the head of the Digital Marketing Group prefers to pay cash.

Owners aboard

UK media owners are joining the Internet rush, but they must ensure their sites offer something different, says **NICK JONES**

The Internet is well established as a medium in the UK. Those who doubt its popularity and permanence should note that the new year brought the Electronic Telegraph its millionth registered user and saw the arrival online of such varied titles as the Express and The Fortean Times.

And it is not only the newspapers which are building new media operations. Brands across the media spectrum are developing Websites and interactive strategies to reach their audiences.

While the launch of yet another print title's Website is no longer news, what is exciting is the titles that are breaking the models associated with early Internet publishing. It is only appropriate that at the front of the next generation is IPC's Loaded. The publishing rule-breaker's site, dubbed with the droll name Uploaded, is keen to avoid Web clichés, proclaiming "this isn't just another tedious waste of Web space or loads of old bits from the magazine that have been rehashed".

Users of the site – www.uploaded.com – can vote on the best looking girls, download seedy screensavers and listen to pirate radio.

Joining Loaded on the electronic news-stand is EMAP's New Woman, the latest addition to the publisher's Connect stable of sites developed for the Web and CompuServe. Like Loaded, New Woman (www.erack.com/ newwoman) breaks a few rules. The monthly title provides a daily update of relevant news, which is important to encourage return visits to the site. But it still serves up a diet of horoscopes, hunks and health advice.

Some publishers are more cautious when taking their properties online. United News & Media has opted to take a well-established formula online by launching the Express holiday brochure ordering service Website. The service ties in with the paper's popular brochure, and existing advertisers are encouraged to place ads on the new site with reduced fees.

Keith Cartwright, group head of travel advertising at the Express, says: "I've been looking for something to expand our Net content. This is the first stage between travel content and potential revenue."

So, how do these new kids on the block shape up against their US cousins?

While praising the couch-potato lifestyle, Uploaded shapes up well against US men's magazines. Men's Health has a site (www.menshealth.com) that tries to mix health with "lad" humour. But despite the irony deficiency, it makes the most of the Web's multimedia features.

New Woman's site launched in the shadow of Cosmopolitan's but it shines in comparison. Sex and health tips can be found on both but New Woman's daily update outshines Cosmo's previews of the print edition.

The Express may be an established name in the UK but in the travel sector, one of the Internet's most exploited areas, that is of little comfort. It could find itself competing against the might of Microsoft for the attention of holidaymakers, if the software and would-be media giant decides to expand its Expedia (www.expedia.com) and Mungo Park (www.msn.com/mungopark) travel sites beyond the US.

Some UK media brands are also keen to go global. The Economist magazine will soon launch a Website that will charge a subscription to access some parts of it. "For our inter-national readers the attraction of getting it speedily and online is a considerable enhancement", says editor Bill Emmott.

One of the most exciting results of going on the Web for radio stations has been the growth of international audiences. One ex-pat IBM executive in Chicago confesses to "tuning in" to Virgin Radio's Website when he gets home-sick.

And since Virgin Radio pioneered Internet radio in the UK last year, many stations have woken up to other ways the Web can help them exploit their brands. At the forefront are LBC and Capital FM.

LBC's site (www.lbc.co.uk) was initially conceived as a means of marketing the station and joint promotions with the likes of restaurants and venues, but it quickly realised it could be used to extract value from the information that came into its newsroom every day.

"LBC listeners aren't interested in chat. They want quality information," says John Williams, the station's new media publisher. So, the site is being used to broadcast events which are too long to squeeze into a hectic radio schedule.

The station's brand values of timely information are not compromised by the site, which offers a live text feed of travel news as well as detailed regional weather.

In contrast, Capital FM is keen that its site (www.capitalfm.co.uk) should set its listeners talking. It features chat "rooms" and enlivens traditional site content, such as entertainment guides and downloads, by exploiting some of the latest Net technologies.

A dedicated new media department helps the station keep on top of developments. According to Douglas McCallum, who heads the department, Capital is looking at how software can be used to build online communities – reinforcing the strategy of building lasting relationships with listeners.

The élan with which print publishers and radio stations in the UK have adapted to the Web is not always matched by the TV companies. While some see the Net as a means of learning about interactivity, others believe it is just another way of publishing schedules.

A site to watch is that of BSkyB (www.sky.co.uk). The satellite channel has developed it beyond the simple schedule model by building its content from successful programming such as The X Files and sport – the site is also home to the official Manchester United site.

The depth of content is due to the site's integration into the station's other operations. News and sports content generated by its 30-strong Skytext teletext team complements the set-piece work undertaken by dedicated journalists working on individual programme and channel areas. "We believe this is a business," explains Simon Howson-Green, head of Internet at BSkyB. He says that the site is not funded from the marketing budget – as many schedule-driven sites

are. Instead, sponsorship and advertising bring in revenue.

Also exploiting programming links is United News & Media's Meridian. Its site (www.meridian.tv.co.uk) launched at the same time as the station's adaptation of Emma and during the first weeks online, the site examined Austenmania. Other content ties in with the Cyberspace series that "explores the marriage of TV and the new interactive media", explains Adrian Tennant, whose Alchemy Interactive Marketing Services created and maintains the Meridian site.

Nearly all major cinema releases in the UK are supported by Websites, unlike most television series. The exception proves the rule. While Polygram Filmed Entertainment made the mistake of not commissioning a Website for the theatre release of Trainspotting it made amends for the video release with an site that exploited the films cult imagery (www.trainspotting.co.uk).

There are lessons that all media brands can take from their involvement in the new media. Primarily that it should be treated as a high stakes game.

Another lesson is to expect to co-operate. In the US, Condé Nast teamed up with Internet search firm

InfoSeek. In the UK, News International and BT will soon launch the Springboard online service. In Japan, daily newspaper Mainichi Shimbun signed up electrical goods retailer Bic Camera to work with it on the Nippon Internet service.

But it may be too late for some media owners to benefit from the most important lesson. The Web is the cheapest way to experiment with new media and learn lessons on how to use interactivity.

The advent of Internet technologies that push content to users over networks is the cause. Pioneering work by PointCast, BackWeb and Marimba and iFusion has demonstrated that it is possible to overcome the limits on using the Internet to serve up a feast of multi-media content to users – even to TV quality in the case of iFusion's Arrive network.

But the cost of redesigning content to suit the nuances of each of these networks could become a barrier to entering the interactive media market for those owners which have not yet understood which model suits them best. Unfortunately, many in this category are British. Jean Louis Bravard, president of iFusion, reports only a lukewarm response to his company's technology from UK media owners.

Safety Net

Given the widespread fears that electronic commerce is not safe, what steps are being taken to reassure consumers?

DAVID REED

Five years ago, the national newspapers were full of stories about junk mail. Life insurance mailings to recent widows were a popular horror story, but so too were mail order frauds. Such incidents may still occur, but they are not a common

experience. Nowadays the papers only occasionally take a swipe at this target.

Instead, they are more likely to run scare stories about security on the Internet. Consumers whose credit card details have been stolen by hackers, or captured by unscrupulous

traders on the other side of the globe, often feature. When direct mail was the target, a popular conspiracy theory among direct marketers was that newspaper barons saw the medium as a threat to their advertising revenues, hence the hostility. The Net could simply be the next perceived challenger to be seen off.

Certainly, those involved in electronic commerce say there is little real justification for the negative coverage. Although credit card issuers are tight-lipped about how much fraud does take place, Internet transactions appear to suffer a lower level of abuse than their telephone-based equivalent, and one-hundredth the level of direct mail problems, according to one source.

Despite this, there is a very real perception in the market that electronic commerce might not be safe. According to research carried out by The Henley Centre, 69 per cent of a sample of 500 early adopters agreed they were concerned about the security of online transactions, 39 per cent of them agreeing strongly. However, analyst Chad Wallen notes: "The more people use the Net, the less strongly they agreed."

He adds: "The way we came to understand it, electronic commerce is not an alien concept that they can't imagine doing at all. But everyone is petrified of buying things. There are a significant number who seem to be buying and a larger number who are prepared to see it as commonplace in the future."

This emerges from a comparison of how people are using the Net now and how they foresee using it in five years' time. The Henley Centre found 59 per cent used it for getting information, 36 per cent for communication, ten per cent for entertainment and one per cent for transactions. In the future, however, 41 per cent said they would use it for communication, 33 per cent for transactions, 28 per cent for information and 16 per cent for entertainment.

Other research sources suggest that transactions over the Net are slowly beginning to reach critical mass. Peter Matthews, managing director of Nucleus Design, says one way to calculate Net use is to combine figures.

"Lou Gerschner, chief executive of IBM, believes 50 million people are online. Forrester Research, a leading US IT research agency, says one in four of all users of the Net claim to have purchased. If you extrapolate from that, that makes 12.5 million transactions," he says.

He points out that Amazon.com, the remarkably successful online bookshop, declared first-quarter 1997 sales of $27m (£17.5m). But he does sound a note of caution about assuming all Net transactions are substitutes for high-street purchases. "You don't know how many of those purchases are legitimate or for pornography – a lot of credit card use is for pornography," says Matthews.

Whatever effect such transactions have on Net users' morals, they may at least have one positive outcome. If a user can give credit card details to a business as shadowy as pornography and not get ripped off, then the chances are a legitimate trader will be even more trusted.

These sites also educate users about the possible ways of buying online, especially if they use one of the three major "virtual credit cards" – Open Market, First Virtual and Cyberbank. These work by opening an account with a Net user who is then issued an online card. The real transactions are processed offline, converting cyber dollars into real ones, reducing the risk of details falling into the wrong hands.

John Sofield is managing director of TDS Internet. His company has the UK rights to Tradex, an online negotiating system which makes use of virtual credit. He says: "Once a consumer has signed up with a virtual bank, there is no filling out forms; they just use a digital code. Once that has been verified, the transaction can be processed."

There is some scepticism about virtual banks, however. David Aldridge, European vice-president of iCat, which markets an online electronic commerce software package, says: "The average guy in the street doesn't know those companies. They only trust Lloyds, NatWest, Barclays and Midland."

For online shopping to take off in the UK, companies will have to become more heavily involved in developing systems and marketing to the general public. "We have been doing a lot of work with the four major clearing banks to get them to endorse what is going on. If they don't say, 'we use the Web and it is fine', nobody will trust it."

"The problem with the Net is that credit card companies are only now starting to make use of security protocols they are happy with, even though there are encryption formats which even the US military can't crack," says Matthews. In fact, issues of national security have held up the release of 128-bit encryption technology into the commercial world, because the FBI has been concerned that criminals and terrorists will use it to encode messages that they cannot then decipher.

However, Matthews says: "Even 64-bit encryption offers a very high level of protection." The current most widely-used format is SSL (Secure Sockets Layer) protocol, which most new browser software can support. Aldridge says that for online traders, "if you are not using SSL, it is like giving your credit card to a tramp downstairs".

What SSL does not have, however, is big-budget backing that will create a sense of reassurance among online shoppers. That is only likely to come as a result of the recently-unveiled SET2 (Secure Encrypted Transaction) protocol. This system is the end-result of a test by Microsoft, Mastercard and Visa whose ambitions are, variously, to dominate the Internet and to make cash a thing of the past.

Reaching agreement on a common standard has been far from easy for these three, and they will not immediately be able to impose SET2 on all electronic commerce sites. But in the UK, at least, the major banks appear to be endorsing the system, which will help get it established. Although once again, secure transactions really means secure for the financial institutions. "SET is only there to protect the credit card issuer, not the consumer," says Aldridge.

For those companies already trying to build a business on the Net, it is a case of "suck it and see". At Book Pages, a newly launched online bookshop, managing director Simon Murdoch says: "We have run trials with encryption systems. Our argument is that SSL is pretty secure, so there is nothing to worry about."

Murdoch says fears about security can be overcome by marketing. "Because of the confusion in the world about security, we offer two other ways of ordering. Customers can place an order with all the details, print it out, handwrite their credit card information and fax or post it to us, or they can use a phone number during office hours and give us their card details," he says. Use of these channels suggests security fears are more perceived than real – only 2.5-to-three per cent of Book Pages customers order by fax and just 0.75 per cent use the phone.

Unlike the US, fewer company buyers in the UK use credit cards to pay for business purchases, preferring to be invoiced.

The type of transactions which the general public might want to carry out online have also yet to be tested. Last year, the Post Office worked with a consortium of hard- and software companies to run an internal test of a transactional system which it called Project Genesis. Among the services it offered was buying travellers cheques online for collection from the nearest Post Office Counter.

According to US research agency Find SVP, 60 per cent of those who have been online for five years or more have bought products from an overseas supplier. While an unknown quantity of those purchases may have been shipped in plain brown wrappers, the event horizon for high-volume electronic commerce is probably closer than you think.

Web or dead

The Web has made the Internet user-friendly, and advertisers daren't miss out. But, says **CAROLINE BASSETT**, surfers are a fickle lot

The World Wide Web changed the face of the Internet, preparing the way for an explosion in consumer use. It made the Net user-friendly, breaking up long screeds of text with graphics. So why are NetScape users turning them off?

The answer is that pictures still take too long to upload. Net surfers choose to see only images they've specifically selected. The practice serves as a salutary reminder of the degree to which Net users control their own consumption. Users go – and see – what they please, by the route they please.

This leaves advertisers with a problem. While it's easy enough to set up a page on the World Wide Web, how do you ensure your target market will visit it? And how do you know if they have? The short answer is that you can't force them; you have to seduce them.

The nature of that seduction, and how to measure its successes and failures, is the subject of a flurry of on-line experimentation as the big agencies, their clients and the content providers race to establish a commanding presence on-line.

The attractions of the Net are obvious: 30 million users worldwide, explosive growth rates and the promise of highly segmented audiences. At current expansion rates, not too far into the next century almost everyone in the West will be on the Net and – while many Internet statistics are disputed, the underlying tendency is clear enough.

Another spur to getting on-line now is the fear of missing out. The US experience suggests that, as media fragments, so do audiences. If they're on the Net, they're not watching TV.

Mark Dickinson, new media development director at Lowe Howard-Spink, cites figures suggesting TV viewing drops by 25 per cent when people surf the Internet. "If we're not there too, we're going to lose them. So there's a fear factor," he says.

So for many of those coming onto the Net the focus is on trial and error, on gaining experience, rather than making profits – and much of the advertising space on offer from the online publishers is organised to facilitate this. With the exception of the giant commercial on-line services (notably CompuServe with its 3.4 million users, 150,000 of them in the UK), spokespeople from agencies and publishers agree few on the Internet are making money. That isn't really the point – yet.

The most direct route onto the Web

is by setting up a site, or series of pages with their own Web address or URL (Universal Resource Locator). This is the route Virgin took with its site, the Raft. It carries clips from different bands and a news section that includes information on new releases. Eventually every artist in the catalogue will have digital material. Paul Sanders, joint founder of State 51, the web production consultancy hired by Virgin to help construct the Raft, said it functions to build links between artists and the people who will buy their work.

Virgin, of course, has all the content it needs, and is in the happy position of catering to a set of consumers hungry for more information, and for more direct links with the bands. Sanders' conception of the Web site he helped build is as a place best used to build awareness and relationships between artists and products and their users. He regards it as a marketing exercise in much the same way a live gig might be, and says its effectiveness cannot be measured purely in terms of sales. For many others, the question of Net content is more problematic. Without compelling content, persuading people to visit and return to sites is already difficult – and it will get harder. Dickinson claims that evidence from the US suggests random surfing has slowed. Commercial Web sites increasingly need not only desirable content but also a profile to attract choosier Net traffic.

This is where advertising and other deals with the fast-growing electronic publications sector come in. On the Net it is irrelevant where a page is based – far more important is what it is linked to. This largely dictates who will know it is there. Setting up links from within the densely populated magazine sites, using flashes, boxes and strategically clickable graphic buttons, is an attempt to work the Net to channel traffic into specific commercial sites.

Links might be laid, for instance, with the Electronic Telegraph, connecting with its general audience, or with Future Publishing's FutureNet or HotWired, which can both lay claim to be purveyors of "Netgeist". Other options include the specialist sites like Ziff Davis's ZD Net, individual magazines such as CD-ROM Magazine, or Top Gear, all of which deliver tightly focused groups of specialist consumers.

There are considerable variations in scale and approach. The Electronic Telegraph has been sitting on the World Wide Web since last November, and claims to be the most popular Web site in Europe with 90,000 registered users and 100,000 pages requested daily. Advertisers include some Telegraph stalwarts, and some more loosely tied into the print version. FutureNet – smaller, but still busy – claims more than 30,000 log-ins weekly. It has attracted consumer brands such as Guinness and Vauxhall and is reaching a constituency beyond its paper-based magazine readers. ZD Net, an example of a more specialised service, aims for depth – and claims 14 of the top technology firms as advertisers.

Vauxhall, the UK's largest on-line advertiser, has linked its home pages with ads appearing in five Web sites – the Electronic Telegraph, Financial Times, Time Out, FutureNet and Top Gear. The choice of specialist and general magazines was an attempt to gauge where and how traffic could be generated, and from which publications. Not surprisingly, Top Gear produced the biggest conversion rate – that is, the largest percentage of visitors to the magazine site moved on to the Vauxhall site.

There are further options to consider within a specific location. Pippa Littler, strategic planner for the Telegraph, gives on-line advertisers the chance to experiment with placing. For £25,000, advertisers get a clickable strip linking to their home page or to an advertisement held within the Telegraph (if they don't have a site of their own). This is shifted across different sections of the newspaper (front page, home news, world news, City, sport, features, gazetter and weather) over a six-week period – advertisers can then gauge an optimum position for themselves, depending on the responses they get. A sum of $40,000 would buy you the entire ZD Net home page rotation – which puts an advertisement in all of its magazine home pages – for a similar period. FutureNet, which also has a portfolio of technology (and Net-based) titles, does the same – at £2,000 a hit.

On-line registration when entering a site can be voluntary or compulsory, and may record different information. The Electronic Telegraph, for instance, gathers information on age, sex and occupation. Every user gets a pin number password. Registration is also used by HotWired, and from October will be adopted by FutureNet. However, some users avoid sites which demand registration, and it can distort traffic figures – users tend to lose their passwords and re-register themselves, or groups may use the same password, so deflating numbers.

The shift towards incentivised voluntary registration may help. Also, however imperfect the magazine sites, users are more likely to register here than at commercial stops. One attraction of advertising within the publications, therefore, is that basic demographic information can be obtained more easily.

Nonetheless, circulation and other figures remain problematic – disputes break out, for instance, over measuring numbers by hits (the number of items clicked within a specific page) or page accesses. The Audit Bureau of Circulations and BPA International are talking to many of the content providers in an attempt to agree a way to validate claims.

Tracking users provides more than demographic information. Profiled consumers are followed around the site as they explore it. What they look at, where they have come from and where they are going to can be logged and analysed.

In this way, tracking can suggest new tactics for positioning ads. Following users through State 51, the lifestyle and music Web site, revealed that only 20 per cent of its readers started at the front page, and substantial numbers never arrived at all.

This is partly a result of random surfing, and partly because users hone their own itinerary – search tools such as Lycos can take surfers directly to the subject of their choice, allowing them to bypass the outer layers of a Web site built around nuggets of attractive information. On-line publications, should not be assumed to work in a similar way to their tree-based counterparts.

If links are one way to re-route traffic to commercial sites, another is to leverage the audience within the publication more directly. Advertisers in the Electronic Telegraph are experimenting with ways of branding; for instance, the TSB sponsors a weekly personal finance section. Most recently, the Electronic Telegraph launched Fantasy Football, sponsored by Littlewoods Pools, which will run for

the the season. Offering £25,000 prize money, it produced 100,000 page accesses in the first three hours it was on-line.

So the choice of location for links, or for other forms of advertising, depends on the audience being sought and – increasingly – the depth and quality of the demographic information provided. Clearly this requires working with the grain of the Net itself.

Tony Burgess Webb, executive vice president of Hill & Knowlton, argues that the Net is not essentially – or not only – an advertising medium. The true currency of the Internet is free information. The point is to work within this paradigm to position the brand and improve communication with its public.

Moves to incorporate the Internet into wider campaigns within other forms of new media – and beyond – make quantifying the gains of specific advertising or Net placement more difficult, but seem to promise greater payback.

Vauxhall is planning a multimedia launch for Vectra. Running alongside the traditional spend will be the Web site and Web-based advertising sign-

posting it, a CD-Rom cover-mounted to Dennis Publishing's CD-Rom magazine – which in turn has its own Web links – and a tip-on card offering a CD-Rom in Top Gear's web site. In a speculative move, Vauxhall plans to produce interactive material for BT's video-on-demand test sites. The intention is to integrate Net-based and traditional media activities – each providing additional visibility for the other. Web addresses, for instance, will feature on print-based ads.

Clearly, while it's easy enough to get onto the Web, doing it effectively requires careful thought and considerable investment. Fortunately, expertise in developing, positioning and monitoring the results of on-line ventures is becoming widely available – for a price.

For example, Hill & Knowlton, an interactive media services group worldwide, offer a tiered range of services, moving from a basic NetAlert service to full Web site design and maintenance. Help, which ranges from the production of a single ad to the creation of an entire site, is at hand from the on-line providers themselves and from many consultancies in the field.

ISSUES

1. **To what extent does the Internet provide a global medium for shopping?**

2. **How does the Internet affect the balance of power and the relationship between marketer and consumer?**

3. **What are the limitations of the Internet for marketing and relationship building?**

4. **What are your views on Internet marketing?**

5　How do you reach potential customers and keep them returning to the Web site?

6　How could a company make advertising on the Internet effective?

EXPLORATION OF ISSUES

1　A marketer's, presence on the Internet is international by definition and compared with other media the Web provides a reasonably level playing field for all players, regardless of size. However, use of the Internet and World Wide Web to foster international consumer relationships may not be possible.

Their use across borders can be hampered by the heterogeneous nature of markets. For example Virgin Atlantic Airways maintained a Web site and displayed details of its trans-Atlantic airfares. The Web site listed a return airfare of under $500, but a prospective passenger wishing to buy one of these tickets was told that this special price was no longer available and the ticket would now cost over $500. Under US law the airline was obliged to keep the information up to date, and as it had failed to do so it ended up paying the US Department of Transport $14 000.

Clearly UK companies that do business with customers in other countries need to be aware of the laws that apply there when promoting their goods and services via the Internet. Perhaps the most problematic area will be the financial services industry, as this sector is closely regulated in most countries.

Still on the theme of international conflicts, the Italian company Tattilo Editrice SpA made erotic pictures available over the Internet. The milder pictures were available to all visitors to the Web site, whether or not they had a subscription. More explicit pictures were available to those who subscribed to a special service.
Tattilo is based in Italy and both services were made available from computer equipment located in Italy. The domain name (that is the Internet address) of the Web site was 'playmen'. Playboy Enterprises Inc – the publisher of *Playboy* magazine – had once failed to obtain protection for its Playboy trade mark *in Italy* in a previous case brought against Tattilo. However Playboy brought proceedings against Tattilo *in the NewYork* courts, claiming that Tattilo had infringed Playboy's US registration of the Playboy trade mark by – among other things – its use of the '*playmen*' address because the service was available to US citizens. The court agreed and ordered Tattilo either to refuse subscriptions from US customers or to shut down its Internet site, even though that site was in Italy. Tattilo was also ordered to pay Playboy the gross profits it had earned from subscriptions to the service by US customers and all gross profits earned from the sale of goods and services advertised on the playmen site. Interestingly, the court stated that 'Cyberspace is not a safe haven' (Sampson, 1999).

2　One of the fundamental building blocks in any relationship is one party's knowledge of another. 'Knowledge is power' is a well established principle, and a major determinant of marketing power has always been the amount of information possessed by agents. From the consumer's perspective, such knowledge might be, in the first instance, limited to what an organisation decides to communicate to the consumer via the Internet, the World Wide Web or other methods of communication. But due to the nature of the Internet and Web, the 'power of information gathering' might be in favour of the consumer. The Web is a powerful tool with which to gather information that might not normally be available to the consumer, such as information on an organisation that has been published by a national or international third party, and this could influence the development of a relationship. This potential for consumer knowledge could actually hamper an organisation's use of this medium. For example a company might be selling the same product in different countries at different prices, and by informing consumers from different countries that they can buy it cheaper elsewhere, the trust in any relationship might be lost instantly. The Internet might lead to a narrowing of price differentials as consumers become more aware of prices in different countries. This potential threat to organisations wanting to build relationships through on-line communications and transactions might be solved by the use of local language, but hindered by an improvement in linguistic ability among consumers in different countries.

Nonetheless, from an organisation's perspective, 'relationship knowledge' can be developed quite naturally via the Internet and the World Wide Web. There are a number of ways in which an organisation can build up its knowledge of consumers:

- the availability of Web site statistics in log files means that Web site visitors can be tracked and traced without their knowledge.
- monitoring 'cookie files' are files within a browser, and through the use of tags a site can recognise whether users have visited the site before and a record can be called up of how they behaved last time.
- On-line forms are 'data entry spaces' on Web sites, linked to a database, that allow users to input information. Forms can be designed to make it optional or compulsory for users to navigate further into the Web site. Forms can be used to gather demographic data, registration information (for example e-mail addresses) or more comprehensive information through on-line questionnaires.

The above can provide valuable information that enables an organisation to develop profiles, tailor its communications and develop 'one-to-one' relationships. The existence of such knowledge by both consumers and organisations (willingly or otherwise) reaffirms the idea of a two-way information flow in relationship marketing.

3 With regard to the limitations of the Internet for marketing and relationship building, first, if an organisation's current or target consumers do not have on-line connections, relationship marketing via the Internet or the World Wide Web will not be feasible. However, as the number of on-line connections, through computers or set-top boxes (which facilitate Internet access though TVs), draws near to the number of telephones and TVs, its attractiveness as a medium will increase. Of course, the limitations placed on employees by employers concerning Internet access in the workplace might impede the development of relationships with consumers who rely on access through the work place.

Second, for effective relationships to flourish over the Internet, the telecom infrastructure should not in any way serve to limit communications. For example frustration with 'download times' or weak or non-existent connections could distinctly damage relationships. From the international or global perspective, this is important as telecom infrastructures in different countries are in various stages of development and this could reduce the effectiveness of on-line marketing strategies.

Third, all private on-line users have an account with an 'Internet service provider' (ISP). There are two main types of account: dial-up, where customers are charged a flat rate fee for a monthly connection, and on-line, where customers are charged an hourly rate. The development of the Internet is partly attributable to the introductory offers made by the larger ISPs such as AOL and Compuserve. This has resulted in consumers taking up one 'offer' after another for free connection for a limited period. From a relationship perspective, this switching is detrimental. Therefore consumer relationships are only likely to flourish over the Internet when consumers stay with one Internet service provider. This could be likened to one of the foundation stones of relationships – 'commitment'. The main problems with account switching from an organisational perspective are traceability and administration. Even though the technology exists to forward e-mail messages to other accounts or access e-mail accounts from around the world using 'telnet', if a consumer switches ISP and there are no other contact details for that consumer, she or he may be untraceable. In terms of administration, the switching of ISP increases the time spent on maintaining databases and so on. This could increase the cost of consumer relationships and offset the the lower cost of communicating by this medium.

Fourth, it is commonly accepted that personal details such as names, addresses and telephone number should be up to date, genuine and not misleading. In formal arrangements, the law often requires this as a prerequisite. However, clients of ISPs often use a codename for the purposes of e-mail communications. Genuine first names, surnames, initials, or aliases or jokey names – all possible and the permutations are virtually unlimited. The only thing that can prevent the use of a particular name or term is if it has already been registered with the particular ISP the applicant proposes to use. However that person can then try another ISP that uses a different domain name and register the preferred name or term there. This can cause confusion and is potentially damaging to on-line relationship building as the person with whom you think you are communicating could be someone totally different.

Fifth, some consumers are likely to have more then one e-mail address – one at work and one at home. In itself this may not limit the building of relationships as consumers normally state which e-mail address they wish to be used, but combined with some of the limitations above, the existence of more than one e-mail address adds to the difficulty of maintaining relationships over the Internet.

Sixth, from an international perspective, whilst it may be feasible to establish Web pages using different languages, including those with special characters, for example Greek and Japanese, e-mail messages are written in ASCII format, which does not support these characters.

Seventh, the Internet and World Wide Web can bypass third parties in conventional supply chains and 'bring the organisation closer to the consumer', irrespective of geographic location,because ISPs or telecommunication companies have so much power over its use, the future opportunities for developing relationships may lie in the hands of such organisations.

Eighth, there are a number of issues to do with privacy, including an increase in the ease at which people can be monitored – as described earlier, most of a users movements can be monitored and logged when visiting a Web, FTP or Gopher site and these site logs or records may not be kept private. Likewise there are organisations that log and list the e-mail addresses of participants in 'themed' discussion groups and then offer these lists for commercial use (for a small fee). There is also the possibility of database information being put to a different use from that intended – databases such as 'USENET/UUCP' were never intended for commercial use.

One way in which organisations can reduce the abuse of privacy is to build into their Web sites forms where visitors can 'voluntarily' provide information. Such volunteered information could act as a valuable foundation for dialogue to prosper and relationships to flourish.

E-mail could be deemed to be 'private', but privacy really depends on the sender and his or her ethical stance. It also depends on the form in which e-mail is sent over the Internet. If e-mail messages are 'encrypted', the likelihood of the message remaining confidential is increased. However the sheer volume of Internet traffic might produce a degree of privacy. This could be significant in all relationships with consumers in trying to develop trust over time. For certain types of communication, encrypted messages will probably be a prerequisite.

In the on-line community there is general feeling that unsolicited or 'junk' e-mail is unacceptable. Therefore organisations should be wary of considering this method to induce dialogue with consumers. In the United States such behaviour is often frowned upon and followed up by abusive reply messages from recipients and possible legal action. Until recently self-regulation has been the norm, but the establishment of an organisation in the United States called the Internet E-mail Marketing Council (IEMMC) might be the first step towards the regulation of unsolicited e-mails. Consisting of five large e-mail advertising companies and a backbone provider, the IEMMC will implement a filtration system that will effectively block the sending of any commercial e-mail, to unwilling recipients whose addresses are held on a list by a third party. This initiative, if successful, may facilitate on-line relationships through unsolicited mass e-mailing, as the recipients will have tacitly consented to receive such communications (Frost, 1999).

④ The Internet is the ultimate interactive and integrated communication system, and it is what relationship marketing will be all about as it will put the consumer, not the marketer, in control of communication. Consumers will seek information about products and services under terms set by them. It may be that this new system will completely transform our concept of marketing. Or perhaps, marketing is not the right term for the electronic arena – 'marketspace' may be more appropriate because location will no longer be important in the transfer of information, and even products and services.

The Internet is not a marketing system in the traditional sense, it is a totally new concept – marketing, customer service and a multitude of other human interactions all rolled into one system. So the use traditional methods of marketing and communications make no sense. The methods we use to plan, develop and measure marketing programmes today will not be appropriate. New terms will be used, for example, instead of word of mouth, we may have 'word of keyboard'.

So what do we make of all this? Firstly, it is clear that the Internet is going to be a major factor in communications in the future, but precisely when is anybody's guess. What will it be like? Most agree that the Internet and the Web will not stay in their present form. There will be changes, perhaps even dramatic ones, but the key ingredients have already been identified. There is little question that consumers will be in control. What that means to traditional marketing, advertising and promotion is not quite clear, but there is little question that advertisers and marketers will have to change or at least adapt their methods.

Traditional media are not likely to be displaced by the Internet, but they will certainly be challenged.

⑤ With the Internet booming, many businesses are eager to get their products and services onto the World Wide Web, but putting your company's information on the screen and providing links to related sites might not be enough. Many consumers and potential customers are skimming through Web sites more often, so you need

something with immediate appeal to potential customers. It is also important to bear in mind that a Web
site is like a storefront, and as the products and promotions in the store keep changing, so should the Web site.
On virtually every page there should be a place to let
people visiting your site know that it is changing; this
could be in the form of an updated section, or a place for
them to 'check here' for new information daily, weekly
and so on.

Another key to a successful Web site is the provision of
customer service. If nothing else, this will promote goodwill as your customers will know that you are there, can
click on a button and get an immediate response, rather
than have to listen to a few minutes of music on the
phone or endure automated voice messages. Customer
service should be easy and visible, so that customers
know how to reach you without too much searching.

Other ideas include building a database of e-mail
addresses so that you can send updates, special offers or
information about new products, and providing a place
where people visiting your Web site can leave messages
and provide feedback; this will make customers feel as
though they are providing direct input into the company.

Another hint for marketers is to make the site easy to
navigate. If people cannot get through to your Web site
easily, the odds are that they will not return to it, even if
it changes regularly.

The opportunities provided by the Internet keep growing for marketers, as does the number of people that
have access.

6 Advertisements on the Internet must be useful
and/or entertaining if they are to win over an audience.
Much of the advertising currently on the Internet represents little more than an electronic Yellow Pages, only
slower, less relevant and with big gaps.

The Internet is not an advertising medium in the normal sense of the word. Rather it is a hugely fragmented,
non-structured information vehicle that many wrongly
believe can be used just like any other advertising medium. Plonk your advertisement on it and, hey presto, 30
to 40 million people will see it. Unfortunately this is not
the case.

Being optimistic, let's say 35 million people worldwide have access to the Internet. Removing those who
have access to the Internet at work but do not actually
use it brings the figure down to 20 million. Now look at
the number who use the Internet on any one day – perhaps 10 million. Now remember that they have a choice
of at least four million Internet addresses to look at.
Consider that they will look for items that are useful or
entertaining. Is it likely that many will browse through
the typical advertisement?

The rush to create sites in the wake of media hype
resulted in thousands of advertisers launching inappropriate sites for Internet users. They offered very little
of value and many directed the hapless user to the
telephone for the real information. A large number of
advertising sites will no doubt be discontinued, but
many will change to become more relevant to users.
Sites need to be useful and/or entertaining. Those that
can capitalise on the unique benefits of Internet technology, such as access from anywhere in the world, data
searching and electronic dialogue, have a better chance
of success.

Some advertisers seem to he heading in the right
direction. Take the Carling Internet site, for example. It is
a vast (and fast) up-to-date compendium of football facts,
news, results, statistics and gossip from the FA Carling
Premiership. This is very useful for the many football
fans who use the Internet in the UK and a useful extension of Carling's sponsorship of the Premiership.

Only a few advertisers can take advantage of Internet
technology. A good example is Federal Express, which
allows its customers, wherever they are in the world, to
tap directly into the FedEx Global Package Tracking
Database, at any time of the day or night to pinpoint the
current status of their package. This saves FedEx an estimated $2million per year in staff costs. The system
includes a facility whereby customers can request their
package status be automatically e-mailed. In addition
customers can download free FedEx document preparation software, providing the tools to complete and print
export forms correctly. However the FedEx site is more
of an integral part of the FedEx product than an
advertisement.

Part 3
Issues in Strategic Marketing Planning

Introduction

In this part we consider more strategic aspects of marketing. Chapter 10 is concerned with organisational issues for the marketing function. This is followed by a doscussion of some developments in distribution strategy (Chapter 11), including brand equity and own label strategy.

Business to business issues are addressed in Chapter 12 in the context of relationship development, customer service processes and competitor cooperation.

In Chapter 13 we delve into some of the issues involved in the strategic integration of marketing communications, including a discussion of the strategic versus tactical use of communications. Chapter 14 contains a collection of clippings on global marketing. These explore topical dimensions of globalisation versus customisation, internationalisation and international brand portfolio strategy.

Chapter 15 looks at the shift in the marketing paradigm – not only in terms of extending marketing applications to relatively new, not-for-profit realms, such as religion, but also the growing fields of relationship marketing. We use a variety of clippings to analyse the growth in interest in relationship marketing and in direct and database marketing – related themes that are highly topical in contemporary marketing. The underlying propositions of 'differential' and 'one-to-one' marketing are also discussed via clippings in the same collection.

A group of clippings on more general strategic issues (Chapter 16), includes one on the package holiday market, which allows us to explore a more integrated view of marketing strategy. There is also coverage of the benefits and problems associated with diversification strategies. Another clipping explores strategic alliances and there is also coverage of the emerging use of game theory in a strategic setting.

10 Marketing Organisation

KEY CONCEPTS

- Marketing department
- Multifunctional team-working
- Corporate organisational restructuring

Top brass fall for false economies

Marketing departments have suffered as blue-chip companies race to restructure their businesses. And the cost-cutting fever has pulled the focus away from consumers' needs. So who is best-placed to win them back? The marketers, of course.

ALAN MITCHELL

Eagle-eyed readers of *MW*'s job pages will notice that two companies – each in the middle of restructuring – were advertising for marketing staff last week. Reckitt & Colman was seeking an assistant brand manager and category manager to work as "part of a European project team", in the same week that it was disappointing the City with lower than expected profits and its second European overhaul in five years.

Barclays Bank, which has shed 2,500 jobs in the past year, was meanwhile advertising for what appeared to be a whole new marketing department. "We want to upgrade our performance in direct marketing, sales promotion, market research, advertising, new product development, product and marketing management," it said. Anything left out?

What's intriguing is just how marketers, and marketing departments, are faring in a corporate environment where restructuring is now almost the norm rather than the exception.

So far, the answer must be – not very well. Here, for example, are some of the comments I've heard recently from senior managers and management consultants: "Despite all the job-cutting in marketing departments, marketers still have it easy"; "They [marketers] are terribly precious"; "They think they are creative, but most of them are simply good bureaucrats"; "They are failing to take part in the corporate upheavals that are going on around them – they prefer to sit in their ivory towers"; "They don't integrate well with other departments"; "They are the least receptive to change"; "They still see themselves as an elite"; No wonder organisations such as McKinsey are asking if marketing has hit a midlife crisis.

But there may be another side to this story. True, we are seeing greater upheavals in corporate structure than at any time since the war – and it isn't hype. The computing and communications revolutions are opening up possibilities, from relational databases through data transfer and computer automated design and manufacturing, and on to the expert systems which are just beginning to appear in marketing departments.

The internationalisation of company structures means that many once-powerful national marketing organisations have effectively been beheaded. The shift away from hierarchical departmental organisations towards flatter, networked, multifunctional team-working means all formerly separate functions are under pressure to justify their existence.

Put all three factors together and no wonder the management consultants are pointing to vast opportunities for cost savings – and that includes marketing. Over the past two years, 28 per cent of all white-collar redundancies have come from sales and marketing.

If you are a Reckitt & Colman facing competitors such as Unilever and Procter & Gamble, which have already announced global cost-cutting exercises, it's clear you have little time to lose.

Yet, there's a darker side to the great change-management crusade – some of its leaders seem to have taken leave of their senses. Religious fanatics think the more they suffer, the closer they get to God.

Now business is spawning its own species, for whom the pain of change seems to have become some sort of test of manhood. One example is the chief executive of a multibillion dollar company who declared in a gushing "businessman-as-hero" article in Fortune magazine last year that managing change in business "is a like a race where you run the first four laps as fast as you can – and then you gradually increase the speed".

He's not a visionary leader – the words and actions just don't match.

The chief executive's rhetoric is all about strategic vision, customer focus, dedication to customer service and being first to market – plus, of course,

"our staff are our biggest asset".

What's actually happening is that the chief executive's restructuring is cost-driven and not marketing-led. Strategy and long-term vision go out of the window because everyone is too busy fire-fighting, and genuine customer focus is almost non existent because everyone's attention is trained inward: the top brass are fussing about the progress of their change-management programmes, while everyone else is fretting about their future place in the pecking order.

While the customer service flag is waved frantically, cost-cutting means customer service actually comes a firm second. And, because the organisation has been so "downsized" and "delayered", there are too few people around to get the jobs done in time. They're running to stay still, not to get ahead of the competition.

Finally, while the human-resource rhetoric winds up to a penetrating shriek, most employees are wondering if they will be handed their P45s the next time their companies announce record profits.

Sure, radical structural overhauls are needed, because of changes in technology and the move towards globalisation. As Lord King remarked at a recent Arthur Andersen seminar

at Strathclyde University, controlling the proliferation of costs in a company is like mowing a lawn. "You think you've done it and next morning there's daisies there."

And sure, marketers have to play their part in the change-management game. If it is the right game. But is it? The total-quality movement went careering down a dead end when, in its obsession with process, it forgot what it was all for – and companies ended up doing the wrong things right first time.

Much of the ongoing restructuring could be falling into the same trap. Marketers' instinctive reluctance to lose sight of the customer, far from being the histrionics of the conservative prima donna, may be the still small voice of sanity that the organisation needs.

This is why Barclays' advertisement for new marketing staff is intriguing. "Barclays is in the course of a large number of major developments aimed at re-engineering the bank," goes the ad. It would "therefore like to strengthen its marketing functions", it added. Marketing – a beneficiary of re-engineering? Now, there's a thought.

ISSUES

1. Discuss some of the trends related to the future remit of the marketing department.

2. How would you define marketing accounts liability?

3. Comment on the new concept of process management

EXPLORATION OF ISSUES

1 The past few years have brought tremendous innovations in marketing organisations. Success in this area has nothing to do with rebuilding marketing departments; when an entire organisation is focused on marketing, the need for a separate department may disappear.

Two key principals of organisation are beginning to emerge. First, in future successful companies will rely primarily on marketing and organise themselves around marketing integrators and functional specialists: integrators will be responsible for servicing particular consumers, channels or product segments. Specialists will create competitive advantage by helping the company to build world-class skills in the two or three most important functional areas of marketing. Second, in a fundamental departure from traditional organisations thinking, successful companies will link these integrators and specialists together through teams and processes, rather than functional or business unit structures.

In tomorrow's marketing organisations, integrators will play the vital role of guiding activities across an industry's entire value chain to ensure that the company is maximising its long-term profitability. They will be charged with tearing down the walls that divide function from function, product manager from product manager and supplier from retailer. They will pool the resources of the whole organisation to provide a better service to the customer.

They will be aware of the real engines of profitability, not only with regard to their own company, but also for their suppliers and customers. They will use this to identify market segments and develop strategies that meet consumers' needs and promote growth in sales and profits. They will lead cross-functional teams to execute these strategies.

Tomorrow's integrators will be fundamentally different from today's brand managers. They will lead teams whose members possess a variety of functional and specialist skills. Compared with today's brand managers, product integrators will need to provide much greater cross-functional leadership – they will be fewer in number, more senior in the organisation and have more experience of different functions than today's brand managers.

The best companies are now using specialists to develop, interpret and communicate models that can predict likely consumer behaviour on the basis of past purchases.

If the building blocks of tomorrow's marketing organisations will be highly qualified integrators and specialists, the mortar that will hold them together will be provided by processes and teams rather than the traditional functions of business units. Teams will be organised around key cross-functional business processes such as building consumer brand equity and ensuring superior customer service. The process focus will be paramount here. The teams, not the functions, will be the linchpin of the organisation. In practice, this will mean offering integrators new, cross-functional career paths and making long-term specialist careers attractive.

The hardest challenge may be instilling a new marketing culture. Making the transition from a relatively simple structure to one in which process-based teams, dispersed throughout the organisation, deliver value to consumers and customers will test the beliefs of even the best marketing companies.

2 Marketing accountability embraces two quite difference concepts. The first is transparency, the most obvious manifestation of which is financial transparency. This has been particularly popular in the past few years as companies have sought to extract the best possible value from their marketing budgets.

However the concept of transparency extends beyond cost into content, which leads us to the second aspect of accountability – responsibility. Who should be held accountable for maintaining ethical and moral standards? Should it be the company, the agency, the regulator or the consumer? We hear a lot about ethical companies, the role of the regulatory systems and the rights of the individual. We also see moral judgements appearing with increasing regularity as more and more issue campaigns are launched: 'Right to Life', 'Meat is Murder', 'Cars Cause Asthma', 'Breast is Best' and so on.

Increasingly, the burden is falling on marketing managers to forge ethical strategies that will not cause offence.

3 Say goodbye the old, inward-looking distinctions between marketing sub-divisions such as advertising, direct mail and sales promotion and say hello to the rich and fascinating world of reputation management, solution design, brand experience delivery, customer acquisition and customer relationship management.

The traditional distinctions between product, service

and delivery/distribution are dissolving into new, all-embracing concepts such as 'customer solutions'. Familiar job titles are disappearing, to be replaced by a bizarre assortment of new tags such as 'development manager, market to collection' or 'manager, customer satisfaction, quality and reengineering'. In short the marketing department of old is being sliced, chopped and dispersed across the whole business. The theory is that marketing is too important to be left to the marketing department. For example Xerox has four key processes: 'time to market', which is responsible for upstream product development, including working out what the market wants; 'supply chain', which includes manufacturing and physical distribution; 'Marketing to collection', which involves most of the other traditional operations, including marketing and selling activities, plus installation and after sales administration; and 'customer service'.

Whether process-oriented structures will last is an open question. One key issue is agility and flexibility. Another is the danger that processes will spawn their own inefficiencies. The development of marketing skill also remains a vital issue. New processes and new cross-functional teams could lead to the slow erosion of the specialist expertise that creates competitive edge. All organisations are compromises and processes are constantly developed and refined

11 Distribution Strategy

Competitive Advantage in Distribution Channels

KEY CONCEPTS

- Own-label competition
- Product positioning
- Brand loyalty
- Private branding
- Brand values
- Door-to-door sampling

Bubble trouble

Having survived two world wars and 150 years of competition, R Whites lemonade is facing its most serious test yet in the form of own-label competition.

SHARON MARSHALL

It is difficult to know whether Robert White, the original founder of R Whites lemonade, would be pleased or horrified by the association his name has in the public's affection in 1995.

As the R Whites lemonade brand reaches its 150th birthday next week, the name is primarily associated with a man in striped pyjamas skulking down to the fridge in the middle of the night to grab a drink.

It is not known whether the original Mr R White was in the habit of breaking from his slumber to seek clandestine refreshment. But it is testimony to the original Allen Brady Marsh advertising campaign that the image persists.

What Mr White is known to have done is set up a barrow business in 1845 selling home-brewed beer. He and his wife, Mary, later expanded the range to include lemonade, ginger ale and pineapple soda. They also expanded the family business to include their sons, who in turn built it into a £500,000 operation by 1894.

But getting the brand to its 150th birthday has been an eventful and difficult task. The company had to fight its way through the devastation of World War I when it was hit by rising raw material costs and the departure of more than 100 R Whites employees and half of its horses to support of the war effort.

Later it was hit by the Blitz, which damaged all its London factories and left the company barely able to celebrate its centenary in 1945.

R Whites became part of the Britvic Soft Drinks portfolio through a complex series of mergers. Having merged with the Whitbread Group in 1969, it and HD Rawlings then merged with the soft drinks division of Bass – Canada Dry – to form Canada Dry Rawlings in 1980. This in turn merged with Britvic in March 1986 to form today's Britvic Soft Drinks.

Although Britvic claims its position is secure and that consumers are remaining loyal to the brand, Nielsen figures for July 1995 show R Whites is taking a severe knocking from own-label.

Once dominated by cheap, poor quality wannabes, the soft drinks own-label sector has recently undergone a turnaround, with companies such as the Cott Corporation bringing out high quality own-label brands at cheaper prices than the branded rivals.

Nielsen figures show R Whites took just a 5.8 per cent share by volume of the lemonade sector in July, compared with own-label brands, which took 57.1 per cent.

Back in July 1992, R Whites held a 4.6 per cent share of the market and so has increased in the past three years. But ominously, its greatest rival – own-label – has grown nine per cent in the same period from 48.1 per cent with the own-label Cresta moving from nothing to 16.5 per cent.

"Private label is so strong," says Tom Blackett, deputy chairman of Interbrand, "I think some of the strong brand values for R Whites have recently fallen away, so the odds are probably stacked against it making it through the next 150 years, although I hope it will."

Part of the problem, says Blackett, is that Britvic is not putting enough advertising support behind the brand – only £260,000 was spent in the 12 months to July. The brand is still primarily known for its "Secret Lemonade Drinker" campaign, developed by Allen Brady Marsh in 1973. With the demise of the agency in 1991 the account was surrendered to Howell Henry Chaldecott Lury – but the creative theme remained. This has resulted in a brand with a 150-year heritage being forever associated with badly cut pyjamas.

Although the campaign has proved popular – even attracting its own fan club of pyjama-clad followers who meet regularly to play football – it has also proved a limitation. The 22-year-old campaign may finally be about to come to an end.

Britvic marketing manager Richard Manaton, who joined the company in February to oversee the R Whites brand says: "The Secret Lemonade Drinker, at the moment, is continuing. But things must move on. This campaign has been very successful in Britain, but the brand is older and has more heritage than the Secret Lemonade Drinker. Some of those elements are not recalled."

The original ad from 1973 featured a father and son singing team on backing vocals – Ross and Declan McManus. Declan later became Elvis Costello. But celebrity connections have since included Paul Daniels, the late Frankie Howerd, Ronnie Corbett and tennis star John McEnroe, who wore a woman's nightdress in R Whites' ads in November 1992.

Britvic is making efforts to regenerate its brand, if not the creative work. The drink was reformulated 18 months ago, introducing real lemons into the recipe. And for its 150th birthday it has commissioned Storyboard to redesign its packaging, adding a transparent label to the bottle. A door-to-door sampling drop and a high-profile birthday party to push the brand's heritage are also being staged this month.

Buyers are also reporting that Britvic is pushing to rebuild its brand at retail level. "We have done quite a bit of work this year to rebuild R Whites' position. Britvic has been putting a lot of support behind the brand and we had an exclusive deal with the company to sell one-litre bottles," says Dean Dawson, trading controller of retail chain Londis.

"The result is that R Whites has made rather impressive gains this summer," claims Dawson. However, he points out that the R Whites sales spurt must be taken in the context of a long hot summer that boosted all soft drinks sales.

The prospect of the brand making it through another 150 years is uncertain. Manaton says it will survive if it can be kept "as fresh and vital as it ever was", but it is unclear how it will evolve.

Growth sectors in the soft drinks market over the past year have included a move to the "cloudy" traditional lemonade drinks, although Britvic insists R Whites will remain clear. They also include a shift towards healthier, sugar-free "New Age" drinks although again, Britvic says that no more reformulations are planned. There is also an unprecedented demand for alcoholic lemonade, but despite its alcoholic roots Britvic says R Whites will not take that path.

In its birthday party invite Britvic talks enthusiastically about its plans for R Whites' 300th birthday in the 22nd century. It is a nice thought. But having survived two world wars the cut-throat battle with the own-label manufacturers could prove a fight too far.

ISSUES

(1) **Comment on the key characteristics of private branding.**

(2) **How would you interpret the 'battle of the brands'?**

(3) **Discuss the underlying concepts and consequences behind brand equity.**

EXPLORATION OF ISSUES

(1) Manufacturers' brands have long dominated the retail scene. In recent times, however, an increasing number of retailers and wholesalers have created their own brands. Buyers are increasingly looking for and demanding private brands. Some companies claim that their own brands offer better value and lower prices.

Private brands (also called store-brands or distributor brands) can be hard to establish and costly to stock and promote. However they yield higher profits for the middleman, and they give middlemen exclusive products that cannot be bought from competitors, resulting in increased store traffic and greater loyalty.

(2) The competition between manufacturers' brands and private brands is called the 'battle of the brands'. In this battle, middlemen have many advantages. They control what products they stock, where they go on the shelf and which ones they will feature in local circulars. They charge manufacturers 'slotting fees' – payments demanded by retailers to stock new products and find 'slots' for them on the shelves. Retailers put a lower price on their store brands than on comparable manufacturers' brands, thereby attracting budget-conscious shoppers, especially in difficult economic times. And most shoppers know that store brands are often made by one of the larger manufacturers anyway. As store brands improve in quality and consumers gain confidence in their store chains, store brands are posing a strong challenge to manufacturers' brands.

Private labels are prominent in Europe, accounting for as much as 36 per cent of supermarket sales in Britain and 24 per cent in France. To fend off private brands, leading brand manufacturers will have to invest in R&D to bring out new brands and new features, and make continuous quality improvements. They must design strong advertising programmes to maintain high customer awareness and preference. And they must find ways to 'partner' major distributors in the search for distribution economies and improved joint performance.

(3) Powerful brand names generate strong consumer preference. Companies around the world invest heavily to create strong national or even global recognition and preference for their brand names. Perhaps the most distinctive skill of professional marketers is their ability to create, maintain, protect and enhance brands.

Brands vary in the degree of power and value they have in the marketplace. A powerful brand has high brand equity in that it has higher brand loyalty, name awareness and perceived quality, as well as strong brand associations and other assets such as a patent, a trademark, and channel relationships. A brand with strong brand equity is a very valuable asset.

Measuring the equity of a brand name is difficult, and because of this companies usually do not list brand equity on their balance sheets.

High brand equity provides a company with many competitive advantages. As stated above, powerful brand enjoys a high level of consumer brand awareness and loyalty, and because consumers expect stores to carry the brand, the company has more leverage in bargaining with retailers. Because the brand name carries high credibility, the company can more easily launch brand extensions. Above all, a powerful brand offers the company some defence against fierce price competition. Some analysts see brands as the major enduring asset of a company, outlasting the company's specific products and facilities.

Branding presents challenging preoblems to the marketer.

12 Business to Business Marketing

Marketers learn to eat humble pie

The fmcg marketers have climbed down from their pedestals and are embracing the fundamentals. They are now using business-to-business tactics – which focus on relationships – as their guide. **ALAN MITCHELL** asks if they should have gone back to basics years ago

A reversal in marketing tactics is happening on the quiet, and the benefits of this much needed about-face would be far greater if they were made public. After decades of occupying the high ground, fmcg marketers are acceding their authority to the business-to-business community.

It may be galling to admit, but many of the "big ideas" being discovered by consumer goods companies are, in fact, well-worn ideas from the backwaters of marketing.

Back in the Eighties, of course, all the traffic was one-way. That was the heyday of marketing. Financial services and business-to-business companies were realising that their solely sales-led operations were not producing the best results. It dawned on them that branding really matters, that even the hardest-nosed business-to-business buyer isn't immune from the influence of a strong brand. They rushed to worship at the fmcg shrine, eager to learn the sophistications of advertising, design and PR from London luvvies.

Headhunters began raiding blue-chip companies for brand-management talent and fmcg notions were soon being touted in new territories. Slick corporate image advertisements became common. Marketers tried to create standalone financial service brands, such as Midland's Vector and Meridien.

These strategies were often pursued to disastrous effect. The banks wasted tens of millions of pounds on advertising before they realised that quality of service meant more to customers than mere ads. Marketers who joined these new companies soon found themselves stifled by a culture that still, despite the rhetoric, saw marketing as a satellite division – nowhere near the heart of things.

The few campaigns that worked, such as BA's 1983 Manhattan ad, only did so because they were the tip of an iceberg of corporate change. They signalled and encouraged BA's newly affirmed commitment to total quality and customer service.

Now the wheel has turned almost full circle. Consumers, marketers have discovered, are rational and calculating about their purchases – rather like the traditional business-to-business buyer. Concepts and practices that have been commonplace among the Cinderellas of marketing have been received as flashes of inspiration – witness the way loyalty marketing has taken off. Most business-to-business marketers held onto the feeling that their existing customers were the meal ticket and have practised loyalty marketing principles for so long they hadn't even come up with a name for it.

In fact, fmcg marketers have been learning from their humbler colleagues in wide range of areas. Business-to-business marketers were among the first to recognise, and use, the power of direct marketing and the database. Business-to-business companies have long realised that the corporate brand – their company's reputation – is crucial to their success, (though many felt almost ashamed of it, Corporate brands somehow weren't "real".) Now, such endorsement is seen as the future for the majority of companies, including many in fmcg.

In addition, it has long been recognised in business-to-business circles that the way to gain an edge in commoditising markets is to add as many layers of bespoke service as possible. Fmcg marketers are only just waking up to the huge potential of this idea.

And it is in business-to-business that the concept of relationship marketing is (again) almost second nature. Of course you try to get to know the individual needs of each, named customer. Of course you try to use this understanding to anticipate these needs and meet them. Of course you try to maximise the two-way flow of information. (Trendies call it "interactive dialogue" nowadays. Fuddy-duddies from business-to-business call it talking to people.)

In fact, if you look at the admittedly highly caricatured portraits of the two different approaches (see box), it's clear where the centre of gravity lies.

There's probably still more for fmcg marketers to learn. The power of the alliance would be one lesson. In tackling the business market, airlines have long tied up with hotel and car-hire groups. Similar strategic marketing alliances, including customer data-sharing between complementary consumer goods companies, could have tremendous power. We have seen only the start of joint promotions.

Another lesson lies in the concept of supplier partnerships. Car companies such as Rover have long realised that by sharing information with a small number of "preferred suppliers" costs can be cut, ideas shared and new product development speeded up. In consumer goods, the idea of the company/consumer partnership has yet to come to fruition. Currently, consumers are still "targets".

In truth, neither fmcg nor business-to-business marketing will ever be "better" than the other, but what is happening is that they are beginning to converge – and the sooner that both sides learn they have a lot to learn from each other, the better.

Only arrogance (usually on behalf of the fmcg marketer) stops it happening. According to Heinz managing director Malcolm Ritchie, one of the most significant changes over the past year is not its direct marketing initiative or even its move into own-label production. Both are predicated on an even more fundamental shift: a reorganisation of the business into three divisions to focus on the specific needs of their [retail] customers.

In other words, Heinz has realised that one of its biggest challenges lies not in its consumer marketing, but in its business-to-business marketing: its ability to build relationships with its retail customers. If fmcg companies had admitted this ten years ago, they might be in a very different position now.

ISSUES

(1) What main steps are taken by a company when establishing a relationship marketing programme?

(2) Define the customer service process.

(3) Comment on the main issues that should be taken into account by a company pursuing a total quality marketing strategy.

(4) Discuss a number of advantages that direct marketing can provide to sellers.

(5) What key forms of formal intercompetitor cooperation can you suggest?

EXPLORATION OF ISSUES

(1) The following are the main stages in establishing a relationship marketing programme:

- Identify key customers who merit relationship marketing. Choose the five to ten largest customers – additional customers can be added if they show exceptional growth.
- Assign a skilled relationship manager to each key customer. The salesperson servicing the customer should receive training in relationship marketing.
- Develop a clear job description for relationship managers. This should include their reporting relationships, objectives, responsibilities and evaluation criteria. The relationship manager is responsible for the client, is the focal point for all information about the client, and is the mobiliser of company services for the client. Each relationship manager will have only one or a few relationships to manage.
- Appoint an overall manager to supervise the relationship managers – this person will develop job descriptions, evaluation criteria and resource support to increase relationship managers' effectiveness.
- Each relationship manager must develop long-range and annual customer relationship plans – the annual relationship plan will state objectives, strategies, specific actions and required resources.

(2) The customer service process involves all activities that make it easy for customers to reach the right parties within the company and receive quick and satisfactory service, answers or problem resolution.

(3) Quality is defined as all features and characteristics of a product or service that bear on its ability to satisfy stated or implied needs. Performance quality refers to the level at which a product performs its functions. Conformance quality refers to freedom from defects and the consistency with which a product delivers a specified level of performance.

- Quality is in the eyes of the customer. A quality programme must begin with the customer's needs and end with the customer's perceptions.
- Quality must be reflected in all company activities. Each functional area and each activity must understand and embody the total quality concept. A system cannot consistently deliver quality if one or more of its components is not operating effectively.
- Quality requires total employee commitment. All company employees must be personally committed to the total quality programme. Commitment requires both professional and personal pride in the outcome.
- Quality requires high-quality partners. Value chain members of the customer delivery system must also embody total quality commitment.
- Quality can always be improved. Nothing is ever perfect.
- Quality improvement may require quantum leaps.

Competitive conditions may demand vast and immediate improvements rather than small and incremental ones.

- Quality does not cost more. Cost savings come from lower rejection rates, better customer satisfaction and new technologies that reduce manufacturing costs.
- Quality is necessary but may not be sufficient. More demanding buyers have ever higher expectations of performance. Companies cannot assume that quality alone will boost competitiveness.
- A quality programme cannot save a poor product. Companies must recognise that a poor product cannot successfully be 'quality imaged'. If the product cannot be changed, it should be dropped.

4 Direct marketing provides sellers with a number of advantages. It allows greater prospect selectivity. The message can be personalised and customised. The direct marketer can build up a continuing relationship with each customer. Direct marketing can be timed more precisely to reach prospects at the right moment. Direct-marketing material receives higher readership, since it reaches more interested prospects. Direct marketing permits testing of alternative media and messages (headlines, salutations, benefits, prices and the like) in the search for the most cost-effective approach. Direct marketing permits privacy in that the direct marketer's offer and strategy are not visible to competitors. Finally, the direct marketer knows whether a campaign has been profitable because of response measurement.

5 Figure 12.1 shows a typology of forms of formal intercompetitor cooperation.

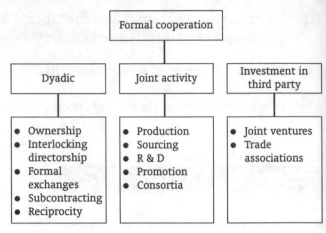

Source: Easton (1990), p. 73.

Figure 12.1

13 Strategic Integration of Marketing Communications

KEY CONCEPTS

- Integration of marketing communications elements
- Strategic use of marketing databases
- Above/below, left/right and 'through the line' marketing communications
- Field marketing

Mailshot in the arm

Birds Eye Wall's, Brooke Bond, Heinz – these are just some of the fmcg bigwigs that have at last seen the benefits of direct marketing. But the redirecting of their budgets below the line does not spell the end of above-the-line advertising, but heralds a long-term relationship between the two disciplines.

HELENA BARTON

At last, it's official. It may have been a long time coming (it's been talked about for more than a decade) but finally the fast-moving consumer goods industry is taking direct marketing seriously.

When a classic marketing-led company such as HJ Heinz gives direct marketing the nod to the tune of about £12m, the industry knows it has won the seal of approval it has long sought.

Heinz sent shockwaves through the marketing fraternity earlier this year when it made dramatic changes to its strategy by redirecting a huge chunk of its marketing budget below the line. The company will continue to use above-the-line media for an umbrella television advertising campaign, but from now on individual products will be promoted using one-to-one direct marketing techniques.

Retailers have recognised the importance of communicating directly with their customers for some time: witness the huge growth in store cards and the plethora of customer-loyalty programmes that have been built on the back of them. The database opportunities afforded by electronic point-of-sale technology has provided much of the impetus for the retail industry's enthusiasm for all things direct.

The fmcg manufacturers have been much slower to embrace the trend. The recent change in their attitude towards direct marketing can be attributed to a number of factors, but is partly because of the retail industry's desire for an increasingly close relationship with its customers at the expense of branded products. These companies are realising direct marketing is one way to regain some clout in their power struggle with the grocery multiples.

There has been much speculation recently about the imminent death of the brand. Such talk may be grossly premature, but the rise of own-label continues unabated, posing yet another threat to the relationship between branded grocery products and their customers.

Matthew Hooper, managing director of multidisciplinary agency Interfocus, says: "It's essential that branded fmcg manufacturers now have a direct dialogue with their consumers rather than talk to them through the grocery multiples. They need to encourage decision-making before the customer goes into the store rather than at the point of sale."

Brands now firmly within the direct marketing frame include Persil Power, Rothmans' Raffles, Gillette, Buitoni, Brooke Bond D Tea, Batchelors and Guinness, as well as new boy Heinz. Manufacturers understood to be on the sidelines include Kraft (the company is believed to be looking at the role direct marketing could play in the company's vision for 2000), Spillers (in the petfoods area) and Birds Eye Wall's with its Menu Master and Healthy Options ranges.

Just two weeks ago Oxo announced it too was to join the fmcg direct marketing ranks. Brooke Bond is doordropping 2.5 million UK homes with leaflets aimed at gathering information on consumer purchasing habits.

The company will use the data to build individual customer profiles on the back of questions about brand preference, which stores people buy stock cubes from and how often. A cashback offer of up to £4 acts as the incentive.

The Oxo campaign has been put together by WWAV Rapp Collins, the agency which will also develop the direct marketing push for Heinz.

WWAV marketing director Jonathan Clark says: "The only way you can make direct marketing work in the context of packaged goods is in the whole area of portfolio management. You don't use it to support a single brand – the margins that most packaged goods companies are working on would rule that out. Its real role

is to support a portfolio of brands."

The argument is that while the margins earned from selling a can of baked beans make fmcg direct marketing a nonsense, when a company such as Heinz comes along with more than 300 products, what previously may have seemed prohibitive suddenly starts to make good business sense.

Clark adds: "The fmcg manufacturers should use direct marketing to target, attract and encourage loyalty from heavy users. They shouldn't use it to generate trial among a specific socio-economic group. The packaged goods companies that will make direct marketing work will adhere to the heavy users' philosophy but for the others, it will always just be a glorified sales promotion through the letterbox."

Clark refutes any claim that the fmcg industry's recent interest in direct marketing dictates that at some point in the future the death knell has to ring for the above-the-line ad industry.

He says: "No one form of communication can do a complete job for a client these days. Advertising is the most intrusive and powerful form of communication and will remain so, but companies have to build on that. They need to develop a relationship with people that says thanks for buying our product, please buy some more and then give them a tangible reason to do so."

The fmcg industry's historic problem with the concept of below-the-line was because of a lack of brand literacy in many direct marketing agencies. They were not as sensitive to brand values as they could have been and any marketing director worth his or her salt was understandably nervous at the prospect of letting an agency loose on a coveted brand that had years of expensive advertising heritage behind it.

The situation has since improved enormously and few marketers would argue that direct marketing agencies

today are not aware of the need to nurture and enhance brand values rather than sabotage them in one fell swoop with a tacky door drop to half the nation.

Clark adds: "We have established a close relationship with many of our clients' above-the-line agencies. We work very closely with Bates Dorland on Heinz and we helped launch Persil Power with J Walter Thompson."

The rising cost of traditional media, coupled with changing consumer lifestyles and media habits (people are not reading and watching the same things as they were ten years ago), is another reason why fmcg manufacturers are showing greater interest in direct marketing. They are finding it increasingly difficult to reach their target market through traditional channels.

Meanwhile, marketing departments are beginning to realise that direct marketing makes sense in the fmcg arena if it is looked at with a long-term perspective. They are evaluating customers over a three or four-year, not six-month, period.

Interfocus' Hooper claims this new long-term vision has come about partly because marketing departments have shrunk and people are realising they may be in their job for five or six years, not two, before they get a chance to move onwards and upwards.

He says: "People are sitting in their jobs for much longer these days. This means they can take a long-term approach to building a brand which starts to make direct marketing feasible. There isn't so much of the short-sightedness there used to be." Short-sightedness included quick fixes to bolster the sales figures before the brand manager's review.

Interfocus runs direct marketing programmes for a number of fmcg brands, including a club for Brooke Bond D tea. The brand now has a database with information on more than 250,000 club members. The principle is simple – customers buy boxes of Brooke Bond D tea and receive tokens in response. The tokens are then put towards a range of prizes including anything from mugs to teddy bears and video tapes.

Hooper says: "It's been more cost-effective to identify the brand's core market – who accounts for most of its volume sales – and mail them rather than target them by any other means. We're building a relationship between the brand and its core customers but there has to be a balance. The margins on these products don't allow us to do mailings every month."

Heinz's commitment to direct marketing is significant, not just in terms of the size of the investment it is making, but more importantly because it was a decision sanctioned at the highest level.

Traditionally, marketing directors of large fmcg brands have not bothered themselves with the lowly world of direct marketing, preferring to concentrate their minds on the altogether more glamorous pursuit of creating glossy TV ad campaigns. Direct marketing has been left to lesser mortals way down the marketing department pecking order who failed to have the

strategic vision that long-term fmcg direct marketing depends on.

There is little doubt that the mighty Heinz's move into direct marketing will provide the catalyst for rival fmcg manufacturers to follow suit rapidly. The fact that a company with the pedigree of Heinz has dared to make the great leap will be encouragement enough for many of its rivals.

Clark says: "Heinz has made the first big move and now other fmcg companies are looking at direct marketing very closely. The dam hasn't burst yet, but there are signs it's cracking."

The missing link

Field marketing can be a valuable promotional tool, yet it is still underestimated by marketers.

LUCY KILLGREN

Let your taste decide!" was the rallying cry of the Pepsi taste test, perhaps one of the most successful marketing drives of all time. It was also one of the few marketing campaigns that linked field marketing directly to advertising with exceptional results.

While strategists at Pepsi may not have known it, they were 20 years ahead of their time in creating a model for the integrated marketing strategy: successfully mixing above and below-the-line activities. But why is it that now, so long after the resounding success of this marketing pi_ce de resistance, so few marketers think of combining field marketing with advertising?

Field marketers will tell you it's no surprise that the link is rarely made once you realise that the discipline is relatively young and as a result has not had much of a voice – at least not until recently. In addition, because field

marketing deals with activities right at the bottom end of the marketing chain, it occupies an unglamorous position.

Eddie Phillips is managing director of CPM International, which had a turnover of nearly £40m last year. He thinks that the reason why field marketing is very rarely combined with advertising is this glamour factor.

"I don't think it's particularly sexy," he says. "Field marketing is the last link in a long chain and there's this feeling that 'my product will sell on its own'. It's the idea that as long as you advertise it will sell, and as long as you get a listing in the major multiples it will sell."

Phillips also points out, rather testily, that while £9bn is spent every year on advertising, the field marketing pie is worth only £135m, which works out as one per cent of advertising spend. It's no wonder he is upset.

Marketers such as Phillips are,

however, increasingly making a noise about this discrepancy and it seems that companies are starting to sit up and take notice. While some have been doing advertising, with sampling bolted on in a tactical way, there is a move to integrate field marketing in a more strategic way to increase sales.

John Bunyard is managing director of Fast Marketing, a company whose raison d'être is linking advertising to high-intensity field activity, such as sampling, as part of a broader strategy. The Fast concept involves the implementation of several integrated activities. These are high-intensity advertising, the use of advertising copy, where the copy conveys the product experience, an experimental bridge to the product sample, heavyweight field marketing and product sampling, and specialised response monitoring.

Bunyard states that advertising linked to field marketing can increase brand sales by over 40 per cent, depending on the product. "The logic is good for sampling," he says. "With advertising you're positioning the brand and creating awareness. With sampling you're giving people the chance to check it out, to see if they like it. What is new is strategically linking the two aspects.

"What we've been doing is using advertising and sampling as the tools to do a very specific job. You use the advertising to set up a very specific expectation, which the product experience delivers. It's not to do with benefits at all – it's purely to do with what it's like to use the product. We call it a realisation. The psychology is that when you have an expectation realised, it's a very rewarding experience. Having expectations borne out is how people get locked into products. We've turned that into a system."

Marketers should be trying to get people to experience the product immediately after they have been exposed to advertising, and the only real way they can do this is through field marketing and promotions, he believes. Instead of using advertising, marketers could directly tie campaigns in with the product's concept.

Many in the industry believe that if manufacturers have experienced the success of linking the two as part of a strategy, they are likely to do the same for all their products.

But what about the manufacturers who have not directly experienced field marketing and advertising working successfully together? The accepted line of attack for reaching these people is, according to experts in the field, through education. In many cases it seems that brand managers may not be aware of field marketing as a discipline, let alone capable of making that strategic link.

Mike Garnham of Milton Headcount believes the reason is a simple lack of awareness on the part of both manufacturers and agencies. He believes that once field specialists get to speak to marketers, they are often quite receptive to the concept.

"We have a pretty good success rate with getting through to companies that are likely to be launching new brands," says Garnham. "These people are generally quite receptive, even if it's a new idea."

For many field marketers it is a question of plugging away with the message from the bottom up, or indirectly through buyers for the multiples. Merchandising Sales Force (MSF), whose managing director is David Carter, has taken the route of approaching those major multiples which are in contact with manufacturers every day.

Garnham is heavily linked with sales promotion agencies and promotes the field marketing message through them. Colleagues are encouraged to talk to these companies and run seminars. Headcount also tends to target directly the marketing managers within companies. Garnham endorses the work of the Field Marketing Association (FMA) in increasing levels of awareness of the strategic importance of linking marketing and advertising. "The FMA is very good at getting to those people who are on marketing courses at university so that when they go out into the commercial world and start planning how to launch and manage brands, field marketing is an integral part of their strategy," he says.

Alison Williams, chair of the FMA, agrees that the key to raising the profile of field marketing in association with advertising is through education. She believes that one of the reasons why manufacturers are not making the most of the link between advertising and field marketing is because they do not understand what field marketing does for them. "Many promotion houses and manufacturers don't understand how an ad campaign can be picked up and translated into reality for the public in the field. Those that do have a tremendous amount of success."

The FMA is working in several ways to address the problem. It is participating with the Institute of Sales Promotion (ISP) and field marketing is now a component of the ISP diploma course and diploma questions. The FMA is also working hard on public relations activities in the marketing press, which has helped increase the profile of the discipline. It also offers free lectures on field marketing to universities with marketing courses.

Williams herself works for FDS International Field Marketing and was heavily involved with the relaunch of the Club biscuit, one of the best recent examples of integrated advertising. Jacob's BURP (Bureau for Unmasking Robotic People) campaign encompassed widespread television and print advertising, backed up by BURP squad teams around the country in shopping malls offering children detector kits to unmask robots with the help of the new Club biscuit.

One million samples were given out as part of the campaign which, in the words of Nick Stephens of Marketing Principles who worked with Jacobs and FDS, had the aim of "getting more bars into people's faces". For Stephens, the campaign was an excellent example of an above-the-line story as a unified theme working hand in hand with below-the-line. "It's a rarity when the two work so closely together. The BURP squads in the shopping malls take the campaign right down to the grass-roots level."

Integrated campaigns such as this one are likely to be remembered for how well they have combined all elements of the marketing mix and how successful this has been in generating sales. As successful integrated campaigns become more common, and levels of awareness of the strategic importance of linking the two disciplines increase, marketers will be forced to look at the lead set by Pepsi 20 years ago and pay more than simply lip service to the idea of integrated marketing.

Between the lines

Above-the-line agencies are increasingly feeling the squeeze as their direct marketing counterparts walk off with traditional advertising business. In the past two weeks alone, work to the value of £55m has gone to non-advertising agencies. **LIZ STUART** asks why

In the space of two weeks the ad agency world has had £55m worth of business pinched from under its nose.

In truth, the £55m represents only two accounts, but many see the decision of Cable & Wireless Communications, followed swiftly by Legal & General, to reject ad agencies for their advertising and media accounts respectively, as evidence that above-the-line agencies can no longer take for granted that they will handle clients' advertising.

In recent months ad agencies have been helpless and aghast, as management consultants and branding agencies have inveigled their way onto advertising pitch lists by offering high-margin strategic advice. "Management consultants have not had a creative idea in ten years," Kevin Roberts, boss of Saatchi & Saatchi Worldwide, said last month about the threat to ad agencies (*MW* June 19).

But the agencies are now even more affronted that the venerable upstarts of the marketing world – direct agencies – are taking their core business. In effect, ad agencies are being squeezed at both ends.

These are not the first advertising accounts to move to direct marketing agencies but they are the most significant.

J Walter Thompson is one of the few major league players without a significant direct marketing division. But chief executive Dominic Proctor says: "Our strategy is to broaden our skills. We are developing capabilities in direct marketing, sales promotion and consultancy in-house. Any agency that fails to recognise the threat from

direct marketing is itself under threat."

Heinz, Unilever, Safeway and the Telegraph Group are among the companies which have already diverted major portions of their marketing budget below the line.

What is changing is the profile of DM agencies themselves. Impact FCA! went as far as buying ad agency Kelly Weedon Shute last week to change its profile. It already handles some advertising for clients, including AT&T and Siemens

This month below-the-line shop Rapier Stead & Bowden, with annual ad billings of only £3.2m, was appointed as the principal agency for the £45m consumer launch of Cable & Wireless Communications (CWC). This decision came on the back of its corporate branding press and cable TV campaign, which broke in June.

The brief, following a pitch against above-the-line agencies ranging from Saatchi & Saatchi to Bartle Bogle Hegarty, is to create a major TV campaign.

The agency's chief executive Jonathan Stead says: "It is the pragmatic attitude of DM agencies which is seducing clients. We did not go in as either an advertising or direct marketing agency – we went in as an agency with a different perspective. But our heritage as a DM agency gave us a unique position in our commitment to thinking beyond advertising."

Ironically, CWC marketing director Ruth Blakemore, who hired Rapier Stead & Bowden, quit last week – only two weeks after making the appointment. This created speculation the account will be moved.

More remarkable still, the insur-

ance company Legal & General hired WWAV Rapp Collins for its £10m media buying business after a pitch against The Media Centre. It previously employed up to six agencies to buy media.

So just how big a threat are these agencies to the above-the-line industry? L&G group marketing director Kate Avery believes ad agencies should be worried. She says WWAV was shortlisted not only because of an existing relationship with the insurer – the original shortlist contained other below-the-line agencies – but because it understood the customer base.

"The key reason I appointed WWAV is because I think that communication with customers is linked into what customers actually need," says Avery. "DM agencies have the vital skills to tap into what people want to buy."

Implicit in her comment is that other advertising and media agencies do not have those skills. However, it should be stressed that much of the media L&G buys is for direct work as it increasingly sells its products directly.

The blurring of disciplines has led to some ad agencies tapping into the benefits of direct response mechanisms to produce DRTV advertising. Ironically HHCL & Partners, one of the losers on the CWC pitch, was one of the first above-the-line agencies to collect data, through its Apple Tango ads back in 1994, which attracted over 2 million responses.

But it has taken years for many advertising agencies to realise the potential threat from the direct marketing agencies, and react. Both BMP DDB and Foote Cone & Belding have only recently announced in-house direct marketing divisions.

BMP DDB managing director Chris Cowpe says: "The lines are blurring between different marketing disciplines, but for the right reasons. There is a trend – marketing organisations are realising that the customer must be at the centre of everything they do." He says BMP's direct division has been set up in part to attract the below-the-line spend of existing clients.

One of the first tests for BMP's direct operation could be the pitch for an estimated £5m below-the-line campaign for its client Vodafone, which is preparing to spend upwards of £20m on a new advertising branding campaign.

Alliance & Leicester, another ad client of BMP DDB, spends 60 to 70 per cent of its £45m annual marketing budget below the line. But head of group direct marketing Simon Knibbs thinks it unlikely that direct marketing could ever replace brand-building advertising.

Considering DM's smart new image, it is strange that some agencies are still keen to distance themselves from their below-the-line heritage. Ogilvy & Mather Direct had one of the best names in the business but switched to Ogilvy One.

One former O&M Direct staffer says: "The change in name was a real slap in the face for the direct industry." He says had the agency really wanted to go for integration, it would have folded the below-the-line agency into the above-the-line operation.

But Ogilvy One chairman Nigel Howlett defends the decision. "In 25 years of being called O&M Direct we have failed to convey the broader meaning of what direct is," he says. "Research told us that people still thought it was just direct mail and mail order."

Which raises the possibility that, if the line between direct marketing and advertising agencies continues to blur, below-the-line agencies could lose their point of difference.

Barraclough Hall Woolston Gray chief executive Simon Hall says no. "We don't want to become just another advertising agency. We have a number of skills, such as getting people to behave in a certain way. We don't want to become another me-too in a sector in decline."

It is also worth noting that the industry is still centred on the traditional tools of the direct marketing trade. Of the £6bn spent on DM in the UK last year, only seven per cent went on DRTV, one per cent on radio, 14 per cent on national newspapers, 11 per cent on magazines and one per cent on outdoor.

Telemarketing, however, accounted for 21 per cent of spend, while direct mail absorbed 20 per cent, with the remainder going on new media, inserts, door to door, database marketing and the regional press, according to figures from the Direct Marketing Association.

If Rapier Stead & Bowden and WWAV Rapp Collins can prove to clients that they should be considered for other non-direct marketing activities, the DMA might have to introduce new spending categories – to include advertising and media buying.

ISSUES

1. **What are the strategic and tactical uses of marketing databases?**

2. **What are the possible stages of development of a strategic role for the marketing database?**

3. **What is the 'integration' issue?**

EXPLORATION OF ISSUES

1. At the strategic level, decisions will need to be taken with respect to segmentation and targeting. In this sense the marketing database can focus on a whole range of categories – for example new prospects, best prospects, loyals and so on – but these can be boiled down into acquisition or retention strategies.

Once created, the database has a variety of uses. It can clearly be used as a list of target customers for direct marketing activities. But it can also provide a wealth of information on the market, customers and potential customers. In this context the database can provide data for both planning and analysis: the database can be analysed to find the most attractive segments for campaign planning and predicting campaign response. Strategically, the database can be used for: (1) changing the basis of competition, (2) strengthening customer relationships, (3) overcoming supplier problems, 4) building barriers against new entrants and (5) generating new products.

On the other hand, when used merely for tactical purposes, the marketing database is not an integral part of strategy planning and is more concerned with the next event than with a longer-term view of customers. It is probably more usual for organisations to employ the database at the tactical than the strategic level.

2 Shaw and Stone (1988) propose a four-stage process when developing a marketing database. In phase one the database is merely a sales database originating from accounting systems and focusing more on product sales than on customers. The second phase is involves multiple databases for different sales territories or retailers, but care must be taken to avoid overlap due to lack of communication and coordination – customers might receive different or even conflicting direct mailings from different parts of the company !

Phase three is more customer-focused and one database coordinates all communication with customers. Analysis is according to profiles, transactions and other relevant factors in order to determine the best way of targeting segments and individuals. In phase four there is true integration, when different organisational functions, not just marketing, are linked with the marketing database.

In parallel with this, Parkinson (1994) identifies three levels of IT application in marketing. The first is concerned with the management of transactions, the second with profiling, targeting and developing effective direct marketing, and the third with marketing productivity analysis, modelling and strategic planning.

If the organisation is not truly customer orientated the database will only have a tactical use, but if used strategically its role will be central.

3 The 'integration' issue concerns lack of both integration and strategic use of the various marketing communications elements. This is actually quite common – organisational structures are often such that PR is a separate function from sales, advertising, direct marketing and so on, and each tries to maintain its own integrity by keeping vital information (even customer lists) to themselves. As Goften (1996) declares, 'there's nothing more sad than the spectacle of an ad agency deploying one concept and a PR agency pursuing another. It's not only a crime against the economic use of resources but no service at all to either client or consumer'. The need for integration in marketing communications is surely overwhelming. The problem of choosing between above- or below-the-line campaigns is partially being resolved by through-the-line campaigns – or even left- and right-of-the-line, where acquisition strategies are 'left' and retention strategies are 'right' of the line.

14 Global Marketing

European Marketing

PepsiCo unveils Euro strategy

JON REES

Over the next five years PepsiCo plans to save $100m (£68m) a year in Europe through improved productivity as a result of overlapping savings from its main brands: Pepsi Cola, KFC, Pizza Hut, Taco Bell and Walkers Smiths.

Given that the company is likely to take about $2.5bn in European revenues this year, it may not be all that big a deal. But those savings are part of a fundamental shift in the way PepsiCo Europe sees itself and its business, and have a direct bearing on the relationship the firm has with its consumers.

"In the past 12 months the heads of each European division have taken a conscious decision to work more close-ly together. We are really leading the way for the rest of PepsiCo world-wide," says KFC vice president Europe, Peter Hearl.

That a lead is needed is evident from PepsiCo's second quarter results. The common factor worldwide was volume growth allied to falling operat-ing profit. International restaurant revenues grew 33 per cent to $383.5m, but operating profit plunged 35 per cent to $12m. And the pattern was repeated to a lesser extent in PepsiCo's worldwide beverage sales. Only the snacks business bucked the trend, with both worldwide sales and operating earnings up, the latter by 15 per cent to $319m.

PepsiCo has long considered cen-tralising its European media buying to save money. Sources suggest it could reasonably look to save five per cent of its media spend if it did so – and it spends $120m to $130m on TV adver-tising in Europe alone.

It also sees the chance of savings elsewhere. KFC, Pizza Hut and Taco Bell all use cooking oil and cardboard, for example, so the chains now buy many of their supplies through one company agency, Pepsi Food Systems.

There are other overlaps. The restaurant chains, snacks and drinks tend to attract the same sort of con-sumer, so it makes sense to site them next door to each other: KFC in the UK is about to open two-in-one sites with Taco Bell, starting with one at

London's Earl's Court in November. Across Europe, especially in the emerging markets of eastern Europe, such as Poland, the process is further advanced. There, three-in-one sites include a Pizza Hut.

"It means you can successfully penetrate more sites because you can lower the break-even point," says PepsiCo president and chief executive Europe Wayne Mailloux. The problem for PepsiCo is to blend this degree of co-operation with the high degree of autonomy for its divisions that the company sees as essential to its success. The need to get close to the "front-line" consumer in order to react more quickly to market change is paramount.

"Our primary mission, over and above anything, is growth. And we are not going to do anything that's going to bureaucratise our operation and jeopardise this. The purpose of enhancing co-operation is to facilitate further growth," says Mailloux.

Clearly, given PepsiCo's results, that means growth in margins and not just volume. With this in mind, the main brand restaurant chains learn from one another in their move towards home delivery. Pizza Hut was the first to change, under pressure from the pizza home delivery market, which has grown rapidly in the UK and the rest of Europe. Now KFC is drawing on its experience. It has been experimenting with home delivery over the past four months in the UK

and Spain. It has four such UK outlets, and will open another four in Birmingham in the next month or so.

"We can get out of the door with our food before the traditional outlets have started cooking the product," says Hearl. "I would be less than honest if I said we had cracked the profit factor yet, but it took Pizza Hut some time to make money from their delivery operations."

As long as it's all incremental sales, Hearl is not worried. He points out that KFC is making more otc sales as a result of increased brand awareness following extensive mailings and other advertising on the new outlets, even if the margins on delivery are slimmer.

Cross-selling opportunities are not neglected either. Since the start of the year KFC has been selling Pepsi in meal combinations at its outlets. And its Pepsi sales have risen 50 per cent.

Good news for a company that is under severe attack elsewhere, and not just from its traditional enemy Coca-Cola (Coca-Cola's second quarter sales were up 11 per cent to $4.3bn and net profit was up 12 per cent to $758m).

PepsiCo also has to contend with formidable new players, such as Sainsbury's and Asda in the UK. Cola supplied to Sainsbury's by Canadian-based syrup supplier Cott sells more in-store than Pepsi Cola and Coca-Cola combined. It is of comparable quality, yet retails at about half the price.

"Sainsbury's is at the cutting edge of own-branding and it's worked very well for it in this most recent instance," says Mailloux. He adds: "I don't expect Sainsbury's to hold its share in the long term."

Saving money through cross-brand co-operation is allied with old-fashioned added value and innovation as the key to future growth and the vanquishing of own-label upstarts.

Pricing, of course, will doubtless play a role. Both PepsiCo and Coca-Cola have reacted aggressively on price in some markets. In Cott's home market, Canada, prices have been lowered and retailer margins have been widened.

For innovation, read "alternative" soft drinks such as Liptonice iced tea, plus new pack sizes and shapes. Most recently there was Pepsi Max – the no-sugar cola that had taken 3.5 per cent of the UK market by volume (Nielsen) a year after launch. It is backed by pan-European promotions such as Club Pepsi Max in Ibiza, which offers action-packed holidays to competition winners. Such event-based marketing is likely to become more common across its brands in the future.

Only about 20 per cent of PepsiCo profits come from its international operations, but by the end of the decade that figure is expected to rise to 50 per cent. Cross-brand co-operation, producing savings as well as passing on lessons, clearly has a fundamental role to play.

ISSUES

1) **What sort of cross-selling opportunities have been developed by Pepsi?**

2) **How should PepsiCo reassess its European marketing approach?**

3) **Comment on the increasing use of event-based marketing by companies such as PepsiCo.**

EXPLORATION OF ISSUES

1 Since 1994 KFC has been selling Pepsi in meal combinations at its outlets and its Pepsi sales have risen 50 per cent. Saving money through cross-brand cooperation is allied with old-fashioned added value and innovation as the key to future growth and the vanquishing of own-label upstarts.

2 The following table suggest how PepsiCo should change its European marketing approach.

Change of approach	
From	To
Local targets	Pan-European targets
Geographic segments	Non-geographic segments
Product/country markets	Global or Europe-wide concepts
Local pricing	Cross-border pricing
Local sales/distribution	European 'key accounts' plus local channels
Local communications	Global core communication strategy
Local marketing organisation and processes	Transnational structures

3 A company can build an identity through the types of event it sponsors. Perrier, the bottled water company, came into prominence by financing exercise tracks and sponsoring health sports events. INM identifies itself as a sponsor of cultural events such as classical concerts and art exhibitions. Other organisations identify themselves with popular causes: Heinz gives money to hospitals and Kraft General Foods makes donations to MADD (Mothers Against Drunk Drivers). One of the best examples of a product that has used a multitude of image building techniques to etch a singular image on the public mind is the Swatch watch from Switzerland. Christies, the auction house, holds periodic auctions of early Swatch watches, and the company sponsors draw to choose the 40 000 lucky collectors who may buy its limited edition watches.

Globalisation versus Customisation

The name droppers

The globalisation of brands is more than just a name-swopping exercise – it helps products to bestow more consistent values. The danger comes when the quest for tidiness defies business logic. **HELEN JONES** reports

If brand owners have their way there will be no corner of a foreign field forever called Andrex, Spillers, Access or any one of a growing number of other well-loved brand names.

Despite sentimentality in local markets about the demise of these brands, which have been nurtured over the years through a combination of careful handling and advertising spend, the twin bridgeheads of a global marketing strategy – uniformity and consistency – are here to stay.

Renegade brands are being swept away in a gigantic tidying-up exercise because they do not fit into a neat and tidy corporate structure. But the new wave of big brand clean-ups is about more than name changes or swopping one name for another – it underlines the increasing globalisation of brands.

The latest casualty is Spillers, which is dropping its name from its branded dogfoods and rolling out the Winalot name as an umbrella brand across Europe. Spillers is tight-lipped about

its plans but it is expected that Spillers Prime, for example, will become Prime from Winalot.

The Spillers name may also disappear from catfoods, to be replaced by Felix, which already has a strong presence across Continental Europe. This is likely to be at the expense of Arthur's, which is strong in the UK, a contender in Germany but unheard of elsewhere.

The timing of the move comes as Spillers parent Dalgety announces plans to spend £67m in the next two years reorganising its petfood interests. This is a direct result of its £440m purchase of Quaker European Petfoods last February.

Interbrand chairman John Murphy says: "It is a common issue for companies going through acquisitions. You have to decide which [brands] will stay and which will go."

Spillers refuses to reveal its full plans. An insider says this is because "there is still quite a lot of the European dimension to be resolved".

But Spillers' has already cut its advertising agency roster. Bates Dorland was last week awarded the Prime account, previously with Ogilvy & Mather and Rainey Kelly Campbell Roalfe which handled new product development. BMP DDB Needham continues to handle Felix.

Spillers spokeswoman Mary McKendry says: "Winalot is a brand we will be looking at very closely in the future and Felix will be our number one focus in catfood. We are refocusing our efforts on Winalot and putting money behind it. Winalot is not used on the Continent but [the name] will have the ability to travel."

The reason for dropping the Spillers name and concentrating on two core names for dogfood and catfood is simple – competition. Spillers is not only facing increasing competition from own-label products but also rival brands, including Pedigree Chum. A source says: "They have to unite behind one brand to take on the might of Pedigree, which has a strong identity throughout Europe."

Interbrand's Murphy says another reason for the recent spate of proposed changes is that "international brand owners want international brand portfolios, rather than a patchwork quilt of local brands in local markets. It makes more sense from the managerial point of view".

Branding specialist CLK's deputy managing director Richard Zambuni says: "The reason an increasing number of multinationals are standardising their brands is quite simple. Apart from sending a consistent worldwide message it also means that they can take greater advantage of growing media opportunities. They can promote one brand, one pack and one positioning across markets."

This is certainly true of Scott Paper, which has declared its intention to kill off the Andrex name – but not its trademark puppy, dog lovers will be relieved to hear – and replace it globally with Scottex.

The Scottex name is already in use in the US, Continental Europe and Asia and, despite Andrex being the UK's seventh largest grocery brand, its familiarity does not safeguard its future. While Scott's UK marketing department concedes that it would be consistent to change the name, Glyn Harper, who was European category leader for toilet tissues at the time of the announcement in May, says that Andrex in the UK "may be a case for an exception".

But Scott's chief executive Albert Dunlap dismisses opposition as "sentimental". And the fact that the European Commission last week initiated an anti-competitive investigation into the $17bn proposed merger between Scott and Kimberly-Clark will not halt the inevitable. Sources say the

axing of Andrex is merely on hold because the investigation is the company's number one priority.

Dunlap may accuse detractors of sentimentality, but does it really matter that much to consumers if a well-loved brand name disappears? Are brand owners taking that much of a risk?

Last year, General Motors announced it was extending the Opel name to cover all Continental Europe, except the UK where Vauxhall has survived because of its robust brand values and its strength in the domestic market. But there is an inevitability, denied by all at Vauxhall, that the name will disappear if General Motors is to reach the logical conclusion of its globalisation plans.

Zambuni thinks the risks are not that great if the change is handled properly. "Clearly, in many instances it is the right thing to do, to divest a company of unnecessary clutter. Consumers weather the change if it is handled well."

He points to the change of Marathon to Snickers in 1991. In many ways this is less complex than either the Andrex or Spillers situation, but it is a good example of how smoothly the process can be handled. Over a period of months Marathon had Snickers emblazoned across the side of the packaging. Snickers was then moved to the front and Marathon disappeared. This was supported by a TV ad campaign to keep the public informed. The net result was an increase in sales.

Slow, steady phasing in would appear, then, to be the correct approach. "They have to handle the baton-change as cleanly as possible, otherwise they risk fracturing the brand equity," says Murphy. "You can change names but you cannot change

everything at once without being in danger of destroying the brand and then having to rebuild it all over again."

Philips white goods, which merged with US domestic appliance manufacturer Whirlpool in 1989, dual-branded its products Philips Whirlpool until 1992 when the Philips name was dropped. The rationale was that consumers had had enough time to become aware of the Whirlpool brand. According to Whirlpool figures, by 1992 awareness of the brand across Europe had reached 97 per cent of the level previously enjoyed by Philips.

This approach is also likely to be adopted by Scott, which is expected to add the Scottex name slowly and to progressively highlight it, before eventually dropping Andrex.

Mastercard is in much the same position. In the UK, Access acts as the local brand but is almost unknown in the rest of the world. Mastercard is understood to be in negotiations with the four clearing banks – Midland, Lloyds, NatWest and Bank of Scotland – which own a stake in it, to regain control and rebrand the card as Mastercard.

Murphy says the move is logical: "Access is a strong brand in a small market. Mastercard is a global company. The rationale for replacing Access becomes overwhelming."

There is a danger that some of the changes now being contemplated in boardrooms could be for the sake of symmetry, rather than for logical business reasons. What is certain is that Andrex, Spillers and Access will not be the last brand names to be surrendered to the needs of a stronger global one.

ISSUES

1. Comment on the debate on globalisation versus customisation of marketing strategies.

2. Discuss the cost considerations of creating a 'global brand'.

3. What is brand equity?

EXPLORATION OF ISSUES

1. Only full-scale international marketing involvement and the globalisation of markets can be seen as the full integration of international marketing into strategic market planning. Traditional full-scale international marketing is based on products customised according to cultural, regional and national differences. In full-scale international marketing, marketing strategies are developed for specific target markets. From a practical standpoint, this means that to standardise the marketing mix, the strategy needs to group countries according to social, cultural, technological, political and economic similarities.

In contrast globalisation involves developing marketing strategies as though the entire world (or regions of it) were a single entity: a globalised company markets standardised products in the same way everywhere. For many years, organisations have attempted to globalise the marketing mix as much as possible by employing standardised products, promotion campaigns, brands, prices and distribution channels for all markets. The economic and competitive pay-offs for globalised marketing are certainly great. Brand name, product characteristics, packaging and labelling are among the easiest marketing mix variables to standardise; media allocation, retail outlets and price can be more difficult. In the end, the degree of similarity among the various environmental and market conditions determines the feasibility of globalisation.

Some companies have moved from customising or standardising products for a particular region of the world to offering globally standardised products that are advanced, functional, reliable and low in price.

Debate about the feasibility of globalised marketing strategies has continued since the birth of the idea in the 1960s. Surprisingly, questions about standardised advertising policies are the leading concern. However it should be remembered that there are degrees of both customisation and globalisation. Neither strategy is implemented in its pure form. The debate will doubtless continue about which products can be fully globalised. For some products – for example soft drinks – a global marketing strategy, including advertising, seems to work well, but for other products – for example beer – strategies must accommodate local, regional and national differences.

2. When a new product is developed, most companies will attempt to make it a global product with a common name and position. The pressure for standardisation is particularly strong in Europe, where there is now considerable media overlap and fewer distinct distribution systems. A more difficult issue is whether or not to create a global brand when regional brands are in place.

When a brand is already established in a country, for example, its equity is based on awareness level and a set of associations that are often very valuable. Changing the name and/or position in order simply to conform to a

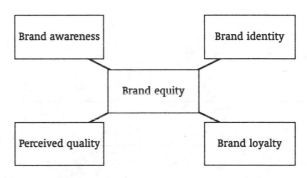

Figure 14.1   Brand equity

Source: Aaker (1995)

standardised global brand may be extremely costly. For example, when Datsun was changed to the global brand Nissan in the United States in the early 1980s it probably cost more than $1 billion, but five years after the change, the Datsun name was still as strong as the Nissan name.

A new name also kills any associations that the old name might have developed. Heinz does not put its name on products it acquires outside the United States because it wants to retain their associations.

If an existing name has weak associations, of course, there is little to lose by changing it. In the late 1980s in the US market, Mars successfully changed the name of its Kal Kan dog food to 'Pedigree' and its Kal Kan cat food to 'Whiskas' to create worldwide names. While Kal Kan was mainly associated with cans, the name Pedigree was associated with aristocratic pets that would only be served the best food, and the name Whiskas was feline-sounding and likeable. Some brands are positioned quite differently in different countries. Clearly it would be foolish to force a common position on such brands in order to achieve a standardised global brand.

The rush to standardise global branding is somewhat ironic as there is also a strong move towards regional marketing. For example in the United States, companies such as Procter and Gamble, Campbell Soup and others are giving local marketing units responsibility for sales promotions and advertising, which were previously centralised.

3 Brand equity is a set of assets and liabilities linked to a brand's name and symbol that add to or subtract from the value provided by the product or service to the firm and/or its customers. The assets and liabilities upon which brand equity is based differ from context to context, but can be usefully grouped into four categories, as shown in Figure 14.1.

These four elements need to be actively managed, and it should be recognised that investment is required to create and maintain them. Furthermore, people and systems should be in place to identify and counter any programmes that may damage them.

15 Extending the Marketing Paradigm

Marketing Religion

KEY CONCEPTS

- Non-profit marketing
- Social marketing
- Market segmentation
- Religious advertising

Prepare to meet thy maker

And on the eighth day, God created marketing directors. As the Church contemplates rows of empty pews, it has turned to the advertising community for divine inspiration.

LINDSAY McMURDO AND HELEN JONES

It is perhaps the ultimate marketing challenge: to revitalise a "brand" that, despite near 100 per cent awareness, has seen "sales" inexorably decline for the past 40 years. As we enter the most important week in the Christian calendar, can marketing help the Church stop the rot?

There is little denying that the traditional Church of England is in trouble. Attendances are falling. There is a very public schism over the ordination of women priests and it's losing market share to a new breed of evangelical churches that have a strong appeal to the younger generation of churchgoers.

But the Church has woken up to the need to hit back. In February the Church of England issued a report called "Paying the Piper, advertising and the Church", which said that in principle there are no ethical reasons why the Church should not use large scale advertising campaigns. The report was prepared by, a working party set up by the Church of England Communications Centre, chaired by the Right Reverend Nigel McCulloch, Bishop of Wakefield. He says: "This report is seminal. It identifies the key questions to be asked about the use of advertising and guidelines for the Church." Basically the Church thinks that advertising can be a creative, effective and amusing means of communication."

Their view will be put to the test this week when radio listeners in several regions will be diverted from their hot cross buns by a religious advertising campaign, devised by production company Commercial Breaks. The script, which is likely to surprise many with its humour, draws attention to the Christian origin of giving Easter eggs, in an attempt to re-establish Easter as a religious event. It ends with the line: "Get the full story this Easter – direct from the maker."

The campaign is the latest attempt by the Church, through the ecumenical Churches Advertising Network, to apply some modern marketing methods to its publicity.

The network has previously achieved some success with its Christmas campaigns, through advertising agency Genesis. Last year's drive, which included radio, posters and billboards, covered a third of England's parishes, and claimed a 15 per cent rise in church attendances.

CAN is co-ordinated by the Reverend Richard Thomas who is also communications officer for the Diocese of Oxford. He has high hopes of the new radio work. "In the past, radio has been a slight weakness," he says. "This time we've got a really sparkling script."

The Easter push will be the last one-off tactical campaign, says Thomas. From this Christmas, CAN will try to produce a more coherent strategy, combining Christmas and Easter.

Future creative work may centre around the familiar visual mnemonics of the Church. "People still use Christian symbols without necessarily understanding the original meaning," says Thomas, citing presents as an example. "Advertising can help to reinvest those symbols with their meaning."

The main obstacles to the Church doing more advertising are partly financial and partly what Thomas calls "ecumenical difficulties".

"We don't really have a set budget," he says. "What's spent has to be raised from scratch each time." He expects a continuing reliance on donated airtime and poster space.

On potential inter-denominational problems, he says: "In ordinary marketing terms, you might expect one brand to take over another. We are expressly set against that; the participants are working together."

Francis Goodwin, managing director of poster company Maiden Outdoor, has been the principal mover in securing free and discounted media space for the CAN campaigns. He expands on Thomas' outline of a longer-term strategy. "Once we've picked off the easy stuff – Christmas, Easter and the other festivals – we'll be tackling more issue stuff," he says. "Of course, that's where it gets more complicated, but we're building up a

head of steam, and a lot of goodwill between denominations."

Goodwin says the churches' approach has been necessarily cautious. "It's still early days, and we're feeling our way very carefully. So far the ads have largely targeted non-Churchgoers, but there are a lot of constituencies to take into account – church leaders, the press, existing church-goers."

He stresses that individual churches must have a follow-up strategy for new attendees. He admits, however: "The Church isn't McDonald's – it can't guarantee product delivery."

Other observers do not share Goodwin and Thomas' faith in the power of marketing. Kevin May, a J Walter Thompson account director who is writing a book on advertising and the Church, says there is an inherent problem with the brand that no amount of advertising can put right. "The problem with formalised Christianity is that it is incredibly unfashionable. On the one hand it has to be in tune with life in the late 20th century', but on the other hand it can't alienate its adherents by, coin promising."

May adds that the Roman Catholic Church has an even bigger problem: "If you ask people about Catholicism you get a list of negatives about issues such as contraception."

However, the Catholic Church appears unconcerned about its image and has never done any advertising for the Church as a whole – though individual churches may run their own local poster campaigns. Jim McDonnell, director of the Catholic Communications Cen. tre, says: "We are distinctly wary of advertising because we do not feel that Christianity is a product or a service. I don't think anyone was ever converted by advertising. It is just a reinforcing mechanism."

May says: "Advertising can work in a limited way. It's like when a brand is in trouble, a costly ad campaign is not

the answer. You have to have the right brand and marketing mix. But advertising could assist with a relaunch and it would be one hell of a creative challenge to get over the unfashionable aspects of Christianity."

Despite May's reservations, CAN is not the only body that is advertising. The Evangelical Alliance, which represents 1.5 million mainly Pentecostalist Christians, is running a national TV ad on Good Friday as part of a £2.2m recruitment drive. The ad, through Birmingham agency Wallis Tornlinson, continues the theme of its poster campaign using a character called Jim in a manner reminiscent of the British Gas "Tell Sid" campaign. The first poster shows a man's tear-filled eyes, and carries the line, "Fear. Emptiness, Despair. Talk to Jim". The second uses the rather more optimistic line, "Hope, Fulfilment and Happiness. Talk to Jim", and a smiling face.

Paul Weaver, assistant general superintendent for the Assemblies of God, which was behind the campaign, says: "It was paid for by donations. Each of the churches involved paid a sum and then we asked churchgoers for a voluntary contribution of £20." He refutes suggestions that the ads play on people's fears and would attract only those that are troubled. "We started off with the idea of a joyous campaign but we commissioned some independent market research and asked the public what they felt about their lives and the state of Britain and it was all very negative." He adds that the latest campaign indicates that there is hope.

Jim – which stands for "Jesus in me" – has caused a good deal of controversy. In the early days the campaign claimed support from Downing Street and prominent politicians, although Weaver attributes this to an over-zealous PR man. However, two weeks ago the Daily Mail and Associated Newspapers ran a disclaimer saying that it had in no way assisted the Jim campaign with a publication called the Jim Times. Associated says: "We have not published any views, one way or the other on this campaign and the claim that this company has supported or endorsed it is untrue." The Jim organisers have agreed to remove Associated's name from all future literature.

Previous attempts to incorporate Christian messages in advertising have also generated their fair share of controversy – but also delivered the goods, in attendance terms at least.

Foote, Cone & Belding earned itself the epithet "God's own agency" with the work it devised in 1989 and 1991 for US evangelists Billy Graham and Morris Cerullo. The former was wellknown, having conducted missions to the UK since the mid-Fifties, and FCB's "LIFE" campaign was sympathetically, even admiringly received. But Cerullo, a product of Eighties tele-evangelism, and a faith-healer to boot, provoked a backlash for the claims, "Some will see miracles for the first time" and "Some will be moved by the power of God for the first time". The posters were exonerated by the Advertising Standards Council, however, and Cerullo played to capacity houses at London's Earl's Court.

FCB board account director Nick Alford ran both campaigns. 'It was all rather virginal territory. It wasn't a case of advertising religion *per se*, but the individuals involved. The aim of the ads was awareness of the meetings.

"Trying to promote spiritual or emotional values is one hell of a task. The Church is in a mess, but it must work out exactly what the proposition is. With Graham and Cerullo, there was a very strong proposition, but with religion as a whole, there's no unity in the product. If it were in fmcg, you'd say, 'Get the product right, then we'll advertise'."

The Jim campaign is barking up the wrong tree, says Alford. "It is targeting a small group of very unhappy people. Religious advertising has to be open to everyone."

ISSUES

1. How would you define marketing in non-profit settings?

2. What are the real hurdles to successful social marketing?

3. Comment on the issues of social responsibility and marketing ethics.

EXPLORATION OF ISSUES

1. One of the most pervasive problems in non-profit marketing is the way in which marketing is defined. Often, marketing is perceived only in terms of promotion. Other components of the marketing mix – product/service development, distribution and pricing strategies – are largely ignored. Marketing, when defined only as aggressive promotion, is a short-lived, surface-level solution for a variety of organisational problems and objectives.

An important factor in such a narrow, incomplete view of the scope of marketing is the fact that marketing was a late arrival to the management of non-profit organisations. The practices of improved accounting, financial control, personnel selection and planning were all implemented before marketing. Nevertheless non-profit organisations have accepted it enthusiastically. Dozens of articles and speeches attest to marketing's popularity. Meanwhile university administrators attend seminars and conferences to learn how to market their own institutions more effectively.

Marketing's rise in the non-profit sector could not continue without a successful track record. While it is often more difficult to measure results in non-profit settings, marketing can already point to examples of success. The Presbyterian-affiliated Church of the Covenant in Cleveland, Ohio, credits a 10 per cent increase in average attendance to a series of radio commercials, which begin with voice-over-music and are spoken by the church's regular Sunday morning announcer. A Midwestern hospital's marketing effort allowed it to reposition itself as a provider of tertiary care services rather than as a community hospital. Marketing is now an accepted part of the operational environment of most successful non-profit organisations.

What is the future of social marketing? The outlook is one of continued growth and application to an ever-widening range of issues. More and more cause-related organisations and government agencies will turn to social marketing in a search for increased effectiveness. The real contribution of marketing thinking is to lead each institution to search for a more meaningful position in the larger market.

2 The main reasons why social marketing pro-grammes are not as successful as consumer product campaigns are:

- Their low visibility
- Lamentable budgets
- Lack of research
- Lack of continuity

Social marketing is the design, implementation and control of programmes calculated to influence the acceptability of social ideas, and involves product/service planning, pricing, communications, distribution and marketing research. What are the real hurdles to successful social marketing?

- The market is usually harder to analyse. Social marketers have less good quality secondary data about their consumers.
- Target market choice is difficult. There is often public pressure to attempt to reach the whole market rather than to zero in on specific target groups.
- Formulating product/service strategy is difficult. The range of product/service innovation options is smaller than is the case with consumer products.
- Social marketers have fewer opportunities to use pricing and must rely more on other approaches that will increase or decrease the cost to consumers of certain behaviour.
- Channels of distribution may be hard to utilise and control.
- Communication strategies may be difficult to implement. Some groups may oppose the use of certain types of appeal that would otherwise be very effective. The budget may be too small to permit the wide distribution of the message, or to evaluate its impact.
- Cause-related organisations are often backward in their management and lack marketing sophistication.
- The results of social marketing efforts are often difficult to evaluate.

3 Ethics relate to moral evaluations of decisions and actions as right or wrong on the basis of commonly accepted principles of behaviour. The most basic ethical issues have been formalised in laws and regulations to conform to the standards of society.

Moral philosophies are principles or rules that individuals use to determine appropriate behaviour. The concepts 'ethics' and 'social responsibility' are often used interchangeably, although each has a distinct meaning. Social responsibility in marketing refers to an organisation's obligation to maximise its positive impact and minimise its negative impact on society; and whereas ethics relate to individual decisions, social responsibility concerns the impact of an organisation's decisions on society.

Although social responsibility may seem to be an abstract ideal, managers dialy make decisions that relate to social responsibility. Social responsibility also extends to marketers in their role as community members. Individual communities expect marketers to contribute to the satisfaction and growth of their communities. Social responsibility deals with the total effect of marketing decisions on society.

One way to evaluate whether a specific behaviour is ethical and socially responsible is to ask other people in the organisation if they approve of it. For social responsibility issues, contact with appropriate consumer groups may be helpful. If other people in the organisation (in this case, the Church) approve of the activity, there is a good chance that the activity is acceptable from both the ethical and the social responsibility standpoint.

A rule of thumb for ethical and social responsibility issues is that if they can withstand open discussion and result in agreement or limited debate, an acceptable solution may exist. Still, even after a final decision is reached, different viewpoints on the issue may remain. Openness is not the complete solution to the ethics problem; but it does create trust and facilitate learning relationships.

Relationship Marketing

Swatch this space

The success of the Swatch brand hinges on the company's unique approach to direct marketing. An extensive membership scheme allows it to build a close relationship with potential buyers.

FRANCESCA NEWLAND

From a cherubic "Putti" designed by Vivienne Westwood to an Eastertide "Eggsdream", Swatch launches more than 150 watch designs each year. The company – conceived by Swiss watch giant SMH in 1983 – manufactures 15 to 17 million watches a year. At the heart of this success story is its unique approach to direct marketing.

Although set up in much of Europe and the US in 1990, The Swatch Collectors Club was not established in Britain until 1993. The club boasts 100,000 members worldwide, 3,000 of whom are British.

The club encourages members to buy several watches, reinforces the value of the brand and creates an international link between Swatch fans. For an annual fee of £45, each member receives an exclusive club watch and a catalogue of every Swatch ever made. The Swatch World Journal is sent to members three times a year and informs them of worldwide Swatch news. Members also receive regular mail-shots that tell them about new product launches – to which they are invited to as special guests.

The Collectors Club database has been built using point-of-purchase information, an insert that comes with every purchase and incentives such as Swatch T-shirts and bags.

Collectors Club manager Nicky Henry says Swatch used direct response ads last year, with inserts in both Sky Magazine and the Clothes Show Magazine. But she says this proved "expensive, and did not get across the concept of Swatch as a collectable fashion accessory".

Henry adds: "In the rest of Europe people buy several watches and wear a particular watch to suit a particular mood. In Britain, however, people tend to buy one watch and wear it until it breaks or is lost. The Collectors Club is designed to promote the purchase of a variety of watches."

This Swatch concept is communicated, in person, to collectors and potential collectors as much as possible. New members have to collect their membership package at one of Swatch's 150 key retail outlets. From then on they are affiliated to that particular outlet. The packages are never sent by post.

These outlets carry point-of-purchase information on the club and Swatch provides the store with a PR pack that gives ideas to retailers to help them build a relationship with members. This is often in the form of cheese and wine parties to announce a new limited edition or a collector's preview evening. At such events, the member is encouraged to bring a guest. This increases public familiarity with the product and broadens the Swatch database. The Oxford Street Swatch store has bi-annual parties for Swatch collectors.

The collection of Swatch watches is boosted by the fact that many limited editions are launched annually, creating a kind of "Swatch frenzy" among collectors, who are told of launches by the company. Rare Swatches have fetched more than £10,000 at auction. Today, one set of watches created in 1988 can fetch £80,000 for a set of six. The Collectors Club enhances Swatch mania as collectors get together and compare the rarity of their collection.

Recent limited editions include one from 1994 when the Italian Pop Artist Mimmo Rotella designed a Swatch

Double Special set of two watches. It was launched as a worldwide limited edition of 22,222. Only 500 sets were available in the UK, so Swatch organised a special draw. Applications were made available to the public and collectors through Swatch retailers.

In July this year Swatch organised the launch of new limited edition watch C-Monsta. Only 750 of the worldwide allocation of 30,000 C-Monsta watches were for sale at a large-scale Swatch extravaganza on Brighton beach. A 14-page invitation was sent out to all collectors to tell them about events that were to take place and emphasise the collectability of the watches and how their value would instantly accrue above that of its £50 selling price.

Entertainment on the day included a barbecue, free bar, limbo dancers, a steel band and a tatooist. There was also a right-to-buy draw for another limited edition, Pacific Beach in a Bottle. Some 1,400 collectors and their guests turned up to swap watches and chat and boast about their collections.

Both the public and guests of the collectors were told about The Collectors Club and encouraged to enter their details on the Collectors Club mailing list. The Club secured 40 new members on the day.

The Swatch success story continues with the launch earlier this month of an entire new concept for Swatch: metal watches; and the announcement that Swatch is the official timekeeper for the 1996 Atlanta Olympic Games.

The secret of a good relationship

Forging successful links between brand and customer is a core part of marketing. But companies must spot the type of relationship their customers actually want, and monitor how it develops. **ALAN MITCHELL** provides advice on establishing and maintaining a successful association.

Much as they hate to admit it, marketers are supreme followers of fashion, and it's interesting to watch fashions come and go. A few years ago, new product development was the craze. Innovation was The Big Thing. Today, this cure-all is being assailed as innoflation, a costly diversion from the essential task of nurturing the core brands.

Not long ago, loyalty and relationship marketing were the bee's knees. Now things are going strangely quiet there, too. Perhaps, just perhaps, a lot of people have invested a lot of money expecting fat returns – and are now beginning to wonder whether they are going to get any returns at all.

Viewed with the luxury of hindsight, marketers may see relationship marketing – the development of a long-term, even intimate association with named customers based on a two-way flow of information – as rather akin to a nation developing a nuclear capability. It may catapult you to world power status, but the technical challenges, costs and risks are enormous.

The first obstacle, at which most brands fall immediately (despite the self-deceiving protestations of their managers), is that most customers simply do not want go beyond an arms' length relationship with brands. Former Henley Centre chief Bob Tyrrell, for example, warns that the best role many marketers can achieve is as a facility, which customers pick up and use when they want to, and then leave aside just as quickly. Better to concentrate your effort on being an excellent facilitator rather than waste time trying to get over-familiar, he suggests. This is a far cry from the common relationship marketing ideal, where customer and brand are supposed to share deeply held values, aspirations and lifestyles.

The second obstacle is, if anything, even more challenging. Assuming that there are grounds for some sort of deeper, more significant relationship between brand and customer, it's not at all obvious what sort of relationship is the best one. Marketers tend to talk about promiscuity and loyalty as though all relationships are marriages. But people have many different types of relationship with other people, and so, potentially, do organisations with their customers.

Here are some possible examples: parent–child (loan marketer), teacher–student (mass marketer of Internet software), leader–follower (fashion brand), comrade-at-arms (pressure group), fellow enthusiast (sports car), confidante (financial services adviser), idol to be worshipped (luxury brand), casual friend (beer, crisps), soul mate (special whisky), old flame (brands your mum used), a friend whom you seek out to escape from everyday reality (holiday).

Of course, advertising agencies have long understood these differences and have sought to build brand personalities around them. But their brands are singular, one-dimensional affairs created for the mass market. The committed one-to-one relationship marketer has a much more difficult task. To succeed, he may need to build many qualitatively different types of relationships with customers, all revolving around the same brand.

Take a PC brand, for instance. For vast sections of the market, its role is to be the friendly, helping hand, showing the ropes to hesitant first-time users. But that's just the beginning. Some customers may seek a "fellow enthusiast feel", all techies and geeks together. Others may want the brand to mean escape and entertainment – "just look at all those gripping computer games!" – or a purely instrumental relationship: "I want to achieve X at minimum cost."

Yet others may seek a coaching relationship: "I want to reach this difficult performance target, can you help me?" Marketers of cars, travel and financial services have a similarly diverse range of potential relationships.

Somehow, the truly successful would-be relationship marketer has to divine exactly what sort of relationship his customer really wants or needs and find a way of consistently tailoring communications and offers to these needs, meshing style, tone and content to the desired relationship over time.

He also has to sense when and how the relationship life cycle is developing. Lovers move from excitement and passion to intimacy and, perhaps, to boredom; and children grow up and assert their independence. Many computer marketers caught a cold when they failed to realise that the first wave of buyers had grown in confidence, moving beyond the need for the reassuring helping hand to seek a less patronising relationship. Customers started buying clones off page, turning to different brands sold through different distribution channels.

For all these reasons, bad relationship marketing is as easy as falling off a log. Many marketers don't even get past the first step: their research techniques just aren't sensitive enough. For example, market research invariably shows that customers want the brand to be helpful and friendly. But these are generic qualities. They tell us nothing of the true nature of the relationship being sought, and achieving them does little to strengthen the bonds between brand and customer.

Then comes the balancing act. The operational capabilities and communi-cations skills needed to develop many different types of relationship simultaneously within one brand are probably beyond most current practitioners. How does one organisation nurture under one roof all the different attitudes, styles and skills you need?

Branding strategies and portfolios may also fall out of kilter. Can one brand really offer a choice of many different types of relationship, as a supermarket offers choice from a range of products? How different can a brand's style and content of communication be to different audiences, bearing in mind that such communications always leak beyond the intended target? Should different brands be created for different groups Ñ with what implications for costs?

The dream of relationship marketing is that it will gather customers ever more tightly around the brand, building and deepening their loyalty to it. The reality may be precisely the opposite as it develops centrifugal forces of its own, pulling the brand in several different directions at once: the marketing equivalent of a nuclear accident.

The few who really are successful at relationship marketing could make current approaches to branding look more like "blanding". But for the rest of us, contentment with excellence in bland management may be no bad thing.

ISSUES

1. What is relationship marketing?

2. What degrees of relationship might there be?

3. The concept of relationship marketing is being transferred from business-to-business marketing – to what extent is it relevant in consumer markets?

4. Comment on the growing use of customer databases.

5. Discuss the concept of direct marketing.

6. How can companies such as Swatch undertake relationship analysis?

EXPLORATION OF ISSUES

1. Relationship marketing involves all activities that are designed to attract, develop and retain customers. It deals with both market and support relationships. Given the number and diversity of relationships that exist, attempts have been made to categorise them. Many of these relationships exist within a business-to-business context, and therefore much of the conceptual and empirical evidence underpinning relationship marketing derives from this context.

By creating strategic alliances, joint ventures and networks, companies can improve the whole value chain and thus enhance their competitive position. It is increasingly accepted that, in isolation, an organisation has limited capabilities, and consequently the network paradigm has gained much ground.

2. There are a number of strategies open to marketers along the marketing strategy continuum. At one extreme, *transactional* exchange involves a single, short-term exchange encompassing a distinct beginning and end.

At the other end of the continuum, *relational* exchange involves a number of linked transactions over an extended period. These exchanges trace back to previous interactions and reflect an on-going process.

Most consumer goods companies are more likely to be at the transaction end; that is, they are more likely to characterised by discrete, one-off transactions and tend to have an anonymous mass of customers. On this basis, the marketing mix paradigm still has much to offer consumer goods marketers, but there have been several attempts to apply relationship marketing concepts to consumer markets.

3. It is not clear whether the transfer of relationship marketing to consumer goods markets is appropriate, but the potential that relationship marketing can offer in this sphere is certainly very attractive.

Modern consumer markets provide many challenges. Core products and services are rendered similar if not identical to those of competitors by technology. There has been a massive upheaval in the social landscape, and increasing market fragmentation. Relationship marketers see long-term relationships with customers as a stabilising element that supports the mastering of these challenges. Long-term relationships, where over time both parties learn how best to interact with each other, lead to increased satisfaction and decreased relationship costs, for the customer as well as for the supplier or service provider. Therefore, in terms of profitability there is clear evidence that intelligent relationship building and management makes sense.

The main objective of relationship marketing in consumer markets is to foster a bond with each customer for mutual benefit. It is implemented using database marketing and integrated marketing communications.

Databases provide the means to identify and track individual customers and their buying habits, calculate 'lifetime' value and generate individualised marketing communications.

Within the academic community there is an understanding that building real relationships goes much further than simply developing a database. While academics and practitioners acknowledge the importance of dialogue as opposed to one-way communication, the extent to which dialogue occurs in practice is somewhat limited. Marketers are not even overly concerned with inviting customers to establish mutual relationships. Consider the following advice to business:

> Relationship marketing . . . requires a two-way flow of information. This does not mean that the customer has to give you this information willingly, or even knowingly. You can use scanners to capture information, you can gather telephone numbers, conduct surveys, supply warranty cards, and use a data overlay from outside databases to combine factors about lifestyle, demographics, geographics, psychograhics, and customer purchases (Shultz, 1993, p.28).

Although inappropriate, this view of relationship marketing remains all too commonplace.

Research in industrial marketing indicates that relationships are complex, long term and mutually beneficial. Literature on topics as diverse as industrial services and social psychology suggests that relationships are characterised by trust, commitment, mutual benefit, adaptation, respect and regard for privacy. If relationship marketing is to be successfully applied in consumer markets, then such relationships should incorporate all these elements.

The idea of classifying interactions on a continuum can be extended to consumer markets: at one end is a discrete, short-term and often mechanical transaction such as buying a soft drink from a vending machine. At the other end is a relationship with one's doctor. Thus relationships with consumers should, in theory, incorporate the integral elements of trust, commitment, discretion and respect for privacy. The extent to which these elements exist in consumer relationships is, however, unclear.

4 Today's companies have a very powerful tool to gather names, addresses and other pertinent information about individual customers and prospects: the customer database. A customer database is an organised collection of current, comprehensive data about individual customers or prospects that is easily accessible and applicable to such marketing purposes as lead generation, lead qualification, the sale of products or services, or maintenance of customer relationships. Database marketing is the process of building, maintaining and using customer databases and other databases (products, suppliers, retailers) for the purpose of contacting and transacting.

Many companies confuse customer mailing lists with customer databases. A customer mailing list is simply a set of names, addresses and telephone numbers. A customer database contains much more information. In consumer marketing, the customer database contains an individual's demographics (age, income, family members, birthdays), psychographics (activities, interests and opinions) and mediagraphics (past purchases and other relevant information).

A well-developed customer database is a proprietary asset that can give the company a competitive edge.

Armed with the information in its customer database, a company can achieve a much greater degree of target-market precision that it can with mass marketing, sequence marketing or niche marketing. The company can identify small groups of customers to receive finely-tuned marketing offers and communications. Some companies are using a technique called 'data mining' in order to improve this process. Most large companies will to need to engage in database marketing if they are to be competitive past the year 2000.

Companies use their databases for four purposes:

- *To identify prospects.*   The database is built up from responses to advertising. The company sorts through the database to identify the best prospects, then contacts them by mail, phone or personal calls in an attempt to convert them into customers.
- *To decide which customers should receive a particular offer.*   Companies draw up criteria for the ideal target customer for a specific offer, then search their customer databases for those most closely resembling the ideal type. By noting the contact's response rates, the company can improve its target precision over time.
- *To strengthen customer loyalty.*   Companies can encourage interest and enthusiasm among their customers by remembering their preferences, sending appropriate gifts, discount coupons, interesting reading material, and so on.
- *To reactivate customer purchases.*   Companies can install automatic mailing programmes (automatic marketing) to send out birthday or anniversary cards,

Christmas shopping reminders or off-season promotions to the customers on their databases. The database can help the company to make attractive offers of product replacement or upgrades just when the customers might be ready to act.

Like many other marketing tools, database marketing requires investment. Companies must invest in computer hardware, database software, analytical programmes, communication links and skilled personnel. The database system must be user friendly and available to various marketing groups, including those in product and brand management, new product development, advertising and promotion, direct mail, telemarketing, field sales, order fulfilment and customer service. A well-managed database should lead to sales gains that will more than cover its cost.

Many things can go wrong if database marketing is not conducted carefully and strategically.

Six classic mistakes are:

- Thinking that you can use database marketing (DBM) only once.
- Not getting the total commitment of upper management.
- Not being 100 per cent certain that everyone involved with the programme fully understands the programme.
- Expecting immediate results from the DBM programme.
- Not recognising the importance of having measurement standards in place before beginning the programme.
- Budgeting the money, allocating the people and material resources, doing the job . . . and then letting the database sit. Use the data you collect!

As more companies move into database marketing the marketing paradigm will change. Mass marketing and mass retailing will continue, but their prevalence and power may diminish as more buyers turn to non-retail shopping. More consumers will use electronic shopping facilities to search for the information and products they need. On-line services will provide more objective information about the comparative merits of different brands. Marketers will need to think of new ways to create effective on-line messages, as well as new channels for delivering products and services efficiently.

5   Direct marketing uses various advertising media to interact with consumers, generally calling for the consumer to make a direct response. Mass advertising typically reaches an unspecified number of people, most of whom are not in the market for a product and may still not want it at a future date. Direct-advertising vehicles are used to obtain immediate orders directly from targeted consumers. Although direct marketing initially consisted mostly of direct mail and mail-order catalogues, it has taken on several additional forms in recent years, including telemarketing, direct radio and television marketing and on-line computer shopping.

Direct marketing has boomed in recent years and is now used by all kinds of organisation: manufacturers, retailers, service companies, catalogue merchants and non-profit organisations, to name a few. Its growing use in consumer marketing is largely a response to the 'demassification' of mass markets, which has resulted in an ever-greater number of fragmented market segments with highly individual needs and wants. Direct marketing allows sellers to focus efficiently on these minimarkets with offers that better match specific consumer needs.

Other trends also have fuelled the growth of direct marketing. The increasing number of women entering the workforce has reduced the time that families have to shop. The higher costs of driving, traffic congestion and parking headaches, the shortage of retail sales help, limited store hours and longer queues at checkout counters have all promoted in-house shopping. The concept of free-phone telephone numbers and the increased use of credit cards have helped sellers to reach and transact with consumers more easily. Finally, the growth of computer power and communication technology has allowed marketers to build better customer databases and communication channels with which to reach the best prospects for specific products.

Direct marketing provides many benefits to consumers. Instead of driving their cars through congested city streets to shop in crowded shopping malls, customers can use their telephones or computers to whiz along the information superhighway. Today's sophisticated communications networks carry voice, video and data over fibre-optic telephone lines, linking buyers and sellers in convenient, exciting ways. People who buy through direct mail or by telephone say that shopping is convenient, hassle-free and fun. It saves them time, and it introduces them to new lifestyles and a larger selection of merchandise. Consumers can compare products and prices in their armchairs by browsing through catalogues at their leisure. They can order and receive products without having to leave their homes.

Direct marketing also provides benefits to sellers. It allows greater selectivity. A direct marketer can buy a mailing list containing the names of almost any group – millionaires, parents of new-born babies, left-handed people or recent college graduates. The direct marketing message can be personalised and customised. The marketer can search its database, select consumers with specific characteristics and send them individualised, laser-printed letters.

With direct marketing the seller can build a continuous customer relationship and produce a steady stream of offers tailored to a regular customer's specific needs and interests. Direct marketing can also be timed to reach prospects at just the right moment, and because of this direct-marketing materials receive greater attention and elicit a better response. Direct marketing also permits the easy testing of specific messages and media. Because the results are direct and immediate, direct marketing lends itself more readily to response measurement.

Finally, direct marketing provides privacy – the direct marketer's offers and strategies are not visible to competitors.

6 Relationship marketing is important for companies' long-term success, since it costs five times more to attract a new customer than to retain an existing one. Clearly, companies that value relationships of commitment and trust with their customers will out-compete those that adhere to the 'hand over the money and we will deliver' school of thought. It is not easy to quantify the quality of relationship marketing; both inputs and outputs need to be examined. Input factors that have a direct bearing on relationship marketing are understanding customers, empowering employees and total quality management. Based on these inputs, various relationship-based outputs can be measured: customer satisfaction, customer loyalty, customer perception of product and service quality, and profitability.

One-to-One and Differential Marketing

KEY CONCEPTS

- One-to-one marketing
- Differential marketing
- Direct marketing
- Market fragmentation

Up close and personal

One-to-one targeting is definitely on the marketing agenda but is that personal touch always welcome?

DAVID REED

Cookies, toasters, triggers: this is the new marketing jargon. Technology is changing the way marketers operate just as they have come to terms with the idea that mass markets no longer exist. The core realisation is that treating customers as individuals may provide real competitive advantage.

As Stan Rapp, keynote speaker at this week's IDM Symposium and chief executive officer of Rapp Collins Worldwide, says: "Everything else exists to make the customer relationship happen."

The starting point for this move to one-to-one communications is often an assessment that other forms are too wasteful. John Orsmond, chairman of ARM, notes that a user of mass direct marketing who relies on rented-in data is likely to be wasting at least 35 per cent of that data through poor targeting.

"You can reckon on enquirer databases of pre-qualified, interested prospects giving you a 40 per cent greater likelihood of purchasing," he says. "If you use fusion techniques for profiling, you can reckon on a 60 per cent improvement in targeting." Those two steps forward are significant ones. First, there is the reduction of waste by using internal data. Second, you can analyse that data to identify the most valuable segments.

Orsmond cites one example of an automotive client, whose database showed that ten per cent of the population accounted for 46 per cent of purchasing behaviour. What role remains for mass marketing once such a finding has been brought to light?

Reaching this stage does require a database, however, which has until recently been a significant stumbling block. As Neil Muranyi, sales director at The Database Group, says: "Analysis is the driver. You can't do one-to-one unless you have in-depth, individual information. That is why you have to move up to group or segment level to deal with data en masse if you don't have it at individual level."

Data has been at a premium, forcing marketers to use aggregated information, which begins with the assumption that individuals can be grouped together. Recently there has been a change, with the population appearing to become more willing to tell marketers what they want to know.

As The Henley Centre found in its Dataculture 1995 report, 69 per cent of consumers want to know more about the companies with which they regularly deal. To allow this to happen, 66 per cent will trade their personal information if it results in better service, while 53 per cent will trade for discounts or promotions.

Similar findings emerged in research carried out by the Direct Mail Information Service. Consumers were asked if companies provide them with enough information. The automotive sector fared best (60 per cent said "yes"), followed by retail (55 per cent). In travel, a slight majority thought they were told enough (51 per cent), but for household goods (47 per cent), appliances (46 per cent) and food and drink (45 per cent) there was clear evidence that consumers want to know more.

This opens the way for communications to deliver more information and convert interest into sales. In the food and drink sector, for example, 57 per cent of consumers said receiving direct mail made them more likely to buy from the company. It is this realisation that is fuelling the growth of customer databases.

Now, more than ever, databases can be populated with rich information. Martin Kiersnowski, managing director of ICD Surveys, notes: "We have 150 different fields of information which can be attached on a standard basis and 3,000 non-standard fields."

With 8 million households on file, which he predicts will rise to 10 million this year, marketers are armed with a tremendously powerful and predictive resource.

"The most powerful indicator is not a complex algorithm or a detailed profile, it is that this person buys a certain product. If you can get sufficient volumes of data on people who buy your brand, you don't need to worry about the other stuff," he says. Nor is ICD alone in having built high-volume databases. The combined NDL/CMT lifestyle survey, marketed by Calyx, now covers 80 per cent of British households.

With the data increasingly available, the focus has turned to the media. According to Miriam Mulcahey, lead media consultant at The Henley Centre: "The technology is there for mass customisation."

Digital TV is about to break in the UK and may change television from a mass to a one-to-one communications vehicle.

The Henley Centre's Media Futures 97 report says: "One of the ironies of digital technology is that it provides television with the opportunity to exploit both mass and niche markets. As such, it could be the ultimate medium for the mass customisation of marketing messages." Combining the database on viewers or subscribers with a marketing communications strategy that wants to talk one-to-one could lead to TV ads that are personally addressed.

Print media is already heading that way. Reader's Digest has announced it can offer a display ad facility which uses the subscriber's personal data to create a totally individual edition. The Internet, of course, is already being driven in this way through the use of cookies – systems that take user information to create an entirely customised Website, different for each person who visits it.

Adrian Baker, business development director at Aspen Direct, says: "Marketers can use the Internet to offer an interactive and bespoke site for each user. The Net is now effectively converging with the database to provide the opportunity to be very personalised about the content and the way in which each consumer views the site."

The Henley Centre predicts that households may soon be infested with toasters – household goods that talk to each other and act on information about the householder. So your fridge could soon be on the phone to the supermarket to order the beer that you have just run out of. Alternatively, the beer company may be able to put a message onto a panel on the fridge saying: "You've just run out. How about a nice cold Brand X?"

To exploit these opportunities, marketers are having to get smarter. The use of triggers for communications is one example of allowing data to drive activity. Tim Pottinger, divisional managing director of The Computing Group, explains: "A lot of people are doing triggered mailings once events happen. To the individual, they appear more personal. It is moving down the road of one-to-one. The trigger could be as easy as the anniversary of a renewal, or date of birth, including age bands, when a product is purchased." It might also be something more complex, such as a change in lifestyle or lifestage, such as the birth of a child or reaching 40.

But this is where that which is technically possible bumps into that which is humanly feasible. Francis Smith, head of data at IMP, believes that putting power into the hands of consumers through interactive media does require a cultural change. He says: "It is difficult to write a business plan to respond to consumers as and when they ask for information. It is easier to say you will mail everybody in January. This is a difficult hurdle to get over, because it is the plan that releases budget in the future and there is a fear of lack of control."

During the past two years, technology has overtaken the industry's ability to exploit it. "Marketers have had a long period of being ahead of technology, of wanting to do things that technology didn't do. Now the technology has leapfrogged, so marketers need to get out of that frame of mind," says Smith.

But there is another disjuncture: between what marketers might want to do and what the public is ready for. John Wood, client services director at Turnbull Wood Hayes, says: "I take issue with consumers being left out of the debate. How much do they want to be treated with that kind of personalisation? The issue is always about getting response, not giving people the information they want. A lot of what is done just irritates people. If you get a response from two per cent, that means the other 98 per cent hate your guts. That is not what you want."

There are also those who doubt whether the potential to communicate one-to-one really is supported by the apparent wealth of data now available. Peter Bell, marketing manager of CDMS, says: "I don't think one-to-one is possible, although that is probably heresy. I don't think we will ever get sufficient data, therefore the communications people receive will of necessity not be as personal as it should be."

And Mulcahey suggests that consumers do not always want to be as interactive as the technology and marketing strategy suggests they should be. How many people will want to interact with their new, flat-screen digital TV rather than just sit on the couch being spoon-fed messages?

As a result, marketers are beginning to recognise that one-to-one communication is not always the best use of their resources. In particular, it is too expensive to be used on customer segments that might not be profitable. The solution could be to adopt mass customisation.

Andrew Robinson, business development director at Harte-Hanks IFM, says: "Mass customisation is about creating the feeling that it is one-to-one, despite the fact that it isn't. It gives you the best of both worlds. It can allow a marketing organisation to maintain a relationship without going into ridiculous detail. Eventually, you get to the point where to take it beyond fine targeting stops being cost effective. Then you have to weigh up the added-value elements of your marketing against the cost of making the sale."

The danger for large organisations is being attracted by the examples quoted by marketing gurus of companies which deal with every customer as an individual. For a florist, this might be easy. But it is exceedingly difficult for companies such as Tesco or NatWest to replicate that same feeling in a different environment. How do you make millions of people feel warm towards you?

What might be concluded is that while everything is possible, not all things are desirable. One-to-one might be too expensive, too hard to manage, or too intrusive. As Robinson says: "The reality is, some people may reject the idea of something completely tailored to them."

The database is here to stay, but don't throw away the old marketing plans just yet.

The power of personal services

Most marketing departments are still built around products and product managers, but there's a whiff of change in the air. Companies are waking up to the fact that their most important asset is their customer base.

ALAN MITCHELL

Using storecard data, mass retailers like Tesco are developing bespoke marketing activities for their most valuable customers

Five years after Bain & Co's Fred Reichheld wrote his Harvard Business Review article, pointing out that a company's most loyal customers are also its most profitable, the customer loyalty revolution is sweeping all before it. Discount the coming backlash against its corruption – loyalty scheme as short-term sales promotion in clever clothing – and we still have a marketing revolution on our hands.

Like most revolutions, the most profound consequences may be the least expected. Take its impact on marketing department organisation. So far there is a miss-match. We have individual customers' names and addresses of, and – if you're an Amex or a store- card holder, a rich history of transactional data – but still the entire machinery is driven by mass-marketing assumptions. If segmentation and targeting is deployed, the main impetus is cost-cutting, not relationship building.

Indeed, most marketing departments are still production-led. They are built around products and product managers whose job it is to shift their wares to as many consumers as possible. But they do not have customer managers. "Customer focus" is merely a means of achieving volume sales targets.

Now there's a whiff of change in the air. Surely, if customer loyalty and maximising life-time customer value is a key priority, should we not have expert staff who concentrate on this, and only this? Yet how many companies are structured to do it? Take banks, whose branch managers, loans managers and savings product managers may all be "focusing" on the same customer, separately, and and at cross-purposes.

Now advocates of "one-to-one" marketing, like US guru Don Peppers, are beginning to suggest a new customer-centred marketing structure is needed. The core of it could be a new-style "customer manager" whose job it is to maximise the relationship with – and value of – a certain group of customers with similar characteristics. Instead of trying to find more consumers for the same product, they would seek to maximise their portfolio of products and services to meet existing customers' needs, thereby relegating product managers to mere "capabilities managers" alongside the rest of production and distribution.

According to Peppers, speaking at this week's Institute of Direct Marketing symposium on The One-to-One Future, marketers' commonplace boast that brands are their companies' most important assets is often mere vanity. For many companies their most important asset is their customer base. While marketers like to think that brands create and sustain customer relationships, increasingly it is the company's relationships with customers that make sales possible, he suggests. "In the long run, all products and services are ephemeral. Only customers are real."

An extreme example is the United Services Automobile Association. Virtually unknown outside the US armed forces, it's hardly a brand, actively limiting its marketing to a relatively tiny market of current and former military officers and their families to sell them insurance, banking, travel services and retirement homes.

But it has found a way to grow without acquiring customers. It simply sells more to existing ones, including other companies' products such as cars, jewellery and white and brown goods. "While brand managers try to increase brand equity, customer managers try to increase customer equity," Peppers commented at a recent Royal Mail conference.

The ultimate, suggests Peppers, is the "learning broker" who, on the strength of a trusting relationship with its customers and close monitoring of their changing needs, makes its money by going out and finding the particular products and services they want. It need not produce any itself, though usually the relationship will have started, say, with a bank account, storecard, or mail order catalogue and developed from there.

Reality check time. Most UK companies are yonks away from having the technology, the database or relationship marketing skills to embark on such a revolution. Yet the intriguing thing is how many companies are beginning to edge in that direction. NatWest's personal account executives started offering bespoke integrated services to high net worth individuals many years ago, for example. The scheme was a great success. Amex's relationship marketing strategy prompted it to split its department to create separate customer loyalty and acquisition managers.

Computer and telecoms companies such as BT, Microsoft and Amstrad Direct are moving away from product marketing to customer marketing: creating packages of products and services for the home-based self-employed, the "edutainment"-crazed kid or the telecommuter. Another example, the increasing popularity of partnership marketing, where the core motive is to gain access to another company's customers.

Even mass marketers are tentatively shifting in this direction. The whole basis of the Heinz direct marketing initiative is to develop bespoke offers and communications for consumers who identify their particular interests, such as dieting or ethnic foods. Next step? Tailor NPD to suit their particular desires.

Likewise, using their storecard data, mass retailers are developing bespoke marketing activities for, say, the most valuable 500 customers in each location. A pilot promotion for Tesco's Clubcard targeting hefty winebuyers with a Chardonnay offer was so successful, that rolling it out across the entire chain would have involved it buying up the world's entire stock. Peppers' chart (above) suggests that as such skills and expertise develop, the line can be moved left, from niche, to mass.

Of course, rumours of the death of the brand manager are now so common it's tempting to dismiss this as just another exaggeration. The difference here, however, is that the rise of both the database and of customer loyalty makes the emergence of the customer manager inevitable. As Brann's Alan Bigg comments: "It is one of the consequences of knowing more about your customers."

Watch this space.

Switching away from the masses

American database marketing guru Garth Hallberg thinks mass marketing will be replaced by 'differential' marketing. In future, marketers will maximise profits by employing distinct marketing programmes for heavy, medium and low product users.

ALAN MITCHELL

Ever since Fred Reicheld and Bain & Co analysed the benefit gained by companies which increased their customer retention rates, the loyalty bandwagon has been gaining momentum. Most marketers simply take it for granted that increased loyalty equals increased profitability – and therefore is "a good thing".

Prepare to think again. Work over many years by Professor Andrew Ehrenberg, now at South Bank University, shows what a dodgy assumption this is. Indeed, if Ehrenberg is right, it's almost a general law of fmcg markets that the bigger the brand, the less "loyal" its customers are.

As he explained at a recent seminar, heavy category users tend to have a repertoire of brands, and big brands are big because, within that repertoire, they are purchased more frequently – say 3.5 times a year – than the number two brand, which is purchased, say, three times a year.

On the other hand, the brand's most "loyal" customers are almost invariably the least valuable. They buy the category once a year and always choose brand X. By normal definition they are 100 per cent loyal – but a complete waste of time. "Your best customers are mostly other people's customers who occasionally buy you," says Ehrenberg.

Ogilvy & Mather database marketing guru Garth Hallberg delivers a few more unsettling messages in his new book, All consumers are not created equal, which is published this month.

One common and reassuring assumption among marketers is that if you are a market leader your customer base is relatively secure and your progress is steady and stable.

But look under the surface, as Hallberg has been doing with brands in the US and you'll find turmoil and chaos. Take US yoghurt brand YopleX. In one year, 51 per cent of its users were new and 45 per cent of its previous users stopped buying. New users accounted for 54 per cent of sales volume, compared with existing users who started buying more, and soaked up 32 per cent of sales. Existing buyers who bought less accounted for 28 per cent of sales loss and defectors, 34 per cent.

According to Hallberg, this incredible shift is by no means unusual.

Kellogg's Corn Flakes had 42 per cent new customers and 40 per cent defectors in one year.

On average, only 35 per cent of car owners (90 per cent of whom insist they are "satisfied" with their current brand) repeat buy.

Another Hallberg target is mass marketing. If you study the dynamics of any category you'll find that "the profits of mass markets do not come from mass market brands", he declares.

Take YopleX again. If you divide its customer base into three equal categories of heavy, medium and low users, you'll find that the heavy users are concentrated in just 16 per cent of all households. Yet they account for 83 per cent of the brand's volume and 110 per cent of its profits.

No. That's not a misprint. Sixteen per cent of households account for 110 per cent of the brand's profits. Hallberg gets this figure by factoring in the cost of what he calls "the mass media tax": the marketing spend that reaches the 52 per cent of households who don't buy YopleX at all. They represent a charge against profits, slicing around 20 per cent off the total. Low users, who only buy the brand about once a year, also end up costing the brand profits as the cost of marketing to them outweighs the tiny revenues they generate.

Again, YopleX is not an oddity. According to Hallberg, in the US, five per cent of households buy 85 per cent of Levi's jeans; eight per cent of households buy 84 per cent of Diet Coke; 21 per cent of cinema-goers account for 80 per cent of attendance. The top third of personal long-distance callers account for 68 per cent of billing and the top third of credit cardholders account for 66 per cent of charges and come from just 15 per cent of all households.

Most brands, it seems, display similar characteristics. The implication? Mass marketing never really existed in the first place. So why continue using its techniques?

Until now, of course, marketers haven't had the information or insight to do anything else. But now that the information is becoming available, Hallberg recommends three things. First, use it to redirect a reduced ad budget towards known heavy users – a far better media-planning strategy than traditional demographics, psychographics and so on, he claims.

Second, rethink promotions. Traditional, indiscriminate, price-related promotions heavily subsidise those consumers who would buy the product anyway. They reduce heavy users' net profitability by 35 per cent, he says. Instead, concentrate a slashed promotional budget on incentivising those consumers identified as most likely to produce the most profitable sales uplift (NOT the biggest volume increase.)

Third, redirect the saved marketing funds into a tightly targeted, direct marketing-based loyalty scheme for heavy users only. And make sure it focuses more on "added value" information about the brand – children's nutrition, dieting, etc. – than on promotions. Results from experiments so far suggest an average sales uplift of 25 per cent. Blue chip companies like Kraft, Unilever, Kimberly-Clark and P&G are all taking note.

Differential marketing, as Hallberg calls it, has its drawbacks. Identifying high users and building a database around them isn't easy or cheap. The likely sales boosts may well be one-off rather than repeating. And the concept is probably best applied to brands with mega budgets, relatively high margins and high degrees of consumer interest. But how many of these still exist?

In his more enthusiastic moments, Hallberg looks forward to the time when supermarkets will combine store card data with manufacturers' loyalty data so that both sides can develop fine-tuned marketing programmes based on differential pricing, differential distribution strategies and even differential product development. In the longer term, he sees differential marketing leading to one-to-one marketing via the information superhighway.

Dramatic shifts are taking place in the heartland of marketing. But how many marketing departments' day-to-day activities remotely reflect this?

ISSUES

(1) **What has changed in the market to cause market fragmentation?**

(2) **What other factors have led to the demand for differential and one-to-one marketing?**

(3) **What has happened to drive marketing's capacity to deliver 'one-to-one' and 'differential marketing'?**

EXPLORATION OF ISSUES

1 It is clear that market fragmentation has taken place. Markets have become 'demassified' and this has been a major trend aiding the growth of direct marketing. This is manifested in greater pluralism within society, evident in the high street where pluralism in clothing styles is observable. The Henley Centre predicted this trend as far back as the 1970s when they discussed household behaviour as 'cellular' rather than 'nuclear' – households were beginning to do things together less and less and were behaving more independently – families were not eating together as often, they had TV and sound systems in their own rooms, and whereas at one time it was typical to have one large 'family sized' packet of Corn Flakes in the kitchen, it was becoming more likely that each household member would have a packet of 'their' cereal in the cupboard.

Another change has been the increase in the number of working women, many of whom are joining their male counterparts in seeking time-saving purchasing methods such as direct mail and telemarketing. Working women are also more independent and partly account for the greater number of smaller households, which require narrower targeting. The divorce rate has risen, and with it the number of small and single households – affecting both sexes. This also means that more men are deciding which washing powder they will buy and more women are buying cars and pensions for themselves. The continuing trend away from cash as the means of payment and towards credit, debit and smart cards, with transactions being conducted by post, telephone or Internet, means that purchases are being made when and where the customer wants it – 24 hours a day and from the armchair, office phone or even portable laptop computer.

2 Companies have become disillusioned with more traditional promotional media in recent years. Market fragmentation has resulted in diminishing audiences for individual media, media costs have soared and consumers are experiencing clutter. Although above-the-line advertising is targeted at specific audiences – those watching a late night Friday show on Channel 4 are unlikely to have the same characteristics as those watching BBC2 on a Wednesday afternoon (or if they are, they might not be in the same frame of mind). However the targeting is still of the 'shotgun' variety rather than the 'sniper's rifle' that is possible through direct marketing.

Audiences are fragmenting as more TV channels appear (satellite and cable) along with more newspapers and magazines – all with advertising space to fill. Furthermore consumers are not helping the advertiser by video recording TV programmes and 'zapping' the commercials. Direct marketing has the potential to overcome the difficulty of this 'clutter' because the message can be personalised.

3 In tandem with consumers' apparent desire to be treated more as individuals and marketing's desire to find more effective media, comes the marketer's search for more detailed and personalised information about customers.

This is based, in part, on the relative decline in the use of demographic segmentation variables, due to their to lack of explanatory depth and their necessary restriction relatively broad targeting applications. In the 1980s the typical 'Mintel' style of market profiling according to age, gender and social gradebegan to give way to psychographic and geodemographic profiling. Indeed the rise of psychographics and geodemographics hastened demographic's decline because of their ability to profile target customers in great detail, even individually, and target them specifically.

One of the more significant factors in the move away from generalised customer profiles towards more individualised ones was the commercial availability of Census data. The 1981 UK Census data were used to cluster analyse some forty variables and the clusters of households that were revealed led to the identification of 39 neighbourhood types. Compare this with one of the leading alternatives of the time – social grade – whereby the entire population was classified into just six groups on the basis of one variable – the occupation of the chief income earner in the household. Whereas demographic profiles are often based on sample surveys of 1000, the marketing industry now has access to a census of 56 million. Names and addresses cannot be obtained from the Census, but the statistics for enumeration districts can. These are groupings of around 170 households. Such data can be linked with the postcode database (there is one postcode for approximately 15 households) and the electoral register database to identify individual households and their characteristics.

There are 'me-toos' of the original Acorn system. Richard Webber, who created Acorn, set up one of the newer competitors after he left CACI to join a similar agency, CCN (Consumer Credit Nottingham, now called Experian, following the link with the American company of that name – one of the origins of direct marketing was credit referencing), and developed Mosaic, which analyses Census data together with credit company records and even a database on county court bad debt cases. The basic rationale behind geodemographics is that 'birds of a feather flock together', making neighbourhoods relatively homogeneous. An easy riposte to this is 'I am not like my neighbour'. However geodemographics have proved to be reasonably robust overall. In other European countries similar systems exist, for example under the names Geo Market profile and Omnidata. Several geodemographic companies now operate in a number of European countries, for example Experian, with its Mosaic brand.

The Target Group Index (TGI) is an annual 34-volume report on buyer profiles in most product markets, based on samples of over 20 000. From this, each geodemographic category's interest in the product concerned can be determined. In fact the TGI sample is now based on geodemographic categories. The National Readership Survey is similarly analysed geodemographically and provides readership profiles for media selection purposes.

The 2001 Census may provide some additional information that is relevant to the direct marketer, and the following questions are being tested prior to the Census:

- Are you in receipt of unpaid personal help?
- Do you provide substantial unpaid personal help for a friend or relative with any long-term illness, health problems or disability?
- Does the household property include a garden or yard?

- Do you belong to a religious group?' (List of categories provided.)
- What is your total gross income from all sources?

These questions could provide some additional data for geodemographics/lifestyle databases, for example income is a useful measure of likely disposable income, the possession of a garden would be of interest to direct marketers of garden products. The existence of personal help might be of interest to service providers and the question about religion could be used by church organisations to target individuals – churches are increasingly turning to direct marketing. The 1991 Census included a controversial question about ethnic origin – could the questions above prove equally controversial?

It can be argued that geodemographics opened the floodgates as far as more individualised targeting is concerned. Before its appearance marketers relied on demographics, with perhaps the odd flirtation with psychographics, often, as mentioned, based on sample surveys of about 1000.

The availability of more individual-specific data, coupled with technological facilitators, is enabling the targeting of individuals based on what we know of their interests and characteristics. The means for storing and retrieving such individual data is the marketing database and it is this that is at the heart of much direct marketing – but not the main focus, because that should be the customer, and nor does the database drive direct marketing, because it is the market that should provide the impetus.

Lifestyle profiles and the nature and use of the database in marketing are explored in the clipping above, and it is clear that all these forces are combining to allow not only differential marketing but even one-to-one marketing.

16 Strategic Issues

Marketing Alliances

KEY CONCEPTS

- Strategic link-ups/alliance marketing
- Cooperative advantage
- Market share building
- Channel conflict
- Market entry and timing
- Managing the marketing mix

Barclaycard runs rings round rivals

While the competition fights it out on price, Barclaycard's link-up with Cellnet provides its 9 million card holders with real added value. The deal offers home banking, bill paying and, possibly, smart cards.

SEAN BRIERLEY

On April 8, viewers of the latest TV advertisement for Barclaycard will see secret agent Bough and his bungling boss Latham lost in a far away location, stranded on someone's roof.

Luckily for Bough and the witless Latham, Barclaycard signed a deal last year with mobile phone operator Cellnet to develop a digital mobile phone to give them – and potentially 9 million other Barclaycard customers who may have strayed off the beaten track – the ability to find out exactly where they are, as well as providing access to emergency services.

The £5m jointly funded advertising campaign, by the country's biggest card issuer and the second biggest mobile phone operator, will promote a product that looks likely to leave the competition standing.

The handsets are offered at a reduced price of £50 to Barclaycard customers – with free connection, a monthly line rental of £15 and a 20 per cent discount on calls. The phone features a Barclaycard button which can call up services such as International Rescue, Road Assist, customer services and bill payments.

The benefits for both brands are clear. Cellnet's general manager Steve Rowley points out that having access to Barclaycard's 9 million customers will obviously build market share in a highly competitive sector. It also bypasses retailers and helps reduce one of the greatest problems of mobile phone marketing: churn – when customers sign up for an initial period and then fail to renew their contracts.

Rowley says 25 per cent of Cellnet's customers quit soon after the initial subscription. "Out of our 2.4 million customers, 600,000 leave each year, though these are replaced by 1.5 million a year," he says. "The fact that many of these customers come in at a discounted rate means it does affect the bottom line."

Barclaycard's commercial director, Shaun Powell, claims the churn rate of his 9 million customers is just 1.5 per cent.

The joint deal also encourages greater use of the phone because customers gain Barclaycard Profile points for calls. In return, the credit card giant takes a cut on each call.

But it has provided some problems for Cellnet. Retailers cannot be happy that the mobile phone operator is bypassing them with a deal that offers more favourable terms, and the mobile phone trade association has tried to take Cellnet to the telecoms watchdog Oftel, claiming the deal contravenes the terms of its licence. The association backed down in the end.

Barclaycard benefits from offering its customers added value, encouraging them to use Barclaycard's services more – customers gain Profile points for paying utility bills on the phone – and offering rival credit card customers an incentive to switch.

Barclaycard is using new product development as an added-value strategy, while its main competitors attempt to fight on cheaper price.

Rewarding customers for using the service with Profile points, for instance, means they are locked into the brand through distribution. Both brands have dominant market positions and access to the resources of larger parent groups, Barclays and BT.

Powell says the Cellnet deal will become central to his marketing efforts.

"This isn't simply an added-value offer, this is full-blown alliance marketing," says Powell. Cellnet is Barclaycard's long-term partner, he says, and the company intends to develop additional facilities with the phone operator.

Though this form of alliance is common in the more saturated US markets, alliance marketing in the UK has largely been confined to mutual endorsements by washing machine and detergent brands.

Powell is evangelical about the need for big brands to form strategic alliances for building market share. "This is where marketing is going," he says.

If this is true, Barclaycard's competitors have been surprisingly slow to get involved. Whereas Powell made clear his intention to get involved in the market as long ago as 1994 – when Barclaycard signed a less ambitious deal with Mercury One-2-One to offer more limited services – other card issuers have done virtually nothing. The deal with Mercury One-2-One is still available, though Barclaycard is not supporting the link-up with advertising.

Powell says Barclaycard benefits from being a standalone brand from parent Barclays. Rival banks such as Lloyds treat their credit cards as an add-on service, rather than as central to their marketing efforts, he says. This gives him greater freedom to innovate.

Other banks have certainly toyed with phone link-ups. Although Midland Bank says that it is not involved in any negotiations with mobile phone operators, TSB announced a deal with Vodafone a day after the Barclaycard-Cellnet deal was struck, though this appears to have foundered. It had intended to develop a similar phone to Barclaycard's using TSB Trustcard (MW October 20 1995), but the plans have been shelved because of the bank's pre-occupation

with its merger with Lloyds.

Barclaycard has also benefited from the discomfort of its main rival, Access, which has seen its marketing and new product development efforts paralysed while unfriendly sale negotiations between its bank owners and Mastercard have continued.

Only NatWest is known to be actively engaged in negotiations to set up a similar deal with a mobile phone company – understood to be Orange – but it would probably be a year late to market.

One obvious service that would benefit from a mobile phone deal would be First Direct, but a spokesman for the bank says it is not involved in talks.

Seemingly, most banks fail to recognise that the technology is already available.

The bulk of new product development by banks has centred on upgrading ATMs (cashpoints) or testing hi-tech PC and television banking, as well as electronic purses.

The hi-tech, low-interest Mondex trial in Swindon, involving the use of stored value cash cards and 300 special stationery BT telephones that refill cards with cash, can easily be performed with digital mobile phone handsets.

Powell confirms that Barclaycard is also considering the possibility of developing a smart card which could load an electronic wallet with cash through the phone, as well as transferring payment from bank accounts and transmitting account details directly to the handset screen.

Rowley says the phone could also be plugged into a computer. Cellnet is looking at the possibility of customers calling up the latest information on how their shares are performing.

The problem for other banks and mobile phone companies is that once customers are locked in, deals can be made to bring in other service providers, such as motoring organisations – Cellnet already has a deal with the RAC – travel and tour operators, high street retailers and even supermarkets.

The problem for Barclaycard's rivals is that they are so obsessed with cheaper competitors gnawing at their ankles that by the time they decide to commit to the new technology, the game may already be in another field.

Ironically they may be condemned to fight it out on price because their brands do not provide enough added-value.

ISSUES

1. **How can a company maintain its competitive advantage?**

2. **Comment on the rise of strategic link-ups and alliance marketing.**

3. **'In defining marketing objectives and marketing strategy, it should be emphasised that they must have a time dimension.' Comment on this statement.**

EXPLORATION OF ISSUES

1. A good strategist seeks not only to 'win the hill, but to hold on to it'. In other words, a business should not only seek competitive advantage but also maintain it in the long term. Maintaining competitive advantage requires barriers to be erected against competitors. Barriers are based on competitive cost differentials and/or price or service differentials. In all cases a successful barrier allows higher margins than those achieved by competitors. A successful barrier must also be sustainable and, in a practical sense, insurmountable by competitors; that is, it must cost competitors more to surmount than it costs the leader to defend.

The nature of the barrier depends on the competitive economics of the business. A heavily advertised consumer product with a leading market share enjoys a significant cost advantage, and perhaps a price-realisation advantage, over its competitors. If a consumer product has, for example, twice the market share of its competitors, it needs to spend only one-half of the advertising pound per unit to have the same impact in the market place. It will always cost competitors more to attack than it costs the leader to defend.

One the other hand, barriers cost money to erect and defend. The expense of the barrier may become an umbrella under which new forums of competition can grow. For example, while advertising is a barrier that protects a leading consumer brand from its other branded competitors, the cost of maintaining the barrier is an umbrella under which a private-label product may hide and grow.

A broad product line, large sales and service capabilities are all examples of major barriers. Each of these has a cost to erect and maintain. Each is effective against smaller competitors who are attempting to copy the leader but can't afford the barrier costs.

The best position in the system is high-barrier and low-umbrella. This is a product or business with a position strong enough so that the costs of maintaining the barrier are insignificant.

Most interesting is the high-barrier, high-umbrella quadrant. Although the business is protected by the barrier, it is at risk because the cost of supporting the barrier is high. Profitability may be high, but the risk of competitive erosion, too, may be substantial. The trade-off is in consumer preferences for more service, quality, choice or 'image' versus lower prices from more narrowly focused competitors.

2 Companies are realising that they might need to form strategic partnerships if they are to be effective, and victory will go to those who set up the better network. Marketing alliances fall into four major categories:

- *Product and/or service alliances*: one company licences another to produce its product, or two companies jointly market their complementary products or a new joint product.
- *Promotional alliances*: one company agrees to carry a promotion for another company's product or service.
- *Logistics alliances*: one company offers logistical support services for another company's product.
- *Pricing collaborations*: two or more companies join together in a special pricing collaboration. Companies need to give thought to finding partners that complement their strengths and offset their weaknesses.

When well-managed, marketing alliances allow companies to achieve a greater sales at less cost. There are eight strategic reasons for entering into an alliance:

- To fill gaps in the company's current market and technological bases.
- To turn excess manufacturing capacity into profits.
- To reduce the risks and costs of entering new markets.
- To accelerate product introductions.
- To produce economies of scale.
- To overcome legal and trade barriers.
- To extend the scope of the existing operations.
- To cut exit costs when divesting operations.

Companies are learning how to craft winning alliances. Three keys to this seem to be:

- *Strategic fit:* before even considering an alliance, companies need to assess their own core competencies. Then they need to find a partner that will complement them in business terms, geographic position or competencies.
- *A focus on the long term:* rather than joining forces to save a few pounds, strategic partners should focus more on gains that can be harvested for years to come.
- *Flexibility:* alliances can last only if they are flexible.

3 Marketing objectives and marketing strategy must have a time dimension. That dimension has two features. First is the time horizon of a strategy. Very large, technologically based companies are especially conscious of the temporal aspects of their strategies. The long planning period required for such firms necessitates careful consideration of the viability of the strategy over time. At the other end of the spectrum is the small firm that views its flexibility as an asset. Here new strategies and marketing programmes that can be quickly launched may be essential. A further dimension is that the consumer packaged goods company should recognise that promotional strategies wear out and must be replaced at some point. Changing marketing conditions and competitive strategies are likely to erode the effectiveness of the best strategies over time.

The second time dimension relates to external consistency. In the case of a new product introduction, an effective marketing strategy must take an evolutionary view. In the earlier stages, substantial market development investment is called for and the promotional copy will emphasise the virtues of the product itself rather than the firm's comparative advantages.

Consumer-Led Marketing Strategy

KEY CONCEPTS

- Consumer demand; consumer-led marketing strategy
- Branding/sub-brands
- Marketing costs
- Price cutting
- Brand loyalty
- Product differentiation
- Consumer behaviour
- Vertical marketing systems

The last resort

After a disastrous year of spiralling discounts, UK tour operators are not optimistic about consumer demand. But as they invest heavily in branding campaigns, the increased cost will have to be passed on to consumers. **PIPPA CONSIDINE** investigates

Bland and naive." That's one verdict on the messages that tour operators are sending to sun, sea and sand seekers. But what's most striking about such summary judgement isn't the condemnatory tone, but the fact that it's a piece of self-criticism.

Richard Carrick, marketing director at Airtours Tour Operations, naturally offers this verdict and promises that his company will change all that. It is a business where operators offer packages with "the same aircraft, same product and same resorts" and customers "end up in a complex shared by other operators". For 1996, Airtours is offering a new "extra special" package that it claims is "the most innovative and extensive series of customer benefits the travel industry has ever seen".

The travel tour operator business of peddling overseas packages to the mass market is dominated by the big three: Thomson, the market leader with a 34 per cent share; Airtours which accounts for 18 per cent; and First Choice, with 13.5 per cent (Stats MR). New brochures are now on the shelves for summer 1996. This year has been disastrous. Operators over-estimated demand and year-round discounting policies ate into profits, so the season for plugging their latest products has come with a clutch of confessions.

Airtours is not the only operator to be hanging out the industry's dirty linen. At First Choice, which made a heavy investment in what is widely seen to have been a successful rebranding exercise last year (it was previously Owner's Abroad), marketing director Kevin Ivie says that industry-wide brand loyalty is "not high".

Even at Thomson Tour Operations, market leader for 20 years, Claire Wilson, director of communications, concedes it's "generally true that there's little product differentiation in the mass market . . . The focus in the past few years has been on price cutting."

Price cutting reached an all-time low this year with a baffling confusion of year-round discounting. Having over-estimated demand for summer 1995, late holidays have had to be discounted by as much as 50 per cent, says Thomson managing director Charles Newbold. In an industry where margins are already tight, at about two per cent, spiralling discounts are particulary harmful to the bottom line. In the short term, this has resulted in profit warnings from Airtours and the Thomson Group – which announced a first half operating loss of $1m (£645,000). There's even less optimism about the consumer's holiday hunger next year and capacity is down by about ten per cent.

But the industry only has itself to blame. "It has an appalling attitude to consumers," says one insider. "It treats them like sheep and is very disdainful." Whether or not selling package holidays is more like selling toilet rolls or selling dreams, tour operators are coming under the same sort of pressures as supermarkets to pay more attention to increasingly picky consumers, looking for customer service along with low prices.

Over the past ten years, the structure of the market has changed. The rise of the multiples means tour operators are paying higher levels of commission (between ten and 17 per cent) to the shops stocking their brochures.

Having a vertically integrated company with a retail chain (Thomson owns travel agent Lunn Poly and Airtours owns Going Places) is not the answer. Even without the threat of the current OFT investigation into uncompetitive practices, Airtours, for example, claims that more than 70 per cent of its product is sold outside its Going Places shops.

Booking patterns seem to have shifted steadily in the past three or four years towards later and later booking. The traditional high points – broch-ure launches in September and at Christmas – have been diluted, with more holidays being booked across the year as consumers second guess the travel companies. "The trick is to sell enough holidays early enough," explains Ivie. The more holidays sold at brochure prices, the better. Late bookings off brochure is where problems arise.

Analyst Wayne Sanderson of Smith New Court says that although the tour operators are "right to be re-evaluating, it's very tough. If they're hoping to break the late-booking mentality, they're not going to do it easily. The trend has set in".

So the real fight for market share is still, for the time being, focused on the more discriminating consumer, the one who wants to know what he or she will get for their money and wants to feel comfortable with the company they pick to put it together for them.

Airtours declares that it is adopting a more consumer-led strategy for summer 1996. Though some are cynical about whether its price-cutting mentality can change overnight, the company now has Thomson's highly regarded former marketing director Peter Rothwell on board as managing director.

Airtours' Carrick says that the industry is guilty of seeing the holiday experience as a commodity. "With consumer expectation changed beyond recognition, we need to emulate the success of the grocery trade," he adds. Summer 1996 will see the introduction of two new sub-brands – Suncenters and Sunclubs – as well as pre-bookable duty-free and airline seats, and lowest price guarantees.

Airtours is also trying to copy other retail sectors with replacement guarantees: if your holiday doesn't live up to reasonable expectations, rather than waiting to claim and complain when you get back, where possible, Airtours is empowering its reps to swap disgruntled customers into alternative accommodation.

This is just the beginning, says Carrick. And, while Airtours has changed, others are "dabbling around the edges", he claims.

It could be argued, however, that the relaunch of First Choice was the true catalyst that sparked the other big tour operators into taking issues such as branding more seriously. The recognition that such a wholesale strategic move was necessary, together with the injection of £7m into advertising through Ogilvy & Mather, has had an impact. "We established the brand last year," says Ivie. "Now we're differentiating on added value with kids clubs and all-inclusives."

First Choice ran a pilot programme in Spain this year offering all-inclusive holidays where food, drink, entertainment and activities are all bundled into the price. This could potentially be a big growth area in the Mediterranean, says the company. These holidays sold six times more quickly than any others in 1995. But a specially commissioned NOP survey indicates that 40 per cent of respondents thought the idea of all-inclusives was "too good to be true".

First Choice is promoting its first dedicated all-inclusives brochure in one of three new ads this month. Another features its children's clubs – Nippers, Surf Seekers and Beach Hounds – which have been tailored to three different age groups.

Thomson, as well as backing the continued growth of long haul, is re-entering the cruise market, following Airtours' success with its own cruise packages. It sees the cruise market as an area where demand is set to outstrip supply.

Wilson takes an authoritative stance on branding – as one would expect of the market leader. "In the wake of price wars and so on, Thomson has come to stand out as the natural first choice in the market." The company's ad campaign this year centred on "Mr Thomson, the man in the white suit, who is the epitome of our attitude to service". New ads are expected to be revealed shortly.

Cathy Reid, a planner at agency BMP DDB Needham, which handles Thomson's business, believes the pressure to brand strongly is increasing. "These days the fact that an operator has a TV presence and is racked in a reliable high street travel agent is sufficient to get it past the consumer's reliability requirements. The big established tour operator brands have to be seen as more than just big and reliable."

Thomson spent £10.8m on advertising last year, First Choice £6.9m and Airtours £5.2m (Register-MEAL). Though the First Choice spend was pumped up to support its relaunch, there is now an ongoing commitment by all three to substantial ad spends.

But brochures are still the main face of the company and they are not without their problems. There's a profusion, some might say a confusion, of tour operators' sub-brands on travel agents' racks, many with the word "sun" somewhere in the name. And the brochures still look dated featuring beaming white smiles and blue skies. Wilson says that, to an extent,

retaining the traditional look is positive. "It's difficult to come away from the white-tooth syndrome; people want to get a feel of the holiday experience."

Tradition, however, is arguably less important than the need to keep up with the customer service standards now expected by the average buyer.

One criticism of the travel industry is that it rarely recruits from outside and is therefore locked into the same marketing merry-go-round. "The same old faces just move from job to job within the industry. They are all locked into the lifestyle and the discounted travel. They never have any new ideas," says one insider. "It is incestuous," admits Carrick. But he defends his own company by pointing

to members of his team with agency experience. And Wilson agrees: "There's no denying it's a good idea to bring in fresh thinking." She cites Thomson's marketing director Richard Bowden-Doyle as an example. He has fmcg experience at Cadbury Schweppes, though his last job was at group company Lunn Poly.

People, like branding exercises, all cost money and, as a result, next year holiday prices are up, in many cases by about ten per cent. Although 1995 has been a lesson in how not to underestimate the consumer, the tour operators can only afford to go so far. The industry has led the consumer to expect good price deals. Now they want more but, on two per cent margins, it's hard to see how they won't be disappointed.

ISSUES

1. Comment on the current and future situation of the package tour and the degree of vertical integration in the travel and tourism industry.

2. Comment on new trends in consumer behaviour in tourism.

3. Elaborate on the growing importance of branding in the tourism industry.

4. Discuss why there is a lack of product differentiation in the travel and tourism industry.

5. Define three major pricing strategies that could be adopted by a large tour operator.

EXPLORATION OF ISSUES

1 Mass tourism certainly had its place and time, but today the tourism industry is in crisis. Mass tourism is no longer best practice. The conditions that gave birth to mass tourism – plus the consumers themselves, technology and production and management practices – are all changing. Tourist product innovation is more likely to be about 'unpackaging' than packaging, providing more individual attention within a number of price bands. Even so, package holidays are not set to disappear. Indeed they may increase in number as Third World countries come into the market. It is the relative importance of package tours that will decline. The price-based market share battle between the major operators has – in reality or perceptually – lowered the quality of the holidays on offer.

European tour operators are more vertically integrated than other industry players. They are also integrated forward into the marketing, retail distribution and sales of their packaged holidays, and integrated backwards into the ownership and control of package components (charter flights, hotels and incoming agencies).

2 The increasing sophistication of the customer will have an impact on product development throughout the industry. There will be an increased requirement for high standards of product design, efficiency and safety. This will be achieved through strong branding and tailoring the product more closely to the needs of specific market segments. New tourists will be more spontaneous and unpredictable – they will want to be different from the crowd and to be in control. Travel will be seen as a chore – the destination will be the *raison d'être* for travel. Tourists will seek quality but with value for money. They will want to experience something different, but will see the holiday as an extension of life. They will see and enjoy but will not destroy. They will appreciate cultural differences, they will be more understanding, better informed and know how to behave. Their interests can be summed up as follows: activity holidays, sports, special interests, interest in local fare.

3 Branding has been growing in importance in the tourism industry. Familiar brands give customers the sense of security they need and provide an anchor for tourism marketing managers. Brands have been found to be a powerful and profitable tool and are being increasingly used by tourism organisations. The importance of the corporate brand is also growing and will become the main marketing mode on the basis of total brand experience. Another major trend relates to the issue of brand equity and its main components: name awareness, brand loyalty, perceived quality, brand association and proprietary brand assets. Brand loyalty is a dangerous idea that, like accounting for brands, can lead to false confidence. The careful arrangement of brand extensions will lead to brand leverage. Tourism companies must beware of the overexploitation of brand names when the extension is applied to brands for which perceived quality and brand associations do not work. There is a trend towards the increased use of 'mixed' or 'endorsed' brands (brands with the benefit of corporate identity and the strength of individual brands. One of the problems with the branding of tourist products is that the promotion and advertising budget is shared across many brands, thereby diminishing its effectiveness and creating consumer confusion. Furthermore, point-of-sale materials make product differentiation difficult. Superbrands (for example, Lunn Poly, Going Places) will become more prominent, and brand comprehension and identity will be vital features of an effective branding strategy in the future. Research indicates that the most important ingredient is not the brand name but what lies behind it. Today's consumer is not only more aware of but also more knowledgeable about the company behind the brand, and is able (and prepared) to use that knowledge to help differentiate competitive offers. Pretty pictures and lofty slogans won't help. Consumers want to know what tourism companies stand for.

4 Today in tourism, product quality is uniformly high and price differences between competitors are negligible. Many competitors copy innovations, which are typically minor and increasingly rare. There is a strong trend towards perceived product parity. The majority of consumers worldwide believe there are no 'relevant differences' between rival brands. They are largely right. Many tourist products are on a par with regard to the main features, so it is the minor features that often determine tourist product choice. Therefore, tourism companies must identify the determinant attributes, not simply the obvious ones. The secret is to learn to live with parity. Tourism companies should learn from the mistakes of those who have gone before and use their marketing resources to redefine the game. Consumers are increasingly aware of the alternatives on offer and the rising standards of service, and so their expectations of service and quality are elevated and they are quick to complain when these are not met. Consumers are being very hard on the 'hard' (functional) features of the tourism brand and softer on the 'soft' attributes (image aspects).

5 Listed below are three major pricing strategies that could be adopted by a large tour operator:

- A heavy emphasis on cost reduction programmes in order to remain price competitive.

- Cost reduction should not be pursued at the expense of quality reduction but as a consequence of a total quality improvement programme.
- Prices should be set according to perceived value rather than cost mark-up. Tour operators should be able to calculate the price of each item that adds value to the product or offer.

Strategic Advantage from Game Theory

KEY CONCEPTS

- Game theory
- Supply-chain efficiencies
- Partnership and relationship marketing

Rules of the game theory

For a company, knowing the next move to make depends as much on what others are doing as any longer term objective. You need to understood the logic of the game before you have any chance of manipulating the rules in your favour.

ALAN MITCHELL

Now that game theory has achieved official recognition (the three Nobel prize winners announced last week – John Nash, John Harsanyi and Richard Selten – were all pioneers), I have a proposal to make. Game theory – the quest to determine the best course of action when what is "best" depends crucially on what others are doing – lies at the heart of all market dynamics and should be a compulsory part of all marketers' training.

Students studying it would become familiar with games such as "chicken", where the biggest pay-off goes to the player willing to go closest to the edge of nemesis (Rupert Murdoch may be the best example of this genre). Then there's "stag hunt", where the benefits of co-operation would be massive except that the players are tempted to fall out over who pays the costs and who gets the biggest share of the spoils. And, of course, there's the agonising "prisoner's dilemma" (*MW* July 1), where long-term self interest cries out for players to do one thing, but mistrust, a lack of communication and short-term necessity drives them to do the opposite.

A key task for the trainee is to analyse ruthlessly exactly what type of game you're getting caught up in. Is it a negative sum game, where all players lose out, such as in a price war? Is it a zero sum game, such as the classic market share battle? Or is it a positive sum game, where, if they play their cards right, contestants create a "win-win" situation?

Mistaking one for another can be fatal.

Most marketers today seem to believe that incentive-based loyalty schemes are a zero sum game – simply a matter of re-dividing existing market shares. Executed properly as partnership marketing exercises, they could even be positive sum games. But the way most are being constructed, the costs involved and the inevitable bidding up of incentives makes them a surefire negative sum hole.

Likewise, until now retailers have been expert at grabbing profits and margins from their suppliers. But now, as retail saturation really kicks in, some are trying to turn an "I win-you lose" confrontation into a win-win partnership. But how?

Game theorist Robert Axelrod charts one course in his influential book The Evolution of Co-operation. Make many small, incremental moves in non-threatening areas to build mutual trust, he suggests. And according to Nielsen UK managing director Jim Rose it's also happening in the grocery trade, as retailers and manufacturers begin to explore the benefits of co-operation over supply chain efficiencies and the like.

"Partnership" and "relationship" are, of course, business buzzwords. As positive sum games, they are won not by "beating the other player, but by eliciting behaviour from other players which allows both to do well", writes Axelrod. Yet how many partnership preachers accept his next lesson: that in such games you do not have to do better than the other player to do well yourself? Many a fruitful relationship will, I suspect, founder as those born and bred in an "I win-you lose" atmosphere fail to come to terms with this insight.

Teaching game theory to brand managers wouldn't be popular. For a start, its conclusions are often unsettling. For example, the sum of many isolated and individually rational business decisions isn't always the supreme, all-knowing perfection we like to call "the market". Often it's the opposite: collective irrationality. This is the dynamic of the gold rush, where 30 individual companies base their business plans on the assumption that they'll capture at least ten per cent of the market. And of the equally remorseless next step: the disastrous slide into a price war.

In competitive situations players are often forced to adopt strategies they would much rather avoid, but can't because of the strategies adopted by their opponents. It would, for example, be a good idea if cross-channel market operators silently agreed to keep their prices up. Last week, Eurotunnel sent out a clear signal that this indeed is its intention. But, if Imperial College's Stefan Szymanski is right, the logic of this game points in the opposite direction. Over time, the temptation for Eurotunnel to exploit its enormous capacity by cutting prices will be irresistible, he argues. And all the others will be forced to respond.

Game theory has its drawbacks. It is very good at rationalising things after the event but not so good at telling you what to do in the midst of battle. The maths are complicated and the results depend crucially on the "pay-offs" you impute to various outcomes. Payoffs that are almost impossible to calculate in real life.

Nevertheless, there are two good reasons why novice marketers should be exposed to it. First, it teaches flexibility. Often a strategy is successful solely because a competitor's behaviour gives it an edge. In a population of cowards, it pays to be a bully. But when everyone turns bully, being a coward is not such a bad idea – the trick lies in knowing when to switch.

An even better trick is knowing how to turn the zero sum game of bullies and cowards into something more fulfilling. Nowadays, "change the rules of the game" has become a cliché, – mere hype for "try to be different". This, in turn, is seen as a matter of will and "creativity".

These qualities may be ten per cent of the answer, if you're lucky. Only those who really understand the logic of the games they're immersed in have any real chance of manipulating the rules in their favour. And that, increasingly, is what modern marketing is about.

ISSUES

1. Explain the underlying concepts behind game theory.

2. Comment on the collaborative versus adversarial approaches to supplier handling.

3. Consider the notion of a relationship marketing system.

EXPLORATION OF ISSUES

1 The recent focus on competition in marketing models has led to much interest in the concept and methods of non-cooperative game theory.

Non-cooperative game theory is about how firms or individuals behave in competitive situations. A competitive situation arises when companies with conflicting interests are interdependent, but are unable to collude explicitly. Interdependence means that the consequences to a company of taking an action depend not just on that firm's action, but also on the actions of its competitors. Conflicts of interest mean that the firms differ in what they would like each of them to do. Finally, inability to collude explicitly means that the firms are unable to enter into enforceable, binding agreements.

Game theory assumes that the competitors are rational and intelligent. Competitors are rational if they make decisions by maximising their subjective expected 'utility'. (For risk-neutral firms – firms whose 'utility' functions are linear in profits – this means maximising expected profits). When faced with uncertainty, rational firms make subjective estimates of the probability of uncertain events and use these as estimates in the calculation of expected utilities of different actions. Firms are intelligent if they recognise that their competitors are rational. Intelligent firms can reason from their competitors' points of view.

'Rules of the game' means a complete description of the game including (1) the number of competitors, (2) their feasible actions at every juncture in the game, (3) their utilities (profits) for each combination of moves, (4) the sequence of moves and (5) the structure of information about moves (Who knows what? When?) A game of complete information is one in which the rules of the game are common knowledge among the firms. In contrast, a game of incomplete information is one in which the opposite is true. Most real-world games are games of incomplete information either because firms differ in their knowledge of the environment or because they do not know the motivations or capabilities of their competitors.

Once a game has been specified, we can distinguish between moves (or actions) and strategies. A pure strategy is a plan of action. A mixed strategy is a probability distribution on the firm's feasible set of pure strategies.

The concept of strategies makes it possible to represent games compactly in what is called the 'strategic form representation' of a game, which consists of sets of possible strategies, one for each form, and the payoffs to each firm for each combination of strategies.

The more detailed description of a game from which the strategic form is derived and makes explicit the flow of moves and information – often represented as a 'game tree' – is called an extensive form representation.

Game theorists provide two explanations of why rational and intelligent firms would use equilibrium strategies. First, a rational firm would, by definition, choose its strategy as a best response to the strategies it assumes for the others. Then, because the company is also intelligent, it must not assume strategies for the other firms that are not themselves the best response to some strategy of the given firm (after all, the other firms are rational too). The other justification of an equilibrium views the essence of competition as the absence of binding agreements.

Games that have a finite number of strategies always have an equilibrium.

2 The way in which the purchasing organisation decides to deal with its suppliers can have a fundamental effect on the future of the buyer–seller relationship. There are two polarised approaches which lead to very different relationships:

- *Adversarial approach*: the purchasing organisation puts pressure on the supplier to minimise prices and, by insisting on short-term contracts and using multiple sourcing, keeps the supplier alert and sweating. The purchaser is unlikely to be interested in helping the supplier unless there is a direct cost saving to be had. The purchaser will rarely need specific products and services and certainly will rarely be prepared to pay for such things. This is a legitimate approach in appropriate circumstances, for example when there are plenty of alternative sources of supply, the product is fairly standard and price really is the driving criterion.
- *The Collaborative approach*: close ties are forged between buyer and seller, and there is much interest and value in close cooperation and integration. Such an approach can support valuable work in product design, specification and quality, advanced production processes, flexible scheduling and delivery, and special inventory. There is, however, a risk of becoming

Table 16.1 Collaborative versus adversarial approaches to supplier handling

Adversarial	Collaborative
Multiple suppliers	Few suppliers
Regular price quotes	Long-term relationship
Adversarial negotiations	Mutual investment
Sporadic communication	Partnerships
Little co-operation	Frequent, planned communication
Quality and timescales to meet lowest threshold	Quality and timescales 'designed in'
Emphasis on lowest unit price	Emphasis on lowest overall cost

too 'cosy' complacent and blinkered, and there is the inherent danger of mutual dependency.

3 Relationship marketing is a marketing system oriented towards a strong, lasting relationship with individual customers, in contrast with transaction marketing, where the company has a more short-term orientation and is mostly interested in immediate sales achievement.

In a relationship marketing system, the profit centre is the customer and not the product, and attracting new customers is viewed as an intermediate objective. Maintaining and cultivating the existing customer base is the key objective, in order to create a long-term, mutually profitable relationship. Relationship marketing is particularly useful in industrial marketing, where the relationship between buyers and sellers is frequently close, long-lasting and important for both parties.

Two types of customer behaviour can be distinguished: the 'lost-for-good' model and the 'always-a-shape' models of behaviour. The 'lost-for-good' model assumes that if a customer decides to leave a supplier the account is lost forever, or, alternatively, that it will be as difficult and costly for the vendor to win back this account as it was to win it in the first place. Because of the high cost of switching, customers change suppliers only reluctantly.

The 'always-a-shape' model assumes that buyers maintain a less intense commitment than they do with the 'lost-for-good' model and that they may have commitments with more than one vendor at a time. The account can easily switch all or part of its purchases from one vendor to another, and therefore may spread its patronage, perhaps over time, among multiple vendors.

These two model provide the end-points of a spectrum of behaviour among industrial customers. Relationship marketing is sensible for customers who fit the 'lost-for-good' model; transaction marketing is appropriate for customers who fit the 'always-a-shape' model.

Diversification Strategy

- Market expansion and diversification
- Marketing innovations
- Brand repositioning
- Brand extension

Car makers switch into the finance lane

Manufacturers, facing a squeeze on traditional markets, are expanding into the financial sector

TOM O'SULLIVAN

Born out of recession, finance firms have become crucial to the future success of their car company owners.

Most of the new marketing innovations, ranging from personal contract plans to free mobile phones have been developed in co-operation with the finance companies. The outbreak of hostilities over the value of personal leasing plans (*MW* last week) illustrates the heightened competition for customers and the rivalry between the players.

"The need to make cars affordable during a difficult time created the schemes which have given the finance companies their power," says one observer. In the most competitive retail market that many can remember – where volume could drop as much as 15 per cent this year – that power and importance can only grow.

Back in 1992, when Ford launched its Options scheme, the logic was simple. With money tight the retail buyer was staying at home. If the car companies could free some money, or make it cheaper to borrow, then they might encourage people onto the forecourt to buy cars.

Ford Credit now estimates that more than half of its retail buyers will use its Options scheme to buy their car next year and by 1998 almost 80 per cent will use a Ford Credit scheme of some sort. The other big players have similarly sized ambitions.

Figures from the Finance & Leasing Association show that almost 20 per cent of new cars sold in the UK last year were paid for through finance company schemes worth £8.9bn. Not all are manufacturer schemes but it is clear they are offering stiff competition to the more conventional sources of car loans.

At the same time, manufacturers who have ventured into the finance business to sell cars are realising there are opportunities to diversify into other consumer banking areas, from home insurance to personal loans.

"Once we have exhausted finance products associated with the car, there is nothing to stop us expanding into other types of financial services," concedes Volkswagen Finance Group managing director Malcolm Hill. "All the major manufacturers are looking down the same road so there is ultimately no limit to how far we can expand – but that is four or five years down that road."

Volkswagen Finance, in line with its Ford and Vauxhall rivals, steered clear of the credit card ventures pursued by their parent companies – the reason being that the cards are "outside core business".

Significantly, the Volkswagen Audi Group took full control of Volkswagen

Finance 15 months ago. It had previously been a joint venture with Lloyds but the takeover underlines its growing importance to the manufacturer. Each brand has its own brand manager in the finance company. All ideas are shared and so incubated with the marketing departments. "No longer can you just sit down and offer a nought per cent finance offer – we have to constantly stimulate the market," says Hill.

The various finance companies offer a similar menu of stimulating opportunities, ranging from dealer support to retail incentive schemes for fleet management. They also offer – at a time when for many manufacturers the core business is losing money or at best breaking even – a very profitable return: in excess of 20 per cent on their equity investment.

Ford Credit Europe (FCE) and the other companies are no longer just about promoting nought per cent finance schemes. FCE is central to the car company's plans to expand in Eastern Europe, has assets of more than £9bn and contributes more than £200m of profit to Ford coffers each year.

"We are repositioning ourselves as Ford's own bank," says Ford Credit UK spokesman David Nash.

"Market research shows that people would go looking for finance in dealerships if they thought we were Ford's own bank. We are a worldwide bank borrowing billions of dollars on money markets and then lending that money to people to buy cars."

The repositioning began in June with the launch of the Acumen personal leasing plan but represents a formalisation of the position in Germany where Ford Credit is already known as the Ford Bank. Volkswagen and other manufacturers have similarly branded operations in Germany.

But Nash is quick to stress that this does not mean Ford will set up a high street operation. "There will be no diversification into non-core financial products. There will be no consumer banking, no personal loans. All we want to do is finance the bulk of Ford sales. The only limit is the size of the individual manufacturer."

But the opportunity to exploit the Ford name and brand values in other product areas could be too good to miss. FCE has become central to Ford's European expansion plans, offering finance to dealers in new markets in the East where there is little infrastructure to provide such funding.

In recent years the finance business has grown from a peripheral to a core activity. Within five years it may well have moved on again to something more than simply offering support to sell cars: standalone business units with a high street presence.

ISSUES

1. Comment on the merits of implementing a brand repositioning strategy.

2. As in the case of Ford Credit and Ford Bank, indicate four types of association that are relevant in making brand-extension decisions as well as three factors that determine which associations will carry over into a new context.

3. Explain the rationale behind a strategy of growth through diversification.

EXPLORATION OF ISSUES

1. Often, a brand or a product may require repositioning. This can happen if (1) a competitive entry has be positioned next to the brand, with an adverse effect on its market shape, (2) consumer preferences have undergone a change, (3) new customer-preference clusters have been discovered with promising opportunities, or

(4) a mistake has been made in the original positioning. Also, over the years brand positions shift to keep up with the changing mood of the market. The risks involved in positioning or repositioning a product, service or brand are high. The technique of perceptual mapping may be gainfully used to reduce those risks substantially. Perceptual mapping helps the examination of the position of a brand relative to competing brands. It helps in:

- Understanding how competing brands are perceived by various consumer groups in terms of strengths and weaknesses.
- Repositioning a current brand in the perceptual space of consumer segments.
- Positioning a current brand in an established market-place.
- Tracking the progress of a promotional or marketing campaign on the perceptions of targeted consumer segments.

There are three main ways of repositioning a brand: among existing users, among new users and among new users. Repositioning among new users requires the brand to be presented with a different twist to people who have hitherto not been favourably inclined towards it. In so doing, care must be taken to ensure that in the process of enticing new customers, current customers are not alienated.

The addition of new users to a brand's customer base helps enlarge the overall market and thus puts the brand on a growth path. Repositioning among new users also helps increase profitability, since very few new investments, apart from promotional costs, have to be made.

2 Three types of association are relevant when making brand-extension decisions:

- An image of high (or low) perceived quality. If the name Ford is attached to a new service, there will be a presumption among some that it will be a high-quality service, backed by a strong company.
- Attribute associations with the brand or product class that are helpful in the new context.
- Associations with product class. It is possible to attach a brand to another product class?

Three factors determine which associations will carry over into a new context:

- The strength of the attribute or quality associations in the existing context. If these associations are weak to begin with, they will be weaker in the new context.
- The fitting of a brand in to the new context. There needs to be a link such as a common use situation, user type, functional benefit or attribute.
- Whether or not it is possible to consider the brand in the new context. Would the makers of the brand be perceived as having the expertise to supply the new product class? If the brand context is implausible, the positive attribute and quality associations will be weak and negative associations may emerge.

The development of brand extensions can start by investigating which products or services a brand name would fit and what associations it would bring to the new product class. Customer trust needs to be transferred.

A brand extension can provide substantial support for a brand name by increasing its awareness level and reinforcing its association. However extensions also have the potential to damage a core brand by creating undesirable attribute associations or weakening those that exist.

Perhaps the worst possible result of an extension is a foregone opportunity to create a new brand equity.

3 Growth through diversification usually takes place outside the value chain, for example the development of new products or services and new markets. Diversification might involve a radical new departure into unknown technical, managerial or marketing areas.

Diversification happens when an organisation decides to move beyond its current boundaries in order to exploit opportunities. It means entering unfamiliar territory in both product and market terms. One of the major attractions of this option is that it spreads risk, moving the organisation away from over reliance on one product or one market. It also allows expertise and resources to be allocated synergistically. There are both offensive and defensive reasons for diversification, with outcomes such as a stronger financial position or greater synergy with existing operations. The danger is, of course, that the organisation will spread its effort too widely into areas of low expertise, and try to position itself against more specialist providers (for example banks).

References

Aaker, D. (1995) *Strategic Market Management*, 4th edn, John Wiley, New York

Anon (1996) *USA Today*, August, p. 7

BBC (1984), *Not By Jeans Alone*. Commercial Breaks

BBC2 (1997) *Money Programme* October 1997

Budd, J. (1997) 'Is the Truth Really Out There? *PR Week*, 4 April, p. 9

Crawford, M. C. (1991) *New Products Management*, Irwin, Homewood, Il.

Croft, M. (1995) 'It's All in the Cards', *Marketing Week (Customer Loyalty Supplement)* 24 March, p. 4–6

Crowe, P. (1995) 'Measures for Success', *Marketing*, 22 June, p. xiii

Dick, A. S. and Basu, K. (1994) 'Customer Loyalty: Towards an Integrated Framework', *Journal of the Academy of Marketing Science*, vol. 22, no. 2, pp. 99–113

Easton, G. (1990) 'Relationships among Competitors' in G. Day, B. Weitz and R. Wensley (eds) *The Interface of Marketing and Strategy*, JAI Press, Greenwich, CT, p. 73

Farrar, L. (1997) as reported by L. Goddard (1997) in 'Freebies Cost Dear under New Tax Laws', *PR Week*, 14 February, p. 2

Frost, F. (1999) 'The use of internet in relationship marketing in consumer markets', Backhaues (1999) *Contemporary Developments in Marketing*, ESKA, Paris, pp. 385–97

Gay Times (1998) reported in Anon (1998) *A-Z of Media*: G: Gay Media, *Marketing*, 9 April, p. 11

Goften, K. (1996) 'Integrating the Delivery', *Marketing*, 31 October, p. viii–viix

IPR (1995) Institute of Public Relations reported in P. Crowe (1995) 'Measures for Success', *Marketing*, 22 June, p. xiii

Joint Industry Committee for National Readership Surveys (JICNARS) (1991)

Lawson, R. W. (1988) 'The Family Life Cycle: A Demographic Analysis, *Journal of Marketing Management*, vol. 4, no. 1, pp. 13–32

Manners, N. (1994) as reported in E. Charles (1994) 'Is the Future Bright? The Rise of PR Consultancies', *PR Week*, November, p. 13

Market Research Society (1981), *Working Party Report on Social Grade*, MRS, London.

Market Research Society (1994) *The Opinion polls and the 1992 General Election*

North, A. and Hargreaves, D. (1996) *BBC You and Yours*, 7 April

O'Brien, S. and Ford, R. (1988) 'Can We at Last Say Goodbye to Social Class?' *Journal of the Market Research Society*, 30, pp. 289–332

O'Malley, L., Patterson, M. and Evans, M. (1997) 'Intimacy or Intrusion? The Privacy Dilemma for Relationship Marketing in Consumer Markets', *Journal of Marketing Management*, vol. 13, no. 6, pp. 541–59

O'Malley, L., Patterson, M. and Evans, M. (1999) *Exploring Direct Marketing*, Thomson International, London

Parkinson, S. (1994) 'Computers in Marketing', in M. Baker (1994) *The Marketing Book*, Butterworth-Heinemann, Oxford, pp. 18–19

Rawlins, M. (1984) 'Doctors and the Drug Makers', *The Lancet*, 4 August, pp. 276–8

Research Services Ltd. (1981), *SAGACITY*.

Rogers, D. (1997) 'How to Sit at the Top Table', *Marketing*, 27 February pp. xiii

Sampson, P. (1999) 'Direct Marketing and the Law', in L. O'Malley, Patterson, M. and M. J. Evans, *Exploring Direct Marketing*, Thomson International, London

Saris,W. E. and de Pijper W. M. (1986) 'Computer Assisted Interviewing Using Home Computers', *European Research*, vol. 14, no. 3, pp. 144–50

Shaw and Stone (1998) 'Competitive Superiority through Database Marketing', *Long Range Planning*, vol. 21, no. 5, p. 24–40

Shultz, D. (1993) 'Marketing from the Outside In', *Journal of Business Strategy*, vol. 14, no. 4, p. 28

Sunday Times/MORI (1992) *Portrait of the Electorate*, 12 April

Taylor Nelson, (1987), *Applied Futures*, Social Value Groups.

The Polls – *http://www.mori.com/ge-1997.htrr*

Toscani (1999) quoted by Kotler, P. (1997) *Marketing Management*, Prentice Hall

Voorhees, R. and Coppett, J. (1983) 'Telemarketing in Distribution Channels', *Industrial Marketing Management*, No. 12

Watson, T. (1996) 'Judgement Day is Coming', *Marketing*, 29 February, p. 26

Westcombe Business Research (1995) reported in 'What Clients Think' in *PR Week*, 16 June, p. 11

Whitehead, J. (1986) 'Keying in to New Data', *Marketing*, 6 March

Index

Index

EXCLUSIVE OFFER!

SAVE £30 when you subscribe to

MARKETING WEEK

That's only £1 per issue for...

- the latest industry developments and issues
- competitive analysis and views
- hundreds of top marketing jobs
  and more...

Simply complete the form below and start saving today!

SAVE £30

☑ **YES! Please arrange my subscription to Marketing Week for:**
1 year/ 50 issues £50 (UK rate only).

Mr/ Mrs/ Ms/ Miss _____ Initials _____ Surname _____

Course title _____ Head of Course _____

University or College _____

Address _____

_____

_____ Postcode _____

Telephone _____ Fax _____

Email _____

☐ I enclose a cheque for £_____ payable to **Marketing Week**

☐ Please debit my Visa/ Mastercard/ Amex/ Diners card by £_____

Card number _____ Expires _____

Signature _____ Date _____

Return to Marketing Week subscriptions, FREEPOST 39, London, W1E 6JZ
Tel: 0171 292 3711 Fax 0171 970 4099

☐ Please tick here if you do not wish to receive direct mail from other companies.

MWSC6